WHERE
THE
IRON
CROSSES
GROW

OSPREY
PUBLISHING

WHERE THE IRON CROSSES GROW

THE CRIMEA 1941–44

ROBERT FORCZYK

First published in Great Britain in 2014 by Osprey Publishing,
PO Box 883, Oxford, OX1 9PL, UK
PO Box 3985, New York, NY 10185-3985, USA
Email: info@ospreypublishing.com

Osprey Publishing, part of Bloomsbury Publishing Plc.

A CIP catalogue record for this book is available from the British Library

Robert Forczyk has asserted his right under the Copyright, Designs and Patents Act, 1988, to be
identified as the Author of this Work.

ISBN: 978 1 78200 625 1
e-book ISBN: 978 178200 9764
PDF ISBN: 978 1 78200 9757

Index by Alan Thatcher
Cartography by Boundford.com
Typeset in Adobe Garamond Pro and Trajan Pro
Originated by PDQ Digital Media Solutions, Suffolk UK.
Printed by Thomson-Shore, Inc., USA.

15 16 17 18   10 9 8 7 6 5 4 3 2

Osprey Publishing is supporting the Woodland Trust, the UK's leading woodland conservation charity,
by funding the dedication of trees.

www.ospreypublishing.com

Contents

Foreword

There is a distant and arid peninsula, surrounded by a dark and brooding sea, where armies and fleets traditionally came to die, like wounded animals. Beneath the surface of this soil lies fragments of the legions of Hitler and Stalin, as well as the civilians they murdered. Bits of bone, perhaps part of a jawbone or teeth, a bent German identity disk, or a moldy Soviet belt buckle, and plenty of rusty bullet casings – this is all that remains of their erstwhile martial glory in the Crimea. Here and there, the land above is still scarred with trenches or antitank ditches or a shard of barbed wire, as well as the ubiquitous shattered concrete bunkers – monuments to man's efforts to deny the inevitable. This was the land where Iron Crosses grew and Red Stars were handed out by the boxful, where reputations were made, or lost, in a matter of hours. These generations had no Tennyson or Tolstoy to note their heroics and sacrifices, just endless lists of awards and casualties, which were then lost.

It is also a place, perhaps unique in modern warfare, where a vicious ethnic and political cleansing was carried out by both opposing sides under the guise of wartime security measures. Warfare in the Crimea was not just about the contest between opposing armies and fleets, but about remaking the human geography with a vengeance. This was a place where opposing views of a better future for their people were implemented by secret policemen armed with submachine guns and unfettered authority. It is a place where horrible crimes were covered up, so as not to tarnish the official version of history. This work is a step toward exposing the long-suppressed truth that the Nazi and Soviet regimes were not so far apart, in terms of behavior, methods, and objectives. To be sure, there were brave and extraordinary soldiers on both sides, but it is a sad truth of military history that some of the most remarkable warriors have fought for some very shabby causes. It is even more remarkable that the tragic events in the Crimea are not confined to distant memory, but are being repeated in the current era, as Russian troops have once again invaded this region in order to aggrandize the notion of a "New Russia."

The military history of the Crimean Peninsula, which stretches back to ancient times, has been shaped by its unique geography. A natural fortress surrounded by water, the Crimea has long been regarded as a place where inferior military forces could create an impregnable bastion to hold off larger enemy armies. Attackers have always had limited options for gaining access into the Crimea, and the traditional route through the narrow Perekop Isthmus has been a tough nut to crack, irrespective of weapons technology. Yet the Crimea has also proven to be a cul-de-sac, where trapped armies were forced to fight a last stand or evacuate by sea. The degree that friendly naval forces could operate along the Black Sea littoral has ultimately determined the ability of both attackers and defenders to achieve decisive results in the Crimea.

While the Crimea was regarded as a "Russian Riviera" since the time of Catherine the Great, it was the creation of a naval base at Sevastopol that brought real strategic value to the Crimea. During the 20th century there were no less than five military campaigns in the Crimea, all of which bear striking similarities. Two of these campaigns, the German invasion of the Crimea in 1941–42 and the Soviet invasion of 1943–44, were major operations but are virtually unknown in the English-language historiography of World War II. Fighting in the Crimea was intense and often desperate, creating heroes on both sides, but their stories are largely forgotten. This book intends to correct that omission, as well as providing historical context for the current Russian military operations in the Crimea. The military history of the Crimea over the past two centuries is exceedingly complex, but presents a rich tapestry of patriots, opportunists, professional soldiers and sailors and not a few villains, all vying for control of this prestigious region, but each in turn facing victory, followed by frustration and defeat.

Prologue

The Russians were drawn to the Crimea by Tatar raiding, which had swept far and wide across southern Russia since the early 16th century. The Tatars were warlike descendents of the Mongol Golden Horde and closely allied with the Ottoman Empire; they were skillful light cavalrymen and for centuries their economy in the Crimea was based upon the sale of pillaged goods and of Russian captives into slavery. The Crimean city of Caffa (later Feodosiya), became the center of a lucrative slave trade with the Ottoman Empire. In 1571, a large army of Crimean Tatars even raided Moscow and burned much of Tsar Ivan the Terrible's capital, then took thousands of prisoners back with them.[1] The Crimean Tatars, who held a position of military advantage, also demanded tribute from Ivan the Terrible and were intent upon seizing more Russian land. Although Ivan the Terrible's army inflicted a severe defeat upon the Crimean Tatars just 40 miles south of Moscow in 1572, this was only a temporary reverse, and Tatar raiders continued to threaten the outskirts of Moscow for another 60 years.

The remote Crimean Peninsula was a natural fortress for Tatar raiding forces, since the only practical invasion route was through the narrow neck of the Perekop Isthmus, just 5½ miles wide. The Crimean Tatars used their plentiful slave labor to build a large fort at Perekop, then supplemented it with a wall across the Perekop Isthmus and dug a 72ft wide and 39ft deep moat in front of it. It was a very strong defensive position, supported by artillery and several forts. Furthermore, the area around the Perekop Isthmus was treeless and devoid of fresh water, which made it difficult for an attacking force to remain long enough to mount a deliberate attack. There were two other lesser land routes into the Crimea, but each was fraught with difficulty. East of Perekop, the Sivash was a shallow, marshy area that was not really sea or land. It could be crossed at two locations – at the even narrower Chongar Peninsula, just half a mile wide, or the 75-mile long Arabat Spit, which was little more than a sandbar. Both routes were easily blocked by small forces; the Tatars built fieldworks at Chongar and a large stone fort to block the southern end of the Arabat Spit. In military terms, the only practical alternative to an assault on the Perekop Isthmus was to land at Kerch, on the eastern end of the Crimea, but Ottoman naval superiority on the Black Sea made this infeasible for two centuries.

Russia, devastated by famine that eliminated nearly one-third of its population during 1601–03, could not immediately respond to aggression from the Crimean Tatars. It was not until May 1689 that Prince Vasily Golitsyn was able to approach Perekop with an army of 117,000 Russian soldiers and plenty of artillery. However, Russian armies lacked the logistical support to operate in such remote, inhospitable terrain, and Golitsyn was compelled to fall back empty-handed.[2] Tatar raiding from their Crimean stronghold continued, with 15,000 Russian captives taken in 1693 alone.[3] Russian tsars became increasingly incensed about eliminating this persistent threat once and for all, but decades passed with no success. Recognizing the deficiency of Russian military training, the tsars were compelled to import foreign military officers to improve the efficiency of Russian armies. One such officer, the German Count Burkhard Christoph von Münnich, led a 62,000-man Russian army in May 1736 that succeeded in storming the heretofore impregnable Tatar Wall at Perekop by use of deception and a night assault. Münnich conducted a feint against one end of the wall, which attracted Tatar attention, while his main body assaulted the other end. The first Russian soldier to reach the top of the Tatar Wall was a 13-year-old nobleman named Vasily Dolgorukov, whom Münnich awarded a field commission. Thereafter, Münnich's army spread out across the Crimea, destroying a number of towns, before disease and lack of supplies forced a withdrawal.[4] The Tatar Khan reoccupied the position at Perekop but another Russian army led by the Irish-born Count Peter Lacy outwitted them again by crossing the Sivash in June 1737 and defeating the outflanked Tatar army. Lacy had discovered an important point about the odd terrain of the Crimea – that under the right conditions of wind and tide, the Sivash was briefly fordable. After these defeats, the military power of the Crimean Khanate fell into sharp decline.

A period of peace followed, but in 1771 conflict was resumed and Prince Vasily Dolgorukov, now a general, returned to Perekop at the head of a powerful army. Tatar resistance was much weaker than before and Dolgorukov easily stormed the Perekop fort on July 10, 1771. Once the defenses at Perekop were breached, the Khan fled to Constantinople and much of his army evaporated. Prince Dolgorukov overran the Crimea in a month, although Tatar survivors retreated into the mountains on the southern coast. He was awarded a title recognizing him as conqueror of the Crimea.[5]

Subsequently, the Treaty of Kuchuk Kainarji with the Ottoman Empire in 1774 recognized the Russian military successes and allowed the nearly defunct Crimean Khanate to be recast as a Russian puppet state. However, the Russian-appointed Khan was rejected by the Tatar people, many of whom retreated into the southern mountains to conduct a guerrilla war. Up to 30,000 Tatars may have been killed during this period of Russian quasi-occupation, but years of guerrilla warfare also strained the Russian Army. After nine years of this nonsense, Catherine the Great finally decided to annex the Crimean Khanate outright in April 1783. She put her lover Prince Grigoriy Potemkin in charge of the region and he encouraged Tatars to leave the Crimea for Ottoman lands; 80,000 left in 1784.[6] Catherine also ordered the deportation of 75,000 Greek Christians from the Crimea and invited colonists from her native Germany to move to the Crimea. Russian rulers since Peter the Great had invited skilled foreigners to come to special economic zones to rapidly build up commerce, and the Crimea was expected to become a rich province.

An expatriate Scot by the name of Thomas F. Mackenzie (1740–86) was in command of the main Russian naval squadron in the Black Sea, and on his own initiative he selected the harbor near the Tatar village of Aqyar as an excellent site for a naval base. In June 1783, crews from Mackenzie's frigates began constructing naval barracks and other shore facilities in the port that would soon be renamed Sevastopol by Prince Potemkin. Another nearby harbor, at Balaklava, was also selected for development. Although the "base" was little more than an undefended roadstead outfitted with a few piers and warehouses, Potemkin announced the formation of the Black Sea Fleet (*Chernomorsky Flot*), from Mackenzie's naval squadron.[7] Another foreigner serving with the fleet at Sevastopol was the American John Paul Jones, who commanded one of Mackenzie's frigates. Mackenzie himself passed quickly from the scene but left a lasting legacy in Sevastopol. It was not long before annexation of the Crimea brought renewed war with the Ottoman Empire, but the Black Sea Fleet, under the capable leadership of Admiral Fyodor Ushakov, handily won a string of naval victories against the Turks between 1788 and 1791. By the end of the 18th century, possession of a warm-water port in the Crimea enabled Russia to become the dominant naval power in the Black Sea.

Due to the remoteness of the Crimea, it took many decades to actually build an effective naval base at Sevastopol. All materials had to be brought in by vessels, across the Sea of Azov, from Rostov. Most of the labor force was comprised of local serfs, who had few tools for digging or construction, but the number of skilled foreigners imported into the Crimea increased significantly after 1805. A cluster of German colonies was built around Neusatz-Kronenthal, 12 miles west of Simferopol, which slowly grew to over 11,000 Germans over the course of the 19th century.[8] It was not until the reign of Tsar Nicholas I (1825–55), that a serious construction effort began to equip Sevastopol as a fully functional naval base. An English engineer, John Upton, was brought to Sevastopol in 1832 to head a five-year project to complete the first dockyard and to design a string of forts around the port.[9] However, Upton's project took two decades to complete and the first Russian warship could not use Sevastopol's dockyard until 1853. Nevertheless, possession of the Crimea and a nascent naval base at Sevastopol emboldened the tsars to consider further expansion at the expense of the Ottoman Empire, since Ottoman naval superiority was no longer unchallenged.

Yet the build-up of the Black Sea Fleet and the naval base at Sevastopol contributed to tensions with Britain and France, which supported the Ottoman Empire. When another war erupted with the Ottomans, a Russian naval squadron led by Admiral Pavel Nakhimov easily crushed an Ottoman squadron at the battle of Sinope in November 1853, but this served as justification for Britain and France to declare war on Russia four months later. It is revealing that the primary objective of the Anglo-French expeditionary forces in the subsequent Crimean War was to destroy the Russian Black Sea Fleet and its base at Sevastopol, which were regarded as the Russian "center of gravity" for further aggression against the Ottomans. The year-long siege of Sevastopol destroyed Russian naval power in the Black Sea; most of the base was laid waste and 14 of 15 ships of the line and four of six frigates were scuttled in the roadstead. After the fall of Sevastopol to Anglo-French forces in September 1855, the Treaty of Paris, signed in March 1856, limited the Black Sea Fleet to only ten small warships with a maximum combined tonnage of 5,600 tons – less than 10 percent of its pre-war tonnage. The treaty also limited Russia's ability to enlarge existing naval bases in the Black Sea and to construct new coastal fortifications.

Although Russia was angered by this punitive peace settlement, it was not until 1871 that Tsar Aleksandr II dared to abrogate the naval clauses of the treaty, but then left it to his son to begin rebuilding Russian naval power in the Black Sea during the 1880s. The weakness of Russia's industrial base made the resurrection of the Black Sea Fleet a long, drawn-out process and it was not until June 1883 that the dockyard at Sevastopol was capable of beginning construction on the *Ekaterina II*-class pre-dreadnought battleships. Nevertheless, most warships of the Black Sea Fleet were still built at Nikolayev, not Sevastopol. Much of the German population that had supported development of the Crimea began to migrate to the United States after Tsar Aleksandr II decided in 1872 to remove their exemption from conscription into the Russian Army. More Russians were brought in to "Russify" the Crimea, but these also included disgruntled workers from cities that brought unrest with them. In June 1905, the Black Sea Fleet was struck by the mutiny of the crew of the pre-dreadnought battleship *Potemkin*, which then spread to other warships in the fleet. Although the revolt was eventually suppressed, it brought out an important political reality in the Crimea. Whereas agitation in the rest of Russia during the Revolution of 1905 was predominantly in the urban proletariat, the Crimean population was primarily agricultural and not disposed to revolution, but the sailors of the Black Sea Fleet were a nexus of unrest.

When World War I erupted in August 1914, the Black Sea Fleet had a clear superiority over the Ottoman Navy, with nine pre-dreadnought battleships versus only two pre-dreadnoughts Turkey acquired from Germany. However, the German decision to transfer the modern battlecruiser *Goeben* to Turkish service eliminated the Russian naval advantage. Adding insult to injury, the *Goeben* (renamed *Yavuz*) boldly bombarded Sevastopol in October 1914, demonstrating the inability of the Black Sea Fleet to even protect its main naval base. It was not until the two *Imperatritsa Mariya*-class dreadnoughts entered service a year later that the Black Sea Fleet gained some measure of superiority. However, the lead dreadnought, the *Imperatritsa Mariya*, suffered a magazine explosion and capsized in Sevastopol harbor in October 1916. Given the scale of the Tsarist investment of resources in the Black Sea Fleet and the naval base at Sevastopol, the return for the Russian war effort was minimal. When the Tsar was overthrown by the February Revolution in March 1917, the sailors of the Black Sea Fleet were quickly radicalized and were hostile to the Provisional Government. Sailor committees demonstrated their revolutionary fervor by renaming the two new dreadnoughts in Sevastopol: the *Imperatritsa Ekaterina Velikaya* became the *Svobodnya Rossiya* (*Free Russia*) and the *Imperator Aleksandr III* became the *Volya* (*Freedom*).

Russian authority all but collapsed in the Crimea after the October Revolution, and local Tatars, although reduced to less than 20 percent of the population, saw in this chaos their chance to recover their independence. Noman Çelebicihan, a 33-year-old Tatar lawyer, proclaimed himself president of the Crimean People's Republic on December 13, 1917. Using a few hundred ethnic Tatar troops demobilized from the Russian Army and some pro-White officers, Çelebicihan established a provisional government in Bakhchisaray. However, the Bolshevik leadership in St Petersburg had dispatched Vasily V. Romenets and Aleksei V. Mokrousov, both former sailors, to whip up revolutionary fervor in the Black Sea Fleet, and their mission was a complete success. On December 16, sailors from the destroyers *Fidonosi* and *Gadzhibey* raised the Red Flag and anarchy spread rapidly across the fleet. While Romenets established a Revolutionary Committee (RevKom) in the fleet, Mokrousov organized 2,500 anarchist sailors into the Black Sea Fleet Revolutionary Force and seized the port of Sevastopol in the name of the Bolsheviks. After receiving telegrammed instructions from the Bolshevik Central Committee in St Petersburg to "act with determination against the enemies of the people," Mokrousov's sailors arrested and executed 128 officers on December 28. Naturally, the Black Sea Fleet Revolutionary Committee refused to recognize Çelebicihan's provisional government and on January 14, 1918 Mokrousov sent a large detachment of his Red Guard sailors northward to Simferopol, where they arrested and executed Çelebicihan. They also murdered about 200 of his supporters, bayoneting and clubbing them to death in the Simferopol train station. Thereafter, the Bolsheviks found it increasingly difficult to control the armed groups of sailors, who favored drunken anarchy over socialist rhetoric. In a three-day orgy of violence, which now extended to families of officers and other members of the bourgeoisie, Mokrousov's gangs of armed sailors murdered between 600 and 700 people in Sevastopol during February 21–23, 1918.[10] Economic activity in the Crimea virtually collapsed as sailors turned to brigandage and hostage taking.

Recognizing that the revolutionary sailors were out of control, Anton I. Slutsky, a professional Bolshevik revolutionary, was sent from St Petersburg to take charge of the Crimea, and his first order of business upon arrival was to institute a Red Terror to crush the rising tide of Tatar nationalism. Slutsky then established a ramshackle government in Simferopol and took charge of the 3rd Soviet Army, which numbered fewer than 5,000 soldiers and sailors. Yet the Bolsheviks had little effective control over the Crimea, and as Professor Peter Kenez described: "The Bolshevik regime [in the Crimea], which lasted for three months, was remarkable only for its senseless cruelty. No one could control the looting and sadism of the sailors."[11]

There was one force that could control the anarchy-loving Black Sea Fleet sailors. Most of the Russian Army was demobilized after the Germans agreed to a temporary armistice in December 1917, but when the Bolsheviks withdrew from peace talks at Brest-Litovsk on February 10, 1918, the Germans were quick to take advantage of Russia's helplessness. Dubbed Operation *Faustschlag* (*Fist Punch*), the Germans advanced into Ukraine virtually unopposed on February 18, 1918 and soon reached Kiev. With German encouragement, Ukrainian nationalists formed an independent government and the Army of the Ukrainian People's Republic (UPR). Although the Bolsheviks quickly returned to the negotiating table at Brest-Litovsk, the Germans forced them into signing away their rights to Ukraine and the Crimea, as well as the Black Sea Fleet. On March 30, 1918, the German government announced that it did not regard the Crimea as part of Ukraine. Privately, a number of senior German military leaders such as Erich Ludendorff wanted to acquire the Crimea as a permanent German colony in the east. However, Ukraine also wanted to seize control of the Crimea and the Black Sea Fleet.

In April 1918, the UPR dispatched General Peter F. Bolbochan, a former Tsarist officer, with the the 1st Division from the Zaporozhye Corps to seize the Crimea. The UPR had quickly begun to form an army

from prisoners returning from Austrian captivity, and Bolbochan's division comprised three small infantry regiments. A small German expeditionary force, initially consisting of General Robert von Kosch's 15. Landwehr-Division and a Bavarian cavalry division, followed Bolbochan's division and tentatively cooperated with the UPR in disarming Russian troops in the area. Slutsky rushed what troops he had to the Perekop, but Bolbochan conducted an end-run at the Chongar crossing, which was seized on April 22, 1918. Once they realized that they were flanked, the Red forces disintegrated in panicked flight, allowing Kosch's German troops to easily pass through the Perekop Isthmus. Local Tatars were eager to join with Bolbochan's division, and when his troops reached Simferopol on April 24 and captured Slutsky, Crimean Tatars avenged the Bolshevik murder of Çelebicihan by executing Slutsky. Two days later, the Germans arrived at Simferopol, but now German–Ukrainian military cooperation came to an abrupt end. Kosch ordered his troops to surround and disarm Bolbochan's division and the UPR was ordered to leave the Crimea, which he pointed out belonged to Germany now. Lenin was furious that the Germans were occupying the Crimea but his protests were ignored.[12]

Control of the Black Sea Fleet now became a primary objective of the Germans, Ukrainians and Bolsheviks. Rear-Admiral Mikhail P. Sablin had saved himself from mob violence in January by openly joining the Bolsheviks – as other former Tsarist officers did as well – and Slutsky had put him in charge of the fleet. Now with German and Ukrainian forces approaching Sevastopol, Sablin was ordered to take the fleet to Novorossiysk, but he was only able to convince the crews of the dreadnoughts *Svobodnya Rossiya* and *Volya*, plus 11 destroyers, to follow him. The rest of the fleet, including the seven pre-dreadnoughts and another nine destroyers, fell into German hands when Kosch's troops seized the city on May 1, 1918.[13] German forces overran the rest of the Crimea forthwith, including the Kerch Peninsula. Alarmed that the Germans might continue eastward to seize the remainder of the Black Sea Fleet at Novorossiysk, Lenin personally ordered Sablin to scuttle his fleet on June 18, 1918. The dreadnought *Svobodnya Rossiya* and five destroyers were scuttled, but the crews of the *Volya* and nine other destroyers refused and opted to return to Sevastopol. A large proportion of the crews of the Black Sea Fleet were Ukrainian and they hoped that the Germans would support the creation of an independent Ukrainian navy.[14]

The Germans enjoyed the Crimea for six months and installed a puppet government in Simferopol, which allowed a limited amount of Tatar autonomy, thereby gaining some degree of local support. The Germans stabilized the situation in the Crimea and even brought the damaged battlecruiser *Yavuz* to be repaired in Sevastopol's dockyards during the summer of 1918 – one could even say that Kaiser Wilhelm II got better use out of the naval facility than Tsar Nicholas II ever had. Yet when Germany agreed to an armistice with the Western Allies in November 1918, the German occupation of the Crimea came to an abrupt end. Concerned about the Bolsheviks regaining control of Sevastopol and the remnants of the Black Sea Fleet, the British Mediterranean Fleet sent a naval expeditionary force to the Crimea less than two weeks after the armistice. Landing parties from the cruiser HMS *Canterbury* were the first to reach Sevastopol on November 24, where they took control over the remaining Russian warships. The next day, a larger force with two British battleships arrived, joined by French and Italian warships. Vice-Admiral Albert Hopman, in charge of the 11,000 German troops in Sevastopol, was allowed to assist with maintaining order until more Allied troops arrived.[15] Although welcomed at first, the British were ignorant of local political factions, and their efforts to encourage a new anti-Bolshevik provisional government in Simferopol were ham-fisted. The famous British spy, Sydney Reilly, was sent to Sevastopol to gather information about political conditions in the area, but much of what he reported was inaccurate or overly optimistic. A contingent of 500 Royal Marines landed on December 1, but the British decided to hand responsibility for the Crimea over to the French, who landed the 176e régiment d'infanterie at Sevastopol on December 26, 1918.[16]

The French, particularly Georges Clemenceau, had ambitious plans for the Crimea and military intervention in southern Russia against the Bolsheviks. Clemenceau regarded the Crimea as the perfect bastion from which to cooperate with local White forces, since the collapse of the Ottoman Empire enabled Allied naval forces to operate freely in the Black Sea. However, Clemenceau's vision of rolling back Bolshevism in Ukraine was not matched by the requisite military muscle. A 2,000-man Greek regiment arrived in January 1919 to reinforce the French, and then several French colonial battalions of Senegalese and Algerians, but the Allied force in the Crimea never exceeded 7,000 men. A French fleet, including the dreadnoughts *France* and *Jean Bart*, also arrived at Sevastopol, but French control did not extend beyond the range of their fleet's guns. Morale among the war-weary French forces was poor and their relations with the Crimean people deteriorated rapidly. Nor did White forces, who opposed the Bolsheviks, have more than a token force in the Crimea. By March 1919, the Bolsheviks began moving to eject both the French and the Whites from the Crimea.

Typically for the disorganized Whites, they left the Perekop Isthmus only lightly guarded, and the Red 14th Army easily stormed the Tatar Wall on April 3. Within five days, Red cavalry reached Simferopol, sending the Provisional Government and Whites scrambling for safety. Red troops reached the outskirts of Sevastopol on 14 April and French naval gunfire repulsed the first tentative assault. However, the French had no stomach for real fighting and a serious mutiny broke out on both French dreadnoughts. A number of rebellious French sailors expressed sympathy with the Bolshevik cause and it was soon apparent that many troops were unreliable as well. The French agreed to a temporary cease-fire with the Bolsheviks, in return for evacuating their forces from the Crimea. Even though the British battleship HMS Iron Duke was in Sevastopol, the Royal Navy decided to focus on incapacitating the remaining Russian warships in the port while negotiations dragged on. The British were particularly concerned about the Bolsheviks acquiring intact submarines. British sabotage parties used demolition charges to destroy the engines on a number of warships, including both Evstafi-class pre-dreadnoughts, four destroyers and all nine submarines. Although the French agreed to a cease-fire with the Bolsheviks, the Royal Navy did not, and HMS Iron Duke and two light cruisers shelled Red positions along the coast on April 25 and April 27.17 On April 28, 1919, the French and Greek troops completed their evacuation from Sevastopol and the Red Army marched in the next day.

Although a large number of Russian civilians left with the French, the remaining White forces retreated to the Kerch Peninsula and entrenched themselves near Ak-Monai. The Reds quickly established the Crimean Soviet Socialist Republic in Simferopol, but due to the outbreak of anti-Bolshevik rebellion in large areas of Ukraine, much of the 14th Army was transferred before victory in the Crimea was complete. Commissar Pavel E. Dybenko, a former sailor and political agitator, was left with only 9,600 troops in the Crimea. Dybenko sent his available troops east to attack the

Whites at Ak-Monai, but the Royal Navy intervened; between May 2 and June 9, the British positioned two powerful naval task groups on either side of the Kerch Peninsula, one in the Sea of Azov and the other off Feodosiya. Naval gunfire from the battleships HMS *Marlborough* and HMS *Emperor of India*, supported by two light cruisers and six destroyers, prevented Red troops from breaching the White defenses.[18] Furthermore, the Royal Navy helped the Whites to move additional forces from Novorossiysk back to the Crimea. General Yakov Slashchev landed near Feodosiya with an infantry brigade and soon joined with local White forces. Alarmed by reports of White landings in the Crimea, Dybenko opted to abandon the Crimea without a fight. Slashchev's troops marched back into Sevastopol on June 24, 1919. Thanks to British naval gunfire support, the Whites had recovered the Crimea and Anton Deniken, the leader of the White Volunteer Army, was determined not only to hold onto it as a bastion but to use it as a springboard for one last counteroffensive that ambitiously aimed for Moscow. However, Deniken's counteroffensive failed, and by early December 1919 the defeated Volunteer Army was retreating to the Crimea, where it would make its last stand. On April 4, 1920, Deniken was replaced by Baron Petr Nikolayevich Wrangel, who assumed command over all White forces in the Crimea.[19]

Wrangel believed that the Whites might be able to hold the Crimea indefinitely, since even his depleted Volunteer Army could defend the only two practical land routes: the Perekop and Chongar. He stationed General-Lieutenant Aleksandr P. Kutepov's 1st Corps behind the old Tatar Wall at the Perekop Isthmus, which was heavily fortified with barbed wire, machine guns, and artillery during the fall of 1919. The 38-year-old Kutepov, last commander of the elite Preobrazhensky Regiment, was one of the best fighting generals of the Volunteer Army and a stern disciplinarian who kept his troops in good order. Kutepov's troops dug three lines of trenches at Perekop, fronted by three to five rows of barbed wire. He had 8,900 troops holding a 5½-mile-wide front at Perekop, with another 7,500 men holding a reserve position at Ishun, 12 miles south of Perekop.[20]

General Yakov Slashchev's 2nd Corps deployed 3,000 infantry on a ½-mile-wide front at the Chongar, which was also heavily fortified with barbed wire, six lines of trenches, and even a few concrete bunkers. Several large coastal guns were taken from Sevastopol to reinforce the Chongar position. Slashchev ordered the Salkovo railroad bridge blown up, leaving a mile-wide gap across the Sivash. Wrangel kept the 12,000 mounted troops of the Don Cavalry Corps back at Dzhankoy as a mobile reserve. Given that the Bolsheviks had absolutely no naval forces on the Black Sea, Wrangel believed that his forces, led by these two skillful and experienced commanders, could hold the only gateways into the Crimea. British military aid continued to arrive in Sevastopol, enabling Wrangel to rebuild the battered Volunteer Army with fresh equipment and uniforms; the British even provided 45 tanks and 42 aircraft to reinforce the White defenses in the Crimea. Meanwhile, those remnants of the Black Sea Fleet that had not yet been scuttled sat rusting in Sevastopol, and although short on both coal and trained sailors, were available to provide Wrangel with naval gunfire support.

With the Russian Civil War in its final spasms by late 1920, the Red Army was finally able to direct sufficient forces to retake the Crimea. Mikhail Frunze's Southern Front dispatched five armies toward the Crimea in October 1920, consisting of 186,000 troops. Yet despite an overall 5-1 superiority in manpower and 4-1 in artillery, Frunze would be able to deploy only a fraction of his forces at either Perekop or Chongar. It was the same kind of situation that faced the Persian army at Thermopylae in 480 BC, where terrain greatly reduced the advantage of superior numbers. With this in mind, Kutepov waited at the Perekop, trusting to barbed wire and machine guns to keep the Reds out.

CHAPTER 1

The Crimea Under the Hammer and Sickle, 1920–41

"We shall now proceed to construct the Socialist order."
Vladimir Lenin, October 1917

The men marched silently in long columns through the cold, ankle-deep mud, which held the stink of a stagnant sea. It was a cold night on November 7/8, 1920, with temperatures around 50° F (10° C) and very windy, which brought a chill to each man, locked in the solitude of the stealthy march. These men were soldiers of Augustus Kork's 6th Army, who were marching 3 miles across the Sivash to outflank Kutepov's White troops at Perekop. Frunze had wanted to make his main effort at the Chongar Peninsula, but the Azov Flotilla could not move its small craft into the Sivash due to ice at Henichesk, which was the only place where shipping could enter the confined waters. Without boats, Frunze did not believe that he could move enough assault troops across the water to overwhelm Slashchev's defensive position. Instead, Frunze was forced to shift his main effort to the Perekop, with Kork's army deployed to conduct a frontal assault on the Tatar Wall.[1] Then by chance, high winds and unusual tide conditions lowered the water level in the Sivash and opened a new avenue of approach. Frunze ordered Kork to send nearly one-third of his army – the 15th and 52nd Rifle Divisions and the 153rd mixed brigade, a total of 20,300 troops – to cross the Sivash during the night. Once the Sivash was crossed, Kork would begin the main attack on the Tatar Wall the next day. Frunze believed that if Kutepov's corps was hit from in front and behind simultaneously, it would lead to a rapid collapse. Neither Kutepov nor Wrangel expected a serious attack across the Sivash, but just in case, they deployed 2,000 Cossack cavalrymen under Mikhail A. Fostikov to screen the coast along the southern side of the Sivash.

Markian V. Germanovich's 52nd Rifle Division began crossing the Sivash at 2200hrs on November 7, followed by the 15th Rifle Division. After about three hours, they landed undetected on the small, flat Litovsky Peninsula southeast of Perekop and, after assembling, advanced half a mile southward. Kork managed to get some light artillery across the Sivash as well, but his assault force was limited to the ammunition they could carry. Around 0400hrs on November 8, the vanguard of Germanovich's 52nd Rifle Division encountered elements of Fostikov's brigade, which slowly fell back toward the base of the Lithuania Peninsula but gained time for Kutepov to dispatch two regiments of the Drozdovskaya Division from Armyansk to reinforce them. By 0900hrs, the Whites had begun a major counterattack near the village of Karadzhanaya, including armored vehicles, which effectively blocked the Soviet flanking maneuver. For the rest of the day, heavy fighting continued around this village and Kutepov fed in more reinforcements from Perekop. The Soviet assault group had limited artillery ammunition, which prevented them from breaking through the White positions, and to make matters worse, the water began rising in the Sivash, isolating them. Just before the waters became too deep, Frunze sent the 7th Cavalry Division across the Sivash to reinforce Kork's two divisions.

By the evening, Frunze's plan was unraveling. The flanking maneuver across the Sivash had been brought to a halt and was being pummeled by White forces with superior artillery. A diversionary attack with a regiment down the Arabat Spit had also ended in disaster, with heavy losses. Frunze was not eager to begin the attack at Perekop until Kutepov's corps was disrupted by the flank attack, but now he had no choice – he ordered Vasily K. Blyukher's 51st Rifle Division to begin the assault on the Tatar Wall at Perekop immediately. Despite the size of Frunze's Southern Front – on paper – Blyukher had only 4,800 assault troops in his division and 55 artillery pieces, of which 34 were light 75mm or 76.2mm guns. His arsenal of heavy artillery was limited to 12 120/122mm and six 152mm howitzers, which was clearly insufficient to create a breakthrough in a heavily fortified line. Blyukher was supposed to begin his artillery preparation at Perekop on the morning of November 8, but heavy fog prevented observed fire. Even once the fog lifted around noon, Blyukher's artillery was unable to inflict serious damage upon the enemy defenses. Under pressure from Frunze, Blyukher committed a reinforced infantry brigade around 1325hrs to attack the Tatar Wall, which succeeded in penetrating through part of the barbed-wire obstacles before being shot to pieces by Kutepov's machine gunners. Soviet armored cars supported the attack, but could not counter White artillery. Blyukher ordered in three more assaults during the course of the afternoon, but all ended in failure. Casualties in the assault regiments amounted to 60 percent or higher. Lacking the requisite 3-1 numerical superiority, and plagued by inadequate artillery–infantry coordination, the Red Army's failure to break the Perekop position was typical for a World War I-type positional battle.

Just when it seemed that the Whites were on the verge of winning the battle, Mikhail A. Fostikov's Cossacks pulled out of the fight at Karadzhanaya and retreated all the way back to the port at Yevpatoriya. Once word went around about the retreat, the morale in Kutepov's 1st Corps cracked and other units began retreating to the reserve position at Ishun. As often happens in warfare, the Whites did not realize that the Reds were in far worse shape, and unauthorized retreats become contagious. With his flank giving way, Kutepov was forced to abandon the Perekop position and try to reform at Ishun. Blyukher's 51st Rifle Division was so badly battered that it did not occupy the undefended Tatar Wall until the morning of November 8, and then lacked the strength to pursue. Kork urged the 15th and 52nd Rifle Divisions, which were also in poor shape, to push on to Ishun.

This was another excellent defensive position, surrounded by four large lakes and marshy terrain. Kutepov was able to assemble at least 9,000 troops and three tanks at Ishun, whereas the pursuing Red divisions had no more than 15,000 combat-ready troops in hand. The Whites had moved two 12in battleship guns on carriages to Ishun and three 8in-gun batteries, and the Black Sea Fleet was able to deploy several warships to provide naval gunfire support – in short, the Whites had a clear superiority in firepower. Kutepov's troops fended off the first enemy probing attack on the evening of November 9, but Blyukher's 51st Rifle Division achieved some success on the west side of the Ishun position on November 10 and was only brought to a halt by naval gunfire. With Wrangel's attention focused on Ishun, Frunze ordered the 30th Rifle Division to launch a surprise attack across the Chongar Narrows on the night of November 10/11 – which succeeded. In desperation, Wrangel ordered a major counterattack on the morning of November 11, spearheaded by their remaining Cossack cavalry, which nearly broke Kork's 6th Army. However, the arrival of the vanguard of Philip K. Mironov's 2nd Cavalry Army led to a costly cavalry battle, which the Whites could not afford. Once it was clear that the White forces had shot their bolt and that their impulsive attack had failed, Wrangel ordered his forces to withdraw from the Ishun position on the evening of November 11.

The Soviet cavalry spread out across the Crimea in hot pursuit, overrunning all of it in less than a week. By the time that Simferopol fell on November 13, Wrangel's forces were already beginning their evacuation of the Crimea. Wrangel had prepared carefully for evacuation and the operation ran smoothly and efficiently; he succeeded in loading a total of 145,693 soldiers and civilians onto an evacuation flotilla of 126 ships within just two days.[2] There were still enough loyal sailors to enable the rump Black Sea Fleet to join the evacuation, with the dreadnought *General Alekseyev* (the former *Imperator Aleksandr III/Volya*), two elderly cruisers, 11 destroyers, and four submarines – a ragged flotilla that was soon dubbed "Wrangel's Fleet." Other disabled warships were towed out of Sevastopol, which was abandoned on November 14. During the evacuation, Wrangel ordered his retreating White troops not to destroy any facilities in Sevastopol, which he said, "belonged to the Russian people." The fleet initially went to Constantinople, depositing the remnants of Wrangel's Volunteer Army at Gallipoli. Three months later, the French granted Wrangel's Fleet asylum and the warships were sent to Bizerte in Tunisia, where they sat rusting at anchor for years until they were finally scrapped.

Frunze claimed that the Red Army lost 10,000 soldiers in assaulting the Crimea in November 1920, but this seems high. Most of the casualties were in Blyukher's 51st Rifle Division, which lost upwards of 3,000 men, but otherwise most Soviet divisions saw only brief combat in the Crimea. The Soviet victory there was based more on luck and determination than skill or planning, as was later acknowledged by the Soviet General Staff's Chief of Operations, Vladimir K. Triandafillov. The forces assigned to storm the Perekop position were grossly inadequate and Frunze based his offensive entirely upon a trick maneuver that succeeded only in part. It was the abrupt collapse of White morale that won the campaign for Frunze, not the tactical skill of the Red Army. Having the means to escape by sea also influenced the White decision to quit a battle that was still in doubt, since many thought it best to run away in the hope of fighting another day than to conduct a last stand.

"There are now over 300,000 bourgeoisie [in the Crimea] who must be dealt with."
Lenin, December 6, 1920

On the morning of November 15, 1920, the troops of Blyukher's 51st Rifle Division and Budyonny's 1st Cavalry Army moved into Sevastopol, led by an armored car marked with a red star insignia and in large red letters, the word "Antichrist." Wrangel's Fleet had not yet steamed over the horizon when the victorious Bolsheviks turned to deal with the remaining "enemies of the Revolution" in the Crimea. While some White commanders had dealt harshly with the local population and Bolshevik sympathizers in the Crimea, allowing their troops license to pillage, rape, and murder on occasion, it had not been officially sanctioned policy. Wrangel had made efforts to clamp down on such excesses, since he realized that such acts turned the population against his side. However, Bolshevik leaders had fewer qualms and were not interested in winning "hearts and minds" in the Crimea. Instead, retribution was the order of the day.

On the day following the Red occupation of Sevastopol, the Revolutionary Military Council of Frunze's Southern Front formed the Revolutionary Committee of Crimea (*Krymrevkoma*), headed by a troika of committed communists consisting of Béla Kun, Rozalia Zalkind (alias Zemliachka), and Georgy L. Piatakov. Kun, a Hungarian Jew, part-time journalist and long-time revolutionary agitator, had returned to Russia after his Hungarian Soviet Republic had collapsed in August 1919. He had already gained a reputation as a violent radical in Hungary, where he was responsible for the murder of over 500 opponents of his short-lived regime. However, the real ramrod on the committee was Zemliachka, a pince-nez-wearing 44-year-old Jewish woman from Kiev. Zemliachka had risen though the Bolshevik ranks since the abortive 1905 Revolution and become a close associate of Lenin. She had also had a fanatic's lust for violence, and a homicidal antipathy to all "enemies of the party." Piatakov, although less prominent than either Kun or Zemliachka, was a close associate of Leon Trotsky and was intent upon eliminating residual ethnic nationalism in the new Soviet Union – particularly Ukrainian and Tatar. These three committed and ruthless communists were tasked by Lenin with implementing the elimination of all "class enemies" in the Crimea, later known as the Red Terror. Three special detachments of the newly formed Crimean Cheka (KrymChK) security troops were put at their disposal. The Cheka formed a special Crimean Strike Group (*Krimskoy Oodarnoy Grooppi*), led by Nikolay M. Bistrih, but also made arrangements to use Red Army troops as well.

Prior to conquering the Crimea, Bolshevik leaders had promised amnesty to all White troops who surrendered, and many enlisted soldiers had opted not to join Wrangel's evacuation in hopes of remaining in their home country. About 3,000 White troops remained in Feodosiya when the Red Army entered the city, and they peacefully laid down their arms. After being disarmed, many White soldiers offered to join the Red Army, but instead, soldiers of the Red Army 9th Rifle Division, under the direction of Bistrih's Chekists, executed 420 wounded White soldiers and put the rest in two concentration camps. As it turned out, this was just the opening act in a five-month terror campaign. On November 17, 1920, the *Krymrevkoma* issued an order for everyone in the Crimea to complete a mandatory registration within three days; predictably, the registration was merely a means to identify "class enemies." In Feodosiya, soldiers from the

25

9th Rifle Division arrested 1,100 people who registered, of whom 1,006 were shot, 79 imprisoned, and only 15 released.

The Cheka and Red Army execution squads quickly spread the Red Terror across the Crimea. Initially, the victims were primarily former White officers and wealthy landowners, but once these were gone the Terror moved on to eliminating common enlisted soldiers, then potential opponents in the general civilian population. People were condemned for just having displayed "sympathy for the White cause," which included dockyard workers in Sevastopol who unloaded supplies from ships during White rule in the Crimea. Soon, members of the clergy, teachers, intellectuals, students, and even medical staff were targeted. In Sevastopol, Cheka death squads and soldiers from the 46th Rifle Division used firing squads and massed hangings to murder at least 12,000 people without trial. Bodies were left hanging all over the city to terrorize the rest of the population. In Kerch, prisoners were loaded onto barges that were then sunk in the Sea of Azov. In Simferopol, capital of the Crimea, at least 20,000 were murdered. Apparently, these numbers were not good enough for Kun and Zemliachka, who accused local Bolshevik officials of being "too soft." In addition to murder, the Chekists employed torture and rape to break those prisoners held in their concentration camps, while the Red Army was allowed to pillage to its heart's content. Not everyone meekly submitted to the Red Terror; some Crimean Tatars slipped off to the Yalai Mountains in the southern part of the peninsula and attempted to wage guerrilla warfare against the Red Army and Chekists. Known as the Green Forces, these Tatars had no chance against the better-armed and organized Red Army.

However, local Bolshevik leaders reported to Moscow that Kun and Zemliachka were losing control of the situation in the Crimea and that their death squads were behaving more and more like bandits. The Communist Central Committee in Moscow responded by recalling Kun and Zemliachka, but sent Ivan A. Akulov in March 1921 to replace them. Akulov tightened up on discipline a bit, but the terror and executions continued. It was not until Mirsaid Haydargalievich Sultan-Galiev, a Tatar who joined the Bolshevik movement and became a member of the Communist Central Committee, travelled to the Crimea and witnessed the Terror firsthand that there was any change in policy. Sultan-Galiev reported back in Moscow that:

Such a reckless and brutal terror has left an indelible mark in the mind of the Crimean people. They all feel a strong, pure animal fear of Soviet officials, along with hidden deep distrust and anger.

Communist leaders in Moscow feigned shock that the Crimean people as a whole would take offense at Chekist efforts to suppress "class enemies," but quietly realized that the Terror could go on for only so long before the region became completely dysfunctional and useless to the party. After April 1921, Akulov began to reduce the number of executions, and these ceased once the Green Forces were defeated by October 1921. At that time, the Crimean Autonomous Soviet Socialist Republic was announced, and a number of Bolshevized Crimean Tatars were included in the regime. According to Soviet figures, at least 52,000 people were murdered (the official term was "repressed") by the Red Terror in the Crimea between November 1920 and April 1921, although the actual number may have been close to 75,000.

When the executions tapered off, the Terror continued in other forms in the Crimea. Imprisonment and deportation were increasingly used to remove potential dissidents; Turkey was sympathetic to the Tatars and agreed to accept some refugees. About 50,000 Tatars were deported either to the Gulag or to Turkey, to reduce their numbers in the Crimea. The Red Army also seized the bulk of the Crimea's agricultural harvest, leaving the population to face a famine in the winter of 1921/22. However, after the famine some concessions on freedom of religion and language were made to placate the Crimean Tatars. For the next six years, the Crimea was allowed to go its own way while the communists in Moscow were focused on the leadership struggle following Lenin's death in 1924. By 1928, Stalin was gaining the upper hand and he was in no mood to make concessions to local ethnic interests. His main domestic objective was forced collectivization of agriculture, which proved just as unpopular in the Crimea as it did everywhere else in the USSR. In 1929–30, Stalin ordered the Cheka to crack down on Tatar nationalism in the Crimea, which led to 3,500 Tatars being executed and 35,000 sent to the Gulag in Siberia.

After Chekist death squads raided several Tatar communities, and Stalin decreed the suppression of their Muslim faith and Turkish language, the Crimean Tatars had had enough of Communist rule. In December 1930, a Tatar rebellion erupted at the village of Alakat on the southern coast of the Crimea after the NKVD executed 42 Tatar prisoners. Stalin sent the Red Army to ruthlessly crush the uprising and to inflict more reprisals on the Tatar community in the Crimea. Forced collectivization resulted in another famine in 1931–33, which reduced the population further. Stalin continued to single the Crimean Tatars out for harsh treatment during the rest of the 1930s, which continued right up to the beginning of World War II. By some estimates, between 1921 and 1941, the communists eliminated about half the Crimean Tatar population, or roughly 165,000 people.

The ethnic German population in the Crimea, numbering 43,631 in 1926, was not targeted in the initial Red Terror. After all, the founders of Marxism – Marx and Engels – had been Germans. Yet the Crimean Germans fell foul of the forced collectivization program in the late 1920s, which appropriated their agricultural communes established in Tsarist times and exiled thousands of them to the Urals.

As an adjunct to the Red Terror in the Crimea, the Soviet regime toyed with the idea of creating a Jewish Republic in the Crimea. Two concepts were behind this proposal: that Jews were regarded as more loyal to the Communist regime and would bind the region to the Soviet state, and that Jewish-operated agricultural colonies could provide hard-currency exports to the Near East. Consequently, the Soviet regime established a committee known as OZET (for "Society for Settling Toiling Jews on the Land"), which encouraged Jewish emigration to the Crimea in 1924–34, doubling the population within a decade. Although the regime provided some funds, OZET was initially quite successful in enticing foreign investments, including over $20 million from the United States. Land was no problem, since the NKVD simply appropriated land from Tatars and *Volksdeutsche* (ethnic Germans), both of whom were regarded as enemies of the regime. Yet by the mid-1930s, it was apparent that this project had produced only mediocre results – mostly due to recurrent famines and the effects of collectivization – so the idea of a Jewish Republic fell out of favor. When Stalin began his purges in 1937, OZET was one of the early victims, and its leadership was liquidated. However, in the minds of local Tatars and *Volksdeutsche*, the Jews in the Crimea were inextricably linked to the Communist regime that they detested and feared.

Once Wrangel's Fleet left, the Black Sea Fleet (Chernomorsky Flot) ceased to exist. The new Soviet state had no naval forces worthy of the name in the Black Sea and the naval facility at Sevastopol was damaged. The Whites, Germans, British, French, and Ukrainians had sabotaged the warships left behind, including those under construction at Nikolayev. A handful of older, less useful warships could eventually be salvaged. By 1922, the Soviets had repaired two obsolete 240-ton *Sokol*-class destroyers and one *Morzh*-class submarine, providing the nucleus of a new Black Sea Fleet. Other incomplete ships were available at Nikolayev, but it would take years to get the shipyard fully operational again.

In the interim, the Soviet regime tried to acquire ships for the Black Sea Fleet by any means. Soviet diplomats approached the French with the proposal to buy back part of Wrangel's Fleet, which was interned in Bizerte, Tunisia. The Soviet Navy was particularly interested in purchasing the dreadnought *General Alekseyev* and some of the newer destroyers, but the French dragged out the negotiations and then decided not to return any of the vessels to the USSR. By 1924, the Nikolayev shipyard was able to repair four incomplete destroyers of the *Fidonisy* class; these four ships became the backbone of the Black Sea Fleet from 1925–30. The elderly light cruiser *Komintern* was also made operational again, as well as four small AG-class submarines. By 1926, the Black Sea Fleet had one light cruiser, six destroyers, and four submarines operational – but just barely.

In 1927, a special underwater salvage unit, known as EPRON (*Ekspyeditsiya podvodnih rabot osobogo naznachyeniya*), was set up to begin raising some of the scuttled warships from the waters around Sevastopol, Nikolayev, and Novorossiysk. EPRON was able to refloat the destroyer *Bystry*, but its engines were wrecked. Subsequently, EPRON divers refloated the destroyer *Gadzhibey* and salvaged its engines, which were then fitted in the *Bystry* – enabling it to become operational again. EPRON made special efforts to salvage material from the two sunken *Imperatritsa Mariya*-class dreadnoughts in the area. The Whites had taken the capsized *Imperatritsa Mariya* into the Sevastopol dockyards in May 1919 in order to begin salvage work, and there it was found when the Red Army entered the city. Although the hull was beyond repair, the armament was worth salvaging and EPRON recovered her 12in gun turrets as well as some of her 130mm secondary batteries. Less successful was the effort to salvage 12in gun ammunition from the sunken *Svobodnaya Rossiya* in Novorossiysk, which resulted in a magazine explosion. Two Tsarist-era light cruisers were also under reconstruction, but it took more than a decade to get them both into service. The Nikolayev shipyard was finally able to begin construction of a few submarines in 1929, but it would not be able to begin building major warships for another six years.

Stalin was not initially concerned about the feeble nature of the Black Sea Fleet, but he changed his mind when the Turkish Government announced that it was going to modernize the battle cruiser *Yavuz* and purchase new destroyers and submarines from Italy. It was unacceptable to Stalin that Turkey should appear to have a superior naval force in the Black Sea, so he directed the Baltic Sea Fleet to transfer the battleship *Parizhskaya Kommuna* and the light cruiser *Profintern* there. When the *Parizhskaya Kommuna* arrived at Sevastopol in January 1930, it became the flagship of the Black Sea Fleet. However, Stalin was unwilling to devote any significant resources toward new naval construction while he was engaged in building up Soviet industry, and first priority went to the Red Army and then the Air Force (VVS). It was not until 1935 that Stalin authorized a naval expansion program, with two *Kirov*-class heavy cruisers, two *Leningrad*-class destroyer leaders, six *Gnevny*-class destroyers, and a large number of submarines intended to reinforce the Black Sea Fleet. Due to disappointing technical performance from Soviet-built destroyers, funds were even appropriated to purchase a destroyer leader from Italy, which entered the Black Sea Fleet in 1939 as the *Tashkent*. The *Parizhskaya Kommuna* was extensively modernized in 1939–40, but all of the *Gangut*-class dreadnoughts still lacked the firepower and protection of modern battleships. Consequently, Stalin approved construction of a new class of 59,000-ton battleships, armed with 16in guns; the one intended for the Black Sea Fleet was designated as the *Sovetskaya Ukraina* and was laid down at Nikolayev in October 1938. The heavy cruiser Molotov, completed in early 1941, was the first and only warship in the Black Sea Fleet equipped with air-warning radar; its Redut-K system could detect enemy aircraft at a range of 75 miles.

Vice-Admiral Filip S. Oktyabrsky took command of the Black Sea Fleet in March 1939. The 41-year-old was a product of the Stalinist purges, which had eliminated many of the more experienced Tsarist-era naval officers. Oktyabrsky came from the merchant marine and had no naval experience from either World War I or the Russian Civil War. He was given a smattering of technical and doctrinal training at the new Naval Academy in Leningrad in 1925–28, but thereafter his command experience was limited to minesweepers and motor torpedo boats. By June 1941 the Black Sea Fleet had blossomed into a considerable general-purpose force, and Oktyabrsky was responsible for a cruiser brigade, three destroyer divisions, and eight submarine divisions, which were equipped with one battleship, two heavy and four light cruisers, 17 destroyers, and 44 submarines. Nevertheless, putting a man without prior command experience of even a destroyer in charge of a fleet of this size and complexity would have a noticeable effect upon the Black Sea Fleet's ability to perform its missions around the Crimea.

Oktyabrsky also had no prior experience with naval aviation, but he had a very powerful force in the Black Sea Fleet Navy Air Force (VVS-ChF), which had 626 aircraft.[3] The two primary missions of the VVS-ChF were to conduct maritime reconnaissance over the Black Sea and to provide fighter cover over the fleet and its bases. The VVS-ChF had 139 Beriev MBR-2 flying boats for the reconnaissance mission within the 119th Reconnaissance Regiment and six separate squadrons. Air cover for the fleet was provided by three fighter regiments equipped with a total of 140 biplane fighters (I-15bis, I-153) and 91 monoplane I-16s. A single modern MiG-1 fighter had arrived at Yevpatoriya by June 1941, but the VVS-ChF lagged behind the VVS in modernization efforts. The fighters could provide a reasonable degree of zone protection over Soviet naval bases, but their limited range and endurance inhibited their ability to cover fleet operations far from the coast. On the other hand, the VVS-ChF had a decent medium-range strike capability in its two bomber regiments, equipped with a total of 117 Ilyushin DB-3F and Tupolev SB-2 bombers, which had the range to strike targets on the Romanian coast. However, barely 20 percent of the aircrews were trained in June 1941, which greatly restricted operational capabilities at the outset of the war.

In March 1910, the Tsarist regime had recognized that the defenses around the main naval base at Sevastopol were outdated. The existing coastal-defense batteries were concentrated around the harbor entrance and consisted of artillery from the 1870s and 1880s. Most batteries had limited arcs of fire and were unsuited for ground defense. The vulnerability of Port Arthur to surprise naval attack and then ground assault during the recent Russo-Japanese War influenced the Russian Navy's decision toward a major modernization of its coastal defenses at its key bases. In particular, the Russian Admiralty became interested in replacing outdated coastal artillery with a powerful new 12in/52cal. naval gun (305mm) developed by the Obukhovskii Works in St Petersburg in 1907. The 305mm Obukhovskii could fire a 446kg shell out to a maximum range of 28 miles, and if mounted in a fully traversing turret, would be ideal for the dual coastal and ground defense role. Funds to update the coastal defenses around Sevastopol were authorized in 1911, and several smaller batteries armed with 120mm guns were completed in 1912–13. However, the main element of the coastal-defense upgrade was to construct two new batteries, each equipped with two twin Obukhovskii 305mm guns mounted in armored turrets. The Russian fortification expert, General César A. Cui (of French-Lithuanian heritage) was sent to head the project, and he selected sites for the two batteries north and south of Sevastopol. General-Major Nestor A. Buynitsky, one of the foremost Russian engineers, took over the actual construction of the two 305mm turret batteries. Cui's design was quite sophisticated, and in addition to building the batteries, Buynitsky was also tasked with building a railroad spur for each construction site and creating a large-scale concrete manufacturing capability in situ. Despite the untimely death of Buynitsky in late 1914, work progressed fairly quickly on the southernmost 305mm battery, later designated Coastal Battery No. 35, but only the initial site preparations had been completed on the northernmost battery site, later designated Coastal Battery No. 30, before the Russian Revolution brought construction to an abrupt halt. The four massive twin-305mm turrets, each weighing over 1,000 tons, had been built by the St Petersburg Metal Works Plant during the war, but some of the guns had been removed for use in coastal defenses on the Baltic and none of the turrets had arrived in the Crimea.

Once Wrangel's forces were driven from the Crimea, the Revolutionary Military Council was mindful of the role played by Anglo-French naval forces in intervening in the Crimea both in 1854–55 and 1918–20 and was eager to deter future reoccurrences. The council decided to resume work on the Tsarist-era coastal-defense program but initially lacked the resources to accomplish much. Virtually all of the 27 coastal batteries around Sevastopol had been rendered inoperative by the Anglo-French before they evacuated the port, and Red Army engineers were able to repair only two 152mm batteries in 1921. Construction of the two 305mm batteries languished for seven years until the council was finally able to provide sufficient resources and labor to resume work on Coastal Battery No. 35 in 1924. Four 305mm guns from the Baltic Fleet battleship *Poltava*, which had been damaged by fire in 1919, were recovered and mounted in the turrets manufactured in St Petersburg during the war.[4] By mid-1926, both turrets were installed in Coastal Battery No. 35 and the installation was declared operational late in 1927, even though the rangefinder and fire-control mechanisms were not installed until the mid-1930s. The battery's command bunker and a magazine holding 800 305mm rounds were protected by 13ft of reinforced concrete, designed to withstand 16in naval gunfire. Coastal Battery No. 35 had a peacetime garrison of 234 naval personnel, but in wartime would be augmented with antiaircraft gunners and more security troops. In July 1929, Stalin visited Coastal Battery No. 35 on an inspection trip, and among his entourage was Generalmajor Werner von Blomberg, head of the Truppenamt. This was during the period of Soviet–German covert military cooperation, and Stalin wanted to impress his German visitors with Soviet defensive capabilities in the Black Sea. Stalin suggested that the battery should demonstrate its firepower by firing a 305mm round, but when informed that each projectile "cost more than a tractor," he demurred.

Construction on the northern Coastal Battery No. 30, located near the Bel'bek River, proceeded much more slowly, and it was not until March 1928 that the Revolutionary Military Council allocated 3.8 million rubles to restart work, which did not actually begin for two more years. The project was badly organized, falling far behind schedule. Coastal Battery No. 30 was declared operational in mid-1934, but its complicated rangefinder system was not ready until 1940. However, the Achilles Heel of both 305mm batteries was that they drew their electrical power from Sevastopol's power grid through a transformer station; if civilian power was lost the massive turrets would become inoperable. Auxiliary diesel generators were emplaced near the command-post bunkers, but only sufficed to provide power for communications and lighting. In fact, both 305mm batteries only became fully operational about six months before the German invasion. Lieutenant Georgy A. Aleksandr had arrived to take

33

command of Coastal Battery No. 30 in November 1937 and Lieutenant Aleksei Y. Leshenko took command of Battery No. 35 in November 1940.

Once Stalin's program of forced industrialization became established by the mid-1930s, the Black Sea Fleet was provided with greater resources, which enabled it to continue to improve its coastal defenses right up to the start of the German invasion. In addition to protecting Sevastopol, the Soviet Navy built three large coastal batteries to protect Kerch. The Black Sea Fleet also was provided with 300 antiaircraft guns to provide additional protection against enemy air attacks on its bases.

The Black Sea Fleet was responsible for the defense of its main naval base at Sevastopol, including coastal artillery and antiaircraft guns, while the Red Army was responsible for the land defense of the Crimea. There were no large naval infantry (*morskaya pekhota*) units formed in the Crimea at the start of the war. The only major Red Army formation in the Crimea in June 1941 was General-Lieutenant Pavel I. Batov's 9th Rifle Corps, comprised of the 106th and 156th Rifle Divisions and 32nd Cavalry Division. This corps had been organized in the North Caucasus Military District and moved to the Crimea in mid-May 1941. Batov arrived at the corps headquarters in Simferopol just two days prior to the beginning of the German invasion. Falling under the authority of the Odessa Military District (to become the Southern Front on mobilization) Batov was instructed that his mission was to defend the Crimea against possible amphibious or airborne attacks, but he received no guidance on coordinating with the Black Sea Fleet. Altogether, Batov's 9th Rifle Corps had about 35,000 troops and could be supplemented by local militia. The Soviet Air Force (VVS) units assigned to the Odessa Military District were grouped around Odessa and had no significant presence in the Crimea in June 1941.

The Soviet General Staff expected to fight future wars primarily on foreign soil, but acknowledged that enemy bombers and warships might be able to attack facilities in exposed areas such as the Crimea. Although Turkey was regarded as an unlikely threat, it had amassed more than 500 combat aircraft by 1940, making it the largest air force in the Balkans and the Middle East. Turkey's acquisition of five foreign-built submarines also aroused Soviet concern. However, the ratification of the Montreux Convention in 1936 eased Soviet concerns by inhibiting foreign fleets from transiting through the Turkish Straits into the Black Sea.

The Kingdom of Romania had not been regarded as a potential enemy during the interwar period, but this changed when Germany and the Soviet Union signed their infamous Non-Aggression Pact in August 1939, which secretly condoned the Soviet acquisition of the Romanian border province of Bessarabia. In June 1940, the Red Army invaded Bessarabia and humiliated the Romanian Army, providing a motive for revenge. Five months later, a coup in Bucharest installed a fascist dictatorship, which quickly signed an alliance with Germany. The new German-Romanian alliance threatened the Soviet position in the Black Sea and for the first time since the Russian Civil War exposed the Crimea to possible enemy air or amphibious attacks. The Royal Romanian Air Force was rapidly developing its offensive capabilities in 1937–40 by taking delivery of Italian-made S79 medium bombers in 1938 and German-made He-111H medium bombers in 1940. By June 1941 the Romanians had formed four bomber groups with 96 bombers. In addition, they had three long-range reconnaissance squadrons equipped with 37 Bristol Blenheims – which posed a credible threat to the Black Sea Fleet.

Although the Soviet High Command was very concerned about the possibility of enemy amphibious landings in the Crimea, there was actually little possibility of that occurring. The Royal Romanian Navy was little more than a coast guard, with only four destroyers, one submarine, a single minelayer, and a few assorted auxiliaries. Romanian vessels were mostly obsolete and too outclassed to risk a head-on action against even part of the Black Sea Fleet. Furthermore, Romania's merchant marine was tiny, with only 35 vessels of 111,678 GRT (gross register tonnage). Five of these merchantmen were modern vessels that would be useful for convoy operations, but the fact is that Romania lacked the ability to move more than limited quantities of troops and supplies across the Black Sea and had no ability to conduct an opposed landing.

MILITARY TERRAIN FEATURES OF THE CRIMEA, 1941–44

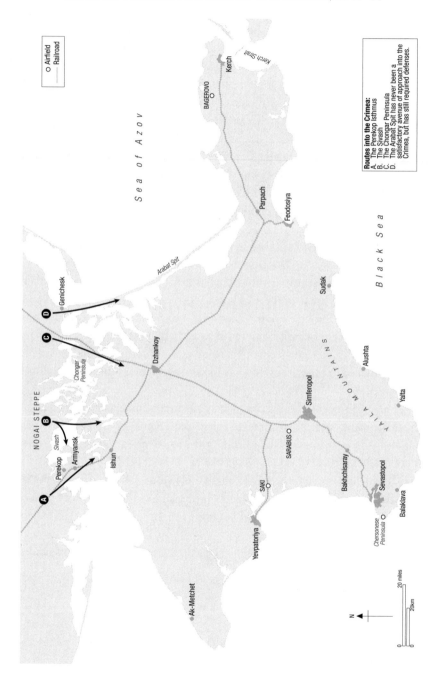

○ Airfield
— Railroad

Routes into the Crimea:
A. The Perekop Isthmus
B. The Sivash
C. The Chongar Peninsula
D. The Arabat Spit has never been a satisfactory avenue of approach into the Crimea, but has still required defenses.

CHAPTER 2

The Onset of War, June–August 1941

"The beauties of the Crimea, which we shall make accessible by means of an Autobahn. For us Germans, that will be our Riviera."
Adolf Hitler, July 5, 1941

The exact details of Soviet strategic planning prior to Operation *Barbarossa* are difficult to quantify, but a number of Stalin's pre-war strategic assumptions are clear. Foremost, Stalin believed that the Red Army was strong enough to deter a German invasion for the time being. Even if the Germans were tempted to commit aggression against the Soviet Union, Stalin believed that there would be adequate early warning to provide the Red Army time to prepare and deploy its forces for combat. Soviet military leaders were not ignorant of the threat posed by Germany after the sudden fall of France in 1940, but believed that their forces and plans would prevail. A series of war games conducted by the Soviet General Staff in Moscow in December 1940 suggested that the Germans would make their main effort in Ukraine, but that their forces would be pushed back to the border long before they reached the Dnepr River.[1]

When war came, the mission of the Black Sea Fleet was to assist the Red Army's Southern Front in defending the coastline of the Black Sea. To that end, one of the primary tasks was laying defensive minefields outside Sevastopol and the other Black Sea ports. However, the fleet also wanted to use its naval air arm and submarines to attack enemy naval targets and facilities in the Black Sea – but little real planning had been put into this concept. At the start of the war in June 1941, the Soviet Stavka (high command) was wary that Turkey might allow Axis air and naval forces to move through her waters in defiance of the Montreux Convention, so Batov's 9th Rifle Corps was ordered to deploy its forces along the coast from Yevpatoriya to Kerch to repel potential amphibious or airborne attacks. No effort was made to construct ground defenses at either Perekop or Sevastopol, since the Stavka believed that the fighting would be confined to the border regions. Instead, the Soviets would use the Crimea as a springboard for air and naval attacks on Romania in order to distract German forces from the main area of battle.

Although *Barbarossa* did not address the neutralization of the Black Sea Fleet, the Luftwaffe included it in its first-strike plan. Before dawn on June 22, 1941, a small number of He-111 bombers from Fliegerkorps IV's 6./KG 4 approached Sevastopol unchallenged and managed to drop their bombs near Vice-Admiral Oktyabrsky's headquarters. It was only a raid, not a serious attack, but it rattled Oktyabrsky and inflicted 230 civilian casualties.[2] Thereafter, Fliegerkorps IV conducted occasional raids and reconnaissance flights on Sevastopol, as well as some aerial mine-laying operations off the port, but the main fighting was occurring in the western Ukraine.

Shortly after the attack on his headquarters, Oktyabrsky initiated defensive mine-laying operations, and his ships emplaced about 3,000 mines by mid-July. He also decided to commit the VVS-ChF to a campaign of attacking the Romanian ports of Constanta and Sulina. The first raid conducted by 3 DB-3F from 2 MTAP and 6 SB-2 from 40 BAP on the afternoon of June 22 met little resistance and succeeded in inflicting minor damage. However, the Royal Romanian Air Force was alert when the VVS-ChF sent 73 naval bombers on June 23, and Romanian Hurricane fighters shot down three. The next day, German Bf-109 fighters from III./JG 52 also got involved and shot down ten of 32 naval bombers.[3] Within the first five days of the war, the VVS-ChF lost 22 naval bombers, including some of their best-trained aircrew. Oktyabrsky was apparently ignorant of the arrival of significant Luftwaffe strength in Romania, which threatened his surface warships and made raids on Romania costly.

Although his fleet's mission was primarily defensive, Oktyabrsky was inclined from the beginning to use his surface warships and submarines to strike at Romania. In the first 24 hours of the war, he dispatched four *Shchuka*-class submarines to attack Romanian shipping, but this was only a preliminary step. On the evening of June 25, Oktyabrsky sent the flotilla leaders *Moskva* and *Kharkov* to bombard the Romanian port of Constanta, with the heavy cruiser *Voroshilov* and two destroyers as a covering force. The two Soviet flotilla leaders approached the Romanian coast and opened fire at 0358hrs on June 26. Although their 130mm shells managed to set some oil-storage tanks alight and damage a rail yard, the Soviet destroyers were unaware that the Germans had installed two 28cm coastal-defense batteries to protect Constanta. Battery Tirpitz engaged the two Soviet flotilla leaders, which caused them to break off the action and turn away eastward – straight into a Romanian minefield. The *Moskva*, moving at 30 knots, hit one or more mines and broke in two, sinking within five minutes; 268 sailors were killed and 69 survivors were picked up by the Romanians. The cruiser *Voroshilov* was also damaged by a mine. Retreating eastward, the *Kharkov* was badly damaged by the German coastal battery and had to be towed. Fortunately for the Soviet flotilla, the Luftwaffe was busy with a raid by the VVS-ChF and did not appear in force to sink the damaged Soviet warships. The result of the raid on Constanta, aside from the damage suffered by the Black Sea Fleet, was to cause Oktyabrsky to be much more cautious in his use of surface warships.

Oktyabrsky continued to send the VVS-ChF to attack targets in Romania with small-scale raids, which also began to bomb facilities further inland. On July 13, six DB-3F bombers attacked the Ploesti oil refinery – a critical source of fuel for the Wehrmacht – and managed to damage a refinery and set 9,000 tons of oil on fire. However, enemy fighters shot down four of the six bombers, and in response the VVS-ChF shifted primarily to night raids to reduce losses. On August 13, Soviet naval bombers damaged the King Carol Bridge over the Danube, which disrupted the Ploesti–Constanta pipeline. Nevertheless, Ploesti was 340 miles from the VVS-ChF air bases in the Crimea, and aircraft like the DB-3F were tactical, not strategic, bombers; at best, each bomber could carry only six 100kg bombs to targets in Romania. While the VVS-ChF raids on Romania did not inflict substantial damage on the Axis war effort, they did help to create the impression that Soviet air bases in the Crimea were a threat.

The original plan for Operation *Barbarossa*, the invasion of the Soviet Union, issued in Führer Directive 21 on December 18, 1940, did not even mention the Crimea or the Black Sea Fleet. Hitler intended that *Barbarossa* would result in the rapid destruction of the best part of the Red Army, followed by the occupation of most of the western Soviet Union, which would satisfy his lust for natural resources and *Lebensraum* (living space). The priority of the German operational effort was weighted on the Leningrad and Moscow axes, and the only specified objectives for Generalfeldmarschall Gerd von Rundstedt's Heeresgruppe Süd was to "destroy all Russian forces west of the Dnepr in Ukraine," and "the early capture of the Donets Basin, important for war industry."[4] The occupation of the Crimea and the elimination of the Black Sea Fleet were only implied tasks at the outset of the German invasion, to be accomplished during mop-up operations. After the issuing of Führer Directive 21, Hitler and the Oberkommando der Wehrmacht (OKW) focused much of their attention and planning efforts on the Balkans, the Mediterranean, and collaboration with Axis partners, rather than further fleshing out operational details of Operation *Barbarossa*. Indeed, it remained a rather vague plan right up to the moment of execution, and this would force the Wehrmacht to constantly shift resources as Hitler changed his strategic priorities.

Yet *Barbarossa* was not the only German planning being made in regard to the Soviet Union. Once Hitler confirmed his intention to invade the Soviet Union, SS-Obergruppenführer Reinhard Heydrich's

Reichssicherheitshauptamt (Reich Main Security Office, or RSHA) began working on Generalplan Ost (Master Plan East), which was intended to conduct ethnic cleansing on a massive scale in conquered Soviet territory. Not only Jews, but also Ukrainians, and, eventually, all Slavs, were targeted for elimination by the SS-Einsatzgruppen. Once the indigenous populations were reduced to a manageable level, where the survivors could be employed as slave labor, German colonists would move in to "Germanize" the conquered territory. Unlike the Wehrmacht, Heydrich did make plans for Ukraine and the Crimea; the Crimean climate was regarded as ideal for colonists, and Ukrainian wheat and Crimean cotton would be valuable resources. Prior to *Barbarossa*, pseudo-scientific archeological research conducted by the SS Ahnenerbe organization pointed to an ancient Gothic presence in the Crimea as a precursor to modern German colonization of the peninsula.[5] Once Generalplan Ost was underway, Heydrich expected that about half the Crimea's population would be ethnic German by the mid-1960s.

At the start of *Barbarossa*, SS-Gruppenführer Otto Ohlendorf's Einsatzgruppe D was attached to Heeresgruppe Süd. Ohlendorf's unit was to follow close behind Rundstedt's advancing armies and eliminate large concentrations of civilians deemed hostile to the Reich. Although many army leaders later claimed ignorance of SS activities in the Soviet Union, the cooperation between the Wehrmacht and the SS-Einsatzgruppen was a vital prerequisite in order for Generalplan Ost to succeed.

It was Oktyabrsky's persistent VVS-ChF air raids on Romania and the threat to Ploesti's oil refinery that finally caused Hitler to take real interest in the Crimea. He was very nervous about any threats to his oil supplies from Ploesti, and recognized that the Crimea was a useful staging base for Soviet attacks on Romania, serving in the role of an "unsinkable aircraft carrier." While Luftwaffe air raids on the VVS-ChF bases in the Crimea succeeded in destroying some aircraft on the ground, the only sure way to permanently stop the attacks on Romania was for German forces to occupy the Crimea sooner than expected.

On July 23, 1941 – ten days after the first VVS-ChF raid on Ploesti – a supplement to Führer Directive 33 was issued. It stated that once Heeresgruppe Süd occupied Kharkov, "the bulk of the infantry divisions will then occupy Ukraine, the Crimea, and the area of Central Russia up to the Don." Less than three weeks later, a supplement to Führer Directive

34, issued on August 12, raised the priority of the Crimea further, stating that Heeresgruppe Süd was "to occupy the Crimean Peninsula, which is particularly dangerous as an enemy air base against the Romanian oilfields."[6] The VVS-ChF had gained Hitler's attention. Once the Dnepr River was crossed, Rundstedt was obligated to send a strong force to occupy the Crimea. Hitler also began to openly talk of the great value that the Crimea would play in post-war German colonization plans in the East.

While Oktyabrsky was using his bombers and submarines to try and harass the Romanian coast, the Soviet Southern Front was being defeated in detail by the Heeresgruppe Süd. On August 2, Panzergruppe 1 surrounded the bulk of the Soviet 6th and 12th Armies in the Uman *Kessel* and crushed the trapped Red Army units within a week. The battered Soviet 9th and 18th Armies, having escaped the Uman debacle, retreated toward the Dnepr River. On August 18, the 16. Panzer-Division captured the port of Nikolayev, which deprived the Black Sea Fleet of its main construction and repair facility. Meanwhile, the Romanian 4th Army had surrounded the port of Odessa, held by the Separate Coastal Army. Outnumbered 4-1 and isolated, the Coastal Army could hold Odessa only if the Black Sea Fleet ensured that supplies and reinforcements could be brought in by sea, as well as providing naval gunfire support as needed. Oktyabrsky had to commit a large portion of his surface forces and VVS-ChF aircraft into the fighting around Odessa. Although Oktyabrsky was able to hold back the battleship *Parizhskaya Kommuna* and his two modern heavy cruisers, he deployed three light cruisers and six to eight destroyers to support the Odessa garrison. For the most part, the Black Sea Fleet played an important part in keeping the siege of Odessa going for ten weeks, and it learned some valuable lessons about convoy operations, mine warfare, and amphibious landings in the process. However, the fighting at Odessa was a doomed effort from the start, and it served to drain resources from the Crimea, which would soon face its own test of fire.

Meanwhile, Generaloberst Eugen Ritter von Schobert's 11. Armee (AOK 11) pursued the battered Soviet 9th Army to the Dnepr, but the Soviets managed to slip across the river, blow up the main bridges, and establish a hasty defense. Recognizing that German forces could cross the

Dnepr at any time, Stavka Directive No. 00931, issued on August 14, activated the 51st Army in the Crimea and it was tasked to "hold the Crimean Peninsula in our hands to the last soldier." Although Batov's 9th Rifle Corps formed the core of the 51st Army, General-Colonel Fyodor I. Kuznetsov was brought down from Leningrad to take command of the new formation. In addition to Batov's two regular rifle divisions, Kuznetsov was provided with two newly formed reserve rifle divisions from the Orel Military District, four militia divisions, and the 5th Tank Regiment. All told, Kuznetsov's 51st Army had about 95,000 troops, but relatively little artillery or transport. Stavka Directive No. 00931 also made the Black Sea Fleet subordinate to Kuznetsov.

Kuznetsov was forced to begin throwing together a defense at the Perekop Isthmus in mid-August with most of his units still en route or severely understrength. Roughly 30,000 local civilians were used to assist the Red Army in fortifying the Perekop Isthmus and Chongar Peninsula, but Kuznetsov was ordered to "immediately clear" these areas of "anti-Soviet elements." On August 16, NKVD detachments rounded up virtually all of the remaining Crimean Germans and deported them to the Urals, where most spent the next decade in labor camps operated by the NKVD. Roughly 20 percent of the Crimean Germans died in these camps.[7]

Kuznetsov's deployment for battle was seriously hindered by faulty intelligence issued in General Staff Order No. 001033 on August 18, 1941:

> According to information from the English military mission, the Germans are preparing sea [amphibious] operations against the Crimea in the most immediate future, while concentrating amphibious assault transports in Bulgarian and Romanian ports. The amphibious assault operation will be supported by airborne forces, which are concentrating in the Nikolayev region.[8]

Despite the fact that the Axis had no appreciable amphibious capability in the Black Sea in August 1941 and their airborne forces were spent after their costly victory in Crete three months earlier, the Stavka was convinced that the threat was real. Accordingly, Kuznetsov deployed 40,000 of his men along the coast to defend against a non-existent amphibious threat and 25,000 in the interior of the Crimea to defend against airborne landings. Consequently, only 30,000 troops were left to defend the vital northern approaches into the Crimea, with just 7,000 troops from Colonel Aleksandr I. Danilin's 156th Rifle Division at Perekop. Since there were no tanks assigned to the 51st Army, the Southern Front scraped together ten T-34 tanks and 56 T-37/38 tankettes from repair depots to form the 5th Tank Regiment under Major Semyon P. Baranov; the tanks were sent by rail to provide Kuznetsov with a small mobile reserve.

On August 30, the 11. Armee conducted an assault crossing of the Dnepr at Berislav and succeeded in building a pontoon bridge across the river. The 9th Army managed to impede the German build-up across the river for a week but Schobert conducted a breakout attack on September 9–10 that shattered the Soviet perimeter and forced the 9th Army to retreat eastward in disorder toward Melitopol. The approaches to the Crimea were now open. Schobert was faced with a dilemma, since he was tasked with both seizing the Crimea and supporting Panzergruppe 1's advance toward Rostov. As soon as he had achieved a clean breakout from the Berislav bridgehead, he directed XXX Armeekorps and XXXXIX Gebirgs-Armeekorps to pursue the 9th Army to Melitopol, while sending General der Kavallerie Erik Hansen's LIV Armeekorps toward Perekop. German intelligence about Soviet force in the Crimea was sketchy, based entirely upon aerial reconnaissance, and they were unaware of the creation of the 51st Army. Schobert ordered Hansen to send a fast advance guard to try and seize the Perekop Isthmus by *coup de main*, hoping that it was poorly guarded. In his moment of victory, however, Schobert was killed when his Fiesler Storch crashed on September 12. Hitler appointed General der Infanterie Erich von Manstein to replace Schobert, but he would not arrive for five days.

On the same day as Schobert's death, SS-Sturmbannführer Kurt Meyer's Aufklärungs-Abteilung LSSAH from the Leibstandarte SS Adolf Hitler (LSSAH) division approached Perekop after a 35-mile dash from the Berislav bridgehead. Oberstleutnant Oskar von Boddien's Aufklärungs-Abteilung 22 was close behind, and together these two reconnaissance units reached the village of Preobrazhenka, 5 miles north of the Tatar Wall, at around 0600hrs. Meyer had a mixed reconnaissance group of *Kradschützen* (motorcycle infantry), a few armored cars, and a *Panzerjäger* platoon with 3.7cm antitank guns, but no artillery or engineers. Upon entering the village, his lead company was fired upon by 76mm guns from the Soviet armored train *Voykovets* and engaged by small-arms fire from dug-in Soviet infantrymen. 2nd Battalion/361st Rifle Regiment from Danilin's 156th Rifle Division was entrenched in a strongpoint in the nearby Chervonyi Chaban State Farm. In addition to this strongpoint, Meyer could see that the area further south around Perekop was heavily fortified with bunkers and barbed wire. He beat a hasty retreat under cover of smoke and reported back to LIV Armeekorps that, "coup against Perekop impossible."[9]

CHAPTER 3

Across the Tatar Wall, September 1941

"... and I will show you where the Iron Crosses grow...."
Feldwebel Rolf Steiner, *The Cross of Iron* (1977)

When Manstein arrived at Nikolayev on September 17 to take command of the 11. Armee (AOK 11), he found that the bulk of his forces were advancing toward Melitopol while Hansen's LIV Armeekorps had moved its 46. and 73. Infanterie-Divisionen up near Perekop but had taken no action to reduce the Soviet defenses. XXX Armeekorps had sealed off the Chongar Peninsula and Arabat Spit with the LSSAH Division, but also had made no effort to penetrate into the Crimea. Schobert's death had given Kuznetsov a vital breathing space in which to enhance his defenses. The difficulty of moving supplies across the Dnepr, with all bridges down, also made it difficult for the 11. Armee to mount a hasty assault at Perekop, since LIV Armeekorps was short of fuel and artillery ammunition.

Danilin's 156th Rifle Division built three lines of defense across the Perekop Isthmus, with the main line of resistance centered upon the Tatar Wall. The outer line of defense consisted of two rifle battalions deployed in forward strongpoints, each supported by an artillery battalion. Colonel Vladimir P. Shurygin, the 51st Army's senior engineer, used civilian labor to dig a 6ft-deep antitank ditch behind this outer covering force, and emplace four lines of tanglefoot-type barbed-wire obstacles. Shurygin's engineers built concrete and timber/stone bunkers for 76mm cannon and 45mm antitank guns in the main line of resistance, as well as digging in several tanks. The Tatar Wall itself was fronted by the ancient moat, which was now 36ft deep and 104ft wide; the wall sat atop a 15ft-high earth berm. The area was completely open, without trees or vegetation, and the Soviets could observe every move that the Germans made. However, the most frightening aspect of the Perekop defenses for the Germans was the extensive use of antipersonnel mines; up to this point in the war the Wehrmacht had not yet had to penetrate a defense of this kind. Not only did Shurygin's engineers emplace thousands of PMD wooden antipersonnel mines, but they buried 50kg aerial bombs and even large naval mines from the depots at Sevastopol. Another innovation was the use of buried flamethrowers with trip wires. Indeed, Kuznetsov got a bit carried away in sending materiel to reinforce the Perekop defenses, including some mines filled with mustard gas; when the Stavka learned of this, Kuznetsov was rebuked and told not to employ chemical weapons without permission.[1]

Luftwaffe aerial reconnaissance was able to detect much of the Soviet defensive preparations at Perekop, which were unsettling for Manstein. He hoped to avoid a costly frontal assault, and set the 11. Armee's engineers to finding a method for bypassing the Perekop defenses, just like his *Sichelschnitt* plan had bypassed the French Maginot Line in 1940. Leutnant Nübling from Gebirgs-Pionier-Regiment 620 conducted an extensive reconnaissance and survey of the Sivash, hoping to find a route across as the Red Army had done in 1920. However, tidal conditions at this time were unsatisfactory; the water at the narrower western end of the Sivash was less than a yard deep, but the bottom was too soft and German scouts sank in to their hips. Manstein asked if assault boats from the 902 Sturmboote-Kommando could be used to cross the Sivash, but Leutnant Nübling found that the water conditions were unfavorable.[2] Furthermore,

THE GERMAN ATTACKS AT PEREKOP AND ISHUN, SEPTEMBER–OCTOBER 1941

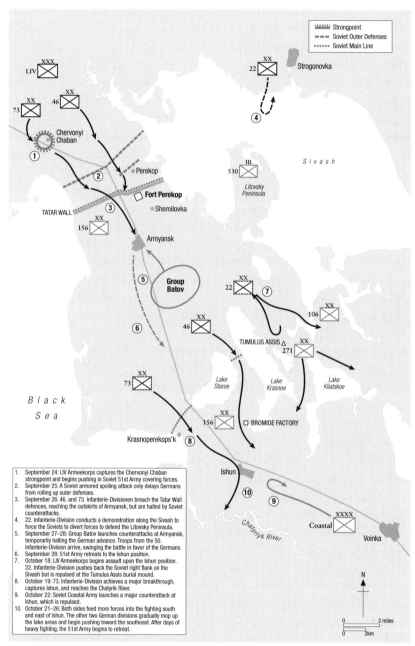

LIV XXX

73 XX   46 XX

Chervonyi Chaban

①

② Perekop

22 XX Strogonovka

Strongpoint
Soviet Outer Defenses
Soviet Main Line

④

530 III

Litovsky Peninsula

Sivash

Fort Perekop

③ TATAR WALL

156 XX

Shemilovka

Armyansk

⑤ Group Batov

22 XX ⑦

106 XX

46 XX

⑥

TUMULUS ASSIS △ 271 XX

Black Sea

73 XX

Lake Staroe

Lake Krasnoe

Lake Kliatskoe

156 XX

□ BROMIDE FACTORY

Krasnoperekops'k ⑧

Ishun

⑩ ⑨

Chatyryk River

Coastal XXXX

Voinka

1. September 24: LIV Armeekorps captures the Chervonyi Chaban strongpoint and begins pushing in Soviet 51st Army covering forces.
2. September 25: A Soviet armored spoiling attack only delays Germans from rolling up outer defenses.
3. September 26: 46. and 73. Infanterie-Divisionen breach the Tatar Wall defences, reaching the outskirts of Armyansk, but are halted by Soviet counterattacks.
4. 22. Infanterie-Division conducts a demonstration along the Sivash to force the Soviets to divert forces to defend the Litovsky Peninsula.
5. September 27–28: Group Batov launches counterattacks at Armyansk, temporarily halting the German advance. Troops from the 50. Infanterie-Division arrive, swinging the battle in favor of the Germans.
6. September 28: 51st Army retreats to the Ishun position.
7. October 18: LIV Armeekorps begins assault upon the Ishun position. 22. Infanterie-Division pushes back the Soviet right flank on the Sivash but is repulsed at the Tumulus Assis burial mound.
8. October 19: 73. Infanterie-Division achieves a major breakthrough, captures Ishun, and reaches the Chatyrik River.
9. October 22: Soviet Coastal Army launches a major counterattack at Ishun, which is repulsed.
10. October 21–26: Both sides feed more forces into the fighting south and east of Ishun. The other two German divisions gradually mop up the lake areas and begin pushing toward the southeast. After days of heavy fighting, the 51st Army begins to retreat.

N

0   2 miles
0   2km

Kuznetsov expected the Germans to try and cross the Sivash and directed Danilin to put two rifle battalions from his 530th Rifle Regiment on the Litovsky Peninsula where the Red Army had crossed in 1920. Nor did the route across the Chongar Peninsula look promising, since the Soviets had blown up the main railroad bridge and emplaced obstacles in the water.

Thus, Manstein was forced to conduct a frontal attack at Perekop. He knew that in order to break a fortified line, particularly in a place where any form of maneuver or surprise was impossible, it would be imperative to add every combat multiplier possible to give the assault a reasonable chance for success. His only armor support came from the assault guns from Sturmgeschütz-Abteilung 190.[3] Since *Barbarossa* had envisioned maneuver warfare, not positional battles or sieges, the 11. Armee had limited artillery and engineer assets, so Manstein would have to rob from Peter to pay Paul. He decided to accept the risk with XXX Armeekorps, involved in the pursuit to Melitopol, and transfer as much of its combat resources as possible to Hansen. Manstein provided Hansen with four additional heavy-artillery battalions (schwere Artillerie-Abteilung 737 with three Czech-made 14.9cm howitzers; schwere Artillerie-Abteilung 641 with four Czech-made 30.5cm mortars; I./AR 814 with two Czech-made 24cm howitzers, four 10cm s.K 18, and three 15cm s.FH 18; and the Romanian 54th Heavy Artillery Battalion with 12 Skoda 15cm howitzers), plus a Nebelwerfer battery. He stripped XXX Armeekorps of its corps-level artillery, transferring II./AR54 and IV./AR207 to Hansen. When added to his two divisional artillery regiments, Hansen's artillery park totaled about 152 pieces. When Manstein first took command, LIV Armeekorps was short of artillery ammunition, but by September 23 Hansen had received enough medium-caliber ammunition to mount a attack. However, the heavy-artillery ammunition was very limited, with only 100 rounds of 24cm and 133 of 30.5cm for each assault division.[4] Hansen also received 2,575 replacements just five days before the attack at Perekop, bringing his two infantry divisions back up to strength. The offensive was set for September 24, and Manstein kept part of the LSSAH Division in reserve to exploit the expected breakthrough.

Generalleutnant Johannes Zuckertort, who was a so-called *Mischling* (halfbreed) of Jewish descent, had to receive a German blood certificate signed personally by Adolf Hitler in order to remain in the Wehrmacht. His younger brother Karl, also a general, had commanded Panzer-Regiment 5 prior to the war but had been expelled from the Wehrmacht in July 1941 (probably for anti-regime attitudes). Thus, Johannes had a strong incentive to toe the Nazi line if he wanted to remain in the Wehrmacht. Now he was responsible for planning the artillery support for Hansen's assault on the Perekop position. Zuckertort directed that HArko 110 (Army-level Artillery Command) would control the light artillery, while HArko 20 would direct the heavy artillery. The artillery preparation commenced at 0500hrs on September 24, with the divisional artillery firing over 2,500 rounds at the Soviet positions. Fliegerkorps IV was able to provide only limited air support to Hansen, but bombers from KG 27 and KG 51 bombed Soviet defenses around Perekop. The Soviet VVS and VVS-ChF were still quite active over the Crimea and neither side had air superiority.

At Y-Hour (0730hrs), assault groups from the 46. and 73. Infanterie-Divisionen moved up to attack Danilin's outer defensive line. Generalmajor Kurt Himer's 46. Infanterie-Division was a Welle 1 (1st wave) formation, consisting primarily of pre-war regulars, but Generalleutnant Bruno Bieler's 73. Infanterie-Division was a Welle 2 formation, made up primarily of reservists. Each division attacked with four or five battalions, supported by pioneers, 2cm flak guns, *Panzerjägers* and a battery of StuG III assault guns. Oberstleutnant Otto Hitzfeld, commander of Infanterie-Regiment 213 led the 73. Infanterie-Division's main effort against the Chervonyi Chaban State Farm strongpoint, held by Captain E. K. Ivashin's 2nd Battalion/361st Rifle Regiment. The Soviet troops were well dug in behind a thick obstacle belt and were supported by plentiful artillery. The engineers from Pionier-Bataillon 173 supporting Hitzfeld's infantry went first, creating a breach in the Soviet obstacle belt under fire, but suffering heavy losses in the process. Finally, a breach was secured and, under cover of smoke grenades, two battalions from Hitzfeld's regiment closed in on the Soviet strongpoint. Intense close combat ensued, and flamethrowers and concentrated charges were used to eliminate Soviet bunkers. Ivashin's battalion was gradually destroyed piece by piece, and the farm strongpoint was overrun after Ju-88s from KG 51 bombed it.[5] However, Hitzfeld had lost four company commanders, and overall the 73. Infanterie-Division suffered 770 casualties on the first day of the offensive. In the eastern sector the 46. Infanterie-Division had a slightly easier time, but still suffered

329 casualties and made only modest progress. At the cost of over 1,100 casualties, Hansen had defeated Kuznetsov's covering forces but had not yet reached the main line of resistance.

Manstein ordered the 22. Infanterie-Division and part of LSSAH to launch diversionary actions at Chongar and along the Sivash, but these failed to impress Kuznetsov. By the end of September 24, Kuznetsov knew that the Germans were making their main effort at Perekop, and he ordered the unengaged 106th Rifle Division to send its 442nd Rifle Regiment to replace Danilin's losses.

At dawn on September 25, Hansen resumed his assault and continued to mop up Danilin's forward security positions. The German *Stossgruppen* (assault groups) were mixed formations, built around an infantry battalion and supported by a pioneer platoon, a section of assault guns, and a platoon of 2cm flak guns. Soviet artillery fire was intense, and inflicted most of the German casualties in the flat terrain, although Soviet machine guns firing from earthen bunkers were difficult to suppress. As the German *Stossgruppen* approached the main line of resistance at the Tatar Wall, Danilin decided to mount a spoiling attack with his reserve: Infanterie-Regiment 530 and Major Semyon P. Baranov's 5th Tank Regiment. However, Baranov sent in only his T-37 and T-40 light tanks, keeping his ten T-34s back, so the counterattack was repulsed by German *Panzerjäger* fire, which knocked out eight light tanks. German losses on the second day of the attack were only 322, but Danilin had lost about one-third of his infantry.

Hansen made his main assault against the Tatar Wall on the morning of September 26, beginning with a terrific artillery preparation that used up much of his remaining artillery ammunition, and dive-bombing attacks by Ju-87 Stukas from StG 77. Fighters from III./JG 77 also appeared in force over the Perekop Isthmus and claimed 27 kills on this day.[6] Both of Hansen's divisions were exhausted after two days of heavy close-quarter fighting, but so was Danilin's 156th Rifle Division. The main strength of the Soviet line was built around the 3rd Battalion, 361st Rifle Regiment. Manstein provided SS pioneers and an artillery battalion from the LSSAH to reinforce the attack. Hitzfeld's IR 213 committed the III./IR 213 and II./IR 170, plus some SS pioneers, to breach the Tatar Wall. Under cover of smoke and support weapons, assault squads reached the ditch around 0900hrs and used wooden boards to ascend the steep wall of the ditch and reach the top, which was covered with barbed wire and trenches. Inside their trenches, invisible from below, Soviet infantrymen hurled grenades into the ditch, inflicting heavy losses on the German pioneers. Soviet return fire was intense, but Gefreiter Willibald Unfried, a machine gunner in 9./IR 213, placed suppressive fire on the parapet, which kept the Soviet soldier's heads down at the crucial moment. German combined-arms tactics, aggressive small-unit leadership, and the presence of skilled soldiers such as Unfried paid off, as assault squads managed to fight their way to the top. The 361st Rifle Regiment fought very well, but by 1030hrs their defense was collapsing. Then, west of Fort Perekop, it suddenly broke. *Stossgruppen* from both divisions surged forward, overrunning mortar and antitank positions. Incredibly, Hitzfeld's troops fought their way into the town of Armyansk, south of the Tatar Wall, and engaged in tense house-to-house fighting against remnants of the 156th Rifle Division, dug in at a brick factory.

By 1100hrs, Danilin's Division was broken and the Germans were across the Tatar Wall in force. Kuznetsov committed Operational Group Batov (the 383rd, 442nd, and 856th Rifle Regiments) under his deputy, General-Lieutenant Pavel I. Batov, to immediately counterattack and restore the main line of resistance. Batov's infantry went in with virtually no artillery support, but they managed to force the 46. Infanterie-Division troops back to the Tatar Wall, and Hitzfeld's men were ejected from Armyansk by 1400hrs. With the attack faltering, Hansen committed a *Kampfgruppe* from 50. Infanterie-Division, just arrived from Odessa. The Luftwaffe also arrived in force, tipping the balance to the Germans. With fresh infantry, the Germans surged forward and captured all of Armyansk by nightfall. The day ended with Kuznetsov's troops still holding the eastern part of the Tatar Wall, but with their operational reserves spent and little infantry left south of Armyansk to stop Hansen from pushing on to the reserve positions at Ishun. The tactical victory of breaching the Tatar Wall had cost Hansen's LIV Armeekorps over 600 casualties.

The Stavka was incensed that Kuznetsov had lost the Tatar Wall line so quickly, and ordered him to keep attacking. At dawn on September 27, Batov renewed his counterattack to push the Germans back to the Tatar Wall. Initially, Batov's infantry retook most of Armyansk, and Hitzfeld's troops retreated to a strongpoint at the brick factory in the northern part of the town. There he held on against Batov's infantry attacks all day long. However, German pioneers from Pionier-Bataillon 173 began building a wooden 16-ton bridge across the western end of the Tatar Ditch, which enabled them to get some StuG III assault guns from Oberleutnant Reinhard Näther's 3./Sturmgeschütz-Abteilung 190 across. Soviet artillery fire caused great losses among the laboring pioneers, and Pionier-Bataillon 173 suffered 118 casualties in creating the crossing over the Tatar Ditch.[7] A sharp German attack by a *Kampfgruppe* from 50. Infanterie-Division, supported by the assault guns and some Stukas from StG 77 retook most of Armyansk and pushed Batov's depleted infantry back.

In one final fling, Batov attacked Armyansk again at dawn on September 28, and not only drove out Hitzfeld's troops, but some of Major Baranov's T-34 tanks even succeeded in reaching the Tatar Wall. Yet the victory was brief, and Batov's last reserves were spent in the process. By 1835hrs, Kuznetsov reported to Moscow that he had no reserves left and his hold on Armyansk was tenuous. Less than three hours later, the Germans recaptured Armyansk and Kuznetsov pleaded for permission to withdraw to his reserve positions at Ishun, which were unoccupied. The Stavka was very displeased with Kuznetsov and believed – probably rightly so – that he had exercised poor use of his reserves and was unable to coordinate effective counterattacks. Yet the Stavka finally acceded and authorized Kuznetsov to withdraw to Ishun. Over the next few days, Major Baranov's tankers fought a series of successful rearguard actions that prevented an effective pursuit, and all but one of his ten T-34s came through intact.

The battle of Perekop cost Hansen's LIV Armeekorps a total of 2,641 casualties, and both of his two divisions were badly mauled after five days of see-saw combat. Hitzfeld's IR 213 had suffered a total of 746 casualties, including two battalion commanders, eight company commanders, and 49 platoon leaders.[8] German material losses were also quite heavy. The 73. Infanterie-Division lost 13 artillery pieces and 12 3.7cm Pak guns, along with a good deal of infantry equipment. However, it was the loss of trained combat leaders, particularly the death of five battalion commanders, that was so painful. On the other side of the ledger, the Germans claimed to have captured 10,019 troops from the 51st Army at Perekop, along with 32 tanks, 68 artillery pieces (incl. 7 150mm howitzers), 43 Pak guns, and 88 mortars – indicating that the 156th and 271st Rifle Divisions were almost totally destroyed.[9] Nevertheless, it is clear that the battle of Perekop was a close-run thing and that the German margin of victory was very slim.

Hansen might have made short work of the Ishun position if the Soviet Southern Front had not recovered and launched a painful counterattack against the Romanians west of Melitopol. In order to feed the fight at Perekop, Manstein had stripped XXX Armeekorps of many of its best resources and pushed Romanian units into the front line, which the Soviets decided to exploit. Just as the Tatar Wall was breached, Manstein was compelled to send the LSSAH, all of Sturmgeschütz-Abteilung 190, and much of his Fliegerkorps IV air support to deal with the crisis near Melitopol. The resulting battle of the Sea of Azov lasted more than a week, resulting in the encirclement and destruction of the Soviet 9th and 18th Armies, but the 51st Army received a vital reprieve.

After Hansen's breakthrough at Perekop, Kuznetsov and Oktyabrsky reported to Moscow that they would have difficulty holding the Crimea without reinforcements and recommended evacuating Odessa, transferring the Independent Coastal Army by sea to reinforce the 51st Army in the Crimea. Reluctantly, the Stavka agreed to this recommendation on September 29, 1941, and four days later the 157th Rifle Division began moving from Odessa to Sevastopol, escorted by the Black Sea Fleet.[10] Distracted by the fighting around Melitopol, Fliegerkorps IV made no effort to interfere with the evacuation of Odessa. Quietly, the Black Sea Fleet picked up the pace in the second week of October, and it was not until the final convoy began loading at Odessa on October 14 that the Luftwaffe took an interest in the Soviet operation. Yet of the 11 Soviet transports, loaded with thousands of troops, the Luftwaffe managed to sink only one small transport and damage another. The bulk of the Independent Coastal Army was delivered virtually intact to Sevastopol – this was perhaps the Black Sea Fleet's finest moment in World War II.

Kuznetsov would need all the soldiers he could get to hold the position at Ishun. Although the 51st Army still had about 50,000 troops in the Crimea, he had to leave one rifle division to guard the Chongar Peninsula and other troops to watch possible crossing sites across the Sivash, leaving barely 15,000–20,000 troops to form a line at Ishun. Furthermore, many of his remaining troops were militiamen, and the cream of Batov's 9th Rifle Corps had been eliminated in the fighting for Perekop. Oktyabrsky

sent Kuznetsov two battalions of naval infantrymen from Sevastopol to reinforce the Ishun position, and the 157th Rifle Division that was the first to arrive from Odessa was en route, but Kuznetsov was short of artillery as well. The Stavka did send aerial reinforcements to the Crimea, including a squadron of the latest Yak-1 fighters for the 32nd Fighter Regiment (32 IAP) of the VVS-ChF, leading to several sharp encounters with the Bf-109s of III./JG 77.

German scouts arrived near Ishun, following in the footsteps of Kuznetsov's retreating army; they found it to be nearly as formidable as the Perekop position. Ishun was a small town at the southern base of the Perekop Peninsula, flanked by three large salt lakes and the Black Sea. Only three mobility corridors existed between these obstacles, and the widest, between the Black Sea and Lake Staroe, where the rail line ran, was only 1,400 yards wide. The terrain was completely devoid of cover and was marshy, making movement of assault guns or other heavy weapons very difficult. Kuznetsov deployed his steadiest units, the 361st Rifle Regiment, a rifle battalion from the 172nd Rifle Division, and the two naval infantry battalions to guard this critical sector. He put the rest of the veteran 156th Rifle Division in the other potential avenue of advance between Lake Staroe and Lake Krasnoe, with a strongpoint built in a bromide factory. In order to cover his right flank, Kuznetsov deployed his 106th and 271st Rifle Divisions between Lake Krasnoe and the Sivash, even though it was a less likely avenue of approach. Indeed, throughout the fighting on the Perekop Isthmus, Kuznetsov consistently put too many forces to cover his flank on the Sivash even though Manstein had found this option impractical – the memory of the 1920 campaign now created a fear in the Red Army of being flanked. In terms of support weapons, Major Baranov still had nine T-34 tanks operational in the 5th Tank Regiment, but Kuznetsov's artillery park was much reduced and limited to mostly older 76mm howitzers. Several improvised armored trains were being hastily assembled in Sevastopol's workshops and the *Voykovets* would soon be joined by the *Smyert' fashizmu* (Death to Fascism), which would provide Kuznetsov with some useful mobile firepower.

Meanwhile, following victory in the battle of the Sea of Azov, Manstein had convinced the OKH that the 11. Armee could not accomplish two divergent operational objectives, and it was decided that AOK 11 would concentrate exclusively on the Crimea, while Generaloberst Ewald von

Kleist's Panzergruppe 1 continued the drive on Rostov. Unfortunately, the OKH also decided to strip AOK 11 of XXXXIX Gebirgs-Armeekorps along with the LSSAH Division, leaving Manstein with just six infantry divisions in XXX and LIV Armeekorps to conquer the Crimea. Hansen's battered LIV Armeekorps had followed rather than pursued Kuznetsov's 51st Army to Ishun, but was in no shape to mount a serious attack until the rest of the 11. Armee began arriving in mid-October.

Since tactical surprise and maneuver were impossible in this restrictive terrain, Manstein decided to surprise Kuznetsov by attacking all three avenues of approach simultaneously. However, he would begin his main effort in the east with Generalmajor Ludwig Wolff's relatively fresh 22. Infanterie-Division, then shift his main effort to the west with Bieler's 73. Infanterie-Division. Himer's 46. Infanterie-Division would conduct fixing attacks in the center, to prevent Kuznetsov from shifting forces between his flanks. Zuckertort was once again in charge of the artillery preparation, but had scarcely more heavy artillery pieces or ammunition than he had at Perekop. Indeed, AOK 11's artillery park was grossly inadequate for a deliberate attack against a fortified position such as this, forcing Manstein to depend even more heavily upon the Luftwaffe to make up the difference. In addition to more Ju-87 Stukas from StG 77, II./JG 3 and III./JG 52 were shifted to Chaplinka airfield to give Fliegerkorps IV a total of three Bf-109 *Gruppen* over the Perekop Isthmus. Oberst Werner Mölders, the Luftwaffe's top-scoring pilot at this point of the war, arrived at Chaplinka to direct air operations over the Perekop. The other three divisions of the AOK 11, the 50., 72., and 170. Infanterie-Division, provided their divisional artillery and pioneer battalions to support the LIV Armeekorps attack, but otherwise were kept in reserve to exploit any breakthrough. Manstein's only armor support was Major Hans Vogt's Sturmgeschütz-Abteilung 190, with about 20 StuG-IIIs, which had been returned after the Soviet defeat at Melitopol. Each of the three assault divisions in LIV Armeekorps were assigned one of Vogt's assault-gun batteries.

At 0600hrs on October 18, Zuckertort commenced his artillery preparation. His main trump cards were a few batteries of 24cm howitzers and 30.5cm mortars, which he used to pulverize the obvious Soviet strongpoints. He directed the divisional 10.5cm and 15cm howitzers against the enemy barbed-wire obstacles and forward trenches. However,

Zuckertort had no accurate long-range guns for counterbattery fire, and he had a tendency to fire small numbers of rounds at a great many targets, failing to achieve sufficient concentration to significantly disrupt the defense. After two hours of pounding away at the Soviet fieldworks and obstacle belt, Hansen's three divisions sent their *Stossgruppen* forward. The biggest surprise came on the eastern flank by the Sivash, where Oberst Ernst Haccius led two battalions of his IR 65 across 490 yards of shallow water and caught the 442nd Rifle Regiment by surprise; Haccius lost a battalion commander killed and three company commanders wounded, but his regiment completely tore apart Kuznetsov's right flank.

However, Wolff's other regiment, Oberstleutnant Albert R. Latz's IR 47, conducted a frontal assault across open ground against the 397th Rifle Regiment atop the Tumulus Assis burial mound. This small rise proved key terrain and Latz's two assault battalions had to conduct a World War I-style infantry assault with predictable results. The German infantry was hopelessly channeled down a narrow mile-wide flat isthmus, with marshy lakes on both flanks. The soldiers advanced in loose formations, followed by pioneer platoons. A battery of Nebelwerfer rocket launchers laid down a smoke barrage in front of the Germans, but the Soviet machine gunners simply fired into the smoke while their battalion 82mm mortars laid down a curtain of high-explosive rounds in front of their barbed-wire obstacle belt. I./IR 47 was decimated, with its battalion commander killed and two company commanders wounded. Latz's men were stopped cold with very heavy losses. Wolff made the mistake of reinforcing failure by sending in his reserve battalion, II./IR 16, which was also shot to pieces. He also failed to employ his assault guns to support his infantry. It had been a painful day for Wolff's 22. Infanterie-Division, with 685 casualties. In the center, the 46. Infanterie-Division made modest gains against the 417th Rifle Regiment, at a cost of fewer than 200 casualties. On the western flank, IR 170 from the 73. Infanterie-Division penetrated only the outer portion of the main Soviet defensive belt between Lake Staroe and the Black Sea. During the day, Soviet counterbattery fire was quite effective, and knocked out a number of German observation posts and reconnaissance elements. Both Soviet armored trains supported the defense near Ishun with fire from their 76mm batteries. The first day was far from a success for Hansen's LIV Armeekorps, which suffered over 1,300 casualties for only small gains.

Still, the Luftwaffe had a good day. Mölders began sending his Bf-109F fighters over the Perekop at 0700hrs and caught the VVS-ChF by surprise. Hauptmann Gordon Gollob, the commander of II./JG 3, claimed to have shot down nine MiG-3 fighters over the Perekop during the course of three sorties – while it is unclear if these claims are all valid, there is no doubt that the Soviet naval fighters suffered heavy losses over the Perekop. Gollob, an Austrian, had 61 aerial victories before coming to the Crimea, and had been awarded the *Ritterkreuz des Eisernen Kreuzes*, but it was in the Crimea that he really established his reputation.

Despite this lackluster start on the first day, Hansen's troops enjoyed remarkable success on October 19. Latz's depleted IR 47 was forced to make another attempt against the Tumulus Assis strongpoint, and this time he sent in Oberstleutnant Rudolf G. Buhse's III./IR 47 and the assault guns. The 36-year-old Buhse was no stranger to critical situations, having fought in the air-landing operation in Holland in 1940 and then having led his battalion in an assault crossing of the Dnepr at Berislav in 1941. He was an aggressive Prussian infantry officer and an excellent tactician. Supported by a battery of StuG III assault guns, pioneers, and a 2cm flak platoon that suppressed some of the Soviet machine gunners, Buhse led his battalion in small assault teams. Eventually, they managed to get through the barbed-wire obstacle belts and get close enough to suppress some of the forward Soviet positions with grenades and automatic-weapons fire. Once they realized that their defense had been pierced, the Soviet 397th Rifle Regiment abandoned the Tumulus Assis strongpoint. Although Buhse's gallant attack, combined with the earlier success by Haccius'ss IR 65, had unhinged Kuznetsov's right flank, the Soviet 106th and 271st Rifle Divisions simply fell further back on the isthmus, which afforded numerous defensive positions.

Infantrymen from Bieler's 73. Infanterie-Division achieved an even larger tactical success on the western side of the isthmus, where Zuckertort finally massed enough firepower to pulverize the obstacle belt in front of the 361st Rifle Regiment. Once the path was clear, two battalions from IR 186 and the III./IR 213 assaulted through the breach, supported by Oberleutnant Hartmann's 2./Sturmgeschütz-Abteilung 190.[11] Zuckertort's bombardment apparently suppressed the defenders, because the German infantry quickly overran the Soviet infantry in the center of their front and captured the fortified village of Krasnoperekops'k. The two battalions of Soviet naval infantry holding the sector along Lake Staroe and a rifle battalion from the 172nd Rifle Division protecting the Black Sea coast were soon isolated by the German advance. As Soviet resistance evaporated in the center, Bieler's *Stossgruppen* continued to advance, and were in the town of Ishun before Major Baranov's tankers, placed there in reserve, knew what was happening – Kuznetsov's command and control had collapsed. Two T-34s were immobilized and captured by German *Panzerjägers* before the remaining seven tanks beat a hasty retreat. Still full of fight, IR 186 pressed on and seized a crossing over the Chatyrlyk River from dumbfounded security troops from the Soviet 42nd Cavalry Division. Bieler's troops had advanced over 5 miles straight through the densest part of the 51st Army's defenses, and at the cost of only 150 casualties.

By the evening of October 19, the 51st Army was near broken and Kuznetsov had lost control over the battle. However, the first element of the Coastal Army, Colonel Dmitri I. Tomilov's 157th Rifle Division, was marching up from Sevastopol and would soon be available for a counterattack. Kuznetsov planned to fling the 157th Rifle Division at the 73. Infanterie-Division's salient at Ishun, supported by the remainder of Batov's two dismounted cavalry divisions. General-Major Ivan Y. Petrov, commander of the Coastal Army, was now subordinate to Kuznetsov but doubtless chagrined that one of his best units would be committed into action piecemeal in order to relieve the 51st Army's situation. On the morning of October 20, two regiments of Tomilov's 157th Rifle Division, supported by 122mm howitzer fire, attacked Ishun from the southeast while Batov's cavalrymen attacked from the southwest. Initially, the attack went well and Bieler's exhausted troops had their hands full trying to hold off a fresh Soviet division supported by Baranov's T-34s. The 73. Infanterie-Division gave ground and evacuated Ishun, while conducting a fighting delay. The commander of the 2. Batterie from Sturmgeschütz-Abteilung 190, Oberleutnant Hartmann, was killed attempting to hold Ishun. However, it was now the Soviet troops who were exposed in the open, and the bombers of Fliegerkorps IV, plus Zuckertort's artillery, mercilessly pounded Tomilov's division. A Luftwaffe air strike found Tomilov's command post and bombed it, wounding him and much of his staff. The Soviet attack faltered and Bieler counterattacked, retaking Ishun and pushing the 157th Rifle Division back to the river. Heavy rain then brought the day's fighting to a close, with little change in positions. Both sides continued to hack away at each other the next day, but with no major moves.

The Stavka was shocked to find out that Kuznetsov had lost the Ishun position so quickly, and following his loss of Perekop it was clear that his skills at battle command were not up to the task of holding the Crimea. A special Stavka representative was sent to the Crimea, who relieved Kuznetsov of command on the evening of October 22. Amazingly, the Stavka decided to put the navy in charge of defending the entire Crimea, and Vice-Admiral Gordey I. Levchenko was put in command of all Soviet ground, air, and naval forces in the Crimea. For all his faults as a commander, Kuznetsov had a better understanding of the situation at Ishun than Levchenko, who had been Stavka's naval representative at Odessa. Levchenko, who had been a crewman on the cruiser *Aurora* during the storming of the Winter Palace in 1917, had impeccable Soviet credentials, but had never commanded troops in ground combat before, and was not familiar with the Ishun position. Whereas Kuznetsov had recognized that the 51st Army was approaching the end of its rope, and recommended retreating to another blocking position, Levchenko dutifully followed his instructions from the Stavka to keep attacking and restore the original defensive line.

Hansen's LIV Armeekorps was near the end of its infantry strength, so Manstein allowed his forces to temporarily shift to the tactical defense while the fresher 132. Infanterie-Division moved up to the front. Manstein had also pleaded with Heeresgruppe Süd for more help from the Luftwaffe, since Zuckertort's artillery was running out of ammunition. Oberst Mölders sent all three of his fighter *Gruppen* in a sweep over the Perekop on October 23 and caught the VVS-ChF by surprise. A squadron from III./JG 52 intercepted six Pe-2 bombers and four Yak-1 fighters attacking the positions of the 46. Infanterie-Division near the Bromide Factory on Lake Krasnoe – shooting down all the bombers and three Yaks for the loss of one Bf-109. On the same day, Hauptmann Gordon Gollob claimed another three MiG-3 fighters. All told, Mölders' fighters destroyed 23 fighters and six bombers for the loss of one of their own aircraft, effectively breaking the VVS-ChF's control over the Perekop.[12]

Levchenko was not able to organize a large-scale counterattack until the morning of October 24, by which point his air support was gone. He decided to base his effort on Petrov's newly arrived 25th and 95th Rifle Divisions, both heavily depleted from months of fighting at Odessa, plus the remaining combat-effective elements of the 51st Army, now led by Batov. The Soviets attacked the 73. Infanterie-Division's positions near Ishun with massed infantry and a few T-34s, but negligible artillery support. Hansen's frontline units were short of infantry but still had plenty of MG-34 machine-gun teams and 8cm mortar squads, which were used to shred the attacking waves. Overhead, the bombers of KG 27 wreaked havoc on the Red Army formations, and probably destroyed the armored train *Smyert' fashizmu* and damaged the *Voykovets*. Although Petrov's infantry courageously advanced several miles into the teeth of concentrated German firepower, they could not break the defense and the attack failed. On October 25 Levchenko ordered Petrov to attack again, but the subsequent heavy losses were too much. Sensing weakness, the Germans waited until Petrov's troops were spent and then committed the fresh 170. Infanterie-Division into a counterattack south of Ishun. The Soviet front began to collapse, and the 170. Infanterie-Division advanced over 4 miles. Soviet command and control disintegrated as Levchenko and Batov both decided to relocate their headquarters to the south but failed to inform Petrov.

On October 26, the initiative clearly shifted back to the Germans, and Manstein released the 132. Infanterie-Division to reinforce Hansen's push to the south. Here and there, the Soviet defenses began to fall apart, and units began retreating without orders, although others continued to cling to strongpoints. Most of Batov's 51st Army troops were retreating in disorder before the day's end, although Petrov had better control over his troops and began a more disciplined withdrawal toward Simferopol on his own authority. Manstein had won the battle at Ishun, but at the exorbitant cost of 7,286 casualties, including 1,515 dead or missing. When the earlier battle at Perekop is included, Manstein's AOK 11 suffered over 12,000 casualties – equivalent to an entire division – to break through Soviet defenses on the Perekop Isthmus. However, the Soviets had little to rejoice about, since the 51st Army and Coastal Army had lost about a quarter of their strength trying to hold the Perekop positions, including 16,000 prisoners taken around Ishun. Batov's retreating 51st Army had very little remaining combat power, particularly after the loss of about 200 artillery pieces. Petrov's Coastal Army was in better shape, since it arrived only in the later stages of the fighting for the Perekop, but it still lost 28,000 of its 80,000 troops.

Manstein had intended to conduct his pursuit with the LSSAH Division, but since this unit was no longer under his command, he had to improvise. He formed a scratch motorized unit known as Brigade Ziegler under Oberst Heinz Ziegler, the chief of staff of XXXXII Armeekorps, to spearhead the pursuit of the defeated Soviet Coastal Army. AOK 11 provided Oberstleutnant Oskar von Boddien's Aufklärungs-Abteilung 22, Major Vogt's Sturmgeschütz-Abteilung 190, two bicycle-mounted reconnaissance companies, some motorized flak guns, and the army-level Panzerjäger-Abteilung 560 (equipped with 3.7cm Pak), but AOK 11 was surprisingly short of trucks due to heavy losses from Soviet air and artillery attacks in the crowded Perekop Isthmus. Instead, a good portion of the ad hoc brigade was composed of Romanian motorized cavalrymen from Colonel Radu Korné's 6th Motorized Rosiori Regiment.[13] Korné was one of the few Romanian tactical leaders who had impressed the Germans in the early stages of Operation *Barbarossa*, and he was known for aggressive and rapid advances. Ziegler was instructed to push hard on Petrov's heels in an effort to keep the Soviets on the run so that they did not stop to form a new line of resistance, but he clearly would not be able to capture a city such as Sevastopol with 2,000 lightly equipped motorized troops.

Once the Soviets were clearly withdrawing, Manstein reorganized and retasked the component formations of AOK 11: General der Infanterie Hans von Salmuth's XXX Armeekorps (22. and 72. Infanterie-Divisionen) would clear the Sivash coast and push toward Dzhankoy; Hansen's battered LIV Armeekorps (50. and 132. Infanterie-Divisionen and Brigade Ziegler) would first clear the port of Yevpatoriya, then head for Sevastopol; and Generalleutnant Hans Graf von Sponeck's XXXXII Armeekorps (46., 73., and 170. Infanterie-Divisionen) would pursue the 51st Army toward Feodosiya and Kerch. Salmuth formed his own ad hoc motorized unit under Major Robert Pretz, commander of Pionier-Bataillon 22, to lead his pursuit. Kampfgruppe Pretz consisted of pioneers, light flak, and *Panzerjägers*. Manstein was also provided the Romanian Mountain Corps, but its forces were screening the north side of the Chongar Peninsula and were not in a position to aid a rapid pursuit into the Crimea.

Petrov's Coastal Army fell back toward Yevpatoriya with the 25th, 95th and 321st Rifle Divisions. There were two main roads heading south from the Perekop: the road to Yevpatoriya and the road to Simferopol. Petrov split his three rifle divisions between these two routes and ordered the

42nd Cavalry Division to act as rearguard and covering force. However, the Soviet units had few motorized vehicles, and initially tried to conduct a slow, fighting withdrawal. One of only four T-34 tanks still operational, commanded by S. Borisov, conducted a single-tank delaying action, pausing to ambush the German advance units before retreating some more. Setting out from Ishun, Brigade Ziegler managed to get past Petrov's ineffectual cavalry screens and not only get between the two roads on which Petrov's troops were travelling, but get ahead of them by the end of October 29. Once past Petrov's troops, Ziegler's mixed German-Romanian force boldly pushed on to the outskirts of Simferopol on October 30, meeting negligible resistance. The main Soviet command post known as "Red Cave" had already been abandoned. The armored train *Voykovets* tried to fight a mobile rearguard action but was caught by Luftwaffe bombers in the Simferopol rail yard and knocked out. LIV Armeekorps was also force-marching southward, shoving Petrov's small rearguard forces out of the way. Petrov continued marching slowly toward Simferopol, but was isolated and in danger of encirclement – if Manstein had had the LSSAH Division, the Coastal Army would have been pinned against the coast and destroyed. Yet German newsreels were already calling this "the victory march in the Crimea," with the attitude that all that was left were mop-up actions.

Meanwhile, Batov's broken 51st Army retreated toward the rail intersection at Dzhankoy where they hoped to link up with the 276th Rifle Division, which had been guarding the south side of the Chongar Peninsula. Although Batov tried to put up rearguards, XXX and XXXXII Armeekorps were hard on his heels and simply bowled them over before they could dig in, capturing thousands more Soviet troops in the process. A feeble effort to defend Dzhankoy failed when the 46. Infanterie-Division fought its way into the town on October 30. Aggravating Batov's situation, Kampfgruppe Pretz was nipping at Batov's flank along the Sivash, threatening to get ahead of the retreating Soviet divisions. After losing Dzhankoy, Batov's retreat became a rout. South of Dzhankoy, Colonel Aleksandr I. Danilin and the rest of his staff from the 156th Rifle Division were scooped up by a patrol from the German 170. Infanterie-Division around 1100hrs. Through a Bessarabian interpreter, a German intelligence officer from LIV Armeekorps interrogated Danilin, and in return for assuring him that he would not be executed, was able to extract important details about the direction of the Soviet retreat and the confusion in the Soviet command structure after the defeat at Ishun.[14] Thereafter, Danilin and his staff disappeared into German captivity, from which few survived.

In Sevastopol, Vice-Admiral Levchenko was out of touch with events at the front, and futilely attempted to direct Petrov and Batov by radio to form defensive positions, unaware that the Germans had already occupied them. Soon, Levchenko lost all radio contact with both armies, and became unable to exercise any kind of command and control over Soviet ground forces in the Crimea. Panic began to set in as the local Soviet military leadership came to realize the extent of the defeat at Ishun and the obvious fact that the Red Army was on the run. Vice-Admiral Oktyabrsky wasted little time, hoisting his flag on the destroyer *Boiky* in Sevastopol on the evening of October 28 and sailing for the port of Poti, with the battleship *Parizhskaya Kommuna* and the heavy cruiser *Molotov*. It was a *sauve qui peut* moment, like that the French army experienced at Sedan in 1940, with little thought for the consequences. Despite the fact that the Black Sea Fleet had already demonstrated an ability to conduct evacuations under fire at Odessa, which could have saved some of Petrov's and Batov's troops who were already cut off by German advances, only a feeble effort was made to save a few troops from Yevpatoriya. Similarly, naval gunfire might have delayed the German advance guard from entering Yevpatoriya and Feodosiya, but aside from two light cruisers and a handful of elderly destroyers, the rest of the fleet was running for cover in the Caucasian ports. Oktyabrsky was finally ordered to return to Sevastopol five days later, but the failure of the fleet to act contributed to the unfolding Soviet debacle in the Crimea.

Nor was there was any unity of command in Sevastopol during the critical days after Ishun. Instead, the newly formed Sevastopol City Defense Committee (Komitet oborana Sevastopolya or KOS) headed by SimferopolCommunist Party boss Boris A. Borisov concerned itself with local defense measures directed by the party, while the Military Council of the Black Sea Fleet (Voyenniy Sovyet Chernomorskogo flota), normally headed by Oktyabrsky, was temporarily headed by his deputy Rear-Admiral Gavrill B. Zhukov, who did little more than proclaim the city to be in a "state of siege." Yet not everyone in Sevastopol lost their heads. Colonel Pavel P. Gorpishchenko, an iron-willed instructor at the Black Sea Fleet's Mine Warfare School, formed an ad hoc defense unit from his cadets, then began recruiting sailors from several dry-docked warships in Sevastopol. In short order, Gorpishchenko organized several thousand armed sailors under his command, which was designated as the 1st Naval Infantry Regiment. The 6ft-tall Gorpishchenko was an experienced combat veteran of the Russian Civil War and a charismatic leader who instilled confidence in his sailors-turned-infantrymen. Three other naval infantry battalions, numbered 15, 16, and 17, were formed on October 29 from naval reservists, crewmen from ships under repair, and VVS base personnel. Soon thereafter, 18th and 19th Battalions were formed as well. General-Major Petr A. Morgunov, commander of all the coastal artillery batteries around Sevastopol, did not have the option of running, and put his batteries on full alert to fire on any approaching enemy ground forces.

Just as Oktyabrsky was leaving Sevastopol, the lead elements of Colonel Vladimir L. Vilshansky's 8th Naval Infantry Brigade were arriving on the cruiser *Krasny Krim* from Novorossiysk. Vilshansky's brigade was made up entirely of naval reservists, most of whom had not yet gone through basic training. His brigade had no artillery and very few automatic weapons. Upon arriving at Sevastopol, Vilshansky was met by Rear-Admiral Zhukov, who ordered him to concentrate his brigade at the Mekenzievy Mountain (named after Thomas Mackenzie, who founded Sevastopol in 1783) railroad station 2½ miles north of Sevastopol. By 1600hrs on October 30, Vilshansky had assembled 3,744 sailors from his brigade, and Zhukov ordered him to occupy a position behind the Kacha River near the town of Duvankoi to block the approaches to Sevastopol from the north.[15] Zhukov also dispatched 16th and 17th Naval Infantry Battalions and a training battalion north to form a blocking position at the Kacha River bridge to delay Brigade Ziegler from moving down the Simferopol–Sevastopol road. The black-clad sailors marched to these positions during the night of October 30/31 and by November 1 Zhukov had a thin screen of fewer than 6,000 sailors, armed mostly with rifles, protecting the approaches to Sevastopol. However, many of the sailors were equipped with AVS-36 automatic or SVT-38 semi-automatic rifles, which provided more firepower than standard bolt-action rifles. Ziegler's troops were surprised when they were assembling to attack the Kacha River bridge and came under fire from Coastal Battery No. 30's 305mm guns; the Soviets claimed that they inflicted very heavy casualties upon the German vanguard, but German records indicate approximately 35–40 casualties and that five trucks were lost.[16]

Without air or naval support and their command and control gone, the Red Army units in the Crimea scattered like a flock of birds. The only intact unit was Colonel Evgeny I. Zhidilov's 7th Naval Infantry Brigade, which had marched from Sevastopol to Simferopol. Zhidilov was an experienced combat veteran who had participated in the Soviet conquest of the Crimea in 1920, and his naval infantrymen were among the best Soviet troops in the Crimea. Yet by the morning of October 31, Ziegler's motorized columns had already blocked the Simferopol–Sevastopol road and captured Bakhchisaray, cutting off Zhidilov's brigade and Petrov's Coastal Army. Lieutenant Ivan A. Eaika's Coastal Battery No. 54, located north of the Kacha River, fired several rounds of 102mm fire at Ziegler's motorized column, but without effect.[17] On the same day, Aufklärungs-Abteilung 132 captured Yevpatoriya, thereby cutting off most of the 321st Rifle Division. Zhidilov's brigade put up a brief fight against the vanguard of the 72. Infanterie-Division north of Simferopol but then joined Petrov's herd of retreating units, trying to evade the German dragnet by heading southeast through the Crimean Mountains to Alushta. The last three T-34 tanks were abandoned in Simferopol due to lack of fuel, as well as many other vehicles. By the end of the day, the 72. Infanterie-Division had occupied Simferopol. Before leaving Simferopol, however, the NKVD executed a number of prisoners, mostly Tatars or people with foreign heritage, who had been rounded up in September as part of the effort to clear the Crimea of "enemies of the people."[18]

After the fall of Dzhankoy, Sponeck's XXXXII Armeekorps continued pursuing the 51st Army toward the Kerch Peninsula, while Salmuth's XXX Armeekorps veered southward to pursue Petrov and clear the Black Sea coast. The Romanian 1st Mountain Brigade succeeded in getting across the Chongar Peninsula and also pushed directly south for the Black Sea. Hansen's LIV Armeekorps advanced more slowly toward the northern approaches of Sevastopol with just the 50. and 132. Infanterie-Divisionen, while Salmuth sent the 72. Infanterie-Division on a wide sweep through the mountains to seize Yalta and then approach Sevastopol from the east along the coast road. The shortage of water had a major impact in slowing the German pursuit, particularly since the bulk of the artillery and supplies in the infantry divisions were dependent upon horse-drawn transport. Nevertheless, Gottlob H. Bidermann, then serving as an enlisted *Panzerjäger* in the 132. Infanterie-Division, noted that his division succeeded in marching over 30 miles per day during the pursuit phase.[19]

Although Manstein preferred a rapid descent upon Sevastopol, his forces were simply not structured for rapid-pursuit operations. Neither the 50. nor 72. Infanterie-Division possessed a reconnaissance battalion, which was usually the basis for forming a *Vorausabteilung* (vanguard battalion) for pursuit operations. Instead, they were forced to form *Vorausabteilungen* from the motorized *Panzerjäger* and infantry-gun companies organic to infantry regiments, which barely amounted to 200–300 troops in a few dozen thin-skinned vehicles. Aside from Ziegler's provisional brigade, Hansen's only other fast asset was Aufklärungs-Abteilung 132, which was split between clearing the area around Yevpatoriya and advancing toward Sevastopol. At best, an *Aufklärungs-Abteilung* in an infantry division had about 600 troops in three squadrons, including one mounted on horses and another on bicycles or motorcycles. The battalion's so-called "heavy squadron" had just three light armored cars, usually Sd. Kfz. 221, and a platoon each of towed 3.7cm Pak guns and 7.5cm infantry guns. These forces were not designed to punch through fortified lines or to operate more than 6 miles forward of supporting infantry and artillery.

It is a sad truth that war is very good to some people. Leutnant Erich Bärenfänger, the 26-year-old commander of 7. Kompanie of IR 123, was enjoying the pursuit. He was part of the *Vorausabteilung* of the 50. Infanterie-Division, and when the senior officer was wounded on the morning of November 2, Bärenfänger assumed command of the advance guard, which consisted of two rifle companies and a heavy-machine-gun platoon. The blond-haired, blue-eyed Bärenfänger was the prototypical Nazi, who had joined the SA at age 18 and received his commission just before the start of World War II. By the Crimean campaign, Bärenfänger already had three campaigns under his belt and he enjoyed a meteoric rise during the war, going from platoon leader to Generalmajor in six years. Pushing his troops to advance rapidly on their bicycles, horses, and a few captured vehicles, Bärenfänger's point squad caught up with the rear of one of Petrov's columns north of the Alma River on the afternoon of November 2. Imprudently, one Russian heavy-weapons column, with five trucks and 80 horse-drawn vehicles, halted to rest near a village without deploying proper security. Once apprised of their location by his scouts, Bärenfänger expertly maneuvered his companies into firing positions without being detected. When Bärenfänger gave the command to fire with all weapons, his heavy machine guns sliced into the enemy column, which disintegrated into chaos. By the end of the short action, Bärenfänger had captured an entire eight-gun artillery battery and 500 prisoners.[20]

While lack of mobility hindered the German pursuit, the Soviet retreat was hindered by multiple problems. Retreats are very difficult for even a well-trained and disciplined army to conduct, and few Soviet commanders had demonstrated much aptitude for this kind of maneuver during Operation *Barbarossa* in 1941. Yet the 45-year-old Petrov proved to be an above-average commander who held most of his army together, despite a complete breakdown in communications and logistics. He managed to keep the bulk of the 25th, 95th, and 172nd Rifle Divisions and Zhidilov's brigade together, moving southeast through mountain trails. He hoped to slide due west and reach the Kacha River north of Sevastopol, but the rapid advance of Brigade Ziegler discouraged this approach. Instead, he was forced to take the Coastal Army on a circuitous and time-consuming route through the mountains to reach Sevastopol from the east. Petrov was also aware that Levchenko had lost control of the situation, so he decided to move ahead of his troops to take command at Sevastopol. If the city fell, his army would be doomed. Leaving General-Major Trofim K. Kolomiets, commander of the 25th Rifle Division, to lead the retreating units, Petrov set out for Sevastopol. By late November 3, Petrov reached Balaklava, although most of his troops were strung out in the mountains and would not reach Sevastopol for another five days. The next day, the Stavka directed Petrov to temporarily take command of the Sevastopol Defensive Region (Sevastopolskogo Oboronitelnogo Raiona or SOR), until Oktyabrsky returned.

Levchenko apparently believed that Sevastopol could not be held for very long, and, like Oktyabrsky, began to quietly make plans to evacuate the naval base. The Stavka had authorized the bulk of the Black Sea Fleet to rebase at ports in the Caucasus, but had not sanctioned the evacuation of Sevastopol. Borisov, in charge of the KOS, recruited thousands of local civilians to complete trenches and antitank ditches on the city's approaches that had been begun weeks before. He also issued orders to stockpile food in anticipation of a siege. The only bright spot was that the Fliegerkorps IV had withdrawn most of its air support after the victory at Ishun in order to support Kleist's drive on Rostov, which left Manstein's AOK 11 with minimal air support. Although a number of VVS squadrons retreated to the Caucasus, the VVS-ChF's 62nd Fighter Brigade remained at Sevastopol and provided Petrov with air superiority over the city.

On the evening of November 2, soldiers from the II./IR 438 of the 132. Infanterie-Division assaulted Lieutenant Eaika's Coastal Battery No. 54, which was overrun after a tough fight. It was the first of Sevastopol's coastal defenses to fall. Despite a punishing Stuka attack that knocked out three of the battery's four 102mm guns, the German battalion still suffered heavy casualties, including 21 dead. Lieutenant Eaika escaped into the hills to join the partisans while 28 of his men swam out to a Soviet patrol boat. Following this hollow triumph, the 132. Infanterie-Division pushed across the Kacha River with two regiments, including Bidermann's IR 437, with the 50. Infanterie-Division coming up close behind. While crossing the Kacha, the German infantry came under fire from Lieutenant Mikhail V. Matushenko's Battery No. 10, which was armed with four 203mm naval guns. Lieutenant Aleksandr's Battery No. 30 also opened fire with its twin 305mm turrets, which the German infantry found unnerving. Between November 1 and November 4, these two batteries fired 276 203mm and 142 305mm rounds at the troops of the 132. Infanterie-Division.[21] Even more worrisome, small groups from Zhidilov's 7th Naval Infantry Brigade (7 NIB) that had been bypassed by Ziegler's Brigade now tried to fight their way through the 132. Infanterie-Division to get to Sevastopol. Gottlob Bidermann recounts how his *Panzerjäger* platoon, attached to a company from IR 437, was attacked from behind several times by groups of naval infantrymen trying to infiltrate through the German lines; Bidermann also described these naval infantrymen as elite troops and noted that their SVT-40 automatic rifles gave them a firepower advantage over German infantry armed with the bolt-action Kar98k.[22]

During November 4–6, Hansen used the 132. Infanterie-Division to methodically begin clearing the Bel'bek River valley around Duvankoi, but ran into increasing resistance from Vilshansky's 8 NIB, the 17th and 18th Naval Infantry Battalions, and the newly raised 3rd Naval Infantry Regiment. In just two days, the 132. Infanterie-Division suffered 428 casualties – the equivalent of a battalion – in minor skirmishing actions. However, Soviet casualties were much higher among the inexperienced naval units. Hansen was trying to jockey the 50. Infanterie-Division to the southeast, to hit Sevastopol's defenses from due east, but this left the 132. Infanterie-Division unsupported and with its hands full against a growing assortment of ad hoc Russian units. Ominously, the first elements of Petrov's Coastal Army had slipped into the defenses around Sevastopol on

November 5, further reinforcing the defense. The Soviet 17th Naval Infantry Battalion was encouraged enough to mount a local counterattack that recaptured Duvankoi from IR 438. Sensing that the 132. Infanterie-Division was vulnerable to a spoiling attack, Rear-Admiral Zhukov ordered Vilshansky's 8 NIB to mount a full-scale counterattack north of Duvankoi at dawn on November 7.[23] Bidermann's IR 437 was on the receiving end of Vilshanksy's counterattack:

> Suddenly and silently, from out of the darkness, poured waves of enemy soldiers. Elite troops of the Soviet Naval Infantry massed toward us... They assaulted our positions from the thick underbrush before Makenziya, pouring toward us in dark waves, hoarse shouts of "Urrah!" erupting from the oncoming line... We opened fire with high explosives point-blank into the rows of attackers.[24]

Although MG 34 machine-gun fire and 8cm mortar rounds broke up the first Soviet assault, the naval infantrymen attacked in waves that stressed the German defense to its limits. Matushenko's Battery No. 10 laid down a prepatory barrage that succeeded in destroying some German vehicles, and, after three hours of fighting, Vilshansky's sailors had seized three hilltop objectives. Vilshansky claimed to have eliminated 250 German soldiers, and Bidermann admitted that his battalion "suffered numerous losses." However, the Soviet sailors could not hold their hard-won ground and were forced to yield to German counterattacks on November 8. Nevertheless, Vilshansky's counterattack caused Manstein to realize that LIV Armeekorps was not strong enough to fight its way into Sevastopol with just two divisions, and he ordered Salmuth to transfer the 22. Infanterie-Division to reinforce Hansen's corps. On the Simferopol–Sevastopol road the German pursuit was now over, and Hansen now had to begin preparing for another deliberate assault, which bought precious time for the defenders.

While Hansen's corps had been trying to push through directly to Sevastopol, the 72. Infanterie-Division had been pursuing Petrov's Coastal Army through the Yaila Mountains. Here and there the Soviets turned to fight when the German pursuit grew too arrogant. On November 4, the 95th Rifle Division ambushed Panzerjäger-Abteilung 72 near the village of Ulu-Sala, destroying half its vehicles and most of its Pak guns. A winter storm that brought heavy rain on November 6 further slowed down the German pursuit, and the Coastal Army steadily won the race to Sevastopol. Nevertheless, the 72. Infanterie-Division had to fight its way into Yalta, which was occupied on the morning of November 8, and an advance guard began to march west along the coast road toward Balaklava. Near Baidary on the coast, Lieutenant Aleksandr S. Terletskiy was in charge of a small group of NKVD border guards retreating toward Sevastopol. On November 9, his group moved through the Baydar Gates, an important mountain pass east of Balaklava. In order to delay the pursuing Germans, Terletskiy's detachment emplaced explosives on a rock overhang over the narrow coast road and then detonated it to block the pass. Terletskiy was later awarded the Hero of the Soviet Union for delaying the 72. Infanterie-Division's advance along the coast from Yalta, although the impact of his feat on German operations appears to have been minimal. Furthermore, Terletskiy's group failed to reach Sevastopol and instead joined a partisan group in the mountains east of Balaklava, as did other Soviet troops who became isolated by the German pursuit.

By November 9, the German pursuit across the Crimea was over. Petrov had managed to save 17,000 troops from his Coastal Army, but had lost a good part of his artillery and vehicles. The 25th Rifle Division Chapaevskaya had suffered 50 percent losses and only 4,233 of its troops made it to Sevastopol; two of its three rifle regiments were reduced to fewer than 500 troops.[25] One exception was Colonel Ivan I. Khakhanov's 52nd Artillery Regiment, which made it to Sevastopol with 13 of their 155mm Schneider Model 1917 howitzers (taken from Poland in 1939). Brigade Ziegler had captured 2,711 prisoners, 52 trucks, and 9 76.2mm guns, while suffering 215 casualties in the pursuit.[26] Nevertheless, the escape of Petrov's Coastal Army was a minor tactical feat for the Red Army, and a major blow to Manstein's plans to seize Sevastopol in a swift coup.

While Petrov was trying to organize Sevastopol's defenses, the remnants of the 51st Army continued to retreat toward Kerch. On the evening of November 3, the 170. Infanterie-Division captured the port of Feodosiya. With the Germans racing across the Crimea and cities falling like nine pins, Communist Party officials and NKVD personnel bolted toward the coast in an effort to save themselves. The Komsomol (Young Communist League) had established Artek camps in the pleasant climate of the Crimea to indoctrinate the next generation of Soviet leaders, and these camps still had thousands of youths stranded by the German invasion; many were the children of party officials who now used their influence to get them evacuated from the Crimea. Everyone who could headed for the ports of Yalta and Alushta, which had not yet fallen.

A number of cargo ships were pressed into evacuating civilians and military wounded from the Crimea ports to Novorossiysk, but Levchenko made little effort to coordinate this effort or to ensure proper air cover and naval escorts. Since Levchenko did not believe that Sevastopol could be held for very long, he permitted the entire medical staff of the Black Sea Fleet to board the 5,770-ton freighter *Armeniya*, which left Sevastopol on the evening of November 6. The *Armeniya* also carried thousands of wounded, and stopped briefly in Balaklava to pick up NKVD personnel. The vessel might have made it to safety had not Communist Party officials radioed for it to dock at Yalta to pick up local politicians, their families, and Komsomol members. Six hours were spent waiting in Yalta for the last people to arrive, by which time the sun was up. The VVS-ChF provided two I-153 fighters as token cover over the *Armeniya* as it left Yalta and the fleet sent two MO-IV sub-chasers to act as escort. However, Luftwaffe reconnaissance aircraft quickly spotted the *Armeniya*, and an He-111 bomber from 1./KG 28 attacked at 1125hrs. A single aerial-delivered torpedo struck the ship's bow, tearing it off. Within four minutes, the ship plunged to the bottom of the Black Sea, taking an estimated 5,000–7,000 passengers with it. There were only eight survivors.

Meanwhile, Levchenko ordered Batov to mount a defense at the Parpach Narrows near Ak-Monai, where army engineers had some good-quality bunkers. This was the narrowest point of the Kerch Peninsula, but it was still 11 miles wide and Batov's army had suffered very heavy losses during the retreat. Nevertheless, the 51st Army turned to fight its pursuers one last time. Sponeck's XXXXII Armeekorps attacked the Ak-Monai position with three divisions at 0700hrs on November 4. The German soldiers were tired from days of forced marching, but they had air and artillery support. Batov complained to the Stavka that he had two battalions of Katyusha multiple rocket launchers, but no rockets for them to fire. It still took Sponeck's troops three days to overcome the

Ak-Monai position, after which Batov's defeated troops fell back to the outskirts of Kerch.

Too little and too late, the Stavka decided to send Batov fresh troops to help defend Kerch. Colonel Nikolay V. Blagoveshchensky's 9th Naval Infantry Brigade was ferried across the Kerch Strait, followed by elements of Colonel Mikhail K. Zubkov's fresh 302nd Mountain Rifle Division. A rough defensive perimeter was formed around Kerch by November 10, using every available soldier and sailor. The initial German probing attack at noon on November 10 was repulsed by Blagoveshchensky's naval infantrymen, but the Germans had no intention of conducting a house-to-house battle against trapped Soviet troops, and Manstein directed Sponeck to pulverize the city with aerial and artillery bombardment. Bombers from III./KG 27 and III./KG 51 dropped bundles of incendiaries in the center of Kerch, setting the city of 104,000 people alight. By November 12, Sponeck's divisional artillery could range the center of the city and added their firepower as well. Stukas from StG 77 knocked out the electrical power plant in Kerch, set military fuel storage dumps alight, and systematically pulverized the port facilities.

Even with the addition of reinforcements, Batov's troops were virtually out of ammunition and could not hold the city. Even before official sanction was given on November 13, an exodus began across the 5-mile-wide Kerch Strait to the imagined safety of the Taman Peninsula. Rear-Admiral Sergei G. Gorshkov's Azov Flotilla assisted the evacuation, using patrol boats and armed trawlers, which could make the crossing in less than half an hour. By November 15, Sponeck's 170. Infanterie-Division was fighting its way into Kerch, and Batov instructed Blagoveshchensky and Zubkov to provide the rearguard while the rest of 51st Army evacuated. Spotting the evacuation in progress, the Germans intensified their air attacks on shipping in the straits, inflicting numerous casualties. Even though Fliegerkorps IV had only a handful of fighters left operating over the Crimea, the VVS-ChF made little effort to protect Gorshkov's flotilla from Luftwaffe raids.

By dawn of November 17 it was over, and Gorshkov's small craft took off the last of Batov's troops that could be saved. Although Blagoveshchensky and Zubkov's units were decimated, both commanders managed to extract a portion of their troops in the final evacuation. Surprisingly, the two pre-war units in Batov's 9th Rifle Corps, the 106th and 156th Rifle

Divisions, managed to save 8,214 of their approximately 25,000 personnel, but all heavy equipment was abandoned.[27] All told, the Soviets claimed to have evacuated 50,000 from Kerch, but fewer than a third were able-bodied combat soldiers. The 51st Army left many troops behind, some of whom were captured, and others went into hiding to form local partisan units. However, the main impact of the loss of Kerch and the bulk of the 51st Army was that Manstein's AOK 11 could now turn its entire attention to the last Soviet foothold in the Crimea: Sevastopol.

CHAPTER 4

The Ring Closes Around Sevastopol, November–December 1941

"Our armies are all advancing
Russia is down on one knee
Our rifles need no enhancing
Victory ours will be
From Finland's snow to Black Sea strand
Forward! Forward!
Eastward, ho! Seize more land!
Freedom is our goal
Victory our destiny
Fuhrer, our sieg is Germany's Heil
German newsreel from Die Deutsche Wochenschau, October 1, 1941

By November 9, it was clear to Petrov that the Germans had missed their best opportunity to seize Sevastopol before the Soviet defenses solidified. The Coastal Army, despite taking a severe beating, had reached the Sevastopol defensive perimeter and joined up with the heterogeneous collection of naval units that had been literally thrown onto the city's ramparts. The Soviet defense of Sevastopol began to coalesce at that point and the fact that Petrov was the man on the spot was clear to the Stavka, which put him in charge of all ground forces and coastal artillery in the SOR.[1] Naval leadership was more complex, with Oktyabrsky in charge of the fleet, Zhukov in charge of the naval base, Morgunov in charge of the coastal guns, and General-Major Nikolay A. Ostryakov in command of the VVS-ChF. Ostryakov was a renowned bomber pilot who had mistakenly bombed the German pocket-battleship *Deutschland* during the Spanish Civil War in May 1937.

The 45-year-old General-Major Ivan E. Petrov did not seem to have the background to lead a joint army–navy command in a desperate siege. Before joining the Red Army and the Communist Party in 1918 he had studied in a theological seminary, and his glasses gave him a studious appearance. Although trained as an infantryman, Petrov spent most of the interwar period in Central Asia in cavalry units and had no previous experience with naval units or combined operations. He had briefly commanded the 25th Rifle Division at Odessa before being given command of the Coastal Army, which is where he gained his first experience with Oktyabrsky's Black Sea Fleet. What Petrov did possess was a determination to hold on and overcome, which he instilled in the defenders of Sevastopol. His first task was to organize a coherent defense from the rag-tag elements under his command, in order to withstand the serious enemy attack that he knew was coming.

General-Major Morgunov had sketched out a defensive perimeter 3–5 miles around Sevastopol in February 1941, but actual construction work did not begin until early July. Initially, two naval construction battalions, supplemented by 2,000 civilian volunteers, began work on building the inner defensive line, which extended only 2 miles out from the city. These defensive lines would be garrisoned by local naval infantry, leaving the defense of the city entirely within the hands of the Black Sea Fleet. Yet it was not until mid-September 1941, when the Germans began attacking the Soviet defenses at Perekop, that the leadership in Sevastopol got serious about building defenses in depth around the city. The new plan was to build three lines of defense, with the outermost layer 7–9 miles out, so that enemy artillery could not bombard the harbor. Obviously, this required a much larger labor commitment, as well as more troops than the Black Sea Fleet could provide. Amazingly, the labor force was able to construct three lines of defense around Sevastopol by early November, with over 300 bunkers, 9,600 mines, and numerous barbed-wire obstacles.[2] None of the defensive lines were complete when Hansen's LIV Armeekorps approached Sevastopol, but the exhausted Russian troops could slip into prepared positions.

Petrov divided the SOR into four defensive sectors, starting clockwise with Sector IV holding the Bel'bek River valley, Sector III holding the Mekenzievy Mountain area, Sector II holding the Chernaya River valley and Fedyukhiny Heights, and Sector I holding the coastal strip around Balaklava. He anticipated that the Germans were most likely to make their main effort against Sectors III and IV, so he placed his best units and commanders there. General-Major Vasily F. Vorob'ev, commander of the 95th Rifle Division, was assigned Sector IV; in addition to his own division, Vilshansky's 8 NIB, 13 ad hoc battalions and two artillery regiments were put under his command. General-Major Kolomiets, commander of the 25th Rifle Division, took over Sector III, which also included Zhidilov's 7 NIB, the 3rd Naval Infantry Regiment, the 1st Perekop Naval Infantry Regiment, and ten other ad hoc battalions. Altogether, Vorob'ev had more than one third of the available forces in his sector and Kolomiets had one quarter in his, which left only weak covering forces in the other two sectors. Zhukov had done a remarkable job forming 30 ad hoc battalions from available resources, including six naval infantry battalions, an NKVD battalion, and a plethora of units composed of VVS ground crews and personnel from the naval schools in Sevastopol. Yet aside from Petrov's 25th and 95th Rifle Divisions and the two naval infantry brigades, none of these were really cohesive units with strong leadership. The question was whether they could they hold out against Manstein's overextended but better led and equipped AOK 11.

Petrov did have a few aces up his sleeve. Although some air units had retreated to the Caucasus, Ostryakov had re-energized the remaining VVS-ChF units at Sevastopol into an effective force that hindered Fliegerkorps IV from making full use of the captured Sarabus airfield, north of Simferopol. The Germans were only able to move two *Staffeln* (squadrons) of Bf-109Fs from III./JG 77 and one *Staffeln* of Ju-87 Stukas from III./StG 77 into Sarabus in early November, but had their hands full fending off repeated low-level air raids by VVS-ChF aircraft. Although the German fighter pilots often proved superior in experience and training,

The defense of Sevastopol, December 1941

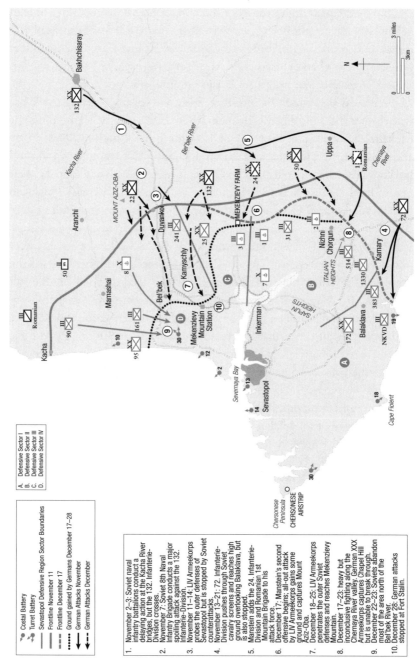

Legend:

- ⚓ Costal Battery
- ⚓ Turret Battery
- —— Sevastopol Defensive Region Sector Boundaries
- —— Frontline November 11
- ‒ ‒ Frontline December 17
- ••• Ground gained by Germans December 17–28
- ↓ German Attacks November
- ⇣ German Attacks December

A. Defensive Sector I
B. Defensive Sector II
C. Defensive Sector III
D. Defensive Sector IV

1. November 2–3: Soviet naval infantry battalions conduct a delaying action at the Kacha River bridges, but the 132. Infanterie-Division crosses.

2. November 7: Soviet 8th Naval Infantry Brigade conducts a major spoiling attack against the 132. Infanterie-Division.

3. November 11–14: LIV Armeekorps probes the outer defenses of Sevastopol but is stopped by Soviet counterattacks.

4. November 13–21: 72. Infanterie-Division pushes through Soviet cavalry screens and reaches high ground overlooking Balaklava, but is also stopped.

5. Manstein adds the 24. Infanterie-Division and Romanian 1st Mountain Brigade to his attack force.

6. December 17: Manstein's second offensive begins; all-out attack by LIV Armeekorps gains some ground and captures Mount Aziz-Oba.

7. December 18–25: LIV Armeekorps penetrates the outer Soviet defenses and reaches Mekenzievy Mountain.

8. December 17–23: heavy but inconclusive fighting along the Chernaya River valley. German XXX Armeekorps captures Chapel Hill but is unable to break through.

9. December 22–23: Soviets abandon most of the area north of the Bel'bek River.

10. December 28: German attacks stopped at Fort Stalin.

the VVS-ChF pilots were improving, and shot down three Ju-88 bombers in the first week of November – the Luftwaffe could not operate with impunity over Sevastopol. By November 7, 1941, the 62nd Fighter Brigade had 61 operational fighters in three regiments, of which the 9th Fighter Regiment (9 IAP) was the strongest, with ten Yak-1 and 11 MiG-3 fighters. There was also a small number of Il-2 Sturmovik ground-attack aircraft, as well as 16 MBR-2 amphibians.[3] In contrast, Fliegerkorps IV was operating only six to 12 Bf-109s, ten to 15 Ju-88s, and eight to ten Ju-87 Stukas over the Crimea by November. The rest of its *Gruppen* were supporting Kleist's advance to Rostov.

Another factor in Petrov's favor was naval gunfire support. Although the Black Sea Fleet's heaviest units had retreated to ports in the Caucasus, the fleet formed a Naval Gunfire Support Group comprising the elderly light cruisers *Krasny Krym* and *Chervona Ukraina*, accompanied by three destroyers. Since his own artillery regiments had lost most of their guns in the retreat, he was particularly dependent upon naval gunfire support. The fleet also provided another armored train, the *Zhelezniakov*, to replace the two lost at Ishun; the *Zhelezniakov* was armed with five 100mm naval guns, eight 82mm mortars, and 15 heavy machine guns. Recognizing the vulnerability of armored trains to Stuka attacks, the *Zhelezniakov* was based inside the Trinity tunnel on the northern side of Severnaya Bay.

Petrov realized that his main task was to parry Manstein's initial offensive long enough for the Stavka to send him reinforcements from the North Caucasus Military District. Winter was approaching fast, and although not as harsh in the Crimea as in central Russia, the weather would hinder the attacker far more than the defender. Despite having a motley assortment of 27,000 ground troops to defend a 29-mile-long perimeter, Petrov was determined to exact a high price from Manstein's assault forces.

Amazingly, Manstein does not even mention his first assault upon Sevastopol in his memoirs, indicating his tendency to skip over unpleasant events. Once Hansen's pursuit ground to a halt against Sevastopol's defenses, it was clear to Manstein that he would have to mount either a siege or a full-scale assault in order to take the city. Characteristically, he opted for the more decisive choice of an assault. However, AOK 11 was in no shape for a full-scale assault upon Sevastopol in mid-November. Since crossing the Dnepr River two months earlier, it had suffered over 26,000 casualties (including 5,400 dead or missing) out of a total strength of 295,000, and fought three major battles. Artillery ammunition was in short supply after the fighting on the Perekop Isthmus and it would take weeks to replenish it by truck convoys from the Dnepr. The 132. Infanterie-Division, which was the closest unit to Sevastopol, only had half of a basic load of ammunition for its 10.5cm l.FH 18 howitzers and four-fifths of a load for its 15cm s.FH 18 howitzers on November 8 – barely sufficient to support one or two days of attacking.[4] Furthermore, AOK 11 was spread across the Crimea, with four of seven German infantry divisions still fully involved at Kerch. At best, Hansen could begin the assault with his LIV Armeekorps (the 50. and 132. Infanterie-Divisionen) with Salmuth's XXX Armeekorps joining in with the 22. and 72. Infanterie-Divisionen within a few days. Manstein assumed that he would be able to get at least two divisions from XXXXII Armeekorps into action at Sevastopol before the end of November, leaving the Romanian forces to conduct mop-up operations in the rest of the Crimea.

However, Manstein's assumptions proved wishful thinking, as the fighting at Kerch lasted longer than expected and Heeresgruppe Süd directed that two of Sponeck's three divisions would go to reinforce Kleist's advance rather than support the attack on Sevastopol. After regrouping his two divisions, Hansen began small-scale probing attacks against the boundary between the SOR's II and III Defensive Sectors on November 11, trying to detect and neutralize Kolomiets' forward security screen. On November 12, the 132. Infanterie-Division finally made a determined effort, with elements of four of its infantry battalions attacking a hill outpost held by the 31st Rifle Regiment, but the attack lacked significant air or artillery support and failed. The next day it was the 50. Infanterie-Division's turn to attack with a few battalions, which also failed to make it through the Soviet forward security screen. Petrov was surprised at how puny Hansen's infantry assaults were, with battalions at half-strength, and saw a chance to knock AOK 11's offensive off balance. Temperatures were already falling to 10° F (-12° C), which further reduced any remaining zest for combat in Hansen's exhausted men, when Petrov struck the front of LIV Armeekorps with a massive but uncoordinated counteroffensive on the morning of November 14. The 7th and 8th Naval Infantry Brigades formed the core of the attacking force, supplemented by three other naval infantry regiments and two Red Army rifle regiments – it was primarily a naval affair. The 132. Infanterie-Division was particularly hard hit by the Soviet naval infantrymen, who attacked in waves and managed to push the German frontline units back. Although Petrov's counteroffensive did not recapture much ground, it forced Hansen's corps onto the defensive for the remainder of November. The only positive note for LIV Armeekorps was that several dozen bunkers had been overrun, which would provide useful winter siege quarters for the frontline German troops. Yet aside from some aggressive patrolling and raids by the 22. Infanterie-Division, which finally got into line north of Duvankoi, Hansen's role in the first offensive was over.

The only major German success in the opening days of the first offensive was a series of Luftwaffe raids on Sevastopol harbor that caught the fleet's Naval Gunfire Support Group at anchor. One idiosyncrasy of Soviet naval gunfire tactics was that their warships preferred to fire from along quayside in the harbor, which made it easier to communicate with forward observers by telephone. It also meant that the Germans knew where to find the source of naval gunfire. The light cruisers *Krasny Krym* and *Chervona Ukraina* had fired 500 rounds of 130mm ammunition at German positions around Sevastopol during November 8–11, provoking several small-scale Luftwaffe retaliatory raids, but these were frustrated by Ostryakov's VVS-ChF combat air patrols, which normally deployed two to four fighters over Sevastopol during daylight hours. After recurrent requests from Hansen to do something about the Soviet naval gunfire, Fliegerkorps IV finally assembled all its available aircraft for a major strike on the port of Sevastopol on the morning of November 12. Although the captain of the cruiser *Krasny Krym* prudently left the harbor before dawn, the *Chervona Ukraina* was still alongside the Count's Quay in Severnaya (South) Bay, leisurely firing her 130mm guns at distant German troop concentrations. Around 0900hrs an air-raid alarm was sounded, but there was little time to react before three Ju-87 Stukas from II./StG 77 pounced on *Chervona Ukraina* from high altitude and hit her with two 250kg bombs, one of which detonated her torpedo tubes. With over 140 of her crew killed or wounded, flames spread across the crippled cruiser as she settled in the harbor. Although her 130mm guns were later recovered, the cruiser itself was finished. Before the VVS-ChF combat air patrol could react, a group of nine He-111 bombers from I./KG 27 and 11 Ju-88s from KG 51 swept over the harbor at low level and dropped their bombs among the dockyard area. The brand-new Type 7U destroyer *Sovershennyi,* already damaged by German air-delivered mines, was struck and would never sail again. The Type 7 destroyer *Bezposhchadny* was also hit and seriously damaged, but was towed to Poti for repairs. Although one of Ostryakov's MiG-3 fighters shot down a retreating He-111, Fliegerkorps IV had scored a major victory over the Black Sea Fleet. Yet in spite of this victory, Fliegerkorps IV was too overextended to interdict all naval traffic in and out of Sevastopol, and consequently on November 17 the elderly freighter *Kursk* arrived from Novorossiysk with the first load of ammunition for Petrov's troops.

Oddly, the initial German offensive against Sevastopol achieved its only success in the sector that Manstein had regarded as merely a supporting attack: Sector I along the coast near Balaklava. On the morning of November 11, the 72. Infanterie-Division was strung out from the Baydar Gate to Yalta, with two battalions from IR 266 conducting an unsupported advance upon Balaklava. The only Soviet forces barring the way into Balaklava were the remnants of the 40th and 42nd Cavalry Divisions. After forcing their way through Lieutenant Terletskiy's improvised roadblock at the Baydar Gate, IR 266 steadily pushed the Soviet cavalry back toward Balaklava and did not encounter any Soviet infantry until November 13. A mile southeast of the town of Kamary, Colonel Mikhail G. Shemruk had deployed part of his 383rd Rifle Regiment on an imposing ridgeline that dominated the coastal road leading to Balaklava. Once Shemruk's infantry were spotted, IR 266 halted its advance and waited for two more battalions from IR 105 and II./IR 124, as well as a few assault guns, to arrive. On November 13, the five German battalions assaulted the ridgeline held by Shemruk's regiment and the few remaining cavalry. Shemruk's troops fought hard for the ridgeline, but Shemruk himself was eventually killed, and the Germans overran the ridge and advanced to the high ground overlooking Kamary. Oberstleutnant Friedrich-Wilhelm Müller's IR 105 occupied Hill 386.6, just 1½ miles from Balaklava harbor.

Over the next week, the soldiers of the 72. Infanterie-Division fought a series of pitched battles for three steep hills just east of Balaklava. Despite losing the high ground early, the Soviets had fortified the town of Kamary and the Blagodat State Farm, which they used as springboards to briefly retake much of the high ground on November 14–15 when the 514th and 1330th Rifle Regiments arrived to reinforce the battered 383rd Rifle

Regiment. Once the Soviet counterattack had run its course, Müller's IR 105 launched an all-out attack on the key piece of terrain in the sector, Hill 212.0, a steep and sparsely vegetated hill on which the vintage Balaklava North Fort sat, and which dominated Balaklava's harbor. After two days of intense fighting on November 16–17, Müller's infantry gained only a toehold on the hill, which they then lost to a Soviet battalion-strength night counterattack. The Soviets also repulsed all efforts by IR 266 to overrun the Blagodat State Farm strongpoint. In one final throw of the dice, Müller's IR 105 was reinforced with two battalions of pioneers in an all-out assault on November 21, which finally captured Hill 212.0. However, the Black Sea Fleet finally committed the battleship *Parizhskaya Kommuna* and two light cruisers to bombard the Germans outside Balaklava, which halted any further German attacks. The 72. Infanterie-Division's strength was spent, with only 20 percent of its infantry left, and it was forced to shift to the defense, thus bringing the first German offensive to a close. The frontline in Sector I now reverted to World War I-style trench warfare, with very little change over the next six months.

Manstein made two mistakes in his first effort against Sevastopol, and both were characteristic of his style of generalship. First, he underestimated the enemy. He believed Petrov's Coastal Army to be a broken reed and discounted the ability of the Black Sea Fleet to form ad hoc naval infantry units. During the November offensive, Petrov received over 9,000 replacements from various quarters, whereas Manstein received none.[5] Altogether, Manstein's AOK 11 suffered about 3,000 casualties in the first attempt to seize Sevastopol, further reducing the combat effectiveness of his infantry divisions. He also underestimated the ability of Morgunov's Coastal Artillery and the Black Sea Fleet's naval gunfire to repel his *Stossgruppen* with heavy-artillery barrages. Manstein's second mistake was to not include the Romanian mountain infantry (*vanatori de munte*) in the offensive, instead relegating them to mop-up duties along the Black Sea coast near Alushta and in the Yaila Mountains. The Romanian 1st Mountain Brigade was the only fresh unit available to AOK 11 and it was a large one, comprising over 10,000 troops in six mountain-infantry battalions, two artillery battalions, and an engineer battalion. If this unit had been teamed up with the 72. Infanterie-Division, Manstein would have gained a clear superiority against Sector I's weak defenses and almost certainly captured Balaklava. However, Manstein was reluctant to include Romanian units in his offensive plans because he did not respect their abilities and did not want to share any victories with them; this kind of attitude would often undermine Axis cooperation in the Crimea throughout 1941–42.

After the defeat of Manstein's first assault upon Sevastopol's outer defenses, which cost both sides over 2,000 casualties, a lull of sorts settled over the frontline positions. Both sides were exhausted and fought-out, requiring weeks to replace casualties and restock for the next round. Operation *Barbarossa* had stalled almost everywhere, from Leningrad to Moscow to Rostov, but Manstein was determined to capture Sevastopol before the end of 1941. Recognizing that hasty attacks with depleted units could not succeed, he set about planning and organizing a deliberate offensive to begin by mid-December. Meanwhile, the frontline soldiers still engaged in desultory combat, with harassing artillery bombardments, air raids, and snipers taking their toll. During the month-long lull between the two offensives, AOK 11 still suffered about 3,000 casualties, or the equivalent loss of one of its depleted companies, every day.

Petrov used the operational pause to re-energize the construction of Sevastopol's three lines of defense, which were directed by General-Major Arkadiy F. Khrenov, one of the Red Army's top engineers. Khrenov had extensive experience building pre-war fortifications, and had been awarded the Hero of the Soviet Union for figuring out how to break through the Mannerheim Line during the Russo-Finnish War. The initial fortifications were primarily trenches, antitank ditches, and wooden bunkers, but Khrenov improved the quality of Soviet fieldworks by directing more tunneling in rock and using the spoil to build stouter artillery bunkers. Engineer equipment was given high priority in supply runs from Novorossiysk, while Khrenov set the naval workshops in Sevastopol to the large-scale manufacture of wooden antipersonnel mines. Khrenov focused on reinforcing the rear and main lines of defense, rather than the forward lines, which were under direct enemy observation. During the month-long lull, his sappers laid 45,000 more mines, including the buried flamethrowers that the Germans detested, and added 20 miles of barbed-wire obstacles.[6] Furthermore, Khrenov was able to tie the defenses of the four sectors together better, which made it more difficult for the Germans to exploit the vulnerable sector boundaries.

Of course, it was just as important to ensure that there were enough defenders to man Sevastopol's three lines of defense, and the Stavka succeeded in directing an increasing amount of replacements to the besieged port. Initially, the North Caucasus Military District was able to send only 3,000 unarmed replacements to Sevastopol on November 18, with rifles to follow later.[7] However, on the night of December 7/8, the cruisers *Krasny Kavkaz* and *Krasny Krym* escorted a five-ship convoy into Sevastopol's South Bay bearing Colonel Aleksandr D. Ovseenko's 388th Rifle Division. This unit was another one of Stalin's "instant divisions" raised in fall 1941, but it was a strong formation, with 11,197 fresh troops and a good complement of artillery (18 76mm regimental guns, 16 76mm mountain guns, and eight 122mm howitzers), mortars, antitank guns, and antiaircraft guns. In addition to Ovseenko's division, Petrov received enough personnel replacements and new weapons to partially restore the combat effectiveness of his Coastal Army. By mid-December 1941, Petrov had about 46,000 troops under his command, and there were 16,000 non-combat military personnel and 51,000 civilians left in Sevastopol. For the first time, Petrov felt that his front line was strong enough to create a central reserve based upon Ovseenko's 388th Rifle Division, Zhidilov's 7th Naval Infantry Brigade, the 40th Cavalry Division, and a rifle regiment from the 95th Rifle Division. Sevastopol's defenses had improved greatly in just a month.

The Stavka also moved to simplify the complicated command structure at Sevastopol, once the first German offensive was defeated. The ineffectual Levchenko, who played no real role in the November fighting, was quietly removed on November 19 and later arrested, being charged with inciting panic because he had planned to evacuate the city.[8] Oktyabrsky was confirmed as commander of the SOR, but Petrov remained the predominant figure in the ground defense of the city, while Oktyabrsky focused more on expediting supplies and reinforcements from Novorossiysk. In practice, all command decisions were exercised through the Military Council of the Black Sea Fleet, comprised of Petrov, Oktyabrsky, Morgunov, and Ostryakov.

In contrast, the situation of Manstein's AOK 11 was getting worse, rather than improving, due to the near-breakdown of Heeresgruppe Süd's logistical infrastructure. Because of the Soviet demolition of all railroad bridges over the Dnepr – which would not be fully repaired until 1943 – no fuel trains could proceed east of the river. Instead, supplies had to be ferried across the Dnepr from the main railhead at Kherson and then either loaded onto the few captured Soviet trains available or moved 210 miles by the depleted number of trucks still operational in AOK 11's quartermaster units. Heavy rains, which arrived in late November, turned the Crimea's roads into slow-go terrain, further exacerbating the problem. Logistical priority went to ammunition, so by mid-December AOK 11's forward divisions had stockpiled over 1,600 tons of artillery ammunition, but the soldiers in the forward positions were left shivering in their summer uniforms and with reduced rations. Gottlob Bidermann noted the poor quality of the rations that were available, and that he and his fellow *Panzerjägers* were forced to scavenge warm overcoats from the corpses of fallen Soviet naval infantrymen in front of their positions.[9] German frontline morale was deteriorating with each passing day, and the cold weather would soon reduce Manstein's half-strength infantry units to combat ineffectiveness. Under these conditions, Manstein probably would have preferred to conduct a siege until his army was strong enough to mount a full-scale assault on Sevastopol in the spring, but once the Soviet Winter Counteroffensive began in early December, Hitler became increasingly adamant that AOK 11 finish off Sevastopol as soon as possible in order to release its divisions for use elsewhere. Forced into action by events elsewhere on the front, Manstein decided to gamble and make another assault upon Sevastopol before Christmas.

There were a few bright notes that improved AOK 11's chances. Since the arrival of the 24. Infanterie-Division at Sevastopol in late November and the imminent arrival of the 170. Infanterie-Division in late December, Manstein could potentially employ six German divisions against the fortress instead of less than three as in the previous effort. Furthermore, much of the heavy siege artillery employed at Ishun – which had been unavailable in November – had arrived at the front to support the December offensive. Zuckertort's super-heavy artillery now included one 35.5cm M1 howitzer, four 30.5cm mortars, eight 24cm Model 39 howitzers, and 36 14.9cm s. FH 37(t) howitzers; except for the M1 built by Rheinmetall, all of the German super-heavy artillery had been taken from the defunct Czech Army in 1939. However, most of the super-heavy artillery pieces were short-range, area-attack weapons with low rates of fire – they were intended to supplement and not replace division-level 10.5cm and 15cm batteries. One specific weakness of Zuckertort's artillery, noted in the battle of Perekop, was a lack of long-range artillery for counterbattery work. Consequently,

AOK 11 received two battalions (II./AR 54 and II./AR 818) equipped with 16 10.5cm s.K 18 cannon and the 6. Batterie from Artillerie-Lehr-Regiment 2 with four 15cm K18 cannon; these weapons could engage enemy artillery out to 13–15 miles and help to even the odds against Morgunov's heavy coastal batteries. A second *Sturmgeschütz-Abteilung* had also arrived in the Crimea, doubling Hansen's assault guns from 21 to 42.[10]

Because of the end of German offensive operations everywhere else, Fliegerkorps IV was also able to support AOK 11 with an additional bomber *Gruppe*, as well as more Stukas and fighters. However, even these additional reinforcements might have been enough, and Manstein opted to increase his vulnerabilities in quiet sectors in order to mass as much of AOK 11's remaining strength into a powerful *Schwerpunkt* (main effort) that could breach Sevastopol's defenses. As part of this risky strategy, he reduced Sponeck's XXXXII Armeekorps holding the Kerch Peninsula to just the 46. Infanterie-Division and two Romanian brigades, assuming that the defeated Soviet 51st Army could not mount any attacks across the Kerch Straits in winter. He also decided to incorporate the Romanian 1st Mountain Brigade into his offensive plan, recognizing that he needed their numbers now.

Manstein's plan of attack was based upon starting with "salami-slicing tactics" to eviscerate and weaken critical parts of Petrov's outer defenses with well-supported battalion-size attacks, then follow through with all-out division-size attacks when a sector began to crumble. Once again, Hansen's LIV Armeekorps would make the main effort. Manstein noted that Petrov's outer defenses were overextended in Sector IV where the 95th Rifle Division and Zhidilov's 8th NIB were trying to maintain control of the area around Coastal Battery No. 10. Here, the Black Sea Fleet wanted this battery held, even though it stretched the defensive perimeter in Sector IV to a dangerous degree. The obvious weak point was the boundary between Sectors III and IV in the Bel'bek River valley, which is precisely where Manstein decided to place his *Schwerpunkt*. He was less certain about how strong the center of Petrov's line was in Sectors II and III, but he wanted to probe aggressively and see what developed. However, he had no intention of XXX Armeekorps renewing an effort to take Balaklava, which he knew had been heavily reinforced; instead, by shifting his main effort from his left to his right, he hoped to catch Petrov by surprise.

At 0610hrs on December 17, 1941, Zuckertort's artillery began a short preparatory barrage, followed by Fliegerkorps IV Stukas and level-bombers attacking Soviet artillery positions. Amazingly, the Soviets were caught by surprise, since they did not expect the Germans to mount a winter offensive. Each of Hansen's infantry regiments had massed their remaining combat-ready infantry into two assault battalions, reducing their third battalions to cadre strength. The Germans attacked in small *Stossgruppen*, as they had learned at Perekop and Ishun, but with refined tactics. A few pioneers would rush forward in "buddy teams" to hurl smoke grenades at sites selected to breach the Soviet barbed wire, which was much less dense than at Perekop. Once sufficient smoke obscured the designated breach site, another pioneer team would move forward and blow up the wire obstacle with Bangalore torpedoes. Once the breach was created, small teams of grenadiers would move forward and hurl multiple *Stielhandgranaten* to suppress any defenders on the other side of the breach. Only then would the assault team move into and through the breach to assault the nearest Soviet defensive position with grenades and flamethrowers. Due to weeks of inactivity, many Soviet sectors were only lightly manned, and the forward outposts fell quickly to this style of blitz assault.

Hansen made his main effort with the 22., 24., and 132. Infanterie-Divisionen against Sectors III and IV, while the 50. Infanterie-Division and the Romanian 1st Mountain Brigade made a supporting attack against Sector II. The greatest success was achieved in the north near the village of Duvankoi and the Bel'bek River valley. Zhidilov's 8th NIB had four battalions deployed along a 4-mile-long front, with a fifth battalion in reserve and the brigade command post situated on the rear slope of Mount Aziz-Oba (which meant "Holy Hill" in Tatar). Generalmajor Ludwig Wolff's 22. Infanterie-Division hit the 8th NIB's two right-flank battalions with two battalions from IR 16, while two battalions from Oberst Ernst Haccius's IR 65 stormed Mount Aziz-Oba and threatened the brigade command post. Given the size of the mountain and the rugged terrain, this was an amazing achievement, which seriously weakened the outer defenses of Sevastopol. Zhidilov quickly counterattacked with his reserve battalion, which temporarily slowed, but did not stop the German advance. Captain Georgy A. Aleksandr's Coastal Battery No. 30 fired 96 305mm shells at Wolff's troops, although the fire was not particularly accurate. By the end of the first day, Wolff's four assault battalions had advanced up to 1¼ miles and seriously damaged Zhidilov's right flank.

South of Duvankoi and the Bel'bek River, the 132. and 24. Infanterie-Divisionen ripped the Soviet forward positions to pieces and advanced up to 2 miles in most sectors. I./IR 438, supported by four assault guns from Sturmgeschütz-Abteilung 197, punched through the 287th Rifle Regiment's defenses and captured Hill 209.9, while III./IR 438 routed Major Ivan I. Kulagin's 2nd Perekop Naval Infantry Regiment and forced it to retreat 2 miles. Hauptmann Wolfgang von Kranenbrock, commander of II./IR 102, sliced through the forward security of the 54th Rifle Regiment and captured Hill 247.1, a key piece of terrain north of the Mekenzievy Farm. Further south, two battalions from Oberst Kurt Versock's IR 31 penetrated the 3rd Naval Infantry's line west of Mekenzievy Farm and captured Hill 287.6. The 50. Infanterie-Division mounted a supporting attack with six battalions that also gained 1¼ miles, and Romanian mountain infantry made a successful attack in the Chernaya River valley. All along the line, the Soviet forward security units suffered heavy losses and were pushed back up to 2 miles. Hansen's assault battalions had achieved surprise, and used the best tactics for the limited resources available, resulting in a significant German tactical victory on the first day of the offensive. However, victory did not come cheap; LIV Armeekorps suffered 1,698 casualties, including 356 dead or missing, on the first day, which was equivalent to about 11 percent of the assaulting troops.

Throughout the siege of Sevastopol, Petrov's ability to exercise effective battle command was hindered by poor communications with his frontline units, which relied heavily upon wire and field telephones.[11] When units abandoned positions and retreated, the phones were often left behind, causing them to lose contact with their divisional headquarters. Few of Petrov's units below division level had tactical radios. Consequently, the German advances on the first day caused great confusion, as one Soviet regiment after another retreated and lost contact. It was not until late in the day that Petrov began to find out how badly Vilshansky's 8th NIB had been hurt, and of the loss of key terrain on the right flank of Sector IV. Once aware of the situation, Petrov committed the bulk of his reserves to restore the front line: Ovseenko's 388th Rifle Division was ordered to send one regiment to help Zhidilov's weakened 8th NIB in retaking Mount Aziz-Oba and the other two regiments to plug the hole caused by the retreat of the 2nd Perekop Naval Infantry Regiment. Petrov also committed the understrength 40th Cavalry Division to Sector IV and Zhidilov's 7th NIB to retake the ground taken by the 24. and 50. Infanterie-Divisionen. Amazingly, Petrov had committed virtually his entire reserve in the first 24 hours of the enemy offensive, leaving only the 161st Rifle Regiment from the 95th Rifle Division in reserve.

Yet even as Petrov's reserves were moving into the front line, Wolff's 22. Infanterie-Division renewed its offensive at dawn on November 18. Zuckertort's gunners began by firing another 10,800 rounds of ammunition in support. Oberst Ernst Haccius's IR 65 had two battalions atop Mount Aziz-Oba, which spotted three battalions of Vilshansky's 8th NIB and the 40th Cavalry Division assembling for their own counterattack to retake the hill. Haccius's soldiers were outnumbered and tired, but from the high ground his MG 34 teams were able to viciously rake the Soviet infantry below. The two German battalions then attacked downhill and caught the Soviet troops completely flat-footed, routing them. All three of Vilshansky's battalions were wrecked as fighting units. Oberst Dietrich von Choltitz's IR 16 enjoyed even greater success against the 773rd Rifle Regiment, moving up to try and restore the ruptured right flank of Sector IV. First calling in a punishing artillery barrage to disrupt the Soviet regiment, Choltitz then attacked with both his assault battalions and routed Ovseenko's riflemen, who were new recruits who had never seen action, and most had only been in uniform for less than a month. Choltitz then proceeded to pursue the fleeing Soviet troops for 2½ miles, tearing a huge hole in the Soviet outer defenses and marking him as a tactical commander of great ability.

Along the rest of the front, the 24., 50., and 132. Infanterie-Divisionen and the Romanian 1st Mountain Brigade continued to attack, making less spectacular advances varying between 500 yards to a mile. Kulagin's 2nd Perekop Naval Infantry Regiment again failed to hold, despite Petrov sending the other two regiments from Ovseenko's 388th Rifle Division to support it. The only area where the Soviets enjoyed any success was in Sector II in the south, where Zhidilov's veteran 7th NIB mounted local counterattacks against the 50. Infanterie-Division and the Romanians. The Soviet naval infantrymen were able to push the Germans back slightly, but engaged in a more difficult see-saw fight over a position known as the Italian Heights (later Chapel Hill), which dominated the lower Chernaya

River valley. The Italian Heights, which overlooked Tennyson's "Valley of Death" where the British Light Brigade made its reckless charge in 1854, was a critical piece of terrain needed to secure access to the eastern route into Balaklava and Sevastopol. It changed hands several times as the Romanian mountain infantry gamely kept counterattacking to reclaim it, but by evening the hill was back in Soviet hands. The second day of the German offensive had again gone poorly for the Soviets, and Petrov's reserves had been committed without accomplishing much. Hansen's LIV Armeekorps had carved out a large area in the boundary between Sector III and IV and had already reached the second line of defense in the north. Petrov's artillery had also taken a beating from constant Stuka attacks and II./AR 818's long-range counterbattery fire, and was suffering from a shortage of ammunition. Morgunov's coastal artillery batteries were still fully effective, but were really only capable of area bombardment. Unable to coordinate an effective counterattack, and faced with declining artillery support, Petrov decided to remain on the defense and stubbornly hold each piece of ground.

Hansen continued to attack on December 19, slowly pushing Petrov's infantry back. Zuckertort's artillery continued to pound Soviet positions; in three days, German artillerymen fired over 52,000 rounds of ammunition and 3,400 Nebelwerfer rockets at Petrov's positions. Aleksandr's battery continued to respond with 305mm rounds, and five other coastal batteries supported the Soviet defense with lighter weapons. However, Zuckertort brought up the 30.5cm Mörser of schwere Artillerie-Abteilung 815 and his one 35.5cm M1 howitzer to bombard Aleksandr's battery, and eventually put one of the turrets out of operation. While the heavy artillery engaged Morgunov's coastal gunners, LIV Armeekorps concentrated its division and corps artillery to support its *Schwerpunkt*. Deluged by fire, Kulagin's 2nd Perekop Naval Infantry Regiment gave way once again and ceded another mile to the 132. Infanterie-Division, while Haccius and Choltitz continued to crush the vestigial right flank of Sector IV. It was increasingly clear that all the Soviet units in Sector IV north of the Bel'bek River were in danger of being isolated, and that Vilshansky's 8th NIB was on the verge of collapse; Aleksandr's battery was ordered to form a 150-man infantry company from its gunners and to replace some of 8 NIB's losses. In the Chernaya River valley in the south, Zhidilov's 7th NIB was pushed off the Italian Heights by Müller's IR 105, which had just joined the battle.

Zhidilov was badly wounded in the fighting for the hill, and his brigade had also lost much of its strength.

Three days of relentless German advances and Soviet heavy losses made the Military Council in Sevastopol quite gloomy, and the naval leaders were no longer certain that Petrov's troops could halt the enemy attacks. Rear-Admiral Zhukov was openly critical of Petrov's failure to stem the enemy and relayed his misgivings to the Stavka, claiming that Sevastopol could not be held without immediate reinforcements from the North Caucasus. The Stavka was not long in responding, directing the dispatch of a fresh rifle division from Novorossiysk to Sevastopol. Furthermore, the Military Council was informed that something bigger was in the works: with the help of the Azov Flotilla and the Black Sea Fleet, the rebuilt 51st Army would make an amphibious landing on the Kerch Peninsula before the end of the month. Petrov was ordered to hold on until this event occurred, which the Stavka believed would surely cause Manstein to abort his offensive.

Although hard pressed, Petrov's infantry dug in their heels and displayed significant tenacity on December 20, preventing the Germans from achieving breakthroughs in any sector. Soviet resistance became particularly obdurate in the Kamyschly Ravine sector, which ran diagonally across the new front line of Sector III. Two regiments of Ovseenko's 388th Rifle Division had reinforced the western side of the ravine, which repeatedly rebuffed efforts by the 132. Infanterie-Division to cross the 500-yard-wide ravine. Indeed, the Kamyschly Ravine would remain the front line of Sector III for six more months. Nevertheless, Petrov was running out of reserves and was forced to start forming rear-area personnel into ad hoc rifle units to keep Sector IV from folding. On December 20, Hansen tried to outflank the Kamyschly Ravine position with a diversion against the south end of the ravine by several battalions from the 24. Infanterie-Division, while the 132. Infanterie-Division committed six battalions against the northern end of the ravine and managed to grab a toehold on the western side of the ravine. However, the limited German success was tempered by a fierce counterattack that ravaged the battalions of the 24. Infanterie-Division – clearly the German infantry were reaching the limit of their combat effectiveness. Only in the 22. Infanterie-Division sector did Hansen continue to achieve significant success, when the assault battalions of IR 16 and IR 65 overran the command post of the 40th

Cavalry Division and killed its commander, Colonel Filipp F. Kudyurov. In the south, along the Chernaya River valley, two battalions of naval infantrymen recaptured the much-fought-over Italian Heights in Sector II on December 20, but then the German XXX Armeekorps committed a regiment from the fresh 170. Infanterie-Division, which retook the heights on December 21.

With both sides exhausted, the situation began to shift in Petrov's favor when Oktyabrsky sailed into Sevastopol's Severnaya (South) Bay aboard the cruiser *Krasny Kavkaz* on the night of December 20/21 at the head of a naval flotilla carrying Colonel Aleksei S. Potapov's 3,500-man 79th Naval Infantry Brigade from Novorossiysk. Oktyabrsky disembarked Potapov's troops on the northern side of the bay and, after assembling into battalions, they marched straight off to reinforce the front near the Kamyschly Ravine. Petrov intended to use Potapov's brigade to spearhead a major counterattack to reduce the dangerous bulge between Sectors III and IV. Oktyabrsky also brought three loads of ammunition for Petrov's troops and ordered his two cruisers and four destroyers to provide more naval gunfire support, which also helped to reinvigorate the defense.

Once again, Hansen pre-empted Petrov's intended counterattack with an all-out assault of his own at dawn on December 22. Before Potapov's brigade could effectively intervene, Wolff's 22. Infanterie-Division finally broke through the right flank of Vorob'ev's Sector IV defenses. Both Choltitz's and Haccius's regiments ploughed the remnants of the 241st and 773rd Rifle Regiments out of their way and boldly advanced over a mile toward the coast. Were it not for one battalion of Potapov's brigade, which force-marched into the gap and brought Haccius's tired soldiers to a halt for the day, Wolff's division probably would have cut off all of Vorob'ev's remaining troops. As it was, Vorob'ev was forced to immediately begin evacuating the remnants of the 95th Rifle Division and 8th NIB from north of the Bel'bek and begin a retreat to the south. Lieutenant Matushenko's Battery No. 10 near Mamashai was blown up and abandoned; the 52 surviving crewmen retreated to Coastal Battery No. 30.[12] Further south, a five-battalion attack by the 32. Infanterie-Division at the northern end of the Kamyschly Ravine put paid to Ovseenko's 388th Rifle Division, which was bowled back in disorder. With the Germans approaching the foot of Mekenzievy Mountain, just a few miles from the northern side of Severnaya Bay, Potapov threw his 79th Naval Infantry Brigade into a furious counterattack, which regained some ground and halted the enemy advance. Petrov relieved Ovseenko of command and pulled his battered division back into reserve to rebuild. Petrov felt as if his frontline units were holding on only by their fingernails, and pleaded with the Stavka for more reinforcements.

Hansen temporarily halted his offensive on December 23 in order to regroup and resupply his forces, but in the interim Oktyabrsky's warships escorted a five-ship convoy carrying Colonel Nikolai O. Guz's 345th Rifle Division from Poti. Guz's division had been preparing to take part in the Kerch amphibious operation and was a relatively strong unit, with 11,274 troops, 34 artillery pieces (including 13 122mm howitzers), 18 medium mortars, 25 radios, and 135 trucks. The division was relatively well trained by Red Army 1941 standards, even if most of the troops were comprised of Caucasian minorities such as Ossetians and Chechens, with only a third being Slavs. In addition, Oktyabrsky delivered the 81st Separate Tank Battalion (81 OTB), which had 30 T-26 light tanks. Petrov kept the tanks in reserve, but hustled Guz's fresh infantry regiments into the center of his line to replace the shattered 388th Rifle Division. Vorob'ev also used the brief respite to build a new front line for Sector IV along the Bel'bek River.

Manstein realized that he had little time left to take Sevastopol before casualties, ammunition shortages, and the winter weather sapped the strength from his offensive. He ordered Hansen to make an all-out attack on December 25, anticipating that Petrov's defenses were ready to crack. Hansen ordered the 22. and 132. Infanterie-Divisionen to mass 12 battalions against the boundary of Sectors III and IV, which now lay around Mekenzievy Mountain, and blast a way through to Severnaya Bay. However, this time the Soviet reinforcements had quick-marched into place before the Germans resumed their attacks, which now came to grief. The 132. Infanterie-Division's five battalions were shocked to run into a regiment from Guz's 345th Rifle Division, which repulsed IR 437's attacks. Likewise, Potapov's 79th Naval Infantry Brigade stood like a rock that IR 438 could not budge. Even Wolff's heretofore unstoppable 22. Infanterie-Division could not penetrate Vorob'ev's new line along the Bel'bek. Vilshansky even led a counterattack that succeeded in pushing back von Choltitz's spent IR 16. Lieutenant Aleksandr in Coastal Battery No. 30 further sapped German frontline morale by engaging Wolff's troops – now visible only a couple of miles away – with 30.5mm rounds fired in direct lay. The Germans were also now face-to-face with the still-intact fortifications of Petrov's main defensive belt, including Fort Stalin. This ferocious display of Soviet firepower and tenacity was not to the taste of the German soldiers, who now began to realize that victory was no longer within their grasp. Even the supporting attack by the 170. Infanterie-Division and the Romanians in the Chernaya River valley miscarried, with heavy losses.

On Christmas morning, Manstein paused his offensive to give AOK 11 a brief respite, then ordered Hansen to resume the attacks with 22. and 132. Infanterie-Divisionen. The Germans focused all their efforts on capturing the area around the Mekenzievy Mountain station, which was believed to be the linchpin of Petrov's defenses in Sector III. However, Petrov had received over 26,000 reinforcements and Manstein had received none, and now the threadbare German infantry battalions – some reduced to just 150–200 combat effectives – were up against the sturdy defenses of the Soviet main line of resistance. Only a few assault guns were still operational and the level of Luftwaffe and artillery support was dwindling, which made it impossible for the soldiers to storm concrete bunkers. Guz's fresh 345th Rifle Division brought the 22. Infanterie-Division's steady advance to a halt and then mounted a furious counterattack against Choltitz's depleted IR 16. Soviet artillery fire was intense, including naval gunfire, and was provided by Petrov's artillery and the armored train *Zhelezniakov*, which ducked out of its cave hideout to pepper the 132. Infanterie-Division with 100mm high-explosive shells. A major Soviet counterattack by Guz's troops hit Choltitz's regiment hard.

Late on Christmas night, Manstein received the first reports of enemy amphibious activity in the Kerch Straits and possible enemy landings, but he was not unduly concerned. He believed that the defeated 51st Army could only mount minor raids, which Sponeck's XXXXII Armeekorps could handle. The offensive at Sevastopol would continue. However, it was clear that AOK 11 was too weak to break Petrov's main line of resistance without substantial forces, and even though Manstein borrowed battalions from the 50. Infanterie-Division to reinforce Hansen's divisions, this was not enough. Hansen's forces were so exhausted that they were only capable of limited actions on December 26–27.

Amazingly, Manstein was able to concentrate all his remaining infantry, supported by the artillery and a few assault guns, against the Mekenzievy

Mountain station sector on the morning of December 28. Four battalions of the 132. Infanterie-Division managed to push Potapov's 79th NIB back over a mile, and capture the Mekenzievy Mountain rail station. On their right, Choltitz's IR 16 found a weak spot in the Soviet main line of resistance, held by the 241st Rifle Regiment, which was defending the approaches to Fort Stalin with only a few hundred riflemen. Choltitz's troops punched through the weak Soviet unit and actually got within sight of the fort before halting. Haccius's IR 65 also managed to flank Guz's 345th Rifle Division and reach the approaches to Lieutenant Aleksandr's Battery 30 (which the Germans had dubbed "Maxim Gorky I"). A group from the 345th Rifle Division was surrounded by the German advance and its commander, Major Maslov, opted to surrender. He later helped the Germans to recruit Soviet prisoners as volunteer labor or *Hilfswilliger* – which earned him a Soviet death sentence in absentia. It was an incredible day, where it seemed that Hansen's troops might actually break Petrov's defenses, but it was not to be.

During the night of December 28/29, another five-ship convoy arrived in Sevastopol bearing Colonel Nikolai F. Skutel'nik's 386th Rifle Division – the third fresh division to augment Petrov's army in December. Formed in Tbilisi just two weeks prior, Skutel'nik's division was composed primarily of less-than-enthusiastic Georgians, Armenians, and Azerbaijanis, but it nonetheless added another 10,000 troops to the defense. It certainly must have brought great chagrin to Manstein that the Luftwaffe had been completely unable to interdict Petrov's naval supply lines, and that the besieged defenders actually enjoyed better logistical support than the attackers.

Although Manstein ordered the offensive to continue on December 29, by 1000hrs he had received further word from Sponeck about Soviet landings at Feodosiya, which caused him to order XXX Armeekorps to cease its supporting attacks and immediately send the 170. Infanterie-Division to reinforce Sponeck's XXXXII Armeekorps. Salmuth's corps had spent the last week in a sanguinary and indecisive struggle over the Italian Heights, which only produced heavy casualties on both sides. Since his troops appeared on the verge of breaching Petrov's main line of resistance, Manstein allowed Hansen to continue his part of the offensive, although only a few battalions were still capable of attacking.

Atop a 65-yard-high hill one mile south of the Mekenzievy Mountain station stood Lieutenant Nikolai A. Vorobyev's 365th Antiaircraft Battery, which the Germans had dubbed "Fort Stalin." It was not a fort intended to stop a serious ground assault but, rather, the position consisted of four 76mm antiaircraft guns in pits, protected by three small concrete machine-gun bunkers. Barbed wire and a few antipersonnel mines provided a perimeter defense. Vorobyev was situated inside a concrete-and-steel command bunker, while most of his crews hunkered in underground bunkers. Choltitz led two battalions of his IR 16 toward the position, anticipating that its capture would open the way to Severnaya Bay. Vorobyev ordered his gunners to fire directly at Choltitz's troops, but the Germans responded by calling in artillery fire that knocked out three of the 76mm guns. Using smoke and short rushes, the German infantry managed to approach the battery position. Assisted by sappers, about 30 of Choltitz's infantrymen managed to penetrate the Soviet barbed-wire obstacles and penetrate into "Fort Stalin." However, at that point another barrage of artillery fire landed atop the hill and inflicted heavy casualties on the German *Stossgruppe*, including its leader. Vorobyev later claimed that he cleverly used a captured German flare gun to call in German artillery fire on their own troops, but he appears to have spent the action entirely in his bunker. It is more likely that Vorobyev was either the unintended beneficiary of accidental German friendly fire or fortuitous Soviet naval gunfire, which was pounding any movement spotted on the hillsides. In any case, Choltitz's attack failed and Hansen's corps had reached its high-water mark. Efforts by Haccius's IR 65 to capture Coastal Battery No. 30 also failed. Vorobyev was quickly awarded the Hero of the Soviet Union for "stopping the German offensive," although he was later stripped of his awards for raping a minor after the war.

Manstein did not call off his offensive entirely until early on December 31, by which time Hansen's LIV Armeekorps was completely exhausted. Hansen's troops had suffered 7,732 casualties during the offensive, including 1,636 dead or missing, which represents about half the assault troops involved. Zuckertort's gunners had fired 5,014 tons of ammunition during the offensive, equivalent to over 100,000 rounds, and had lost nine artillery pieces to Soviet counterbattery fire. Hansen's infantry and Zuckertort's firepower had certainly demolished the outer defensive line of Sevastopol, but had barely dented the main line of resistance. Indeed, it was only through imaginative small-unit tactics and excellent leadership that the Germans were able to make any significant progress at all. Wolff's

22. Infanterie-Division had particularly distinguished itself as the most aggressively led unit in AOK 11. On the other hand, the sanguinary brawl over the Italian Heights cost Salmuth's XXX Armeekorps 863 casualties and the Romanians 1,261 casualties, which was costly for a single position. Manstein had gambled on winning at Sevastopol, and failure to do so meant that most of his divisions were now reduced to combat ineffectiveness.

Petrov's Coastal Army had also taken a horrendous beating, with at least 17,000 casualties suffered, including 6,000 captured, but help appeared to be on the way with the amphibious landings at Kerch and Feodosiya. Soviet material losses were also significant, and both Coastal Battery No. 30 and Coastal Battery No. 35 had fired so many 305mm rounds during the first and second German offensives that the barrels were worn out; until new barrels were installed, Sevastopol's heaviest guns would remain silent.[13]

CHAPTER 5

Winter War, December 1941–March 1942

"Any weakling can take victories, but only the strong can endure setbacks."

Adolf Hitler, Berlin, January 30, 1942

Only two days after the winter counteroffensive began at Moscow, the Stavka sent orders to General-Lieutenant Dmitri T. Kozlov, commander of the Transcaucasian Front, directing him to begin planning to send the bulk of his forces across the Kerch Straits to liberate the Crimea. Kozlov and his chief of staff, General-Major Fyodor I. Tolbukhin, were given just two weeks to plan and execute the first major amphibious operation ever conducted by the Red Army. Kozlov was directed to land as large a force as possible, first to establish a secure lodgment in the Kerch Peninsula and then, once sufficient forces were across, to begin advancing westward to link up with Petrov's Coastal Army in Sevastopol and liberate the Crimea. It was a grand vision, based upon Stalin's belief that the Wehrmacht was a spent force, and that the moment had arrived for the Red Army to strike a death blow against the invaders.

Tolbukhin was generally regarded as a capable staff officer, but he had sat out the bulk of the 1941 campaign in the backwater Transcaucasus Military District and was eager to show off his talent in his first operation of the war. He developed an overly complicated plan that he hoped would quickly compromise the German ability to hold the Kerch Peninsula by making many small landings at multiple points, rather than one large landing. In the first echelon of Tolbukhin's landing plan, five different transport groups would land 7,500 troops from the 224th Rifle Division and 302nd Mountain Rifle Division from General-Lieutenant Vladimir N. Lvov's 51st Army on separate beaches north and south of Kerch. Then, after the Germans had reacted to this landing, General-Major Aleksei N. Pervushin would begin landing elements of his 44th Army to their rear, at Feodosiya. Oktyabrsky was expected to provide a significant part of the Black Sea Fleet to support the landings and provide naval gunfire support, while Rear-Admiral Sergei G. Gorshkov's Azov Flotilla would assist in bringing troops across the Kerch Straits. The VVS and VVS-ChF were expected to provide air support from bases in the Taman Peninsula. Despite the availability of troops and shipping, the Red Army had no experience with a complicated joint operation of this sort, and the short time provided for planning led to multiple failures of coordination. On top of this, the winter weather in the Black Sea at the end of December was predictably stormy, which greatly complicated the loading and unloading of troops. The constant siphoning of the best units and shipping to reinforce Petrov's Coastal Army at Sevastopol further disrupted operational planning.

Although the weather over the Kerch Strait area was poor on Christmas eve, Bf-110 reconnaissance aircraft from 3.(F)/11 spotted unusual enemy naval activity and reported it to the Luftwaffe liaison officer within Generalleutnant Hans Graf von Sponeck's XXXXII Armeekorps headquarters in Islam-Terek, located northwest of Feodosiya. Sponeck had commanded the 22. Luftlande-Division during the airborne invasion of Holland in May 1940 and was badly wounded; afterwards he was awarded the *Ritterkreuz* and continued to lead his division ably in the advance across southern Ukraine until promoted to command XXXXII Armeekorps in October. Now he was tasked with defending the Kerch Peninsula and much of the eastern Crimean coastline, but Manstein had stripped his corps to the bone in order to reinforce the offensive at Sevastopol. Consequently, Sponeck's only combat units were Generalleutnant Kurt

Himer's 46. Infanterie-Division, two coastal artillery battalions equipped with obsolete artillery from World War I, a pioneer regiment and a Luftwaffe flak battalion. Himer's division consisted of three infantry regiments (IR 42, 72, and 97) and three artillery battalions, but it was overextended and badly deployed. Oberst Friedrich Schmidt's Infanterie-Regiment 72 had its three battalions concentrated around the old Yenikale fortress northeast of Kerch, guarding the coastline that was closest to the Taman Peninsula. Oberst Ernst Maisel's Infanterie-Regiment 42 had just two battalions with 1,460 troops to guard a 17-mile stretch of coastline south of Kerch.[1] That left only Oberstleutnant Alexander von Bentheim's Infanterie-Regiment 97 holding positions in depth, with one battalion at Feodosiya and two battalions near the northern coast along the Sea of Azov. The southern coast of the Kerch Peninsula was only lightly screened by Aufklärungs-Abteilung 46.[2] In a pinch, Sponeck could also call upon the Romanian Mountain Corps for help, which had the 8th Cavalry Brigade guarding the coast near Alushta. After receiving the aerial reconnaissance report about enemy naval activity in the Kerch Strait, Sponeck issued the *Weihnachtsmann* ("Santa Claus") alarm, which put all units in XXXXII Armeekorps on alert to defend the Kerch Peninsula against amphibious landings.[3]

On the evening of December 25, 1941, the Soviet amphibious operation began when elements of the 51st Army's 224th Rifle Division and the 83rd Naval Infantry Brigade loaded aboard small craft on the Taman Peninsula and began the short, but frozen, transit across the Kerch Strait. It was not a very impressive invasion flotilla. Group Two, heading for Cape Khroni, 4 miles northeast of Kerch, consisted of the gunboat *Don* (equipped with two 130mm and two 45mm guns), the transports *Krasny Flot* and *Pyenay*, a tugboat, two self-propelled barges that carried three T-26 tanks and some artillery, and 16 small fishing trawlers. Lacking landing craft that could deposit troops on beaches, Gorshkov's Azov Flotilla was forced to use whaleboats to transfer troops from the transports to the shore – a tedious and dangerous process in turbulent seas. The weather was roughly Sea State 5 (waves 2–3 yards high, wind speed at 17–21 knots) with strong westerly winds and rain – similar to that experienced on D-Day in June 1944 – but was trending towards a more intense storm in the next 24 hours. At Cape Khroni, 697 troops from 2nd Battalion/160th Rifle Regiment succeeded in getting ashore by 0630hrs on December 26, but a number of troops trying to wade ashore through the surf either drowned or became hypothermia

Soviet return to the Crimea, December 26, 1941–January 1, 1942

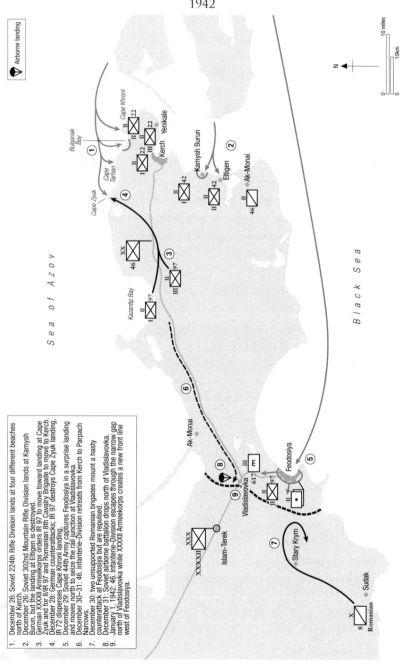

Airborne landing

1. December 26: Soviet 224th Rifle Division lands at four different beaches north of Kerch.
2. December 26: Soviet 302nd Mountain Rifle Division lands at Kamysh Burun, but the landing at Eltigen is destroyed.
3. German XXXXII Armeekorps orders IR 97 to move toward landing at Cape Zyuk and for I/IR 97 and Romanian 8th Cavalry Brigade to move to Kerch.
4. December 28: German counterattacks; IR 97 destroys Cape Zyuk landing, IR 72 disperses Cape Khroni landing.
5. December 29: Soviet 44th Army captures Feodosiya in a surprise landing and moves north to seize the rail junction at Vladislavovka.
6. December 30–31: 46. Infanterie–Division retreats from Kerch to Parpach Narrows.
7. December 30: two unsupported Romanian brigades mount a hasty counterattack at Feodosiya but are repulsed.
8. December 31: Soviet airborne battalion drops north of Vladislavovka.
9. January 1, 1942: 46. Infanterie–Division escapes through the narrow gap north of Vladislavovka while XXXXII Armeekorps creates a new front line west of Feodosiya.

102

casualties. Later in the day, another rifle battalion was landed at Cape Khroni, along with a platoon of T-26 tanks and some light artillery. The landings at the more distant Cape Zyuk were problematic; only 290 troops succeeded in getting ashore in six hours and several vessels were grounded on the rocky coastline. At Cape Tarhan, there were only two whaleboats available and just 18 soldiers out of the 1,000-man landing force actually reached the beach. The most successful Soviet landings were in Bulganak Bay, just west of Cape Khroni, where the Azov Flotilla managed to land 1,452 troops from the 224th Rifle Division's 143rd Rifle Regiment, along with three T-26 tanks, two 76mm howitzers, and two 45mm antitank guns. Other planned Soviet landings at Kazantip Point and Yenikale were aborted due to the weather. By midday, the Soviets had five separate beachheads on the northern side of the Kerch Peninsula, with barely 3,000 lightly equipped troops ashore. Enemy resistance initially was minimal, since very few Germans were stationed along this stretch of coastline, but the Luftwaffe arrived over the invasion areas by 1050hrs with He-111 bombers and Ju-87 Stukas. Gorshkov's Group 3, wallowing in heavy seas off Cape Tarhan, was particularly hard hit, and the 3,900-ton cargo ship *Voroshilov* was bombed and sunk with 450 troops aboard. Group 2 off Cape Zyuk was also bombed, and one vessel with 100 troops sank.[4]

Tolbukhin's amateurish landing plan, apparently made with little input from the Navy, simply dumped frozen, poorly supplied troops on remote beaches and assumed that they would somehow link up and seize the port of Kerch. Instead, the troops moved less than a mile inland and began to dig in against the expected German counterattacks. The isolated regimental and battalion commanders, with little or no communication between each other or their higher headquarters, decided to wait until the rest of the 224th Rifle Division and the follow-on 83rd Naval Infantry Brigade arrived before advancing further inland. However, after the initial landings were completed, the weather worsened, preventing any further large-scale landing operations across the Kerch Straits for the next three days.

The landing of the 302nd Mountain Rifle Division at Kamysh Burun, south of Kerch, was the only opposed landing on December 26. Here, the German I./IR 42 and II./IR 42 held excellent defensive positions on high ground overlooking the sandy beaches. The first wave of the invasion at 0500hrs ran into a deluge of German machine-gun, mortar, and light-artillery fire, which prevented most of the improvised landing craft from approaching the shore. An attempt to land on the beach at Eltigen was slaughtered by II./IR 42. A company of Soviet naval infantry managed to land at Stary Karantin, but was quickly overwhelmed by Major Karl Kraft's I./IR 42. The second wave arrived at 0700hrs and was also repulsed. However, some Soviet troops managed to land at the dock area at Kamysh Burun, where they had some cover from German fire, and the third wave was able to establish a tenuous foothold there by the afternoon. Yet only 2,175 of 5,200 troops succeeded in getting ashore at Kamysh Burun, and the Luftwaffe sank a number of ships off the beaches.

Generalleutnant Kurt Himer had taken command of the 46. Infanterie-Division only nine days prior to the Soviet amphibious assault. By 0610hrs he was aware of several landings, but the disjointed nature of the Soviet plan made it difficult for him to assess the enemy's main effort. Oberst Ernst Maisel's IR 42 appeared to have repulsed the landings south of Kerch, but the landings to the north were largely unopposed. Himer ordered Oberst Friedrich Schmidt's IR 72 to crush the landings at Cape Khroni, but there were no forces near Bulganak Bay or Cape Zyuk. After considering more reports on enemy activity, Himer ordered the *Stabskompanie* (headquarters company) of Oberstleutnant Alexander von Bentheim's IR 97 and its alarm unit – Hauptmann Karl Bock's III./IR 97 – plus a battery of 10.5cm howitzers, to rush toward Cape Zyuk. Bentheim's regiment was the most spread out of Himer's regiments, with II./IR 97 in Feodosiya and the other two battalions in central reserve. The roads were in bad condition due to heavy rain but Bentheim moved out with a horse-mounted platoon, and the lead elements of his regiment crawled eastward along the northern coast of the Kerch Peninsula toward Cape Zyuk. By midnight, Bentheim had both his I. and III. Battalions, along with two batteries of artillery, moving into position for a counterattack the next day.[5]

Kurt Himer had few forces available and was compelled to deal with multiple dispersed enemy landings and insufficient information on which to base his command decisions. At 1350hrs, IR 72 reported that they had captured a Soviet officer in skirmishing near Cape Khroni, and that under interrogation he had revealed that the Soviets intended to land a total of 25,000 troops near Kerch. With only six battalions to defend the entire eastern Kerch Peninsula, Himer – with Sponeck's approval – began making decisions that would shape the battle. He decided to commit all of IR 72 to crush the Cape Khroni landing as quickly as possible and bring up all of IR 97 – including II./IR 97 in Feodosiya – to crush the Cape Zyuk landings. He directed IR 42 to contain the Kamysh Burun landings until the other counterattacks were completed. A small alarm unit known as *Eingreifgruppe Bulganak*, consisting of one rifle company from IR 72, an artillery battery, and some pioneers, was sent to contain the landings at Bulganak Bay. Meanwhile, Sponeck requested that the Romanian 8th Cavalry Brigade be dispatched to reinforce Himer's forces near Kerch. It was a typical German operational plan: decisive, expeditious, and based upon a faulty intelligence picture.

Due to the muddy roads, the two battalions from Bentheim's IR 97 were not in a position to counterattack the Soviet beachhead at Cape Zyuk until 1300hrs on December 27. The terrain near the Soviet beachhead was flat and devoid of any vegetation, offering no concealment to either side. The Soviet troops – members of the 2nd Battalion/83rd Naval Infantry Brigade – spotted the Germans and immediately launched a spoiling attack against Hauptmann Karl Bock's III./IR 97 as it was deploying, committing three T-26 tanks and several companies of infantry. The Germans were briefly knocked off balance but a *Panzerjäger* platoon from 14./IR 97 was able to deploy a 3.7cm Pak, and Obergefreiter Max Freyberger fired 42 rounds into the attacking Soviet tanks, knocking all three out. A few Luftwaffe aircraft also arrived overhead and bombed the Soviet infantry, who fell back to their beachhead, but the German counterattack was postponed until the next day. Both sides hunkered down for the night on the open terrain, with a strong, cold wind chilling the troops.

At dawn on December 28, a cloudy day with light frost, the two battalions of IR 97 converged on the Soviet beachhead from the southwest, supported by two 10.5cm howitzers from 3./AR 114, while a pioneer company blocked the eastern exits from the beach. The Soviet landing force was in an indefensible position, crammed between the coast and Lake Chokraks'k, which made any defense difficult. Around 1000hrs, a few Stukas from StG 77 and six He-111 bombers arrived to bomb the Soviet beachhead.[6] Hauptmann Karl Bock's battalion quickly smashed through the Soviet defenses and headed toward the beach. The 42-year-old Bock was an unusual battalion commander in the German Army, being both a veteran of World War I and a member of the Nazi Party who had served six years in the SS. By 1200hrs, Bock's troops had the beach in sight. The Soviets fought from rock outcroppings and then were pushed back further, some troops fighting standing waist-deep in the surf. Yet by late afternoon, Soviet resistance at Cape Zyuk was broken; and IR 97 took 458 prisoners and counted about 300 dead. Bentheim's regiment suffered roughly 40 casualties in reducing the Soviet beachhead.

In the meantime, IR 72 had moved with I. and II./IR 72 and crushed the Soviet beachhead at Cape Khroni. At dusk on December 28, a Soviet follow-on convoy approached Cape Khroni with reinforcements and observed German troop activity all along the coastline. One Soviet officer and 11 men managed to swim out through the frigid waves to a patrol boat, where they revealed that the beachhead had been destroyed. There were still pockets of resistance inland to be mopped up, and over 1,000 troops were still ensconced on the shore of Bulganak Bay, but by late on December 28, Himer and Sponeck had reason to be satisfied – over 1,700 prisoners had been taken and the bulk of the Soviet landing forces had been defeated. The Soviets had gained a sizeable lodgment at Kamysh Burun, but IR 42 had them surrounded and they could be dealt with as soon as IR 72 and IR 97 completed their mop-up operations. If the storms over the Kerch Straits had remained for another day or so, a significant German tactical victory would have been in hand, but the weather began to subside on the evening of December 28/29 and the Soviets were now ready to spring the second phase of their invasion upon Sponeck.

At 1300hrs on December 28, two assault regiments from General-Major Aleksei N. Pervushin's 44th Army began loading aboard an invasion fleet at Novorossiysk comprised of two light cruisers, eight destroyers, 14 transports, and numerous small craft. Four and a half hours later, the advance elements steamed out of Novorossiysk aboard the light cruiser *Krasny Kavkaz*; the elderly *Fidonisy*-class destroyers *Shaumyan*, *Zhelezniakov*, and *Nyezamozhnik*; and a group of patrol boats and coastal minesweepers. The weather improved briefly, allowing the flotilla to travel at 16 knots for most of the way, until the destroyer *Sposobnyi* struck a mine and suffered 200 casualties. Many of the troops spent the whole voyage on exposed, ice-crusted decks, and were frozen and seasick after a few hours. Off the port of Feodosiya, two Soviet submarines waited on the surface, ready to mark the harbor entrance with lights when the assault force approached.

Inside Feodosiya, which had a pre-war population of 28,000, the German garrison was not expecting action, since Sponeck had dispatched the only infantry unit, II./IR 97, to support the battle around Kerch. The main units left defending the port of Feodosiya were II./AR 54 (equipped with four 10cm and 11 15cm howitzers of World War I-vintage) and I./AR 77 (equipped with six captured Czech 15cm howitzers). Both artillery battalions were deployed in coastal-defense positions around the port, but had limited transport and means of ground defense. Also available in or near Feodosiya were 700–800 engineers from Oberstleutnant Hans von Ahlfen's Pionier-Regimentsstab z.b.V. 617 (two assault-boat companies, one Brücko B bridging company, and Landungs-Kompanie 777), although they were equipped only with light small arms. Ostensibly, the harbor entrance was protected by a raft boom, preventing enemy access.

Once the Soviet 51st Army began landing on the Kerch Peninsula, Sponeck ordered the Romanian Mountain Corps to send first its 8th Cavalry Brigade then its 4th Mountain Brigade to reinforce Himer's 46. Infanterie-Division, leaving only the 3rd Rosiori motorized Cavalry Regiment near Feodosiya. By the evening of December 28, the bulk of Colonel Corneliu Teodorini's 8th Cavalry Brigade had marched halfway to Kerch, but Brigadier-General Gheorghe Manoliu's 4th Mountain Brigade and General-Major Gheorghe Avramescu's Mountain Corps headquarters was still located at Stary Krym, 14 miles west of Feodosiya.

At 0350hrs on December 29, the Soviet flotilla approached Feodosiya and the destroyers *Shaumyan* and *Zhelezniakov* fired star shells that illuminated the port, followed up by a 13-minute naval bombardment. Then four MO-IV type sub-chasers sprinted toward the outer edge of the long harbor mole where the lighthouse sat at the end. Pulling up alongside the mole, about 60 naval infantrymen led by Lieutenant Arkady F. Aydinov leapt onto it and quickly secured the lighthouse. They then began clearing the mole, capturing two unmanned 3.7cm Pak guns, and Aydinov used green flares to signal to the fleet that the harbor entrance was clear. German gunners from II./AR 54 engaged the patrol boats ineffectually, and the Soviet naval infantrymen seized the entire mole before the Germans could effectively react. Amazingly, the raft boom was found to be open, apparently due to negligence. At 0426hrs the destroyer *Shaumyan* entered the harbor, moved alongside the mole, and disgorged a company of naval infantrymen within 20 minutes. The destroyers *Zhelezniakov* and *Nyezamozhnik* repeated the maneuver, further reinforcing the Soviet lodgment. Although the *Shaumyan* was damaged by German artillery fire, the Germans never expected the Soviets to attempt anything so bold, and had not properly fortified the harbor entrance. Soviet audacity and the speed of the initial landings caught the Germans completely by surprise.

Once the three destroyers had disembarked their assault troops, Captain 1st Rank Aleksei M. Guscin brought his cruiser *Krasny Kavkaz* alongside the mole at 0500hrs and began landing 1,853 troops from the 633rd Rifle Regiment of the 157th Rifle Division. By this point, the Germans were fully awake and concentrated all their fire on the Soviet cruiser, hitting her 17 times, setting her No. 2 turret on fire. However, Guscin was far from helpless, and he directed his 180mm batteries to fire point-blank at the enemy artillery and machine-gun positions, winking at them from the shoreline. After more than three hours of intense combat in the port, Guscin finally maneuvered his damaged cruiser away from the mole, having accomplished his mission.[7] Belatedly, the Luftwaffe showed up and sank a minesweeper and patrol boat, but were too late to impede the Soviet landing operation.

By 0730hrs the Germans had completely lost control of the port and the Soviet transports had begun to land artillery and vehicles. Once Soviet infantry began moving into the city, the German artillerymen began abandoning their positions and the German defense quickly collapsed. Ahlfen's pioneers briefly tried to put up resistance but they soon retreated as well. By 1000hrs, Sponeck learned that the Soviets had seized most of Feodosiya and were pouring ashore. Indeed, the remarkable thing about the Feodosiya landing is the speed that Oktyabrsky's fleet was able to land 4,500 troops in the morning and have elements of three rifle divisions from Pervushin's 44th Army ashore by the end of the day. Sponeck realized that no substantial German forces were near Feodosiya and that the Soviet landing represented a clear threat to his corps' lines of communications. He immediately ordered Teodorini's 8th Cavalry Brigade to turn around and march back to Feodosiya, while Manoliu's 4th Mountain Brigade was ordered to form blocking positions west of the city. In a telephone conversation with Manstein, Sponeck requested permission to withdraw the 46. Infanterie-Division from Kerch back to the Parpach Narrows, where it could contain the Soviet bridgehead at Feodosiya and establish a viable defensive line until reinforcements arrived. Manstein refused, and ordered Sponeck to hold on; he promised Gruppe Hitzfeld from the 73. Infanterie-Division, that the entire 170. Infanterie-Division would be sent to retake Feodosiya.

What happened next was – and remains – highly controversial, and is known as "the von Sponeck affair." Having been ordered not to withdraw Himer's 46. Infanterie-Division, the 53-year-old Graf von Sponeck did something almost unheard of in the Wehrmacht – he severed communications with AOK 11 headquarters in Simferopol and decided to disobey Manstein. At 0830hrs, Himer was ordered to force-march his entire division westward in order to prevent it from being cut off in the Kerch Peninsula. Was Sponeck justified in retreating, or did he panic, as was suggested at his subsequent court martial? While it is true that there were no significant German troops left near Feodosiya, the Romanians had close to 20,000 troops converging on the city, as well as German reinforcements from AOK 11. It had been Sponeck's decision to pull these troops away from Feodosiya toward Kerch and now he reversed himself, leading to countermarches that exhausted the Romanian troops. Sponeck insisted that the two Romanian brigades launch a counterattack against the Soviet lodgment at Feodosiya on December 30 – without air or artillery support – and they were quickly repulsed. Pervushin's three rifle divisions then pushed northward, threatening to isolate XXXXII Armeekorps forces in the Kerch Peninsula.

Himer's division spent December 30–31 marching 75 miles westward in a snowstorm toward Sponeck's corps headquarters, which was still located at Islam-Terek, 18 miles northwest of Feodosiya. Shortages of fuel caused some vehicles to be abandoned, and the division's heavy weapons lagged behind. Yet by the time that the vanguards of IR 97 and IR 42 reached the important crossroads town of Vladislavovka on the morning of December 31, they were shocked to find that the Soviet 63rd Mountain Rifle Division had already seized the town and created a roadblock. Himer tried to push both regiments to crash through the Soviet position, but it was far too formidable, and his troops were exhausted and lacking in artillery support. Unable to break through the Soviet roadblock, the 46. Infanterie-Division retreated west cross-country across the flat, snow-covered landscape through a 6-mile-wide gap between the Sea of Azov and the Soviet pincer. The retreat of the 46. Infanterie-Division was a near-run thing, with isolation from the rest of AOK 11 a distinct possibility, but it was no *Anabasis* (Xenophon's 4th century BC history of the march of the Ten Thousand through the Persian

Empire). Himer's division abandoned a good deal of material, but personnel losses were light. Between December 24 and December 31, 1941, Infanterie-Regiment 42's battle strength was reduced from 1,460 to 1,279, a 12 percent loss rate. By the time that his division formed a new defensive line east of Islam-Terek on January 1, 1942, Himer still had over 4,300 of his infantry remaining.[8]

As if the situation was not bad enough for the Axis, on the night of December 31 a 250-man Soviet airborne battalion led by Major Dmitri Ya. Nyashin leapt from 16 TB-3 bombers into the black void north of Vladislavovka. The Soviet paratroopers were obliged to climb out of a hatch onto the bomber's wing and then slide off, one at a time, which resulted in a very dispersed drop. Nyashin's paratroopers were scattered in the corridor that the 46. Infanterie-Division was retreating through, and engaged in a number of small skirmishes with the retreating Germans, who were panicked by the sudden appearance of Soviet paratroopers. Darkness concealed the small size of Nyashin's force, and increased Sponeck's apprehension about his vulnerable position. Soon thereafter, Nyashin linked up with Pervushin's ground forces.

By January 1, 1942, XXXXII Armeekorps had established a new line of defense 12 miles from Feodosiya. The lead elements of Gruppe Hitzfeld were arriving, led by Oberstleutnant Otto Hitzfeld with his Infanterie-Regiment 213 of the 73. Infanterie-Division, I./AR 173, Panzerjäger-Abteilung 173, a platoon of four StuG III assault guns from Sturmgeschütz-Abteilung 197, and a flak detachment from 3./Flak 14. Manoliu's 4th Mountain Brigade had also established a stable defense around Stary Krym, although the 236th Rifle Division was pushing against their lines. By this point, Pervushin's 44th Army had carved out a 7½-mile-deep lodgment from Feodosiya and was probing northward and westward. On New Year's Day, Soviet infantry and light tanks attacked toward the XXXXII Armeekorps command post at Ismail-Terek, but Panzerjäger-Abteilung 173 had just arrived at the front and succeeded in knocking out 16 T-26 tanks. German historian Paul Carell claimed that in this action, "the armored spearhead of the Soviet Forty-fourth Army had been broken," but in fact, Pervushin still had at least 18 tanks left and more on the way.[9]

The 51st Army had also taken advantage of Himer's retreat from Kerch to break out from the Kamysh Burun beachhead, and Colonel Mikhail K. Zubkov's 302nd Mountain Rifle Division liberated Kerch on December 31. By the next day, the 51st Army began liberating the rest of the eastern Kerch

Peninsula. Soon, XXXXII Armeekorps would have to face two Soviet armies, determined to push west toward Sevastopol. Could this paper-thin defense hold? If not, the entire German position in the Crimea was at risk. However, this was no longer Sponeck's problem, since Manstein relieved him of command on New Year's Eve. Within three weeks, Sponeck was court-martialed in Germany for disobedience and retreating without orders. Although many other German commanders had done the same during the Soviet Winter Counteroffensive, the regime chose to make an example of Sponeck, who was sentenced to death, thereafter commuted to six years' imprisonment. Manstein said nothing on behalf of his subordinate, and allowed the new commander of Heeresgruppe Süd, Generalfeldmarschall Walther von Reichenau, to impose group punishment upon the entire 46. Infanterie-Division. Reichenau ordered that, "because of its slack reaction to the Russian landing on the Kerch Peninsula, as well as its precipitate withdrawal from the Peninsula, I hereby declare 46. Infanterie-Division forfeit of soldierly honor. Decorations and promotions are in abeyance until countermanded."[10]

Inside his underground headquarters in Sevastopol, Vice-Admiral Oktyabrsky planned to mount an amphibious diversionary operation to prevent Manstein from sending any of his limited reserves to interfere with the 44th Army's landings at Feodosiya. He reckoned that the Germans were stretched so thinly that they could not afford to deal with another crisis. An obvious target was the port of Yevpatoriya, located on the coast only 40 miles north of Sevastopol. Oktyabrsky and Petrov envisioned a lightning amphibious raid to seize the harbor at Yevpatoriya – believed to be lightly guarded by Romanian troops – which would then be used to host a larger landing by a brigade-size force. There was talk of a paratroop landing and using partisans to support it, but details were sketchy. If a large enough force could be landed at Yevpatoriya, Manstein would be placed on the horns of a dilemma: being forced to choose between sending his limited reserves to the east or west, but not both. Oktyabrsky wanted the landing to occur shortly after New Year, but the winter storm that had plagued the Kerch landings returned and made this impossible for several days. It was not until the evening of January 4, 1942, that the weather abated enough for the landing to be attempted.

At 2330hrs on January 4, a small flotilla consisting of the *Tral*-class coastal minesweeper *Vzryvatel'*, seven MO-IV sub-chasers, and the tugboat SP-14 under the command of Captain 2nd Rank Nikolay V. Buslaev left Sevastopol harbor and headed north along the coast in the darkness. Embarked aboard the flotilla was Captain Georgy K. Buzinov's separate Naval Infantry Battalion, augmented with engineers, reconnaissance troops, and an NKVD detachment. Three hours later, Buslaev's tiny flotilla arrived off the entrance of Yevpatoriya harbor. The wind and sea were extremely rough, knocking his formation about and surely inducing seasickness in the naval infantrymen, who were almost all loaded above deck. Buslaev directed his ships to land their troops on three piers jutting out into the harbor.

Although there was only a German coastal artillery unit, a platoon of military police, and a few Romanian troops in Yevpatoriya, they were not caught by surprise. After the rapid loss of Feodosiya, Manstein had put all other coastal units on high alert, no matter what the weather. As Buslaev's small craft approached the piers, searchlights switched on and caught the Russians in the act of landing. The largest contingent of 500 troops landed at the main passenger pier, with Buslaev bringing his minesweeper *Vzryvatel'* alongside. The Germans and Romanians opened fire with machine guns and mortars, killing about 50 naval infantrymen just as they landed on the pier. Subsequent groups jumped directly into the shallow-but-freezing water and waded ashore, using the pier for cover. A nearby coastal battery fired on the pier and one round struck the bridge of the *Vzryvatel'*, killing Buslaev. German forward observers directed fire against the landing from the roof of the nearby Crimea Hotel. The pier itself was damaged by an explosion, which made it difficult for the other Soviet ships to unload heavy weapons and supplies. Eventually, Lieutenant Vladimir P. Tityulin rallied enough troops underneath the pier to push inland and overrun the Crimea Hotel by 0500hrs. Two other companies had landed separately on two smaller piers and also gradually fought their way into part of the city. Not long after the landing, the *Vzryvatel'* ran aground on a sandbar just 50 yards offshore, and became hopelessly stuck. One sub-chaser and a tugboat remained to offer assistance, but the rest of the flotilla departed before dawn, since the Luftwaffe was sure to arrive once the sun came up.

In Yevpatoriya, the Soviet naval infantrymen expanded their control over the southern part of the city, but German blocking positions equipped which machine guns prevented them from moving too far inland.

"The Bolsheviks will be driven off and never return!" proclaims a propaganda poster distributed by 11. Armee in the Crimea. This poster ties in with Manstein's secret memorandum about annihilating the "Judaeo-Bolshevik" system and depicts the Wehrmacht acting as exterminators under the Nazi banner. (NARA)

German infantry cautiously advance into a Crimean village, 1941–42. (Nik Cornish, WH 721)

This photo was taken in 1920 from the bottom of the ditch below the Tartar Wall. At top left, the remains of barbed wire from the White trenches atop the wall are still visible. (Nik Cornish, RCW 111)

This is the point of Wrangel's defenses on the Litovsky Peninsula along the Sivash where the Red Army took advantage of the weather to outflank the Perekop position by wading through the lower-than-usual water. Rows of barbed wire were established to bar the movement of small boats, but the fieldworks defending the obstacle were primitive and virtually unmanned. (Nik Cornish, RCW 94)

Since the time of Catherine the Great, Russian naval power in the Black Sea was based upon possession of the naval base at Sevastopol and the possession of capital ships to operate from that base. The battleship *Parizhskaya Kommuna* was transferred to the Black Sea in 1930 to serve as flagship for the fleet, but it subsequently proved to be ill-suited to operate in Crimean waters that were dominated by enemy air power. The Black Sea Fleet's sole battleship and handful of cruisers did play a major role in stopping the initial German assault upon Sevastopol in November–December 1941, but afterwards sat out much of the rest of the war in obscure backwater anchorages. (Author's collection)

Soviet coastal gunners at Coastal Battery 30 (later dubbed "Fort Maxim Gorky I" by the Germans) in Sevastopol before the German attack. The 305mm gun turrets were designed to traverse 360 degrees and could fire against naval or ground targets. Like the British at Gibraltar, the Russians at Sevastopol were more concerned about attack from the sea and put more effort into preparing for a naval attack that never came, rather than the landward attack that did. (Author's collection)

Soviet VVS-ChF MiG-3 fighters of the 32nd Fighter Regiment based at the Chersonese airstrip south of Sevastopol in 1941–42. A small number of Soviet naval fighters tenaciously defended the skies over the naval base for six months until overwhelmed in June 1942. (Author's collection)

German soldiers from Hansen's LIV Armeekorps observe Soviet positions on the Perekop Isthmus, September 1941. The 11. Armee was forced to mount a deliberate assault against a Soviet defense in depth, yet was not properly equipped with siege artillery or combat engineers. (Author's collection)

German infantry are seen here having occupied positions in the Soviet outer defenses at Perekop and are observing an artillery preparation of Fort Perekop. The Soviets planted steel beams in the ground to form an antitank barrier, and behind the barrier were numerous antipersonnel mines. (Author's collection)

Fort Perekop, the main Soviet defensive position behind the Tartar Wall (the ditch is marked with a "T"). This obsolete field work, extant since the 17th century, was improved by Red Army engineers with protective trenches and a dense minefield on the approaches. Hansen's troops never actually captured the fort, which was abandoned once the town of Armyansk (located to the south) fell into German hands. (NARA)

Hansen's LIV Armeekorps used small *Stossgruppen* (assault groups) consisting of grenadiers and flamethrower-equipped pioneers to overcome the tough Soviet forward security positions at Perekop, before even reaching the Tartar Wall. Here, a grenadier flings a *Stielgranaten* at a Soviet position. Note that the entrenched Soviet defenders are virtually invisible, while the upright German attackers are fully exposed and vulnerable. (Author's collection)

German infantry from the LIV Armeekorps crossing the Tatar Ditch on September 26, 1941. The steep walls formed an excellent defensive parapet and it was only through the use of aggressive combined-arms tactics that the Germans were able to breach this position so quickly. (Author's collection)

Soviet prisoners taken at Perekop, September 1941. The 51st Army failed to hold either the Perekop or Ishun defensive positions, and lost about half its troops and the bulk of its field artillery. (Author's collection)

German infantry advance south from Ishun into the Crimea. Most of the 11. Armee could only advance at a walking pace. The flat, grassy terrain made movement easy but also rendered attackers very vulnerable to defensive fire when Soviet rearguards chose to stand and fight. (Author's collection)

Once the Soviet defense at Ishun was broken on October 26, 1941, Manstein initiated a pursuit operation. Brigade Ziegler was an extemporized motorized unit, which consisted mostly of thin-skinned wheeled vehicles. Note the alertness of the German troops – looking out for Soviet rearguards or ambushes – and the air-recognition flag on the hood of the vehicle. (Author's collection)

A Soviet I-153 "Chaika" fighter patrols over the entrance to Sevastopol's Severnaya Bay in 1941. At this point, naval traffic in and out of the port appears still normal, with a minesweeper and transport in the background. However once the Luftwaffe appeared over Sevastopol, most naval traffic only moved at night, in order to avoid attacks. (Author's collection)

Romanian motorcycle troops from the 6th Motorized Roșiori Regiment were used in the pursuit after Ishun in November 1941, as well as during Operation *Trappenjagd* in May 1942. Note the German vehicle in the foreground, likely belonging to a liaison officer. (Nik Cornish, WH 1410)

A Soviet 152mm howitzer in a wood-framed firing position. Most of Sevastopol's perimeter defenses in late 1941 were still fairly basic in layout, and it was not until the winter that most of the artillery was emplaced in more robust positions. (Nik Cornish, RA 105)

When the destroyer *Sovershennyi* was crippled by German bombers in Severnaya Bay, the Soviets stripped the wreck of its 130mm gun turrets and deployed them in two batteries on the Malakhov Hill. Matyukhin's Battery 701 had two 130mm guns deployed in open concrete pits, which continued to operate until the final days of the siege. (Author's collection)

A German infantry NCO cautiously peers around a shell-pocked building in a Crimean village. Note that he is prepared for unexpected close combat, with an entrenching tool in one hand. By the time that the 11. Armee reached the outskirts of Sevastopol in November 1941, its infantry units were severely depleted. (Author's collection)

German troops from the 132. Infanterie-Division fought their way into Feodosiya on January 18, 1942, routing the Soviet 44th Army. Note that the weather is cold and that the German infantry are outfitted only with standard greatcoats. Manstein's 11. Armee was greatly aided by the mild Crimean winter and suffered relatively few frostbite casualties, unlike the rest of the Wehrmacht on the Eastern Front. (Author's collection)

A German soldier at Yevpatoriya scans the sea for further Soviet landings, with the shattered wreck of the Tral-class coastal minesweeper *Vzryvatel'* behind him. After running aground during the raid on the night of January 6, 1942, the *Vzryvatel'* was riddled by point-blank fire from German 10.5cm howitzers. However, the defiant resistance of the doomed vessel served as an example of selfless service for the Black Sea Fleet and an indication to the Germans of the willingness of the Soviets to mount near-suicidal amphibious raids. (Author's collection)

Caught by surprise by the Soviet capture of Feodosiya, Manstein was forced to abort his offensive against Sevastopol and hurriedly transfer elements of three divisions to retake the city. The 11. Armee did not possess much wheeled transport by January 1942, but unlike the rest of the Eastern Front, the Crimea did not receive sufficient snowfall to immobilize the German Army. (Süddeutsche Zeitung, 00403719)

After retreating from Kerch, the German 46. Infanterie-Division was forced to construct hasty defenses across the Parpach Narrows to prevent a Soviet breakout. The Soviet Crimean Front made four efforts to break through the Parpach Line between February and April 1942. Note the open nature of the terrain, which meant that troops were often under enemy observation. There were several stone quarries in the area, which the Germans used to gather material for their fighting positions. Due to a high water table, it was difficult to dig trenches in this area. (Süddeutsche Zeitung, 00403804)

Manstein received the newly-raised 22. Panzer-Division in March 1942, but the unit was badly defeated in its first action on March 20, 1942. However, the division performed much better during Operation *Trappenjagd* in May 1942. This division was primarily equipped with the Czech-built Pz 38(t) tank, which could not stand up to the T-34 or KV-1 tanks encountered in the Crimea. (Süddeutsche Zeitung, 00403725)

Two T-34 tanks lie wrecked near Koi-Assan on the Kerch Peninsula after the Soviet offensive in March 1942. The Soviets were unable to use their superiority in armor to break out from the Kerch Peninsula, and the Parpach Narrows became a lethal killing ground reminiscent of World War I battlefields. (Author's collection)

German pioneers and StuG III assault guns advance through the Soviet defenses at Parpach during Operation *Trappenjagd* in May 1942. Note the use of smoke to conceal the breach site in the Soviet obstacle belt. Manstein was able to overcome well-prepared Soviet defenses through the use of skillful combined-arms tactics and overwhelming air support. (Süddeutsche Zeitung, 00403782)

Manstein's trump card in the Crimea was the assault boats of 902. Sturmboote-Kommando, which he used to outflank the Soviet defenses at Parpach in May 1942, and then to cross Severnaya Bay in June 1942. Using the element of surprise, these assault boats enabled the Germans to conduct a new form of maneuver warfare in coastal waters. (Nik Cornish, WH 1336)

The *Svobodnyi*, a Type 7U class destroyer, was the newest destroyer in the Black Sea Fleet, having been commissioned in January 1942. It was involved in the regular supply run from Novorossiysk and was caught in daylight hours by Ju-87 Stuka dive-bombers in Sevastopol's Severnaya Bay on June 9, 1942. After being struck by multiple bombs, the destroyer sank near the Count's Quay. (Author's collection)

Tracers and parachute flares arch over the frontline trenches around Sevastopol in June 1942. Although most combat occurred during daylight hours, frontline units received regular harassing fire during the night, and the Soviet naval infantrymen were particularly fond of conducting local trench raids during hours of darkness. (Süddeutsche Zeitung, 00403699)

Meanwhile, news of the Soviet landing at Yevpatoriya had reached Manstein's headquarters, and he ordered several units to head there immediately. Oberstleutnant Oskar von Boddien's Aufklärungs-Abteilung 22 was in the lead, followed by Oberstleutnant Hubertus-Maria Ritter von Heigl's Pionier-Bataillon 70 and Oberst Friedrich-Wilhelm Müller's Infanterie-Regiment 105 of the 72. Infanterie-Division. The lead elements of these units began to arrive after 1000hrs, but the Germans decided to wait until all the reinforcements were assembled before launching their counterattack.

Oktyabrsky tried to send reinforcements to Yevpatoriya. Another naval infantry battalion was loaded aboard the destroyer *Smyshlyonyi*, the coastal minesweeper *Yakor'*, and four MO-IV sub-chasers, but could not land at Yevpatoriya on the night of January 5/6 due to a violent storm. On the morning of January 6, the German counterattack started, supported by artillery and the Luftwaffe. German artillery demolished the Crimea Hotel and began reducing other Soviet strongpoints. Engineers from Pionier-Bataillon 70 used flamethrowers to burn Soviet pockets of resistance. A battery of 10.5cm howitzers was brought up to engage the stranded *Vzryvatel'* with direct fire, and they repeatedly punctured its hull. Soviet sailors bravely refused to abandon their ship until it was reduced to a burning wreck; there was only a single survivor. By the evening of January 6 there were only 120 naval infantrymen left out of the original landing force of 740 men. Captain Buzinov led a breakout effort, hoping to reach either Sevastopol or nearby partisan units. The naval infantrymen mounted a desperate frontal attack against one of the German blocking positions, manned by troops of the Aufklärungs-Abteilung 22. A wild close-quarter melee ensued, with submachine guns and grenades in the dark. Sixty Russians were killed, but Oberstleutnant von Boddien was also killed. The remaining Russians fled into the darkness, but Buzinov and a group of 17 naval infantrymen were cornered the next morning in a nearby village, where they made a last stand. Only four sailors, led by Captain-Lieutenant Ivan F. Litovchuk, managed to reach Soviet lines at Sevastopol.

The Germans stamped out the last resistance in Yevpatoriya on the morning of January 7. One sailor escaped by swimming out in the icy water using a float and was picked up by a Soviet patrol boat. Altogether, the Germans claimed 600 Soviets killed and 203 captured, which was virtually the entire landing force and the naval crews. The Soviets later claimed that the Germans executed wounded naval infantrymen – which is quite possible – and then began rounding up civilians in the city who had aided the landing force. Thousands were imprisoned, deported as forced labor to Germany, or simply turned over to Einsatzgruppe D for elimination.

When Oktyabrsky lost contact with the landing force, he decided to send a small naval reconnaissance team to ascertain their status. A 13-man reconnaissance team was landed from the submarine *M-33* near the Yevpatoriya lighthouse on the evening of January 8. It did not take long before they realized that Buzinov's battalion had been annihilated, but before they could re-embark, the stormy weather returned in full force. For six days the team remained near the lighthouse, awaiting a chance to return to the submarine, but the Germans eventually detected them and destroyed the team, except for a sole survivor. The Soviet landing at Yevpatoriya proved to be a forlorn hope that was mostly undone by adverse weather conditions and rapid enemy reaction.

General-Major Aleksei N. Pervushin's position at Feodosiya seemed very good on January 1, 1942: his 44th Army had three rifle divisions with 23,000 troops ashore and the enemy forces in front of him were weak and disorganized. General-Lieutenant Vladimir N. Lvov's 51st Army was advancing to join him with another four rifle divisions and, together, they would crush the Axis forces before they could establish a firm defense across the narrow neck of the Kerch Peninsula. Yet while the Black Sea Fleet had brilliantly pulled off the surprise landing at Feodosiya, the Red Army proved less adept at exploiting this victory. Pervushin's three divisions had occupied so much ground around Feodosiya that he lacked the manpower to mass for a real offensive to destroy either the Romanian Mountain Corps of XXXXII Armeekorps. Gruppe Hitzfeld had arrived and had established a rock-solid defense in the gap between the Romanian Mountain Corps and XXXXII Armeekorps. Instead, Pervushin settled into a semi-defensive posture around Feodosiya, waiting for Lvov's army to arrive before mounting a joint offensive. Unfortunately, this decision handed the initiative back to Manstein's AOK 11.

Once it was clear that the Soviet forces in Feodosiya were not pushing westward in any strength, Manstein resolved to organize a counteroffensive to retake the city. Although the Germans was not particularly adept or equipped for winter offensive operations, Manstein sensed an opportunity to inflict a reverse upon an overconfident and overextended enemy. He began by sending General der Infanterie Franz Mattenklott, former commander of the 72. Infanterie-Division, to replace Sponeck as commander of XXXXII Armeekorps. Mattenklott was an iron-willed officer who would hold the line until reinforcements arrived. Initially, Manstein was only going to send the 170. Infanterie-Division to reinforce XXXXII Armeekorps, but he decided to add the 132. Infanterie-Division and two battalions from the 72. Infanterie-Division as well. The only remaining armor support was three StuG IIIs from Sturmgeschütz-Abteilung 190 and a handful from the newly arrived Sturmgeschütz-Abteilung 197, which were sent as well. Committing this many reinforcements required AOK 11 to abandon some of the hard-won positions gained in the December offensive, which irritated Hitler, but Manstein argued that a counteroffensive capable of achieving operational-level objectives required this kind of tactical sacrifice. The Romanian also agreed to send Brigadier-General Nicolae Costescu's 18th Infantry Division to reinforce XXXXII Armeekorps.

For the next two weeks, the front assumed a static character with only minor combat activity on either side. The vanguard of Lvov's 51st Army reached the Parpach Narrows by January 5, but took no offensive action against the opposing 46. Infanterie-Division. Lvov's army moved into place very slowly, and even by January 12 he still had only two rifle divisions deployed forward. Meanwhile, Axis reinforcements poured in, and by January 13 Manstein had amassed more than four divisions outside Feodosiya. He also brought up the XXX Armeekorps staff, now under Generalmajor Maximilian Fretter-Pico, to spearhead the counteroffensive while Mattenklott occupied the attention of Lvov's 51st Army. Manstein also requested greater help from the Luftwaffe, and General der Flieger Robert Ritter von Greim was sent to Sarabus airfield in the Crimea to take charge of the Sonderstab Krim (Special Staff Crimea).

On the Soviet side, General-Lieutenant Dmitri T. Kozlov's Caucasus Front still directed the operations of the 44th and 51st Armies, but he believed that the Germans were too weak to threaten either of these armies before he was ready to make his own "big push." He violated one of the primary tactical lessons learned during World War I – entrench your forces whenever they stop advancing – and did not emphasize defensive measures.

Prior to launching a major offensive, Kozlov also wanted to conduct another landing behind enemy lines on the Black Sea coast in order to divert Manstein's reserves – a tactic which had already demonstrably failed at Yevpatoriya. On the night of January 5/6, 218 soldiers from the 226th Infantry Regiment were landed from the destroyer *Sposobnyi* near Sudak, 25 miles southwest of Feodosiya. The Germans detected the landing but regarded it as a nuisance and sent only a single company of *Panzerjägers* to contain it, which Kozlov interpreted as weakness.

Generalmajor Vasiliy K. Moroz's 236th Rifle Division had its main line of resistance 9 miles northwest of Feodosiya on the Biyuk–Eget ridge, which towered over the flat plain. He also had a forward security zone, deployed 3 miles forward of the ridge. Moroz was an experienced cavalryman and his division was close to full strength, sitting atop the best terrain in the area. At dawn on January 15, 1942, Manstein's counteroffensive kicked off with a brief artillery preparation on Moroz's forward security positions, followed by Stukas and He-111s bombing the ridgeline. Then three battalions of Oberstleutnant Otto Hitzfeld's IR 213 advanced, along with I. and II./IR 42 from Himer's division. Hitzfeld was one of the best German regimental commanders in the Crimea and an aggressive tactical leader. Apparently caught by surprise, Moroz's forward security positions were quickly overrun by Hitzfeld's soldiers. Three StuG IIIs supported the advance and knocked out two T-26 light tanks, but then one assault gun was knocked out by a Soviet 76.2mm antitank gun.[11] During the day, German bombers found Pervushin's command post and blasted it to pieces; Pervushin was badly wounded and the 44th Army's command and control was disrupted at a critical moment. His chief of staff, Colonel Serafim E. Rozhdestvensky, took over command, but the situation was too chaotic to make informed decisions. The rest of the 46. Infanterie-Division and the Romanian 8th Cavalry Brigade conducted feint attacks against the 51st Army, which further confused the Russians, who wasted their reserves in this unimportant sector. By evening, Hitzfeld's infantry had captured virtually the entire Biyuk–Eget ridgeline, and German forward observers could now observe virtually all of the 44th Army's lodgment. Moroz's division had been badly defeated in a single day by just five German infantry battalions – a stunning upset from an enemy who had seemed on the ropes. Nevertheless, Fretter-Pico's corps suffered 500 casualties on the first day of the offensive.[12]

On January 16, Fretter-Pico's XXX Armeekorps continued to pound against the 44th Army's faltering defense north of Feodosiya, reinforcing Gruppe Hitzfeld with more battalions from the 46. and 170. Infanterie-Divisionen. The Soviets mistakenly interpreted the German operational objective as seizing the town of Vladislavovka, near the juncture of the 44th and 51st Armies, and committed most of their reserves in this sector, leaving Feodosiya itself poorly protected. The Soviets attempted to assemble a battalion-size armored counterattack to save Vladislavovka but ran straight into the assault guns of Sturmgeschütz-Abteilung 190, which knocked out 16 T-26 light tanks.[13] Meanwhile, the main German effort steadily pushed the 63rd Mountain Rifle Division back toward the sea and threatened to isolate the 236th Rifle Division in Feodosiya. Since the VVS-ChF was still flying from airfields in the Taman Peninsula, the Luftwaffe was able to operate over Feodosiya with little interference from enemy aircraft. By the evening of January 16, Fretter-Pico brought up the 32. Infanterie-Division to attack directly into Feodosiya.

With the port of Feodosiya hanging in the balance, Kozlov – who was only vaguely aware of the 44th Army's critical situation – made a nearly insane command decision. He decided to commit the 44th Army's remaining reserves and most of the Black Sea Fleet's available warships into a larger diversionary landing at Sudak. Escorted by the battleship *Parizhskaya Kommuna*, the cruiser *Krasny Krym*, and four destroyers, a flotilla deposited Major Georgy N. Selikhov's 226th Rifle Regiment at Sudak. Naval gunfire scattered the small Romanian garrison in the town and the Soviet troops were able to gain a small lodgment, but to what end? Once ashore, the Soviet troops entrenched themselves and waited for the enemy to react. Unfortunately, Manstein was moving in for the kill at Feodosiya and was unwilling to be distracted. Aside from a few blocking detachments sent to keep Selikhov's troops under observation, they were ignored for the time being.

On the morning of January 17, the 132. Infanterie-Division attacked directly into the northern part of Feodosiya, ripping apart the remaining defenses. Gottlob Bidermann's *Panzerjäger* unit from IR 437 was involved in the final push toward the suburb of Sarygol, on the Black Sea. Soviet resistance became desperate as the Germans pushed into the city outskirts, and Bidermann's platoon was suddenly attacked from behind by a bypassed Soviet infantry unit:

The attackers poured out of the depression. There were at least one hundred Russians streaming with a loud "Urrah!" toward our seven-man Pak crew and one machine-gun position. Rifle shots slammed into the side of the vehicle and ricocheted off the gun shield of our Pak gun. Hans took charge of the machine-gun position. Laying his machine gun across the ammunition trailer, he fired a long burst from a standing position... An unteroffizier lying next to me near the wheel of the carriage was firing short, sustained bursts from his machine pistol when he suddenly rolled backward, screaming with pain. We had no time to assist the wounded, only to fire, fire, and fire to save our lives.[14]

Bidermann's platoon eventually repulsed the sudden Soviet attack, but suffered several casualties. His battalion then moved into Sarygol, thereby isolating the remaining Soviet troops in Feodosiya. Thick black smoke from burning buildings languished over the city while Stukas relentlessly bombed the harbor area without mercy. Despite the Black Sea Fleet's attempt to conduct an emergency evacuation, few troops from the 44th Army escaped by sea. Kozlov authorized the broken remnants of the 44th Army to retreat northeast toward the Ak-Monai or Parpach position. The next day, German troops entered the shattered city, after rounding up 5,300 prisoners.[15] Although his 236th Rifle Division was annihilated, General-Major Moroz managed to escape – only to be convicted by a military tribunal three weeks later and executed. The right wing of the 44th Army escaped the debacle at Feodosiya, but its two remaining divisions were in poor shape and virtually leaderless.

Rather than halting, the German counteroffensive actually accelerated on January 19, as Fretter-Pico's XXX Armeekorps wheeled along the coast, pursuing the remnants of the retreating 44th Army. Lvov's 51st Army had no real ability to counterattack since most of its artillery had still not reached the front and even its rifle divisions were far from complete. While the 302nd Rifle Division managed to repulse IR 97's attack on Vladislavovka, that position became increasingly untenable as the headlong retreat of the 44th Army caused the Soviet front to unravel. Having misjudged the German capabilities, Kozlov now exaggerated them to the Stavka and believed them capable of "throwing our forces into the sea."[16] By January 20, both Soviet armies were in retreat, and XXX and XXXXII Armeekorps were able to advance to the Parpach Narrows, which greatly simplified their ability to block any Soviet exit from the Kerch Peninsula. Thereafter, the new front line settled into a World War I landscape of trenches, dugouts, and barbed wire. Overall, the German counteroffensive crippled the 44th Army at a cost to Fetter-Pico's XXX Armeekorps of 995 casualties, including 243 dead and missing.[17]

Once Kozlov's main armies had been defeated, Manstein was able to dispatch five German and two Romanian infantry battalions from Fretter-Pico's XXX Armeekorps to deal with the Soviet lodgment at Sudak. Fretter-Pico sent two *Kampfgruppen* against the Sudak lodgment, one from the east and one from the west, but by the time they arrived Selikhov's regiment had had a week to entrench itself. The Germans quickly found that the Soviet position was a strong one, and settled down into a siege, using artillery and air attacks to grind down the Soviet regiment. In an arrant display of stupidity, Kozlov decided to reinforce failure, and on the night of January 24/25 the Black Sea Fleet landed Major Sergei I. Zabrodotsky's 554th Mountain Rifle Regiment at Sudak. An additional 1,300 troops were landed the next night, bringing the total landed at Sudak to 4,264 men. However, the additional troops only extended the death throes of the Soviet lodgment, which the Germans began to crush in late January 1942. By January 28, XXX Armeekorps declared that the enemy forces at Sudak were eliminated and that 876 prisoners had been taken, but failed to mention that the prisoners were executed. About 2,000 Soviet troops died in battle at Sudak and a few hundred were evacuated by sea, but the vast majority simply disappeared into the mountains. Perhaps 350–500 joined local partisan groups, but others simply went into hiding. Fretter-Pico was forced to leave a Romanian mountain-infantry battalion around Sudak in mop-up operations until the summer, and they continued to discover small groups of survivors until June.

Manstein's winter counteroffensive at Feodosiya was a unique German triumph that stood in stark contrast to Soviet successes on many other parts of the Eastern Front during the winter of 1941/42. In just a matter of days, he had managed to inflict a signal defeat on Soviet forces in the Kerch Peninsula that threw Kozlov's forces onto the defensive. It was not a decisive victory, since Kozlov's armies would soon be back for a rematch at the Parpach Narrows, but Manstein had gained time to build a better defensive front and had greatly leveled the playing field. Had his forces not recaptured Feodosiya, he would soon have had to contemplate evacuating the Crimea and falling back toward Perekop.

On December 31, 1941, Hansen was forced to evacuate a good deal of territory captured during the December offensive in order to release the 132. and 170. Infanterie-Divisionen to participate in the counteroffensive to retake Feodosiya. With only the 22., 24., 50., and 72. Infanterie-Divisionen plus the Romanian 1st Mountain Brigade left in the siege lines around Sevastopol, Hansen could not afford to hold everything that had been seized. Consequently, LIV Armeekorps withdrew from the area around Mekenzievy Station and, once again, the Kamyschly Ravine became the front line. At the end of the year, Hansen's LIV Armeekorps did begin receiving some replacement batallions, but rail traffic across the Dnepr was still so sporadic that some troops were required to walk from Perekop to Sevastopol. German logistics in the Crimea were still very primitive during the winter of 1941/42, meaning that Hansen's troops were desperately short of food, fuel, ammunition, and winter clothing. There was no food for the 50,000 horses in AOK 11 at all, so they were evacuated to the logistics depot at Kherson, leaving most of Hansen's division-level artillery immobile for the duration of the winter.[18] The defenders also faced severe food shortages, and were not much better off than those in encircled Leningrad, which was also under siege.

Both sides settled into a routine of desultory trench warfare, with occasional raids. Most of the German troops were able to construct underground shelters, but a typical day on the front line was monotonous and dangerous. However, static warfare afforded an opportunity for German scouts to covertly tap Soviet field telephone lines at night, which led to an intelligence coup on January 21 when the Germans learned about an imminent Soviet sortie against the 24. Infanterie-Division. Forewarned about the timing of the enemy attack, German artillery shredded the Soviet infantry as soon as they left their trenches.[19]

Aside from lax communications security, another major problem facing the Soviet defenders was that most of Morgunov's coastal artillery had worn out their barrels by firing too many rounds during the November–December fighting. Even the 305mm gun turrets in Coastal Batteries No. 30 and No. 35 were no longer fit for combat; Lieutenant Georgy A. Aleksandr's Battery No. 30 had fired 1,238 rounds since the beginning of the siege and was non-operational. Now only a mile from the closest German positions and visible to enemy forward observers, Morgunov's engineers came up with a bold plan to replace the 50-ton gun barrels in late January 1942. It took 16 nights' worth of heavy, dangerous labor, but the barrels were replaced and the battery operational again by February 12. Following this, Soviet naval engineers replaced the barrels of Coastal Battery No. 35, then of six 152mm guns, three 130mm guns, and four 100mm guns. Soviet engineers also stripped the guns from the crippled cruiser *Chervona Ukraina* and the destroyer *Sovershennyi*, both lying in Sevastopl's inner harbor area, in order to provide for five new naval artillery batteries to defend the landward side of the city. Captain-Lieutenant Aleksei P. Matyukhin led 65 sailors from the destroyer *Sovershennyi* to the Malakhov Hill, famous from the 1855 siege, where they established Battery 701 with two 130mm guns. By the end of March, Morgunov's coastal batteries were restored to full effectiveness.[20]

It helped that Sevastopol was not really under tight siege during the winter of 1941/42, and that naval convoys could deliver supplies and spare parts from naval depots in Novorossiysk with only modest opposition from the Luftwaffe. Petrov received nearly 6,000 replacements in January, and 2,194 of his wounded were evacuated. The Romanian Navy was far too weak to interfere with Russian convoys, and although the German Kriegsmarine was planning to dispatch light naval forces to the region, they had not yet made an appearance. Fighters from the VVS-ChF were able to maintain air superiority over Sevastopol because the only German fighter unit in the Crimea – III./JG 77 at Sarabus – was forced to concentrate most of its limited sorties over the Parpach front. However, Manstein prevailed upon the Luftwaffe to increase its efforts to interdict Soviet naval supply lines to the Crimea. At the end of January 1942, the Luftwaffe sent Oberleutnant Hansgeorg Bätcher's 1./KG 100 to the Crimea specifically to interdict Soviet shipping in the Black Sea. Bätcher's *Staffeln* had only eight operational He-111 bombers, but he was one of the greatest bomber pilots of World War II and his unit's aircrew among the elite of the *Kampfflieger*. Bätcher's aircrew had no experience in anti-shipping operations, but they learned low-level bombing tactics that began to inflict a toll on Soviet ships going to Sevastopol and Kerch.[21] The VVS-ChF in Sevastopol responded by launching repeated raids on Bätcher's squadron at Saki airfield, but failed to put the German anti-shipping unit out of business.

Although Bätcher's attacks were initially more of a nuisance than lethal, Petrov did not receive all the replacement troops and equipment he requested, though enough arrived to rebuild many of the battered units in his Coastal Army and restore its fighting effectiveness. By February 8, he had 69,853 troops in his Coastal Army, plus 12,128 naval infantry. Three convoys during February 12–15 brought in another 7,746 troops and 1,900 tons of supplies. However, the Stavka would not allow Petrov to spend the entire winter quietly rebuilding his army, but required him to launch attacks against the German siege lines concurrent with Kozlov's offensive to break out of the Kerch Peninsula. On February 26, 1942, Petrov mounted a large attack with the 345th Rifle Division, the 2nd Perekop Naval Infantry Regiment, the 3rd Naval Infantry Regiment, and the 125th Separate Tank Battalion against the German 24. Infanterie-Division near Mekenzievy Mountain. The German troops were not expecting such a serious attack and the Soviet troops were able to advance 1,300 yards into the German lines before being stopped by a counterattack. Desultory combat continued in this area until March 6, which cost the 24. Infanterie-Division 1,277 casualties, including 288 dead or missing. Petrov's assault forces suffered much heavier losses, including 1,818 dead and 780 captured. After this, the German siege lines were forced to maintain greater alertness against the possibility of more Soviet sorties.

Recurrent Soviet landings along the Black Sea coast forced Manstein to create a large number of ad hoc coastal-defense units, such as Gruppe Heigl to defend Yevpatoriya and Gruppe Schroder to defend the area around Yalta. Indeed, much of the German 170. Infanterie-Division, Romanian 10th Infantry Division, and Romanian 4th Mountain Brigade were tied down on coastal-defense duties for much of the winter, which severely strained AOK 11's meager resources. Troops deployed along the coast were often bombarded at night by the Black Sea Fleet and harassed during the day by VVS-ChF air raids. In return, Zuckertort established some of his long-range artillery to shell Severnaya Bay whenever convoys appeared in the harbor. The Black Sea Fleet continued to operate weekly supply convoys into Sevastopol all winter, relying heavily upon the light cruisers *Komintern* and *Krasny Krym*; the flotilla leaders *Tashkent* and *Kharkov*; the destroyers *Boiky*, *Bditelny*, and *Bezuprechny*; and the freighters *Abkhazia*, *Belostok*, *Pestel*, and *Lvov*. The Italian-built flotilla leader *Tashkent*, commanded by Captain 2nd Rank Vasiliy N. Eroshenko, was one of the star players on the Novorossiysk–Sevastopol route and almost invulnerable to German air attacks since it was capable of bursts of speed up to 39 knots and armed with six 37mm 70-K antiaircraft guns. Eroshenko made multiple trips in and out of Sevastopol with impunity throughout the winter. Overall, the convoys brought in 35,000 replacements between January and May 1942 and evacuated 9,000 wounded, as well as thousands of civilians.

The winter around Sevastopol was much milder than elsewhere on the Eastern Front, and temperatures rose above freezing after the first week of March 1942.[22] By mid-March, Hansen's troops often didn't need to wear their bulky overcoats during the day, and spring arrived in the first week of April. During the late winter, once the ground was clear, each of Hansen's divisions set up close-combat courses to teach the new replacements how to breach obstacles, clear trenches, and knock out bunkers, all of which had been learned in the December offensive. In the Soviet lines, Petrov's troops also prepared for renewed fighting, but had to be more circumspect about training in the open. Soviet artillery harassed the German siege lines with sporadic firing, discouraging movement in daylight. German artillery did the same to Petrov's men, firing 50 tons of ammunition even on a quiet day. Daily frontline "wastage" was similar to World War I, with Hansen's LIV Armeekorps suffering five to ten dead and 15 to 25 wounded every day from enemy snipers, artillery fire, and air raids.[23] One sniper, Lyudmila M. Pavlichenko from the 25th Rifle Division, began to rack up an impressive number of "kills" with her SVT sniper rifle, although probably nowhere near the 257 Germans from AOK 11 that she claimed. Petrov's Coastal Army included a number of women in combat roles, but it is difficult to confirm their actual accomplishments. Soviet "kill" claims were often highly inflated by unit-level commissars, eager to prove that their unit was fulfilling its duty to the *Rodina* (Motherland). Another female soldier, Senior Sergeant Nina A. Onilova, also from the 25th Rifle Division, fought as a machine gunner in a number of actions around Mekenzievy Mountain and was awarded the HSU after being mortally wounded in action on March 1. German soldiers were often surprised when they captured Soviet female soldiers, which happened on a number of occasions around Sevastopol.

Another inspirational leader in the Soviet defense at Sevastopol was General-Major Nikolay A. Ostryakov, the VVS-ChF commander, who even flew his own Yak-1 fighter on patrols over the city. His 3rd Special Aviation Group (3 OAG) had coalesced into an elite aviation group, with some of the best Soviet naval fighter pilots available. Unfortunately, the Luftwaffe also became aware of Ostryakov's role in the defense and made efforts to target him. On April 24, General-Major Fedor G. Korobkov, the deputy commander of Soviet naval aviation, arrived in Sevastopol on an inspection trip for the Stavka, and Ostryakov took him to see the main VVS-ChF facility in Kruglaya Bay, west of the city. Thirty minutes after the generals and their staffs entered a hangar to look at ongoing maintenance activities, six Ju-88 bombers zoomed in from the sea and headed straight for the airbase. Before anyone could react, the Ju-88s dropped their bomb loads on the facility, and one 500kg bomb entered through the hangar roof, killing the two Soviet generals and their staffs. Soviet sources make no mention of how such a catastrophe could occur, but it is unlikely that it was a serendipitous event. Soviet communications security was often lax and it is likely that Luftwaffe radio intercept units noted the arrival of a senior figure like Korobkov and gleaned details of his itinerary in order to plan an air strike – this was essentially the same method that the Americans used to target Japanese Admiral Isoruku Yamamoto in 1943. In any case, the death of Ostryakov was a major blow to the VVS-ChF.

In late February 1942, Bätcher's 1./KG 100 was joined by Major Horst Beyling's II./KG 26, which had been trained as a torpedo squadron. Beyling brought 34 He-111H-6 bombers to Saki airfield on the coast near Yevpatoriya, with more than half outfitted to deliver two aerial torpedoes. Beyling's torpedo bombers damaged a Soviet freighter in the Kerch Straits on the night of March 1/2, and Bätcher's low-level bombers damaged the Soviet tanker *Valerian Kuybyshev* at Kerch on March 3; the tanker was delivering a critical load of fuel to sustain the offensive by Kozlov's Crimean Front. Increasingly, Soviet ships bound for Sevastopol or Kerch came under air attack and suffered damage. In retaliation, the VVS-ChF mounted raids on the German air bases in the Crimea and managed to destroy five of Bätcher's He-111s on the ground. Nevertheless, one of Beyling's He-111H-6 bombers torpedoed and sank the transport *Vasiliy Chapaev* on March 23. The III./KG 51, a Ju-88 bomber unit based at Nikolayev, was brought in to raid the Soviet Caucasian ports of Novorossiysk and Tuapse. At midday on March 24, Hauptmann Werner Baumbach led nine Ju-88s from KG 51 over the Black Sea and caught the port of Tuapse completely by surprise. There was no flak or fighter opposition, enabling the German bombers to inflict considerable damage on ships and facilities.[24] In response, the VVS-Crimean Front hastily tried to establish air cover over the ports and the Kerch Strait, but inter-service coordination was not a Soviet strong suit and most of the Soviet fighters were too short-ranged to operate effectively over the Black

Sea. In March, the three German bomber units sank five small Soviet freighters totaling 10,338 GRT, which might not seem like much, but the Soviet merchant marine in the Black Sea was beginning to run out of ships and could not replace them. It was also apparent that the Caucasian ports were no longer safe, which boded poorly for Sevastopol's lifelines.

In April 1942, the German anti-shipping campaign became increasingly painful for the Soviet merchant marine in the Black Sea as He-111 bombers seeded the shipping routes across the Kerch Strait with air-delivered mines. The tanker *Valerian Kuybyshev,* after being repaired, attempted another run to Kerch on the evening of April 2, escorted by a destroyer and two MiG-3 fighters overhead. Nevertheless, five He-111s from Beyling's II./KG 26 swooped in low and launched torpedoes, one of which struck the tanker's stern, turning it into a ball of flame. Soviet officials in Sevastopol had been evacuating as many civilians as possible by sea during the winter in order to reduce the logistical needs of the isolated city and to minimize casualties from a renewed German offensive in the spring. Unfortunately, the passenger ships were large targets, and on the afternoon of April 17 the 4,125-ton passenger ship *Svanetia* was sunk, attacked by a group of He-111H-6 bombers and struck by two torpedoes; the ship sank in 20 minutes, taking 750 of the 950 passengers and crew aboard to the bottom with her. Lacking long-range fighters that could patrol over convoys at sea, the VVS-Crimean Front commander decided to employ his handful of Pe-2 tactical bombers as "heavy fighters," believing that they could deter He-111 attacks on shipping. They did not. Further raids on Tuapse and Novorossiysk sank two merchantmen and damaged four others. On April 28, the Luftwaffe made a maximum effort with 43 He-111s raiding Kerch and 21 Ju-88s raiding Novorossiysk, losing just one bomber to Soviet fighters.

The end result of the winter siege was that the Luftwaffe had failed to interdict Sevastopol's sea lines of communication, which enabled Petrov's defenses to improve considerably. On the other hand, German air attacks had cost the Soviet merchant marine losses that it could not sustain indefinitely, and the VVS had been unable to prevent the Luftwaffe from attacking shipping and ports. Sevastopol's sea lines of communication remained intact by the onset of spring, but they were vulnerable. On the ground, both sides had used the winter months to rest and replenish their forces, as well as to improve their positions. Petrov's Coastal Army was well suited to defending the fortified naval base, but it lacked the armor and mobile artillery to break through the German siege lines and link-up with Kozlov's forces. Help would have to come from outside, and thus, both the Germans and Soviets looked to a decision first in the Kerch Peninsula before the fate of Sevastopol could be decided.

Kozlov's 44th and 51st Armies were so disorganized after the retreat caused by Manstein's Feodosiya counteroffensive that they were incapable of offensive action for more than a month. However, reinforcements began to flow steadily into the Crimea after part of the Kerch Strait froze over on January 20 and remained frozen for three weeks. Soviet engineers built an ice road across the frozen strait, which enabled 96,618 troops, 23,903 horses, and 6,519 vehicles to cross from the Taman Peninsula to the Kerch Peninsula in this period.[25] A 47th Army was created at Kerch with two rifle divisions, but remained a second-echelon holding command for some time. On January 28, 1942, the Stavka rationalized the command structure in the Crimea by placing Kozlov in command of the new Crimean Front and subordinating the Black Sea Fleet and the SOR to the front. At the same time, the Stavka issued a directive for Kozlov to begin preparations for a major offensive to break out of the Kerch Peninsula and advance westward to link up with Petrov's Coastal Army in Sevastopol. The 45-year-old Dmitri T. Kozlov, a former junior officer in the Tsarist Army, had been a decent regimental commander in the 1920s but was in over his head trying to run a joint command structure involving four armies, a fleet, and various air units. Kozlov's staff was equally amateurish and incapable of developing anything but the most basic of plans, and were further burdened with Stalin and his Stavka representatives constantly pushing them to attack. Commissar Lev Mekhlis, the head of the Red Army's Main Political Administration, arrived as the Stavka's representative to the Crimean Front in late January and immediately began interfering with operational planning.

Stalin and Mekhlis wanted Kozlov to attack and retake the Crimea by mid-February, but this was simply not possible, as the logistical situation in the Kerch Peninsula was still quite rudimentary, since preference had been given to combat units moving across the straits, not service-support units. Three regiments of 76mm USV guns had arrived without any ammunition and food was in very short supply for the Crimean Front. The transportation

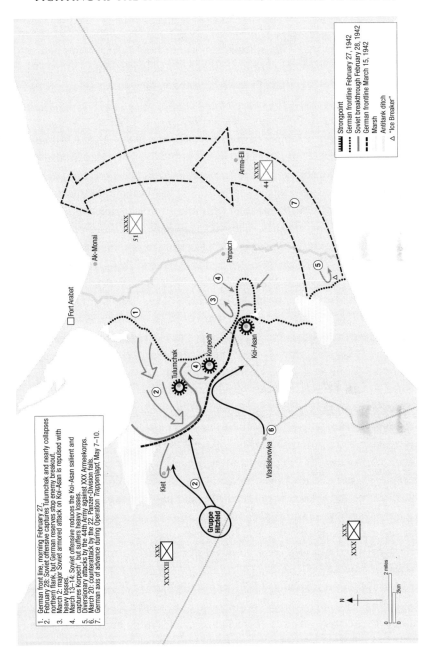

Strongpoint
German frontline February 27, 1942
Soviet breakthrough February 28, 1942
German frontline March 15, 1942
Marsh
Antitank ditch
△ "Ice Breaker"

Arma-Eli

Ak-Monai

Parpach

Fort Arabat

Tulumchak

Korpech'

Koi-Asan

Vladislovovka

Kiet

Gruppe Hitzfeld

1. German front line, morning February 27.
2. February 28: Soviet offensive captures Tulumchak and nearly collapses northern flank, but German reserves stop enemy breakout.
3. March 2: major Soviet armored attack on Koi-Asan is repulsed with heavy losses.
4. March 13–14, Soviet offensive reduces the Koi-Asan salient and captures Korpech', but suffers heavy losses.
5. Diversionary attacks by the 44th Army against XXX Armeekorps.
6. March 20: counterattack by the 22. Panzer-Division fails.
7. German axis of advance during Operation *Trappenjagd*, May 7–10.

N

0   2 miles
0   2km

network in the Kerch Peninsula was primitive, and heavy rains made the dirt roads impassible to traverse even for Soviet trucks. After the recapture of Feodosiya, the Luftwaffe shifted its focus to battlefield interdiction, and began bombing Kerch's port facilities and regularly sinking cargo ships crossing from Novorossiysk. Consequently, Kozlov was not able assemble a combat-ready force of five rifle divisions in the 51st Army and four rifle divisions in the 44th Army until late February.

Kozlov decided to make his main effort with Lvov's 51st Army in the northern part of the Parpach Narrows, in the area between Koi-Asan and the Sivash. This area, roughly 5½ miles wide by 6 miles deep, was a flat, grassy steppe with no significant elevations, and would become the most fought-over terrain in the Crimea for the next three months. Aside from a handful of small villages in this area, there was very little cover and concealment, which made any kind of movement susceptible to artillery and air attacks. The Germans built *Stützpunkt* (strongpoints) in the villages of Tulumchak, Korpech', and Koi-Asan. Mattenklott's XXXXII Armeekorps held this area with General Nicolae Costescu's Romanian 18th Infantry Division and Himer's 46. Infanterie-Division, while the 132. Infanterie-Division held the southern end of the Axis line. Gruppe Hitzfeld was in reserve. This was excellent defensive terrain, and the narrowness of the front enabled Mattenklott and Fetter-Pico to establish defensive positions in accordance with German doctrinal norms; unlike other places on the Eastern Front, where German divisions were required to hold 12–15 miles of front line, here a division was required to hold only a 2–4-mile-wide front. Yet both sides made costly mistakes at the Parpach Narrows. The Germans chose to hold on to a salient jutting out from the Koi-Asan position and required the Romanian 18th Infantry Regiment to defend an exposed position in the north, along the Sivash. Soviet offensive planning was made with very little regard for terrain or weather, which was atrocious in late February. Unlike other parts of the Eastern Front, which were still receiving large snow storms, the warmer Crimea received less snow but far heavier soaking rains, which lasted for days.

At 0630hrs on February 27, 1942, Kozlov began his first offensive, beginning with an artillery preparation from about 230 artillery pieces, although the vast majority were lightweight 76mm guns. The German strongpoints, usually reinforced with stones from nearby rock quarries, were not damaged much by 76mm high-explosive rounds, and Kozlov's heavy artillery was limited to just 30 122mm howitzers. Nor did he have any long-range guns for counterbattery work to suppress the German artillery. Nevertheless, when Kozlov committed his armor against two battalions of the Romanian 18th Infantry Regiment, they achieved quick success. Despite heavy rains that made the low-lying ground too soft for his battalion of KV-1 heavy tanks to advance, the lighter T-26 tanks moved forward and overran the *Stützpunkt* at Tulumchak. The Romanian infantry regiment was routed, opening up the northern end of the Axis defensive line. A German artillery battalion, supporting the Romanians, was overrun and lost all 18 of its 10.5cm l.FH 18 howitzers, as well as 14 3.7cm Pak guns.[26] Kozlov's armor and infantry were able to advance 2½ miles on the first day of the offensive, until Gruppe Hitzfeld was rushed up to halt them. Thereafter, the Soviet assault units were blocked by marshy terrain and determined German infantry, preventing any further advance. The stalled Soviet tanks and infantry were then exposed to persistent artillery and antitank fire, which eroded their numbers. Although Kozlov had attached sappers to his armor units, they had fallen behind, and seven Soviet tanks were knocked out by German Teller antitank mines near *Stützpunkt* Tulumchak. On the left flank of the Soviet penetration *Stützpunkt* Korpech' remained in German hands, and its machine guns and mortars concentrated on anything moving upright in the open terrain. The Soviet assault literally bogged down. The ground near the Sivash was so waterlogged, with large standing puddles of water, that Soviet troops could not even lay prone in some places. The Axis defense was also undermined by the lack of air support; the Luftwaffe managed only three sorties over the battle area on the first day, against over 100 sorties from the VVS-Crimean Front.

Encouraged by his success on the right, Kozlov kept reinforcing this sector in the hope of achieving a breakthrough. He directed the reserve 47th Army to send its 77th Mountain Rifle Division to support the right hook around the enemy line. Mattenklott responded to this alarming situation by repositioning Hitzfeld's IR 213 and I./IR 105 to backstop the battered Romanians, while the 46. Infanterie-Division committed all its strength to holding the center of the Axis defensive line at Koi-Asan. Hitzfeld was inclined to take the offensive, and he aggressively led an attack on the morning of February 28 that temporarily recovered some ground on the northern flank. The crisis of the battle developed during the afternoon, as Kozlov committed his best remaining infantry against the Romanians, and they gave way. The fresh 77th Mountain Rifle Division succeeded in a minor breakthrough, which captured the village of Kiet, nearly outflanking the entire Axis defensive line. The 51st Army claimed the capture of over 100 Romanians. However, Gruppe Hitzfeld and the I./IR 105 were able to counterattack and retake the village. Blocked by the marshy and waterlogged terrain around Kiet, it proved impossible for Kozlov to expand his position in this sector and he was left holding an exposed salient. The wide marshes just north of Kiet were no-go terrain even for infantry.

While Mattenklott fed part of the 170. Infanterie-Division into the northern sector to allow Costescu's battered division to go into reserve, the rest of the front was reduced to desultory combat levels on March 1. During the first three days of the offensive the 44th Army had conducting little more than nuisance attacks against the German XXX Armeekorps sector on the right, which allowed Manstein to concentrate his reserves against Lvov's army. Kozlov was frustrated by his lack of progress in the center against *Stützpunkt* Koi-Asan, held by IR 42 and IR 72, which was the key to the Axis position, and by his inability to convert his success on the right into a real tactical advantage. Instead, Kozlov became fixated on mounting diversionary attacks to draw Manstein's reserves away from Koi-Asan, but this proved wishful thinking. He ordered the Black Sea Fleet to bombard Axis positions around Feodosiya and Yalta, and, over the course of four nights, the battleship *Parizhskaya Kommuna* fired 100 rounds of 305mm against these targets, with the heavy cruiser *Molotov* and eight destroyers joining in as well.[27] A minor naval landing was made at Alushta on March 1, then withdrawn after four hours having achieved nothing.

Resolved to accomplish some signal success before weather and logistics brought his offensive to a premature end, Kozlov decided to make an all-out attack against *Stützpunkt* Koi-Asan on March 2. He deployed two rifle divisions, supported by the newly arrived 39th, 40th, and 55th Tank Brigades, and the 229th Separate Tank Battalion (OTB), against the strongpoint, but the Soviet armor piled up against the still-intact German obstacles and was shot to pieces by *Panzerjägers* and artillery. Furthermore, the Luftwaffe was finally able to provide some air cover, including 40 Stuka sorties from III./StG 77 that targeted the massed Soviet armor.[28] The Soviets admitted that they lost 93 tanks on this one day, in addition to about 40 other tanks lost in the opening days of the offensive. Nonetheless, Kozlov's assault did overrun a battery of four 14.9cm s.FH 37(t) howitzers, and a VVS bomber raid on Vladislavovka destroyed an ammunition dump containing 23 tons of munitions.[29] Yet it was apparent that Kozlov's offensive had failed to dent the Koi-Asan or Korpech' positions, and he suspended his offensive on March 3, after losing a great deal of infantry and most of his armor, including 28 of his 36 KV-1 tanks. The 51st Army was left holding a salient in open terrain across the northern part of the front, but only security troops could be posted in this exposed area. At great cost, Kozlov's first offensive had bent back the left wing of XXXXII Armeekorps, but the Koi-Asan strongpoint held firm in the center. In his memoirs, Manstein downplayed the Soviet offensive by writing that "we eventually succeeded in containing the enemy breakthrough in the northern sector," while omitting the near-disaster on the first day.[30] He did decide to mass all his assault guns at Koi-Asan, including the newly arrived 2./Sturmgeschütz-Abteilung 249.

Failure to achieve a clean breakthrough brought instant recriminations, with Kozlov blaming the weather. Although Tolbukhin was certainly at fault, as chief of staff, for the poor planning, Mekhlis put the brunt of the blame on him and had him relieved. Stalin ordered Kozlov to immediately begin preparing for another offensive, to start within ten days. The plan for the second attack paid more attention to the German defenses and decided to concentrate most of the 51st Army's offensive power against *Stützpunkt* Koi-Asan in the center of the enemy line, reckoning that its loss would allow Lvov to punch through Mattenklott's line. Kozlov also directed that this time, the 44th Army would play a greater role in the offensive by mounting a diversionary attack against the 132. Infanterie-Division positions along the Black Sea coast. Mekhlis, who had no tactical experience, bragged that "we'll organize the big music for the Germans!" and then foolishly directed Kozlov to split up his 224 tanks among the rifle divisions, rather then keep them as a mobile exploitation force.[31] Rather optimistically, Kozlov claimed that his forces could advance 2½ miles in a three-day offensive. Stalin also ensured that the VVS-Crimean Front was greatly reinforced, and by early March it had 581 aircraft, although most were older I-16 fighters, I-153 fighter-bombers, and DB-3 bombers. The Germans used the respite to reinforce the Koi-Asan position with over 2,000 Teller antitank mines.[32]

It was snowing when Kozlov's second offensive began at 0900hrs on March 13. Lvov attacked with three rifle divisions across terrain that was still too waterlogged to prevent rapid tactical movements, and the initial results were the same as before: all Soviet attacks were repulsed with heavy losses.

Mekhlis ordered the armor committed in order to support the infantry, but they ran into antiarmor ambushes established by two assault-gun companies. But 1. Kompanie of Sturmgeschütz-Abteilung 197 had a great day, with Leutnant Johann Spielmann's section claiming 14 T-34s destroyed and Oberwachtmeister Fritz Schrödel personally claiming eight enemy tanks, including three KV-2s. The Soviet armor did manage to inflict some losses, including a direct hit on Oberleutnant Nottebrock's StuG III, which mortally wounded the commander of 2./Sturmgeschütz-Abteilung 249.[33] It is clear that the Soviet armor was destroyed in piecemeal fashion, with 157 tanks lost in the first three days of fighting. More than half of these losses came from the 56th Tank Brigade, which lost 88 of its tanks. Spielmann was awarded the *Ritterkreuz* for his battlefield accomplishment.

However, XXXXII Armeekorps was beginning to suffer from losses, and air attacks by the VVS-Crimean Front were becoming increasingly painful. Once again, Soviet DB-3 bombers blew up the main ammunition dump at Vladislavovka, detonating 60 tons of munitions. While II./JG 77, newly arrived in the Crimea from refitting in Germany, inflicted heavy losses upon the older fighters of the VVS-Crimean Front, it could not gain air superiority over the Parpach sector. Heavy expenditures of infantry finally paid off, and the 51st Army captured *Stützpunkt* Korpech' from IR 105 on March 14, as well as a battery of three 10.5cm f. FH 18 howitzers and nine Nebelwerfer launchers. Mattenklott's defenses were seriously dented, but Kozlov's artillery had expended most of its ammunition and a pause was necessary before the offensive could be renewed.

Manstein was sufficiently concerned by the loss of *Stützpunkt* Korpech' that he decided to mount an immediate counterattack with the 22. Panzer-Division, which had just arrived in the Crimea. The OKH had sent the new division to AOK 11 in order to spearhead a major counteroffensive against the Crimean Front, but now Manstein decided to use it in a local counterattack to retake a battalion-size strongpoint. Nor was the 22. Panzer-Division complete, since parts of it were still arriving from France and the unit was untested in combat. Nevertheless, Manstein imprudently decided to employ Oberstleutnant Wilhelm Koppenburg's Panzer-Regiment 204 without much infantry or engineer support. Furthermore, the bulk of Koppenburg's tanks were ex-Czech Pz 38(t) models, which could not stand up to Kozlov's T-34s and KV-1 if encountered. When Koppenburg's two *Panzer Abteilungen* crossed the front line at 0600hrs on March 20, a thick fog limited visibility to 100 yards or less. Unfamiliar with the terrain, one of Koppenburg's battalions became disoriented in the fog and the other ran into a minefield. The counterattack then became a confused meeting engagement in the fog, which went very badly for the Germans. Alerted to the approach of German armor, the Soviet 55th Tank Brigade quickly appeared with a battalion of T-26 light tanks and four KV-1s, which blocked access to Korpech'. Attempting to maneuver, I./Pz. Regt 204 ran into a nest of Soviet 45mm antitank guns and suffered 40 percent losses. Eventually, Koppenburg aborted the counterattack by 0900hrs, having completely failed in his mission. The 22. Panzer-Division's counterattack at Korpech' was one of the most badly bungled German armored attacks of the entire war on the Eastern Front; 32 of 142 tanks had been lost (including nine Pz IIs, 17 Pz 38(t)s, and six Pz IVs) and the division had to be sent to the rear to refit.[34] Using tanks without proper battlefield reconnaissance or the use of air, artillery, infantry, or engineer support went completely against German combined-arms doctrine, and the failure to properly plan or support the attack was entirely Manstein's fault. Kozlov's second offensive had failed to achieve a breakthrough, but he had dented the German main line of resistance, and the decimation of the 22. Panzer-Division prevented Manstein from gaining the initiative.

After taking just a week to replace losses and restock his artillery ammunition, Kozlov began his Third Offensive on March 26, intent upon taking the tenacious Koi-Asan *Stützpunkt*. However, this attack fizzled out very quickly, and the Crimea Front was incapable of making a serious effort until early April. The Luftwaffe mounted continuous raids on the port facility at Kerch, which seriously disrupted Soviet logistic operations, and, consequently, Kozlov could not resume his offensive until April 9, but with fewer tanks and artillery pieces than required.[35] Once again, Mehklis pressed Kozlov to commit his armor while German lines were still unbroken, which was akin to smashing against a wall at high speed. Manstein had also begun to receive reinforcements in the spring of 1942, including the 28. leichte Infanterie-Division, which was equipped with the new 2.8cm s.PzB 41 tapered-bore antitank guns. On the first day of the latest Soviet offensive, Obergefreiter Emanuel Czernik destroyed seven T-26 tanks and one BT with the new weapon, at ranges of 70–660 yards.[36] Unlike larger antitank guns, the low-silhouette s.PzB 41 could be easily concealed even in flat terrain like the eastern Crimea. After three days of unsuccessfully pounding on German defenses at Koi-Asan, Kozlov finally decided to halt his offensives and rest and resupply his exhausted divisions. As a result of these four offensives, most of the Crimean Front's combat power was concentrated on its right flank in the 51st Army, while the 44th Army had not received priority and the 47th Army was little more than a holding command. Unwittingly, lax Soviet radio communications during the March–April fighting had enabled German signals troops to intercept traffic between the Crimean Front's army-level headquarters and to determine their positions – which were then provided to the Luftwaffe.[37]

During the four months from January to April 1942, Kozlov's Crimean Front (including the forces in Sevastopol) suffered a crippling 352,000 casualties for the liberation of just the Kerch Peninsula. Most of these losses were incurred during the four offensives conducted between February 27 and April 11, which made only modest tactical gains. In the same time period, Manstein's AOK 11 suffered a total of 24,120 casualties, indicating an extremely unfavorable 14-1 casualty ratio for Kozlov. Indeed, it is clear that AOK 11 made an impressive stand against long odds at the Parpach Narrows, while maintaining the siege of Sevastopol – a great feat of generalship. On the other hand, after making a daring amphibious landing at Feodosiya in December 1941, the Crimean Front reverted to a dull, plodding form of operations. Given the excessive casualties of the attackers for marginal gains across unsuitable terrain, Kozlov's four offensives bear a striking resemblance to British offensives at Passchendaele in 1917, but these equally large battles have been almost completely forgotten today.

CHAPTER 6

The German Conquest, May–July
1942

*"For the Soviets, there is only surrender or
annihilation."*
German newsreel commentary, May 20, 1942

As spring arrived, Hitler began issuing orders for the upcoming summer
offensive with which he intended to knock the Soviet Union out of the war.
This time, the main effort would be made in the south with Heeresgruppe
Süd, toward the Caucasus oil fields and the Volga, while Heeresgruppen
Nord and Mitte remained on the defensive. Yet Hitler and the OKH
recognized that it would be necessary to clear up the Soviet Barvenkovo
Salient south of Kharkov and to finish off Soviet resistance in the Crimea
before embarking upon the larger task. By eliminating Soviet resistance in
the Crimea, Manstein's AOK 11 would be free to support the advance into
the Caucasus. In accordance with Führer Directive 41 issued on April 5,
Manstein was directed to eliminate Kozlov's forces in the Kerch Peninsula
first, then Heeresgruppe Süd would deal with the Barvenkovo Salient with

Operation *Fridericus*, and then, afterwards, Manstein would complete operations in the Crimea by capturing the fortress of Sevastopol. Manstein flew to Rastenburg in East Prussia to discuss his future plans with Hitler, and stated that substantial Luftwaffe air support was an essential requirement for rapid success in the Crimea. Hitler agreed, and promised to send the elite Fliegerkorps VIII to support his attacks. However, unlike *Barbarossa*, Hitler stressed that the Luftwaffe no longer had the resources to conduct simultaneous major offensives, but instead would have to shuttle its resources between the Crimea and the other armies of Heeresgruppe Süd, meaning that Manstein's attacks would have to stick to tight schedules.

Even before Kozlov's fourth offensive ended, Manstein and his staff began developing an operational plan to crush all three armies of the Crimean Front in one bold stroke. The offensive was named Operation *Trappenjagd* ("Bustard Hunt") and would begin in early May, once the ground had hardened. Unusually, Hitler granted Manstein considerable autonomy on how he conducted his offensive, as long as it was completed on time. A key part of the plan relied upon the transfer of Fliegerkorps VIII to the Crimea prior to *Trappenjagd* in order to seize air superiority at the outset of the offensive. Manstein believed that if the Luftwaffe could gain air superiority over the Crimea he could then mass enough combat power to smash in Kozlov's weaker left wing, comprising General-Lieutenant Stepan I. Cherniak's 44th Army, then exploit the situation before Kozlov could react. The plan was typical of Manstein's philosophy of war, based upon risk, maneuver, and concentration of force at the decisive point. By normal principles of military science, success was unlikely, since Manstein was able to assemble only the 22. Panzer-Division, five German infantry divisions, and two and a half Romanian divisions to attack a total of 19 Soviet divisions and four tank brigades. Outnumbered by more than 2-1, Manstein's forces seemed better suited for defense, but he counted on this disparity to lull Kozlov into a false sense of security.

Kozlov's forces certainly appeared formidable. In the north, Lvov's 51st Army defended a 5½-mile-long front with eight rifle divisions, three rifle brigades, and two tank brigades. In the south, Cherniak's 44th Army defended a much shorter sector with five rifle divisions and two tank brigades. Although both first-echelon armies had prepared three lines of defense, including an antitank ditch that bisected the entire width of the Parpach Narrows, almost all the rifle units were deployed within 2 miles of the front line. Tank brigades and cavalry were deployed further back in reserve. In the second echelon, General-Major Konstantin S. Kolganov's 47th Army was deployed in reserve with four rifle and one cavalry division. Under pressure from Stalin to mount another offensive, Kozlov intended once again to use Lvov's 51st Army as his battering ram and had massed the bulk of his forces in the northern salient to support this concept. Kozlov was confident that General-Major Yevgeniy M. Nikolaenko's VVS-Crimean Front, which had 176 fighters and 225 bombers available, would continue to maintain air superiority over the eastern Crimea and that this would deter any attempt by Manstein to go on the offensive.[1] However, Kozlov failed to appreciate that Nikolaenko's air strength was based on quantity, not quality, and that the bulk of his units were intended for close-air-support roles, not air superiority. Only the three fighter squadrons in the 72nd Fighter Division (72 IAD) were equipped with modern Yak-1 or LaGG-3 fighters; the other six fighter regiments were equipped with obsolescent I-16 fighters or I-153 fighter-bombers. Another serious but subtle weakness was that Nikolaenko had only three reconnaissance squadrons equipped with a dozen SB bombers and U-2 or R-5 biplanes.

Not surprisingly, Nikolaenko's limited reconnaissance assets failed to note that Generaloberst Wolfram von Richthofen, commander of the elite Fliegerkorps VIII, established his headquarters at Kischlaw, west of Feodosiya, on May 1. Over the next five days, Fliegerkorps VIII brought over 400 more aircraft into the Crimean theater, thereby radically altering the air balance in favor of the Luftwaffe. In particular, the Luftwaffe fighter strength in the Crimea swelled from one *Jagdgruppe* with 45 Bf-109F fighters to four *Jagdgruppen* with 166 Bf-109E/F fighters. Many of these fighters were based at newly built airfields south of Simferopol and west of Feodosiya, which had not previously been used by the Luftwaffe. A number of Soviet reconnaissance aircraft disappeared over the Crimea in early May – the first victims of Fliegerkorps VIII in this sector – but it did not cause any undue alarm in Kozlov's headquarters. In addition, Richthofen's command brought German bomber strength in the Crimea up to five *Kampfgruppen*, with 160 bombers and all of StG 77 with 106 Ju-87 Stukas. Sarabus, the main German airbase in the Crimea, swelled from hosting about 70 aircraft to over 250 in a few days. On May 6, two *Gruppen* from Schlachtgeschwader 1 (SchG 1) began to arrive at an airstrip near Feodosiya; I./SchG 1 was equipped with Bf-109E-7 fighter-bombers and II./SchG 1 was equipped with 43 of the new Hs 129 B-1 ground-attack planes. These heavily armored aircraft were intended as tank destroyers and equipped with two 20mm and one 30mm cannon, as well as antipersonnel fragmentation bombs. By May 7, Richthofen had quietly assembled 555 combat aircraft in the Crimea to support Operation *Trappenjagd*.[2]

Manstein had learned from his experience in developing his version of the Fall Gelb plan for the attack through the Ardennes in 1940 that significant operational-level surprise could be achieved by attacking in places that the enemy did not expect and by using methods they had not considered. He deliberately chose to place his *Schwerpunkt* in the least favorable terrain: the swampy southern sector held by Cherniak's 44th Army. He intended to use three infantry divisions from Generalleutnant Fretter-Pico's XXX Armeekorps in the first echelon to breach the Soviet lines, then, once a breach was achieved, to push the 22. Panzer-Division to exploit the hole in Cherniak's front. It is apparent that Manstein learned from the debacle with 22. Panzer-Division in March, and this time he intended to hold his armor back until Fretter-Pico's infantry breached the enemy's defenses. Instead of using paratroopers – which were not available – Manstein intended to conduct a small-scale amphibious landing behind Cherniak's front, using the assault boats from the 902. Sturmboote-Kommando. This was a high-risk operation – if Fretter-Pico's troops did not break through quickly, the amphibious force would be isolated and destroyed. Based upon his experience from the December offensive at Sevastopol, Manstein had also developed new tactics for breaking through enemy fortified lines, based upon the close cooperation of infantry *Stossgruppen*, assault guns, pioneers, *Panzerjägers*, and flak troops. Consequently, Manstein provided Fretter-Pico with the tools to unlock Cherniak's defense: a total of 57 StuG III assault guns from the 190., 197., and 249. Sturmgeschütz-Abteilungen, two batteries of 8.8cm flak guns, and plentiful engineer support. Furthermore, at least a dozen of the StuG IIIs were equipped with the new L/48 long 7.5cm cannon, which greatly improved their antitank capability. Manstein also integrated deception into the *Trappenjagd* plan by having Mattenklott's XXXXII Armeekorps conduct feints against the 51st Army, which made it look as though any German counterattack would occur in the northern sector, while Fretter-Pico's troops did not occupy assault positions until the night before the attack. In fact, Mattenklott's northern sector was seriously denuded of troops in order to strengthen Fretter-Pico's corps, leaving just the 46. Infanterie-Division and the Romanian Mountain Corps to keep the 51st Army at bay. For once, Axis operational-security measures worked, and AOK 11 was able to conceal the fact that more than half of its combat forces were massed against the southernmost point of the Soviet line and that the rest of the front was only lightly held.

General-Major Yevgeniy M. Nikolaenko, commander of the VVS-Crimean Front, was a 36-year-old fighter pilot who had earned an HSU decoration in a fighter melee over China in August 1938. He was an up-and-coming star of the VVS, but it all vanished on the morning of May 8, 1942, when Operation *Trappenjagd* kicked off. Fliegerkorps VIII mounted a maximum effort, flying over 2,100 sorties during the course of the day, beginning with attacks on Nikolaenko's forward airfields at Bagerovo and Marfovka. It was like June 1941 all over again, with the VVS caught flat-footed as Luftwaffe bombers swept in and destroyed parked aircraft on the ground. Richthofen then allowed his four *Jagdgruppen* to conduct fighter sweeps across the Kerch Peninsula during the day, resulting in a claim of 57 air-to-air "kills" on the first day of the offensive. By noon, Nikolaenko had lost perhaps one-quarter of his aircraft and had clearly lost control of the air over the Kerch Peninsula. During the first two days of *Trappenjagd*, Fliegerkorps VIII flew 3,800 sorties and shattered the VVS-Crimean Front; the Luftwaffe admitted losing 23 of their own aircraft against over 100 Soviet aircraft.

Cherniak, born into a Belarusian peasant family, was a 41-year-old career infantryman who had served as an advisor in the Spanish Civil War and had later been awarded the HSU for his performance as a division commander during the Russo-Finnish War. He had an admirable record for a Soviet commander, having dodged the purges and managed to avoid suffering any notable reverses in the field. Like Nikolaenko, Cherniak's heretofore-laudable reputation was wrecked in the opening hours of *Trappenjagd*. Three minutes before sunrise, XXX Armeekorps' artillery began a ten-minute artillery preparation on Cherniak's forward units at 0415hrs. Four Nebelwerfer batteries poured smoke and high-explosive on the identified Soviet positions. The 44th Army had two divisions – the 63rd Mountain Rifle and the 276th Rifle Division – holding a 4-mile stretch of front line, then an antitank ditch located 2 miles further back, guarded by the 157th and 404th Rifle Divisions. Cherniak's reserve consisted of the 39th and 56th Tank Brigades, located near Arma-Eli.

At 0425hrs, German infantry from the three lead divisions began moving forward. Although the Soviet 251st Rifle Regiment (63rd Mountain) held a very strong position on the 40m high "Tatar Hill" north of the Feodosiya–Kerch road, the unit was not completely tied in with the neighboring 346th Regiment to the south. Stukas from StG 77 blasted the top of the hill just as troops from Generalleutnant Johann Sinnhuber's 28. leichte Infanterie-Division crossed the line of departure. The dust from the air raid had barely settled when *Stossgruppen* from Jäger-Regiment 49 of Sinnhuber's division, supported by 21 assault guns and a company of 18 captured Soviet tanks, was able to first bypass then overwhelm the isolated 346th Rifle Regiment. Less than 2 miles to the south, the 132. Infanterie-Division's two lead regiments and 22 assault guns were able to overwhelm the 291st Rifle Regiment's strongpoints on the coast by 0445hrs, and by 0540hrs IR 438 had reached the west side of the antitank ditch. After "Tatar Hill" was overrun, the Jäger-Regiment 49 spearhead pushed rapidly up the 1½-mile stretch of road to reach the west side of the antitank ditch. Despite the fact that the 11-yard-wide antitank ditch was protected by a minefield and barbed wire, as well as steel girders to stop tanks, Jäger-Regiment 49 was able to overcome the stunned Soviet defenders and to secure a bridgehead across the ditch by 0755hrs. In only three and a half hours, the 63rd Mountain Rifle Division's frontline regiments had been shattered, and the Soviet second line of defense had been pierced. Soviet tanks appeared to contest the crossing, but a one-sided duel with Sturmgeschütz-Abteilung 190 resulted in the loss of 24 Soviet tanks in exchange for the loss of just one StuG III.[3] The only sector where Fretter-Pico's XXX Armeekorps encountered difficulties was south of Koi-Asan, when the 50. Infanterie-Division, supported by 14 assault guns, attacked the 276th Rifle Division. The German infantrymen from the 50. Infanterie-Division had to cross very swampy terrain and then attack through three rows of obstacles before reaching the antitank ditch late in the day.

The collapse of Cherniak's 44th Army was accelerated by a coordinated attack upon the second-echelon defenses as well. Shortly after the initial artillery bombardment, one infantry company from Infanterie-Regiment 436 (132 ID) and a pioneer platoon were moved by a flotilla of assault boats from the 902. Sturmboote-Kommando from Feodosiya to land 1,500 yards behind the antitank ditch. Amazingly, not a single vessel of the Black Sea Fleet interfered with this German amphibious operation, although one or two small warships would have annihilated the flimsy speedboats. Some Soviet mortars and light artillery did engage the assault boats as they approached the shore, but they failed to hit any. This attack was an extremely bold move, and it helped to unhinge the Soviet second line of defense. The German infantrymen quickly overwhelmed two bunkers covering this stretch of coast and then radioed for the next wave to come in. During the day, the 902. Sturmboote-Kommando ferried in most of the rest of the infantrymen of IR 436, which proceeded to overrun the antitank-ditch defenders from behind. Very effective Luftwaffe close-air support kept any Soviet counterattacks away during the early hours of the landing, although Soviet artillery and mortar fire succeeded in destroying 13 assault boats. The two second-echelon formations from the 44th Army – the 157th and 404th Rifle Divisions – were hard hit by Stuka and Hs 129 B attacks during the day and failed to redeploy in time to either deal with the amphibious landing or the penetration up the center by the 28. leichte Infanterie-Division. Once the antitank ditch was breached, Manstein committed his only mobile unit – the Groddeck Brigade – to move through the gap, and its units soon linked up with the IR 436 beachhead and pushed 2 miles further east. Fretter-Pico's XXX Armeekorps had suffered only 104 killed and 284 wounded on the first day of *Trappenjagd*, but it had captured 4,514 prisoners and ripped open the 44th Army's left flank.

Based upon the experience gained with Brigade Ziegler during the pursuit operations in November 1941, Manstein decided to assemble an even larger and more capable motorized *Kampfgruppe* for the pursuit phase of *Trappenjagd*. Oberst Karl Albrecht von Groddeck, an experienced commander of motorized infantry, was brought to AOK 11 to take command of an ad hoc brigade comprised of Aufklärungs-Abteilung (mot.) 22, I./ Infanterie-Regiment 391, Panzerjäger-Abteilung 560, schwere Artillerie-Abteilung 154 (12x 149mm s.FH 37(t)), the 6./ Artillerie-Regiment 818 (4x 10cm s.K 18), one battery of six StuG III assault guns from Sturmgeschütz-Abteilung 197, a special-forces company from z.b.V. 800 "Brandenburg," one Nebelwerfer battery, two flak batteries, one company from Pionier-Bataillon 173, and the Romanian 3rd Motorized Cavalry Regiment. In addition, Gruppe Müller was attached to Brigade Groddeck, with truck-mounted Infanterie-Regiment 401, I./Infanterie-Regiment 105, Panzer-Abteilung 223, a panzer company with 18 captured Soviet tanks, two Romanian 15cm batteries, a battery from

Sturmgeschütz-Abteilung 190, and more pioneers and *Panzerjägers*. Altogether, Groddeck had a division-size task with five infantry battalions, 30 armored fighting vehicles, and 30 artillery pieces.[4] Every truck, car, and motorcycle that could be temporarily spared in the Crimea was given to Groddeck's brigade to motorize as many sub-units as possible, but some of the infantry still rode on bicycles, pulled on ropes behind trucks.

Belatedly, Cherniak committed his 56th Tank Brigade and 126th Separate Tank Battalion (OTB) with 98 tanks, including seven KV-1, to attack the 28. leichte Infanterie-Division's breakthrough. However, by the time that the Soviet armor assembled on the open steppe, Stukas from StG 77 and Hs 129 Bs from SchG 1 arrived and blasted them to pieces in a hail of bombs and cannon fire; 48 tanks were knocked out, including all seven KV-1.[5] Kozlov did not realize how badly the 44th Army's front had been breached until German pioneers had almost completed bridging the antitank ditch, thereby opening the way for Brigade Groddeck to begin rushing eastward toward Kerch.

The day of decision for Operation *Trappenjagd* was May 9, and it quickly went badly for Kozlov's Crimean Front. Soviet command and control was apparently badly disrupted in the initial Luftwaffe raids – the 51st Army commander, General-Lieutenant Lvov, was mortally wounded in one raid, and Kozlov still failed to comprehend the extent of the German breakthrough in the 44th Army sector – he merely ordered Cherniak to clear it up with local counterattacks. He did give Cherniak one rifle division from the 47th Army reserve, but this was too little and too late. German pioneers had spent the night of May 8/9 filling in the 12-yard-wide antitank ditch and removing mines, wire, and steel beams in order to clear a path for the 22. Panzer-Division, but pockets of bypassed Soviet troops prevented this task from being accomplished until midday on May 9. In the interim, the 28. leichte Infanterie-Division boldly moved northeast and seized Arma-Eli, while the 132. Infanterie- Division and Brigade Groddeck continued to advance eastward against light resistance. Cherniak continued counterattacking with his remaining forces, but these uncoordinated regiment-size operations were easily defeated by XXX Armeekorps. The Stukas of StG 77 and the Hs 129Bs of SchG 1 also eliminated most of Cherniak's armor, and Bf 109 fighters shot down 25 Soviet aircraft attempting to support the 44th Army counterattack. Cherniak's counterattack was a dismal failure.

During the fighting around Arma-Eli, Brigade Groddeck managed to skirt around the 44th Army's shattered left flank and to boldly advance over 15 miles into the Soviet rear areas. Kozlov had left only the 11th NKVD Division and the depleted 72nd Cavalry Division in the rear to secure the final defensive line along the so-called "Turkish Rampart," another example of ancient fortifications in the Crimea, but in reality little more than a time-worn berm and ditch fieldwork. Unfortunately, Soviet command and control was so disrupted that neither unit was aware that German forces were approaching their positions. Suddenly, a motorized raiding party of the Groddeck Brigade descended upon Marfovka airfield on the afternoon of May 9 and destroyed some 35 I-153 fighter-bombers on the ground. Kozlov was shocked when he heard this, and the growing fear that the Germans were running amok in the rear areas helped to shatter Soviet morale.

Manstein was finally able to commit the 22. Panzer-Division and its 200 tanks in the late afternoon of May 9, but the unit had barely crossed the antitank ditch and begun moving north when a drenching rain began to fall. The heavy rains created mud that temporarily slowed the panzers and grounded the Luftwaffe, which gave the Soviets a brief respite. Despite Lvov's death, Kozlov tried to block the 22. Panzer-Division by shifting the 40th Tank Brigade and 229th OTB, with 53 tanks including 21 KV-1s. Yet when the rain stopped the next morning, the Luftwaffe easily spotted the Soviet heavy tanks and pulverized them – 11 KV-1s were destroyed and others immobilized. With the Soviet armor knocked out, the 22. Panzer-Division resumed its advance and quickly reached the Sea of Azov, cutting off the entire 51st Army by midday on May 10. The 28. leichte Infanterie-Division followed hard on the heels of the panzers, and with the help of the 50. and 170. Infanterie-Divisionen, they sealed off the *Kessel* pinned against the Sea of Azov.

By this point, the Stavka began to realize that the Crimean Front was in serious trouble, and ordered Kolganov's 47th Army – which was not inside the *Kessel* – to counterattack, but his handful of second-rate infantry units had little artillery or tank support and could not even form a new front line. There were still five intact RVGK artillery regiments, but communication with these critical fire-support assets was lost on the first day of the German offensive and no effort was made to restore it, so they sat inactive and without orders to support either counterattack or defense.[6] It was not long before Kozlov realized that the only viable course of action was to order an immediate retreat to the Turkish Rampart, but it was too late. Brigade Groddeck's vanguard captured several crossings over the southern part of the virtually unguarded "Turkish Rampart" on the morning of May 10. Manstein also increased the pressure on the trapped 51st Army by ordering the German XXXXII Armeekorps and Romanian 7th Corps to begin attacking the western side of the pocket. Once this happened, Soviet command and control completely collapsed and Kolganov's 47th Army began a disorganized stampede to the rear, with all units not already encircled attempting to reach the imagined safety of Kerch. There was only one main paved road running from Feodosiya to Kerch and the Luftwaffe had a field day, conducting merciless low-level strafing and bombing runs on the retreating Soviet columns. However, Soviet antiaircraft units were still operational, and when KG 55 proved overly bold, they lost eight He-111s to ground fire on May 10.[7]

Less than 24 hours elapsed before the eight divisions of the encircled 51st Army realized that their situation was hopeless and surrendered, which quickly released XXX Armeekorps to pursue the retreating Soviet fragments. Once through the "Turkish Rampart," the only unit between Brigade Groddeck and the southern approaches to Kerch was the Soviet 11th NKVD Division, a well-equipped and full-strength formation assigned to rear-security duties. On May 11 the NKVD troops managed to ambush the German vanguard, and Groddeck himself was badly wounded. However, once the NKVD troops realized that the German brigade had armor and artillery, they broke contact and fell back toward Kerch, intent only upon saving themselves. Once it became clear that his front was collapsing, Kozlov began organizing an evacuation from Kerch by calling upon Gorshkov's Azov Flotilla and about 80 local fishing craft. However, Fliegerkorps VIII concentrated its bombers on interdicting the Kerch Strait and sank three transports with 900 wounded aboard between May 10 and May 12, as well as sinking a gunboat, six patrol boats, and various other craft. The decimated VVS-Crimean Front put up a better effort over the straits and managed to inflict some losses on Fliegerkorps VIII, but could not stop Richthofen's bombers from savaging the evacuation flotilla. Richthofen's forces dropped 1,780 bombs around Kerch in one day, setting the city aflame.[8]

By May 13 the Germans were across the "Turkish Rampart" in strength and quickly shoved the small Soviet rearguards out of the way. Curiously, Oktyabrsky and his Black Sea Fleet remained aloof from the Kerch evacuation, and he sent some of his destroyers on meaningless night bombardment missions against German positions near Feodosiya, which had no impact upon *Trappenjagd*. On May 14, the 132. and 170. Infanterie-Divisionen had fought their way into the west side of Kerch. One *Stossgruppe* from IR 391, supported by four assault guns from Sturmgeschütz-Abteilung 190, got too far ahead and found itself encircled by Soviet troops and attacked at close quarters. Soviet infantry swarmed over the assault guns, trying to knock them out with grenades and explosive charges. In desperation, the Germans fought their way out of the encirclement, but every member of the assault-gun platoon that escaped was wounded.[9] Warily, German troops entered the shattered port the next day, clearing out stragglers, and then set up 2cm and 8.8cm flak guns on the piers to engage fleeing Soviet vessels with direct fire.

Colonel M. Yagunov, a staff officer from the Crimean Front, had been assigned the task of conducting the rearguard during the evacuation. He gathered a motley crew of naval infantrymen, rear-area troops, and aviation cadets for his rearguard and they succeeded in holding the Germans back from the port area for a time, but ultimately found themselves cut off. Unable to reach the embarkation areas and with German artillery and air attacks pounding the entire port area, Yagunov made the decision to pull his rearguard force back to the Adzhimushkay Quarry, 2½ miles northeast of the port. The Soviets did manage to evacuate a multiple rocket-launcher battalion and some artillery, but the majority of the Crimean Front's equipment was abandoned to the enemy. In the end, Gorshkov's vessels were able to evacuate somewhere between 37,000 and 73,000 troops from the Crimean Front to the Taman Peninsula, of whom at least 20 percent were wounded.[10]

For several days after the fall of the port, small Soviet armed groups held out in various positions around Kerch. One group of about 2,000 troops made a stand in the 1890s-vintage Fort Totleben south of Kerch, while a somewhat larger number held a position near Yenikale. These forces were finally annihilated by May 20 through the use of massed German artillery and bomber attacks. Yagunov's group in the Adzhimushkay Quarry held out for 170 days before being eliminated.

In one of the more astonishing victories of World War II, Manstein's outnumbered AOK 11 had smashed Kozlov's Crimean Front in less than two weeks. The three Soviet armies suffered about 28,000 dead and 147,000 captured out of 250,000 troops engaged, with nine out of 18 divisions completely destroyed and the others reduced to combat-ineffective fragments. All the Soviet tanks and artillery in the Kerch Peninsula had been lost and the VVS-Crimean Front and VVS-ChF lost 417 aircraft. German losses were light for a success of this magnitude, with a total of 7,588 casualties in XXX and XXXXII Armeekorps (including 1,703 dead or missing), as well as 12 tanks, three assault guns, and nine artillery pieces.[11] More significant was the expenditure of 6,230 tons of ammunition, which was more than Manstein had expended in his December attack upon Sevastopol and which would require two weeks for AOK 11 to replenish. Operation *Trappenjagd* was an exquisitely executed set-piece offensive, with near-perfect use of a combined-arms *Schwerpunkt* to quickly achieve decisive results. Although Manstein had to return the 22. Panzer-Division and some of the Luftwaffe units to Heeresgruppe Süd for the counterattacks at Kharkov, which began even before *Trappenjagd* had finished, for the first time he could now turn to deal exclusively with fortress Sevastopol.

On the Soviet side, Stalin was quick to punish failure of this magnitude. Kozlov was demoted to general-major and given secondary assignments for the next year, before finally being shuffled off to the Trans-Baykal military district for the rest of the war. Mekhlis tried to deflect the blame upon others but Stalin saw through this and reduced him two ranks – in the Red Army, commissars were more culpable than commanders for defeats. Lvov had the good sense to die of his wounds, but Nikolaenko, Cherniak, and Kolganov were all relieved of command and reduced in rank to Colonel; Nikolaenko and Cherniak served in secondary roles for the rest of the war, but Kolganov managed to shine in the final East Prussian campaign of 1945 and retire as a general-lieutenant. Thousands of bypassed Soviet troops went to ground in the Kerch Peninsula, in quarries and other isolated places. Most would surrender or be captured in days, but for a few determined stalwarts, surrender was not in their vocabulary.

In order to capture Sevastopol, Manstein knew that he would need an unprecedented amount of firepower to break through Petrov's multiple lines of defense. Recognizing that his previous offensives had lacked sufficient air and artillery support, Manstein was determined that his next attack would have as many combat multipliers in his favor as possible. While executing *Trappenjagd*, he and his staff drafted Operation *Störfang* (Sturgeon Haul) for the final offensive against fortress Sevastopol. Before sending his combined-arms *Stossgruppen* into the attack, he wanted a massive five-day air and artillery bombardment to neutralize as much of Petrov's defenses as possible.

Traditionally, the German Army relied upon 10.5cm and 15cm howitzers to provide the backbone for its division-level medium artillery in both World War I and II. Heavier artillery of various calibers, including rail artillery, fell under control of the *Heeresartillerie*, which reinforced army and army group-size operations. Corps-level artillery usually consisted of pieces between 15cm and 21cm caliber weapons, although it did include the 10.5cm s.K 18 cannon. In 1940, the Wehrmacht began fielding Nebelwerfer units equipped with multiple rocket launchers, which also fell under the *Heeresartillerie*. Although German armies had a reputation for possessing powerful heavy artillery, they actually had very little of it, and most of the weapons they had were not of German origin. Since German operational-level doctrine was based upon the concept of *Bewegungskrieg*, or maneuver warfare, greater emphasis had been placed upon medium-artillery weapons that could support mobile operations, not heavy artillery intended to break through heavily fortified lines or to conduct siege warfare. Consequently, the German preference was to go *around* fortified areas like the French Maginot Line, and if forced to mount a siege, as at places like Warsaw or Leningrad, to rely upon the Luftwaffe to pound the enemy into submission. However, at Sevastopol in 1942, Manstein did not have this luxury, since he was under tight time constraints to release Fliegerkorps VIII back to Heeresgruppe Süd in time for the main German summer offensive – *Fall Blau* – set to begin on June 28.

Yet as war approached in the mid-1930s, the Wehrmacht's leadership became concerned about its limited ability to overcome either the French or Czech border fortifications. The German Heereswaffenamt (Army Weapon's Office) issued requirements to Krupp and Rheinmetall-Borsig in 1936 to develop a variety of heavy-artillery pieces. Ideally, these two companies would have cooperated in developing a few practical weapons for the Wehrmacht

OPERATION *STÖRFANG*, JUNE–JULY 1942

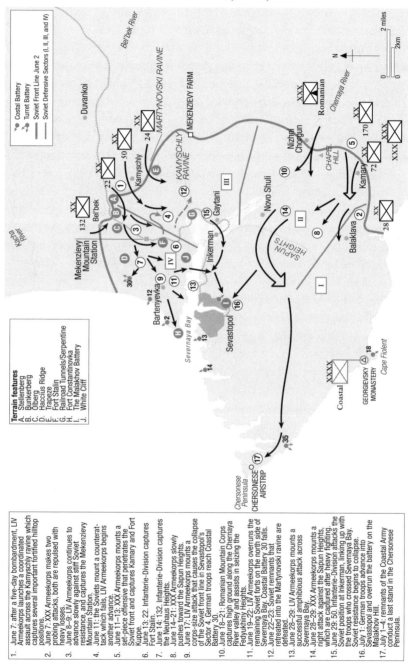

Terrain features
A. Stellenberg
B. Bunkerberg
C. Ölberg
D. Haccius Ridge
E. Trapeze
F. Railroad Tunnels/Serpentine
G. Fort Stalin
H. Fort Constantinovka
I. The Malakhov Battery
J. White Cliff

Coastal Battery
Turret Battery
Soviet Front Line June 2
Soviet Defensive Sectors (I, II, III, and IV)

1. June 7: after a five-day bombardment, LIV Armeekorps launches a coordinated assault across the Kamyschly ravine which captures several important fortified hilltop positions.
2. June 7: XXX Armeekorps makes two probing attacks, both are repulsed with heavy losses.
3. June 8–9: LIV Armeekorps continues to advance slowly against stiff Soviet resistance, and captures the Mekenzievy Mountain Station.
4. June 11: the Soviets mount a counterattack which fails, LIV Armeekorps begins another advance.
5. June 11–13: XXX Armeekorps mounts a set-piece offensive that penetrates the Soviet front and captures Kamary and Fort Kuppe.
6. June 13: 22. Infanterie-Division captures Fort Stalin.
7. June 14: 132. Infanterie-Division captures the Neuhaus Heights.
8. June 14–21: XXX Armeekorps slowly pushes toward the Sapun Heights.
9. June 17: LIV Armeekorps mounts a corps-size attack that causes the collapse of the Soviet front line in Sevastopol's Sector 4. German troops reach Coastal Battery 30.
10. June 18–21: Romanian Mountain Corps captures high ground along the Chernaya River valley and assists in seizing the Fedyukhiny Heights.
11. June 19–22: LIV Armeekorps overruns the remaining Soviet forts on the north side of Severnaya Bay. Coastal Battery 30 falls.
12. June 22–23: Soviet remnants that retreated into the Martynovski ravine are defeated.
13. June 28–29: LIV Armeekorps mounts a successful amphibious attack across Severnaya Bay.
14. June 28–29: XXX Armeekorps mounts a night attack against the Sapun Heights, which are captured after heavy fighting.
15. June 29: 50. Infanterie-Division attacks the Soviet position at Inkerman, linking up with the troops who crossed Severnaya Bay. Soviet resistance begins to collapse.
16. July 1: German troops advance into Sevastopol and overrun the battery on the Malakhov Hill.
17. July 1–4: remnants of the Coastal Army conduct a last stand in the Chersonese Peninsula.

148

that could be produced in quantity. In reality, both companies took different directions and allowed their engineers to present to the Heereswaffenamt a wide variety of often-impractical artillery prototypes with non-standardized calibers. Little or no thought was given to ease of manufacturing, ammunition logistics, or deployment issues – instead, the bigger the gun, the better. When war came sooner than expected in 1939, the Wehrmacht was forced to accept a number of these prototypes into service, even though they were expensive and available in only token numbers. Krupp had begun simply enough by rebuilding its original 1906-vintage 42cm howitzer into the "Gamma" howitzer, of which only one was provided to the Wehrmacht in 1940. However, Krupp engineers endeavored to show off their talent in building a new generation of 28cm rail artillery as well as a massive 80cm cannon that would be named "Dora." Building a small number of 28cm railroad guns made sense since they were inherently mobile and could easily achieve ranges of 20 miles with a 284kg shell. On the other hand, the 80cm Dora became an iconic weapon during the assault on Sevastopol in June 1942 – just as Nazi propagandists had intended – but it was inherently impractical as a weapon due to its huge size, low rate of fire, and exorbitant requirements for personnel and other resources. Rheinmetall initially took a similar direction as Krupp and developed the 35.5cm M1 howitzer; the Wehrmacht accepted one M1 in July 1940 and it arrived at AOK 11 in late October 1941. Yet Rheinmetall's engineers became very interested in the benefits of plunging fire provided by heavy mortars and began developing the 60cm "Karl" series of super-heavy mortars. While the 124-ton Karl was semi-mobile on tracks and could fire an impressive 1,700kg or 2,170kg concrete-piercing shell, it had an effective range of only 3–4 miles, which required it to fire from practically the front line, and exposed it to enemy counterfire.

Generalleutnant Johannes Zuckertort's HArko 306 (Higher Artillery Command) began assembling its artillery park for *Störfang* in mid-May 1942. Except for the sole M1 howitzer in AOK 11, most of the super-heavy weapons such as "Dora," "Karl," the "Gamma" howitzer, and the pair of 28cm "schwere Bruno" railroad guns did not arrive at Sevastopol until late May 1942. In fact, the Wehrmacht had difficulty assembling an adequate siege train for Sevastopol, and much of Zuckertort's heaviest artillery was of Czech origin, including a 42cm M17 Skoda howitzer, 16 30.5cm Mörser M17 L/12s, four 24cm H39 howitzers, and 16 14.9cm s.FH 37(t) howitzers. Including the corps- and division-level artillery, Zuckertort's artillery had 20 different types of calibers at Sevastopol, which greatly exacerbated the logistic situation. While Zuckertort had amassed 183,750 10.5cm and 47,300 15cm rounds for the medium artillery, as well as over 23,000 Nebelwerfer rockets, his German-built heavy guns had very little ammunition to shoot. When schwere Artillerie-Abteilung (E) 672 arrived with Dora on May 26 it possessed only 48 rounds, and schwere Artillerie-Abteilung 833 brought only 122 60cm rounds for its three Karl mortars. The two 42cm howitzers had 276 rounds between the two of them and the M1 had just 352 rounds of 35.5cm ammunition.[12] Rather than the photogenic Dora and Karl, Zuckertort's real heavy firepower would reside with the Czech-built 30.5cm mortars and 14.9cm s.FH 37(t) howitzers and their large stockpiles of ammunition. That did not fit the propaganda ideal of German engineering prowess.

In preparation for the artillery bombardment, Zuckertort had directed his three *Beobachtungs-Abteilungen* (Observation Battalions), to conduct a thorough survey of all visible Soviet fortifications and fieldworks. During April–May, the survey platoons from these invaluable units developed very detailed maps of the enemy's defenses, which were registered in a grid system. Essentially, each grid became a "kill box," with every bunker and enemy position assigned a unique number. These maps became the basis for Zuckertort's artillery fire plan and Richthofen's Fliegerkorps VIII bombardment plan. Zuckertort's HArko 306 would direct all of AOK 11's *Heeresartillerie* during the bombardment, as well as LIV Armeekorps' subordinate corps- and divisional-level artillery batteries. The XXX Armeekorps artillery would be directed by General der Artillerie Robert Martinek's Arko 110, while the Romanian Mountain Corps artillery was semi-autonomous but was also worked into the fire-support plan. Richthofen would direct the concurrent Luftwaffe air strikes on Sevastopol. Although often described as "the heaviest German artillery barrage" or "the most intense barrage" ever laid down on the Eastern Front, Zuckertort's artillery preparation was not based upon massed, continuous bombardment as in World War I. Rather, it was based upon methodical shoot-observe-shoot tactics that would sweep the targets in each grid until they were damaged or destroyed. Once this was achieved, the infantry would go in.

At 0540hrs on June 2, the Czech-built 14.9cm s.FH 37(t) howitzers of schwere Artillerie-Abteilung 737 fired the opening rounds of Operation *Störfang*. Manstein observed the bombardment through Zeiss-made *Scnfernrohr* (scissors binoculars). The shelling started slowly, while registration fire gradually zeroed in on Soviet positions in the main defensive belt around Mekenzievy Mountain. Then the division-level 10.5cm and 15cm howitzers joined in at 0600hrs, firing three-round missions against specific targets in the enemy security belt. However, most medium guns fired no more than six to 12 rounds on the first day. German forward observers would then wait for the dust to settle and assess the effect on targets – either ordering a repeat fire mission or recommending moving on to the next target on the list. Overhead, the Hs 126Bs of 3.(H)/13 also passed on spotting reports to HArko 306. The two 60cm Karl mortars – "Odin" and "Thor" – each fired one test round, then remained silent for the next four days. Most of the other heavy artillery fired a few rounds each, but the two 28cm "schwere Bruno" railroad guns fired 104 rounds and two batteries of obsolete 28cm howitzers fired 330 rounds. At 1100hrs, the corps-level artillery joined in with 21cm mortars firing at forward Soviet positions. Zuckertort was hoping to provoke Petrov's artillery into responding so that they could be targeted and destroyed, but most of the Soviet batteries remained silent on the first day.

Richthofen's Fliegerkorps VIII actually dropped more high explosive on Sevastopol on the first day of *Störfang* than Zuckertort's gunners. Since most of the bombers were based less than 60 miles from the city, they could fly three or more sorties a day with maximum bomb loads. On day one, Fliegerkorps VIII dropped 525 tons of bombs on Sevastopol. Major Werner Hoffmann's I./KG 100 specialized in dropping the Luftwaffe's largest bombs against critical targets like Morgunov's coastal batteries. On June 2, Hoffmann's He-111H-6 bombers dropped one 1,700kg SD 1700 "Sigismund" semi-armor-piercing bomb and seven 1,400kg PC 1400 "Fritz" armor-piercing bombs.[13] Initially, Richthofen concentrated his effort against the harbor area and the two VVS-ChF airbases, which were under constant observation. Captain Konstantin S. Alekseyev, who commanded the 1st Squadron of the 6th Guards Fighter Regiment, was stationed at the Chersonese airfield. Alekseyev was the top-scoring ace in the VVS-ChF with about eight "kills" by the start of *Störfang*, and his squadron, equipped with Yak-1 fighters, was badly outnumbered by Fliegerkorps VIII, but gamely took to the skies every day to attempt to intercept German bombers.[14]

On June 3–4, Zuckertort's gunners fired less ammunition and mostly medium artillery, with only minor contributions from the 30.5cm mortars. Much of the bombardment was focused on a few key hills on the right flank of Sector IV, which is where LIV Armeekorps intended to make its main effort. Haccius Ridge and the Ölberg – as designated by the Germans – were held by the Soviet 3rd Battalion, 514th Rifle Regiment, and offered a commanding view of the Bel'bek River valley. The Gamma mortar fired 30 42cm rounds against the Ölberg, while Haccius Ridge was pummeled by 24cm howitzers rounds. Nevertheless, the 514th Rifle Regiment reported only 32 casualties during the five-day bombardment. On their right, the 79th Naval Infantry Brigade held a trio of hills at the junction of the Bel'bek River and Kamyschly Ravine, which the Germans dubbed the Bunkerberg, the Stellenberg, and the Eisenbahnberg. Zuckertort's artillery pounded these hills daily, and the Eisenbahnberg was singled out for attention with 20 "Gamma" rounds, 30 30.5cm rounds, and 40 28cm rounds, but only managed to kill or wound about 20 percent of the dug-in Soviet naval infantrymen. Most of Zuckertort's artillery was focused against Petrov's III and IV Defensive Sectors, with only a single battery of 30.5cm mortars supporting the XXX Armeekorps barrage in the south.

On the other side, Petrov had expected a German offensive, but the Stavka did not believe that it could last for more than two weeks and thus had not provided him with the means to sustain a longer battle. Instead, they had put the bulk of available resources into Kozlov's Crimean Front, which now no longer existed. In fact, Petrov's artillery was unprepared for a protracted slugging match against Zuckertort's guns. His artillery commander, General-Major of Artillery Nikolai K. Ryzhi, had direct control over six army-level artillery regiments: three medium and three light. These units possessed a total of about 156 artillery pieces: 36 152mm ML-20 howitzers, 12 155mm Schneider M1917 howitzers, four 122mm A-19 guns, 40 107mm M1910/30 guns, and about 60 76.2mm F-22 guns. While the ML-20s had better range than the German s.FH 18 15cm howitzers, many of Ryzhi's guns were in poor condition after more than ten months of continuous use; in the 18th Guards Artillery Regiment, for example, the ML-20s had used 80–90 percent of their barrel life and the 107mm guns had used 90–100 percent. Firing guns with worn-out barrels greatly decreased their accuracy and increased the chance of malfunctions, including burst barrels that could injure the crew. Ammunition was also in short supply; the ML-20s were in decent shape with 390 rounds per gun, but the 155mm howitzers only had 75 rounds per gun, the 122mm had 100, and the 107mm 158. This meant that Petrov's heaviest artillery had to conserve its fire and that there was insufficient ammunition for a long battle. Even if the Black Sea Fleet brought in more ammunition, most of the guns were so worn out that many were operating in a degraded condition. The 76mm guns were in much better technical shape and had about 300 rounds per gun, plus another 900 rounds per gun stored in warehouses in Sevastopol, making them the most reliable – if not most effective – Soviet artillery during the final battle for Sevastopol. In addition, there was a single multiple rocket-launcher unit – Major Dmitri D. Kush-Zharko's 53rd Guards Mortar Battalion, with 12 BM-8 82mm launchers. In contrast to Petrov's impoverished artillery ammunition supply, most of Manstein's medium artillery started the battle with five or six basic loads of ammunition, with more en route.

Meanwhile, Fliegerkorps VIII continued to make the greatest impression on the Soviet defenders, particularly as the Stuka attacks became more accurate. Although most of the bombs dropped were 50kg, 250kg, or 500kg general-purpose bombs, Hoffmann's I./KG 100 continued delivering heavy bombs of 1,000–2,500 kg against targets in Sevastopol. Meanwhile, Richthofen's fighters laid waste to the Soviet naval pilots attempting to defend the city. A young German Bf-109F pilot in 5./JG 77, Oberleutnant Anton Hackl, claimed a LaGG-3 fighter and a Yak-3 fighter on June 3–4; he was to become the top-scoring Luftwaffe pilot during *Störfang*, with 11 kills claimed over Sevastopol in June. Nevertheless, the outnumbered VVS-ChF's 3 OAG put up a very tough fight over Sevastopol, and it had gained considerable combat experience against some of the Luftwaffe's best pilots. Nor was it only fighter pilots who built their reputations at Sevastopol; Feldwebel Herbert Dawedeit, a Stuka pilot from 8./StG 77, would fly 120 combat missions over the city – up to eight per day. Dawedeit enjoyed great success against both ground and naval targets and would eventually complete 806 combat missions; he was later awarded the *Ritterkreuz*, and he survived the war.

There were a number of targets that Manstein wanted destroyed or neutralized before beginning his ground offensive, but, amazingly, Aleksandr's Coastal Battery No. 30 (dubbed "Fort Maxim Gorky I" by the Germans) did not have a particularly high priority since it was assumed that the 305mm guns were no longer operational. The Soviets had successfully managed to conceal the repair of these guns during the spring, and Petrov wanted them to remain silent until the German ground assault began. Thus, when the men of schwere Artillerie-Abteilung (E) 672, along with hundreds of Organization Todt engineers, were finally able to emplace the 80cm Dora railroad gun in a position near Bakhchisaray, it was not directed to fire at this most obvious target. Instead, at 0535hrs on June 5, Dora fired a single round against the abandoned military barracks near the Mekenzievy Mountain station. Zuckertort then instructed Dora to fire at Coastal Battery No. 2, equipped with four 100mm guns, near the harbor. Eight rounds were wasted on this pathetic target, which was not even armored. Meanwhile, Aleksandr's Coastal Battery No. 30 suddenly opened fire, lobbing five rounds at a German observation post – and missed. In all likelihood, the hasty field repairs had probably failed to boresight the turrets correctly, and they were no longer capable of accurate shooting.

Although Zuckertort now knew that Coastal Battery No. 30 was still operational, he did not commit Dora against this target. Instead, on June 6, Dora fired six rounds at "Fort Stalin" – which was simply an antiaircraft battery – with one round falling within 40 yards of the target. Another eight 80cm rounds were fired at "Fort Molotov," which was just another fortified hilltop. Major Hoffmann's I./KG 100 dropped ten 2,500kg "Max" and four 1,800kg SC 1800 "Satan" bombs around Aleksandr's battery on June 5, but scored no direct hits.[15] Finally, Major Freiherr Rüdt von Collenberg, commander of schwere Artillerie-Abteilung 833, was ordered to silence Aleksandr's battery. During the night of June 5/6, the "Thor" mortar was sluggishly maneuvered onto a hillside north of the Bel'bek less than 4,000 yards from Aleksandr's battery. At 1700hrs on June 6, "Thor" began firing the first of 16 60cm concrete-piercing shells, and its seventh shot scored a direct hit on the eastern 305mm turret. A great chunk of the armor plate was torn off the top of the turret and one gun barrel was damaged. In addition, a fire started in the turret and the ventilation system caused smoke to spread throughout the underground battery complex. Aleksandr himself was still secure inside his command post, known as "Bastion I" to the Germans, but the bombardment also knocked out his internal communications lines. Although Coastal Battery No. 30 continued to fire occasionally from its other turret – which was damaged by a bomb the next day – its active role in the defense of Sevastopol was nearing an end.

On June 6, Dora continued to waste its limited ammunition against a variety of mundane targets. Zuckertort wasted "Dora's" ammunition on too many secondary targets, instead of concentrating it against a single target. Furthermore, Dora was a very fragile weapons system and suffered from technical defects after a few rounds. Dora fired 25 of its 48 rounds before the actual assault on Sevastopol began, and it appears that the biggest gun ever built achieved virtually nothing, aside from making some very large craters. In contrast to the complete inaccuracy of Dora, Manstein relied upon Oberst Friedrich-Franz Rittner's Flak-Regiment 18 for precision fire against the numerous Soviet bunkers. Rittner had four mixed flak battalions with a total of 48 8.8cm flak guns and deployed single guns in forward areas as bunker busters. It turned out that many of the Soviet bunkers hastily built during the winter of 1941/42 could not withstand direct hits from rounds larger than 7.5cm, and the high-velocity rounds from 8.8cm flak guns proved adept at cracking them open. Rittner's flak gunners would fire a total of 181,787 rounds during *Störfang* and inflicted far more damage upon Petrov's defenses than Dora.

By the end of the fifth day of the bombardment, Zuckertort's artillery had fired 42,595 rounds of ammunition at Sevastopol, equivalent to 2,449 tons of munitions. Rather than the popularly depicted super-heavy weapons like Dora and Karl, it was the ubiquitous 10cm s.K 18 cannon, 15cm s.FH 37 howitzer, and 21cm Mörser that were the predominant weapons used in this phase. During these five days, Fliegerkorps VIII dropped over 2,264 tons of bombs on Sevastopol, including 14 2,500kg, five 1,800kg, three 1,700kg, and seven 1,400kg heavy bombs.[16] How successful was five days of sustained air and artillery attacks upon Petrov's defenses? Many frontline bunkers were destroyed or damaged, but the trench works and underground shelters were more resistant to artillery fire, as well as the railroad tunnel on the south side of Mekenzievy Mountain. Soviet personnel losses were relatively light. For example, the 514th Regiment defending on Haccius Ridge suffered only 12 dead and 20 wounded during June 2–6, less than 3 percent losses, despite being the target of daily heavy-artillery fire and Luftwaffe attacks.[17] Given the level of effort put into the German artillery preparation, AOK 11's infantry realized little actual benefit. Despite five days of pounding, the Soviet infantrymen waited in their bunkers and dugouts, filled with grim determination to hold the line. Political officers spent the time haranguing the troops about fulfilling their duty to the Motherland, and the penalty of failure.

Even before Zuckertort's artillery opened fire on June 2, Petrov and Oktyabrsky knew that a German assault upon Sevastopol was imminent after the destruction of Kozlov's Crimean Front, and they began pleading for reinforcements from the North Caucasus Military District. Kozlov had repeatedly short-changed Sevastopol for replacements and supplies during the spring of 1942, but now the Military Council of the Black Sea Fleet requested 15,000 replacements, 50 brand-new Yak-1 fighters, more fuel for 3 OAG to maintain a high sortie rate, and triple the amount of ammunition allocated to the SOR. Amazingly, Petrov requested 10,000 rifles and 1,500 light machine guns, indicating that many of his troops were poorly armed. In addition, Petrov wanted to evacuate as many of the remaining civilians and naval-base personnel as possible in order to reduce the need for food, so that naval convoys could concentrate on bringing in replacements and ammunition. On May 25, the evacuation of civilians began in earnest. Thus far, the Luftwaffe units based in the Crimea had enjoyed only limited success, and against stationary naval targets in Sevastopol's harbors and slow-moving and unescorted merchant ships in coastal waters. Soviet convoys to Sevastopol had successfully delivered 35,000 reinforcements and evacuated 9,000 wounded from January to May, without excessive losses.

Oktyabrsky committed the cruisers *Molotov* and *Krasny Krym*, six destroyers (*Tashkent, Bezuprechny, Bditelny, Kharkov, Soobrazitel'ny*, and *Svobodnyi*) and eight *Tral*-class coastal minesweepers to the June supply runs. Except for the elderly *Krasny Krym*, these vessels were relatively fast and capable of 30 knots or better, and the Italian-built *Tashkent* was a greyhound that could conduct 39-knot dashes. The Luftwaffe pilots simply could not hit a warship that was maneuvering at these speeds. Yet while the destroyers could bring in 300–400 troops each and a cruiser 1,000–2,000, the warships were ill-suited for carrying and offloading heavy cargo such as vehicles and palletized ammunition. The Soviet merchant marine contributed three cargo/passenger vessels (*Abkhazia, Belostok,* and *Gruziya*) and the tanker *Mikhail Gromov* to the Sevastopol run. None of these vessels could move faster than 12 knots, so the fast Soviet escorting warships were chained to slow-moving targets. This is where the Achilles Heel of the Soviet Black Sea Fleet became apparent: a lack of air-warning radar and inadequate antiaircraft ammunition. The heavy cruiser *Molotov* was the only one of Oktyabrsky's fleet to carry an air-search radar, and it was a primitive set at that. Almost all of Oktyabrsky's warships relied upon the obsolescent 45mm 21-K antiaircraft gun in single mounts as their primary antiaircraft weapon, but this weapon was inadequate for dealing with multi-aircraft attacks. The *Molotov* and the Type-7 (*Gnevnyi*-class) destroyers carried the 21-K, which had a very low rate of fire and ammunition unsuited for engaging aerial targets. The *Tashkent* and new Type 7U destroyers received the 37mm 70-K gun just before the start of the war; this weapon was similar to the Swedish 40mm Bofors gun and combined a high rate of fire with improved HE-Frag rounds. Despite the lack of up-to-date antiaircraft weaponry, Soviet convoys to Sevastopol during the spring were often aided by morning fog, which could rise 100 yards or more and make it difficult for aircraft to spot vessels.[18] Thus, Oktyabrsky believed that his warships would continue to be able to run the Luftwaffe's aerial gauntlet into Sevastopol at acceptable cost.

During the night of May 27/28, the heavy cruiser *Molotov* and two destroyers delivered Colonel Nikolai V. Blagoveshchensky's 9th Naval Infantry Brigade from Novorossiysk. Instead of providing the 15,000 replacements that Petrov had requested, the Stavka sent a single brigade with 3,017 troops. Blagoveshchensky's brigade consisted of survivors from the fighting in the Kerch Peninsula and had a high percentage of recently wounded men, released from hospital and sent right back to the front. As *Störfang* began on June 2, the destroyers *Tashkent* and *Bezuprechny*, plus the passenger ship *Abkhazia*, brought 2,785 replacements right into Sevastopol harbor without much interference from Richthofen's Fliegerkorps IV. Captain Vasily N. Eroshenko was fond of using the 39-knot speed of his *Tashkent* to evade German bombers, and when a trawler instructed him to slow to 14 knots while moving through a lane in the outer harbor minefields, he ignored this and swept into Severnaya Bay at maximum speed:

> Bombers caught the Tashkent approaching the Chersonesus. We defended ourselves, without reducing speed. Bombs were falling pretty close, but they are not from dive-bombers. It is terrible for the army troops, encamped on the deck, where there is overcrowding and one fragment can hit ten men.[19]

Once in Severnaya Bay, the ships unloaded during the night and left before daylight. German artillery would fire on the harbor area when ships were sighted, inflicting some shrapnel damage, but it was too inaccurate to sink any shipping. However, the tanker *Mikhail Gromov*, sailing with two minesweepers, was less fortunate and was pounced on 37 miles south of Yalta by the He-111 torpedo-bombers of Major Horst Beyling's II./KG 26. One torpedo struck the tanker's bow at 2055hrs and set her ablaze, which caused her destruction. After this, Oktyabrsky decided not to send any more tankers to Sevastopol and instead submarines would be used to bring in small quantities of aviation fuel. Yet the loss of the *Mikhail Gromov* seemed like something of a fluke, since the Black Sea Fleet continued to enjoy success with using high-speed supply runs with destroyers on June 3, 5, and 6, which brought 2,500 more troops into Sevastopol without loss. Even the 4,857-ton passenger ship *Gruziya*, built by Krupp at Kiel in 1928, managed to slip into the port unescorted on June 7, with another 750 troops. During the first week of June, the Black Sea Fleet also managed to evacuate 1,612 wounded and 3,434 civilians. But time was running out.

Unknown to Oktyabrsky, the Axis had decided in January 1942 to transfer light naval forces to the Black Sea to assist in interdicting Soviet naval convoys. The Italian Regia Marina created a composite unit designated as the 101st Squadron with four 24-ton MAS boats and six 35-ton mini-submarines under the command of Capitano di Fregata Francesco Mimbelli. The German Kriegsmarine also decided to send the 1. Schnellbootsflottille under Kapitänleutnant Karl-Heinz Birnbacher, but his 92-ton boats were considerably more difficult to transport and had to be disassembled, then sent by barge down the Danube to Romania, so Mimbelli's squadron arrived in theater first. Mimbelli established his squadron at Yalta and Feodosiya in mid-May, and his MAS boats and mini-submarines commenced patrolling activities off the Crimea just as *Störfang* was beginning.[20] The first two of Birnbacher's S-Boats did not arrive at the Romanian port of Constanta until May 26, and they did not begin patrols off Sevastopol until June 6.[21]

Meanwhile, the air battle over Sevastopol rapidly turned against the VVS-ChF's 3 OAG. Richthofen's fighters, which now had a 3-1 numerical superiority over Sevastopol, ripped into the 3 OAG on June 7, claiming 17 "kills." Even Captain Konstantin S. Alekseyev, the VVS-ChF's top ace was shot down and badly wounded on June 8. His 6th Guards Fighter

Regiment lost a number of other experienced pilots in the opening days of June. One German ace, Oberleutnant Anton Hackl claimed five Soviet fighters and four Il-2 Sturmoviks over Sevastopol in the first nine days of *Störfang*. On June 10, the 45th Fighter Regiment arrived in Sevastopol from the Caucasus with 20 brand-new Yak-1 fighters, but the pilots were mostly inexperienced, and nine were shot down in their first two days of combat. During the period June 7–12, the three *Gruppen* of JG 77 inflicted crippling losses on 3 OAG, which lost the ability to protect the port or shipping against large-scale Luftwaffe attacks. By mid-June, Fliegerkorps VIII was dominant over Sevastopol and the sea lines of communication were now at great risk.

As the battle for air superiority over Sevastopol was being decided, Fliegerkorps VIII began to shift its focus to severing Sevastopol's sea lines of communications. On the evening of June 9, the destroyers *Svobodnyi* and *Bditelny* and two minesweepers were escorting the 4,727-ton transport *Abkhazia* into Sevastopol when they came under attack from the He-111H-6 bombers from Beyling's II./KG 26. Over the course of two hours, the German bombers launched 24 torpedoes against the convoy, but none hit, and the ships reached Severnaya Bay intact. Normally, the convoys unloaded during the night and left before dawn to avoid becoming stationary targets for the Luftwaffe. Captain 3rd Rank P. I. Shevchenko's destroyer *Svobodnyi* had unloaded its cargo of ammunition by 0430hrs, but as the sun rose on the horizon the transport *Abkhazia* had only begun to unload a cargo that included new trucks for Petrov's army. Shortly thereafter, the first He-111 bombers began appearing over the port and the Soviets activated a smokescreen system used to obscure the port area.

Shevchenko's *Svobodnyi* was the newest destroyer in the Black Sea Fleet and had only entered service in January 1942. Consequently, the *Svobodnyi* had received five of the improved 37mm 70-K antiaircraft guns, rather than the obsolescent 45mm 21-K gun. The smokescreen helped to conceal the vessels in Severnaya Bay, and Shevchenko's antiaircraft gunners were able to fend off a number of attacks by individual He-111 bombers. Then – for reasons never explained – Oktyabrsky personally ordered the smoke screen turned off around 0640hrs. Most likely, Oktyabrsky wanted to conserve the limited supply of diesel fuel for the smoke generators when the ships were not under serious air attack, but the generators remained off even as Fliegerkorps VIII began to appear in strength around 0800hrs.

Shevchenko moved the *Svobodnyi* into Korabelnaya Bay and moored alongside the long wharf. At 0915hrs, a group of He-111s from Major Bätcher's I./KG 100 attacked the *Abkhazia* and scored a direct hit that set the transport on fire. Ten minutes later, Ju-87 Stukas from StG-77 scored more hits on the burning *Abkhazia*, which heeled over against a pier. Although Shevchenko's destroyer had suffered light hull damage from two near-misses, it was still operational, and it is not clear why he decided to remain in Sevastopol after the *Abkhazia* was sunk. At any rate, the *Svobodnyi* was still moored along the wharf when a full Stuka *Gruppen* launched a multi-directional "hammer and anvil" attack against the destroyer at 1315hrs, which overwhelmed its antiaircraft gunners. A 50kg bomb hit the gun shield of the second 130mm gun, then two bombs hit the bridge and wounded Shevchenko, then six more bombs ripped her apart from stem to stern, killing 67 of the crew. The wounded Shevchenko ordered the remaining crew to abandon ship, and the survivors assembled on the wharf to watch their burning destroyer heel over and sink. Nearby, the *Abkhazia* burned all day, and its vital cargo of ammunition finally exploded around 2200hrs. It had been a bad day for the Black Sea Fleet.

Neither of the Soviet antiaircraft batteries, nor the 3 OAG, had been able to save the *Svobodnyi* and the *Abkhazia*, because they were both becoming rapidly combat-ineffective. The flak batteries were running short of ammunition and their barrels were worn out. Replacement pilots and aircraft continued to arrive from the Caucasus, but 3 OAG was reduced to the role of a guerilla air force. As the amount of air-to-air combat declined, the Luftwaffe transferred I./JG 77 out of the Crimea.

On the night of June 11/12, the heavy cruiser *Molotov* and destroyer *Bditelny* conducted a high-speed run into Sevastopol that successfully delivered 3,341 troops from the 138th Naval Rifle Brigade, as well as 190 tons of ammunition. However, when the German-built transport *Gruziya* tried to make it into Sevastopol with the minesweeper *T-413* and an *MO-IV*-class patrol boat on June 13, it was spotted. The *Gruziya* was carrying an enormous load of 1,300 tons of ammunition, including artillery shells filled with Mustard Gas and Lewisite, a chemical weapon that acts as a blister agent (this was confirmed by post-war divers on the wreck). The convoy was spotted by German aircraft at first light and a single bomb hit the *Gruziya*'s aft cargo hold, detonating the ammunition. A massive explosion broke the ship in two, leaving no survivors. The T-413 and the patrol boat survived this air attack, but both were sunk at 1145hrs off Cape Fiolent. It is uncertain why the Soviets were shipping chemical weapons into Sevastopol, but most likely it was based upon the fear that AOK 11 would use chemical weapons to reduce the fortress.

After mid-June, the Black Sea Fleet's convoys became increasingly at risk from both Axis air and naval attacks. The cruisers *Molotov* and *Bezuprechny* made another high-speed run into Sevastopol on June 15/16, which delivered 3,855 troops and 442 tons of ammunition, but on June 18 the flotilla leader *Kharkov* was damaged en route to Sevastopol by German aircraft and forced to turn back. The 2,048-ton passenger vessel *Belostok* succeeded in making it to Sevastopol and, although damaged by artillery fire, left by 2130hrs with the minesweeper *T-408* as escort. On its return trip, the *Belostok* carried 375 wounded and 43 civilians. Off Cape Fiolent, the small convoy was approached by unidentified craft. It was two of Kapitänleutnant Karl-Heinz Birnbacher's S-Boats – the *S-72* and the *S-102*. The Kriegsmarine had finally arrived in the Black Sea. Kapitänleutnant Werner Töniges, captain of the *S-102*, had started his career in the merchant marine before transferring to the Kriegsmarine. By the summer of 1942 Töniges was an accomplished ship-killer and had already been awarded the *Ritterkreuz*. The two S-Boats attacked individually, and the Soviet escorts failed to react in time, which enabled the two boats to fire off five torpedoes. One of Töniges' struck the *Belostok* at 0148hrs, and the ex-Spanish passenger vessel sank quickly, taking 388 souls down with her.[22] This was the first Kriegsmarine victory in the Black Sea and the last attempt to run slow-moving merchant ships into Sevastopol.

On June 24 the destroyers *Tashkent*, *Bezuprechny*, and *Bditelny* managed to bring 1,871 troops from the 142nd Naval Rifle Brigade into Sevastopol. Encouraged by this success, the Soviet destroyers quickly returned to Novorossiysk to bring the rest of the naval brigade to Sevastopol. Captain 3rd Rank Petr M. Buriak loaded 320 troops and 16 medical personnel onto his destroyer *Bezuprechny* and started back to Sevastopol on the morning of June 26. Eroshenko's *Tashkent* followed soon after, overloaded with 944 troops. Initially, the VVS provided fighter cover over the destroyers, but by late afternoon the destroyers were on their own. Buriak's *Bezuprechny* was still equipped with the obsolescent 45mm 21-K antiaircraft guns, but managed to fend off two small-scale air attacks. However, a large group of Ju-87 Stukas from II./StG 77 attacked the

Bezuprechny 37 miles off the Crimean coast at 1857hrs. Oberfeldwebel Werner Haugk of 5./StG 77 scored a direct hit on the destroyer, which broke it in two.[23] Hit by two more bombs, the *Bezuprechny* sank in two minutes, but dozens of men made it into the water. Soon, the *Tashkent* appeared on the horizon. Eroshenko witnessed a huge plume of black smoke hanging over *Bezuprechny's* grave and bobbing heads amidst a floating lake of fuel oil. Now the Ju-88s turned their attention to Eroshenko's *Tashkent*, and he was only able to survive by high-speed turning and furiously firing off one-third of his antiaircraft ammunition. Under these conditions, he could not stop to rescue survivors. On the way into Sevastopol, Italian MAS boats ambushed the *Tashkent* off Cap Fiolent, but Eroshenko's luck held, as two torpedoes passed under his bow without exploding. Eroshenko made it into Sevastopol, but only three out of 572 aboard the *Bezuprechny* were eventually rescued.[24]

On the return trip, a German reconnaissance plane spotted the *Tashkent* at 0415hrs, and a large force of He-111s from I./KG 100 arrived overhead around 0600hrs, followed by Ju-87s from III./StG 77. The He-111 bombers employed a new tactic, attacking one after another in a shallow diving attack, rather than with intervals of several minutes between each attack. Eroshenko's ship weaved from side to side, avoiding bombs, but his antiaircraft gunners were running out of ammunition. After more than three hours of dodging, and after avoiding 355 bombs, Eroshenko's luck finally ran out when Feldwebel Herbert Dawedeit of 8./StG 77 dived on his ship and dropped a 250kg bomb close to the stern of the *Tashkent*, which disabled the destroyer's steering and caused massive flooding.[25] Unable to maneuver and with speed dropping off to 14 knots, the *Tashkent* suffered two more near-misses and 1,900 tons of seawater poured into her ruptured hull. Amazingly, Eroshenko's crew made emergency repairs that enabled the destroyer to keep limping eastward and survive further attacks. Eventually, Soviet fighters from Novorossiysk appeared and the attacks stopped, while other ships were sent to tow the damaged *Tashkent* into port. Yet the fact that even the high-speed *Tashkent* was no longer invulnerable indicated that Richthofen's Fliegerkorps VIII had finally achieved their goal of isolating Sevastopol.[26]

The air battle over Sevastopol was also finished. On June 25 the Stavka ordered the survivors of the 6th Guards Fighter to evacuate to the Caucasus, while a dozen Yak-1 fighters from the 9th and 45th Fighter Regiments conducted a last-ditch stand over Sevastopol's air space for another week, until their airfields were in danger of being overrun. Richthofen left to participate in the opening phase of the main *Fall Blau* summer offensive and took III./JG 77 with him. By late June, only II./JG 77 remained in the Crimea, but it was enough.

In one last desperate gesture, Oktyabrsky sent two minesweepers on June 28 to deliver the last 330 troops from the 142nd NIB, and they managed to survive constant air attacks on the way out. Another 300 wounded and civilians were evacuated. Yet this was the end. During June, the Black Sea Fleet had delivered over 17,600 reinforcements into Sevastopol, but had lost two destroyers, a minesweeper, and five merchant ships sunk and most of the other warships had suffered damage from near-misses. As June ended, the last 31 operational VVS-ChF aircraft in Sevastopol flew to the Caucasus, while all damaged aircraft were destroyed. Without even a token amount of air cover, the Black Sea Fleet was no longer willing to send surface ships to certain death off the Crimea, and resorted to using only submarines for supply runs to Sevastopol in its final days.

The Kamyschly Ravine ran for 2 miles diagonally from the southern side of the Bel'bek River. It was less than 400 yards wide at its narrow northern neck, but widened out to over 600 yards as it moved south toward the village of Kamyschly. Both sides of the ravine were bounded by steep hills, studded with small trees and brush. The hill on the western side – known as Hill 124 to the Russians or the "Stellenberg" to the Germans – was a key piece of terrain that controlled the northern half of the ravine and provided excellent observation over the Bel'bek River valley to its front. The Stellenberg sat atop a large, rolling ridge, which provided ample concealment, and to its left the so-called "Haccius Ridge" ran almost all the way to Coastal Battery No. 30. The bottom of the Kamyschly Ravine was often wet and marshy, with drainage from the nearby river or hills. The ravine formed a perfect moat and an excellent natural defensive position.

During the December offensive, the 132. Infanterie-Division had captured the western side of the Kamyschly Ravine, but had been forced to withdraw from this terrain after Manstein called off the offensive. In

January, Colonel Aleksei S. Potapov's 79th Naval Infantry Brigade entrenched themselves on the western side of the Kamyschly Ravine, stretching along a 2-mile front from Hill 124 in the north to a fortified position known as the "Trapeze" in the south. During the spring, Major Vladimir V. Shaslo's 747th Rifle Regiment from the 172nd Rifle Division took over defensive positions west of the "Stellenberg" along "Haccius Ridge." The key position on this ridge was a hilltop known as the "Ölberg," which overlooked the rail line that ran up the escarpment to the Mekenzievy Mountain station. Potapov's brigade had taken heavy losses in the December 1941 fighting but still had three battalions with a total of over 3,500 veteran troops by the start of *Störfang*; he placed his 1st Battalion and the 5th Company around Hill 124, his 3rd Battalion around the Trapeze, and kept two companies from the 2nd Battalion in reserve.[27] In contrast, Colonel Ivan A. Laskin's 172nd Rifle Division had been badly gutted in the retreat from Ishun in November 1941 and barely 1,000 of its troops reached Sevastopol; due to these losses, both the 383rd and 747th Rifle Regiments had been disbanded. Eventually, sufficient replacements reached Sevastopol by sea to enable Laskin to reform the 747th Rifle Regiment in March and the 383rd Rifle Regiment in May. Filled with fresh conscripts, most with no previous battle experience, these units took over positions on the escarpment overlooking the Bel'bek River. Laskin assigned his only veteran outfit, the 514th Rifle Regiment, to defend forward combat outposts around the town of Bel'bek. The boundary between Sevastopol's Sector III (commanded by General-Major Trofim K. Kolomiets of the 25th Rifle Division) and Sector IV (commanded by Colonel Aleksandr G. Kapitokhin of the 95th Rifle Division) lay between the Stellenberg and the Ölberg, which is precisely where Hansen's LIV Armeekorps intended to make its main effort.

By early June, the entire western side of the Kamyschly Ravine was densely entrenched, and Zuckertort's artillery preparation (*Vorbereitungsfeuer*) inflicted only moderate to light damage on the fieldworks and barbed-wire obstacles that lay at the base of the steep slope of the Stellenberg. Hansen's assault plan for his LIV Armeekorps was to cross the Kamyschly Ravine with all three regiments of the 22. Infanterie-Division and two regiments each from the 50. and 24. Infanterie-Divisionen. A total of seven German infantry regiments with more than 10,000 troops would attack across the 2-mile-long Kamyschly

Ravine; in contrast, the US Army landed just two infantry regiments on a 5-mile-wide front in the first wave at Omaha Beach in June 1944. This was the *Schwerpunkt*, where Manstein would mass all his resources on a narrow front to smash through the hard outer core of Petrov's defenses.

Across from Hill 124, Generalmajor Ludwig Wolff's 22. Infanterie-Division had assembled two battalions from Oberstleutnant Rudolf Buhse's IR 47 and two battalions from Oberst Dietrich von Choltitz's IR 16 on Hill 191.8 on the eastern side of the Kamyschly Ravine, overlooking the Soviet positions. This was a very dangerous space, as both sides regularly traded sniper and mortar fire across the 400-yard-wide ravine, so neither could move troops around much in the daylight. Nevertheless, the Germans managed to manhandle three batteries of 28/32cm Nebelwerfer 41 multiple rocket launchers from III./schweres Werfer-Regiment 1 up onto their hill during Zuckertort's five-day artillery preparation – apparently without being noticed.[28] Petrov expected that an attack against Sectors III and IV was imminent, and on the night of June 6/7 he ordered all frontline units to conduct counterfire against suspected German assembly areas at 0255hrs on June 7. Potapov's brigade had limited organic artillery – just four 122mm howitzers and 8 76.2mm field guns – so it relied heavily upon artillery support from Laskin's neighboring division. Laskin's division was supported by Colonel Josef F. Shmelkov's 134th Howitzer Regiment, equipped with a rather obsolescent collection of ten 152mm M1909/30 howitzers and about 20 122mm M1910 howitzers. Shmelkov's artillery fired against positions held by the 22. Infanterie-Division for 20 minutes, but achieved little since they had to conserve their ammunition.[29]

At 0315hrs on June 7, Zuckertort's artillery opened fire again, but this day was different. This day was "X-Day" – the beginning of the German ground assault. The *Heeresartillerie* fired with everything they had, attempting to lay waste to the Soviet frontline positions in a crushing artillery barrage.[30] The Stellenberg, currently occupied by the 5th Company from Potapov's brigade, was hammered by sustained fire from 30.5cm howitzers for nearly an hour, but worse was to come.[31] Without warning, the 18 Nebelwerfer 41 multiple rocket launchers began to hurl over 100 incendiary and high-explosive rockets onto the "Stellenberg," setting underbrush afire and filling the Soviet trenches with dense, choking smoke. The blast affect was horrific even for troops in trenches, and the overpressure likely left many Soviet troops unconscious or shell-shocked. Even before the Nebelwerfers had finished launching their first volley, a red flare ascended into the morning sky, signaling the beginning of the ground assault. *Stossgruppen* from the 22. Infanterie-Division began to emerge from their assault positions and rush into the Kamyschly Ravine.

In the lead was I./IR 47, led by Major Gustav Alvermann, who had been awarded the *Ritterkreuz* for leading an air assault into Holland in 1940. Close behind was III./IR 16. The German *Stossgruppen* did not attack in large units, but advanced using infiltration-type tactics, in small, well-armed groups. Each group comprised a mix of infantry and pioneers, the latter of which were essential for breaching the enemy obstacles. Rushing across the bottom of the ravine, which was swampy in places, the assault troops came under sporadic automatic-weapons and mortar fire, but the enemy was firing blindly into the smoke created by the Nebelwerfer barrage, so casualties were initially light. Hearts pounding, the first assault teams approached the base of the western side of the ravine and began to suffer casualties from Soviet PMD wooden antipersonnel mines. The pioneers began marking lanes through the minefield, while the rest of the assault troops covered them from prone firing positions. After this tedious task was completed, with more casualties from enemy shrapnel, the pioneers began cutting through the barbed-wire obstacles, some of which had probably been smashed about by the German artillery preparation. At this point, members of the 9th Company of Potapov's brigade, deployed in combat outposts along the edge of the Kamyschly Ravine, began to engage the German troops attempting to breach the obstacle belt. The Germans were prepared for this and a 2cm flak platoon had moved forward in direct support of the *Stossgruppen*; the flak gunners engaged flashes from Soviet automatic weapons with 150 large-caliber rounds per minute, which quickly suppressed them. Awed by the firepower display, many Soviet infantrymen did not fire, but simply made themselves as small as possible at the bottom of their trenches. As the pioneers cut through the wire, some troops threw smoke grenades to cover them while others hurled *Stielgranaten* to suppress enemy troops on the far side. Then they were through – a thin corridor at first – but as more *Stossgruppen* reached the wire and began to breach it, the penetration widened. After a brief fight for the forward trenches, the Germans began to climb up the western side of the ravine.

Off on the left flank of the 22. Infanterie-Division, troops from Generalleutnant Friedrich Schmidt's 50. Infanterie-Division's IR 121 and IR 123, supported by Sturmgeschütz-Abteilung 197, were crossing the ravine further south, heading toward the village of Kamyschly and the "Trapeze." Oberleutnant Erich Bärenfänger, who had performed so well during pursuit operations in November 1941, had been partly in charge of leading the assault elements from III./IR 123. Bärenfänger led a *Stossgruppe* from the front, racing across the open terrain of the valley floor toward the Soviet trenches. He and his troops hurled a barrage of a dozen *Stielgranaten* before leaping into the trench and engaging in close-quarter combat with the naval infantrymen of Potapov's brigade. After clearing the frontline trenches, Bärenfänger boldly pushed up a trail toward the heights, and his battalion was soon 1,000 yards ahead of the rest of his regiment. Small groups of naval infantrymen attacked his open flanks, forcing Bärenfänger to stop and deploy his machine guns to prevent the Soviets from encircling him.[32]

Simply moving up the steep, cratered sides of the "Stellenberg" in full combat gear was very difficult for Alvermann's soldiers, and it was virtually a job for the *Gebirgsjäger*. Nevertheless, Alvermann led the I./IR 47 up the southeast corner of the hill while the III./IR 16 climbed the northeast corner. Atop the Stellenberg, the 5th Company was apparently stunned by the German artillery barrage and initially put up relatively little resistance until the Germans were at close quarters. Then a few troops rallied around Chief Petty Officer Bel'tikov, who manned a machine-gun position – his fire repulsed the first effort by III./IR 16 to rush to the top.[33] However, Alvermann led his battalion south of the Stellenberg, overran trenches held by Potapov's 3rd Company, and managed to isolate the 5th Company and other troops from Potapov's 2nd Battalion by 0550hrs. Potapov's intent to reduce casualties from the artillery bombardment resulted in too few troops deployed on the forward key positions at the critical moment, and his limited reserves could not move quickly enough to reinforce threatened sectors in broad daylight under artillery and air bombardment. Schmidt's 50. Infanterie-Division's IR 123 had quickly overrun the village of Kamyschly, while IR 31 from the 24. Infanterie-Division was attempting to advance west toward the Trapeze. Potapov was faced with a typical dilemma of battlefield command – based upon limited information from his forward units, where should he send his limited reserves and direct his brigade fire support? Due to loss of contact with their forward observers, Potapov's 120mm mortars and 76mm guns could only fire against pre-plotted engagement areas.

While all this was happening, two battalions of Oberst Ernst Haccius's IR 65 began advancing west along the Bel'bek valley in front of the Stellenberg in an effort to attack the position from all sides, but they were held up by heavy enemy fire from the Ölberg and the "Bunkerberg," both held by Major Shaslo's 747th Rifle Regiment. Automatic weapons fire was also coming from an abandoned industrial building known as "the Tomato Factory" on the south side of the Bel'bek River. The Tomato Factory was another key position since it controlled the railroad cut that led up the ridge to the Ölberg, and blocked east–west movement along the Bel'bek River. The bombed-out facility itself was held by Lieutenant Vasil'kov's machine gunners and 78 soldiers of the 5th Company of the 514th Rifle Regiment, while the 4th and 6th Companies were deployed in combat outposts north of the river. Captain Ivan A. Sharov also commanded a battery of entrenched 45mm antitank guns near the Tomato Factory. Haccius's IR 65 had the unenviable task of clearing this obstacle with little or no cover, and while under enemy fire from several directions. Once again, the Nebelwerfers proved to be the deciding factor; III./ Werfer-Regiment 54 with 18 15cm Nebelwerfer 41s was brought onto the escarpment on the north side of the Bel'bek River, and Haccius's forward observers directed fire against the Tomato Factory and the Bunkerberg.[34] Both targets were plastered with volley after volley of point-blank rocket fire. Haccius's infantry then moved in, supported by assault guns from Sturmgeschütz-Abteilung 190. This incident highlights one of the key differences between the attackers and the defenders in the third battle of Sevastopol; the Germans could generally call in timely artillery or air support to reduce strong enemy positions, but Soviet artillery was hindered by inadequate command and control, resulting in long response times and poorly directed fire missions.

Nevertheless, Sharov's antitank gunners hit four of the German assault guns, but lost six of their guns in an unequal duel. Sharov was an ideal junior officer in the Red Army: coming from a peasant background, he was a veteran of the Russo-Finnish War and a Communist Party member. The fighting around the Tomato Factory soon involved close-quarter infantry combat, but Sharov and a few others managed to make it back to the Soviet lines.[35] It proved to be a bad day for Sturmgeschütz-Abteilung 190, which had three more StuG IIIs knocked out by mines near Bel'bek, and the commander of 1. Kompanie was killed by a Soviet sniper.[36]

Choltitz's IR 16 was not stopped by the fire from the top of the Stellenberg for very long, and by 0700hrs part of the hill was secured by III./IR 16. Some naval infantrymen from the 5th Company held out for a while on top of the hill, but organized resistance was broken. Later, a few survivors from the Stellenberg managed to evade to the south and reach Soviet lines. While Choltitz continued to advance west across the top of the escarpment toward the Bunkerberg, to help IR 65, two battalions of IR 47 boldly pushed toward Potapov's second line of defense at the Eisenbahnburg. III./IR 16 soon encountered dense minefields that stopped them cold, but Major Alvermann's I./IR 47 found a gap in the Soviet defenses and managed to reach the Eisenbahnburg by 0755hrs. Alvermann's advance was assisted by at least a platoon of StuG IIIs that had crossed the Kamyschly Ravine and made it up the western escarpment and through the minefields – an amazing achievement in less than four hours. Potapov's mortar battalion was located in this area, plus two reserve rifle companies, but they were apparently stunned by the sudden appearance of German infantry and assault guns at the second line of resistance, and Alvermann's battalion succeeded in capturing the Eisenbahnburg after just 20 minutes of fighting. In the process, the 9th Battery of Smelkov's 134th Howitzer Regiment was overrun, along with an observation post with several staff officers.[37] Although only a 2-mile advance, Alvermann had cleaved Potapov's 79th NIB in two.[38]

After four hours of non-stop attacking, the 22. Infanterie-Division's regiments paused to regroup before tackling the Ölberg and the Bunkerberg, which controlled both sides of the railroad cut. Haccius's IR 65 was still tangled up in reducing the 514th Rifle Regiment strongpoint at the Tomato Factory, while IR 437 from the 132. Infanterie-Division conducted a supporting attack against the adjacent Soviet positions in the town of Bel'bek. When the German advance paused, Potapov launched a local counterattack against I./IR 47 on the Eisenbahnburg with two companies of his second battalion, but failed to recover any lost ground.[39] At 1200hrs, II./IR 65 and two battalions from Choltitz's IR 16 conducted a probing attack against the Bunkerberg, which consisted of three bunkers surrounded by a large minefield. Initially, the German infantry had difficulty breaching the minefields, and enemy sniper fire made movement difficult. Nevertheless, IR 16 secured the Bunkerberg by 1330hrs.[40]

In the early afternoon, the Soviet artillery and VVS-ChF began to intervene in the battle. Pairs of Il-2 Sturmoviks from the 18th Ground Attack Aviation Regiment began low-level strafing runs against German troops south of the Bel'bek River. Around 1315hrs, two Il-2s tried to strafe IR 47's positions at the Eisenbahnburg, but Oberfeldwebel Herbert Kaiser of 8./JG 77 pounced on them and shot both down. However, another pair of Il-2s found one of the 28cm "Schwere Bruno" railroad guns of the Eisenbahn-Artillerie-Batterie 688 and scored a direct bomb-hit on its ammunition wagon; the explosion of 22 rounds of 28cm ammunition damaged the rail gun and caused casualties among the crew.[41] Soviet artillery was also becoming increasingly effective as forward observers came back on line and directed effective fire missions into the Kamyschly Ravine, which hindered German supply columns trying to push ammunition across to their assault battalions. Aleksandr's Coastal Battery No. 30 managed to fire several 30.5mm rounds during the day, but Major von Collenberg's two Karl mortars kept lobbing 60cm rounds at the two turrets throughout the afternoon.

Hitler was keenly following the attack from his headquarters near Rastenburg and received regular updates, particularly about the activities of Dora. On X-Day, Dora fired ten 80cm rounds, including seven at a Soviet ammunition depot on the north side of Severnaya Bay known as "White Cliff." The White Cliff naval depot – so named because of the chalky cliffs – had a series of tunnel adits built into the side of the escarpment and had a number of separate munitions bunkers buried deep underground. It is often claimed that Dora scored a direct hit on White Cliff and detonated the entire storage of ammunition, but this is unlikely. Most rounds from Dora tended to be "over" the target, which meant that they landed harmlessly in Severnaya Bay. Furthermore, the depot was on a reverse slope and would have required a very high-angle plunging round or dive-bombing to hit; rounds from Dora would have been more likely to impact on the escarpment above the depot. Based upon the terrain, if the White Cliff depot was hit – and this is not confirmed by Soviet or German sources – then it was more likely from air attack than Dora. At any rate, at 1300hrs Manstein received a message relayed from Heeresgruppe Süd that, "the Führer was much upset because Dora fired at the ammunition dump 'White Cliff'. The Führer stated that this gun is only intended to fire at concrete emplacements." Oddly, the LIV Armeekorps claimed that it did not have any information about Dora firing against White Cliff and the journal indicated that someone had sent this report directly to the OKH in Berlin. Manstein told Hansen, "please determine who sent it."[42] Hitler was right to be upset that the heaviest weapon provided to AOK 11 was firing at an obscure target instead of supporting the *Schwerpunkt*, but the accuracy of Dora was so poor that it made little sense to dump 80cm projectiles on targets that were so close to German troops.

In the southern part of the Kamyschly Ravine, the German attack had not gone as well. Coming out of the Melzer ravine on the eastern side of the Kamyschly Ravine, Oberstleutnant Erich Reuter's IR 122 from the 50. Infanterie-Division had both assault battalions badly shot up by an artillery concentration from Colonel Shmelkov's 134th Howitzer Regiment. The 50. Infanterie-Division's other regiment, Oberst Albert Ringler's IR 121, had difficulty reaching the escarpment on the western side of the ravine, and the terrain was too rough for its attached assault guns to help much. Bärenfänger's III./IR 123 had made a mile-deep advance onto the escarpment but was isolated for part of the day. It was not until the late afternoon that the 50. Infanterie-Division could mount a serious attack against the Trapeze position. After heavy casualties, IR 121 captured the Trapeze at 1615hrs. However, the 24. Infanterie-Division had failed to get across the Kamyschly Ravine at all during the morning due to heavy Soviet fire and was forced to follow in the tracks of the 50. Infanterie-Division.[43] While the 50. Infanterie-Division succeeded in advancing a mile into the Soviet defensive positions on June 7 and protecting the 22. Infanterie-Division's left flank, the 24. Infanterie-Division only succeeded in capturing one minor enemy position at the cost of over 600 casualties.

Hansen was determined to capture the Ölberg on the first day of the ground offensive, but the assault battalions were tired and running short on ammunition, so the attack was put off until the late afternoon. In addition to the eight operational StuG IIIs still with Haccius's IR 65, Hansen sent Panzer-Abteilung (FL) 300 to reinforce the assault troops. This unit had 14 Pz IIIJ tanks, six KV-1 tanks captured during *Trappenjagd*, and the untried B IV and Goliath radio-controlled demolition vehicles.[44] In addition, the 132. Infanterie-Division, which had been clearing up the Soviet combat outposts along the southern side of the Bel'bek River, sent two battalions from IR 436 to reinforce Haccius's attack. At 1455hrs, Zuckertort's artillery began pounding the Ölberg for 30 minutes, followed by rolling Stuka attacks, but the infantry was not ready to move until 1730hrs. Just as the infantry assault with I./IR 65 and II./IR 65 was beginning, Zuckertort reported to Hansen that "ammunition was scarce" and that his artillery could not fully support the attack.[45] Despite a heavy pounding, the heretofore-inexperienced conscripts of the 1st Battalion, 747th Rifle Regiment, put up a good fight for the Ölberg. Although Haccius's soldiers secured a toehold on the hill by 1835hrs, fighting continued on the position until after 2100hrs. The 1st Battalion, 747th Rifle Regiment, virtually fought to the death, with most of its officers killed and two companies obliterated.[46]

Just as this German tactical success was occurring, the Soviets launched a battalion-size counterattack against IR 47's position at the Eisenbahnburg at 1805hrs. This Soviet counterattack was better planned and received strong supporting fires from division-level artillery and Morgunov's coastal batteries. After heavy fighting, the counterattack was repulsed, but Major Alvermann was killed. As night descended, the fighting tapered off as both sides began to reorganize for the next day's fight. The assault across the Kamyschly Ravine cost Hansen's LIV Armeekorps over 2,000 casualties, including 423 dead or missing. Wolff's 22. Infanterie-Division had achieved the most and bled the most, having suffered 801 casualties – equal to about a third of its assault troops. Thanks to strong artillery and air support, the 22. Infanterie-Division succeeded in breaking through the outer Soviet defenses and capturing four important fortified positions: the Stellenberg, the Bunkerberg, the Eisenbahnburg, and the Ölberg. The 22. Infanterie-Division Kriegstagebuch (war journal) noted that, "the day's fighting was characterized by extraordinary violence. The enemy showed extraordinary cunning in the division's attack on the high ground. Enemy snipers and small groups of stragglers, that had kept themselves hidden behind our lines, shot individual troops."[47]

Soviet losses in Sector III were also very heavy on the first day of the German ground offensive, with Potapov's brigade suffering about 30 percent casualties, and Laskin's 172nd Rifle Division had at least two battalions decimated. The 22. Infanterie-Division captured 153 Soviet prisoners on the first day, while overall Soviet casualties in this sector were roughly 2,000–3,000. On X-Day, Zuckertort's artillery had fired 3,939 tons of artillery ammunition – 60 percent more than that fired during the entire five-day preparation.[48] In addition, Richthofen's Fliegerkorps VIII made a maximum effort and dropped 1,300 tons of bombs on Soviet positions. Altogether, over 5,000 tons of high explosives were employed on the first day of the German ground assault, and mostly against Sevastopol's Sector III. By day's end, Hansen had begun to split the seam between Sectors III and IV. The successful assault across the Kamyschly Ravine was an impressive German tactical success that gave LIV Armeekorps the initiative and set the stage for the advance upon Severnaya Bay.

By nightfall on June 7, Petrov realized that the Germans had captured at least half of the critical high ground on the boundary of Sectors III and IV and that the enemy was now within 4½ miles of Severnaya Bay. Having had six months to prepare for this German offensive, Petrov should have had a contingency plan and the resources to mount a major counterattack against the German assault divisions, which had suffered heavy casualties and were low on ammunition. Yet ironically, Petrov had neither the plan nor the resources to deliver a timely riposte when it might have made the most difference. On paper, there were a total of 101,238 Soviet military personnel within the Sevastopol Defensive Region (SOR) at the beginning of *Störfang*.[49] Petrov's Coastal Army had seven rifle divisions with a total of 68,360 personnel, including just over 50,000 combat troops. Of Petrov's seven rifle divisions, six were already assigned to defend sectors of the outer defensive perimeter, but he managed to position Colonel Nikolai Guz's 345th Rifle Division in reserve at Mekenzievy Mountain station behind Sectors III and IV. The Black Sea Fleet contributed another 15,000 combat troops in its six naval infantry units, with the newly arrived 9th Naval Infantry Brigade assigned as the reserve for Sectors I and II in the south. This meant that Petrov started the battle with about 65,000 combat troops holding a 23-mile front, with roughly 15 percent of these deployed in sector reserve. However, Petrov had almost no reserve units under his direct control. Within Sevastopol, there were another 18,000 rear-area support and naval-base personnel, some of whom would eventually be drafted as infantry replacements, but not until the very end of the fighting. Yet it is clear that Petrov was attempting to hold too large a perimeter with insufficient forces and that he could not sustain a protracted battle with heavy casualties unless the Black Sea Fleet regularly delivered replacement units.

Nor did Petrov set a good example with his own headquarters, which was bloated with over 200 officers, many of whom should have been leading troops at the front. Before *Störfang* began, Petrov relocated his headquarters to an abandoned coastal battery on the Chersonese Peninsula south of Sevastopol – which kept him out of range of most of the German artillery, but exacerbated his already poor communications with his frontline units. Due to the limited number of tactical radios in Soviet frontline combat units, Petrov was almost totally dependent upon field telephones for command and control, which greatly delayed his reaction time to any German initiative. Most of the landlines were not buried very deep, so Zuckertort's heavy bombardment disrupted much of Petrov's connections with his frontline units. During the night of June 7/8, Petrov ordered General-Major Kolomiets, commander of Sector III, to organize a counterattack against LIV Armeekorps with the reserves located around the Mekenzievy Mountain station, but the fallacy of delegating control over the reserves to the sector commanders was revealed. Instead of using Guz's 345th Rifle Division to mount a major counterstrike, Kolomiets decided to leave Guz's division in place and commit only small forces to a counterattack, without significant artillery support. Consequently, the Soviet counterattack at dawn on June 8 was little more than a pathetic gesture, consisting only of the 1st Battalion of the 2nd Perekop Naval Infantry Regiment and six T-26 light tanks from the 81st Separate Tank Battalion. Furthermore, rather than attempting to recover any of the heights overlooking the Bel'bek River, Kolomiets misdirected this counterattack toward the Trapeze position in order to relieve some of the units from his own 25th Rifle Division that had been encircled. This puny effort struck II./IR 32 and accomplished nothing.[50] It is also a good example of how Soviet commanders tended to make decisions that benefited their own command, rather than their overall objectives. Often, Soviet commanders assumed that "someone else" would deal with German breakthroughs, and selfishly conserved their own resources.

Hansen waited until 1000hrs before resuming his offensive, allowing his forward troops time to receive ammunition and rations. Zuckertort's HArko 306 provided a 30-minute artillery preparation, focused on the Mekenzievy Mountain station area and the western end of Haccius Ridge. The German attack on July 8 was more narrowly focused than on the previous day, relying once again upon Wolff's 22. Infanterie-Division as the *Schwerpunkt*, reinforced by IR 437 from the 132. Infanterie-Division. The battered regiments of Laskin's 172nd Rifle Division still held good ground in front of them, but no longer had a continuous front, and were defeated in detail. IR 437 pushed west from the Ölberg along Haccius Ridge, rolling up the 514th Rifle Regiment's positions, while Wolff's three infantry regiments and a battalion's worth of assault guns smashed through the remnants of the 383rd Rifle Regiment and advanced 1¼ miles southward from the Ölberg. The lead German battalions advanced to within 600 yards of the Mekenzievy Mountain station and were not stopped until they ran into the second line of defense held by Guz's division, which was situated behind a 2-mile-long antitank ditch. However, Guz could do nothing for the collapsing right flank of Colonel Aleksandr G. Kapitokhin's Sector IV. Kapitokhin's troops had been little engaged on the first day of the German offensive and he still had the bulk of his 95th Rifle Division defending positions north of the Bel'bek River. With German infantry advancing deeply into his right flank and heading toward Coastal Battery No. 30, Kapitokhin was forced to pull a battalion from his 241st Rifle Regiment to block IR 437's advance. Altogether the 22. Infanterie-Division took 232 prisoners on June 8, mostly from Laskin's 172nd Rifle Division.[51] Meanwhile, the German 50. and 24. Infanterie-Divisionen continued to push back Potapov's 79th NIB and the 25th Rifle Division on Kolomiets's right flank. At the cost of another 1,745 casualties, Hansen had gained a firm foothold in Sevastopol's outer defenses.

Oddly, Guz had only his 1163rd Rifle Regiment on the line, defending behind the antitank ditch and centered upon the Mekenzievy Mountain station, while he kept the 1165th and 1167th Rifle Regiments further south, near the position known as Fort Stalin. Although many Russian officers were prejudiced against the ethnic Caucasian troops in this unit, the division had performed well in stopping the German offensive in December 1941. Since then, Guz's riflemen had transformed the bombed-out artillery barracks west of the train station into a fortified strongpoint, and they manned a half-dozen bunkers overlooking the antitank ditch. Another key position – called the "Forsthaus" by the Germans – was located on the boundary of Guz's 345th Rifle Division and Potapov's depleted 79th NIB, but held by the 2nd Perekop Naval Infantry Regiment. Most of the Soviet artillery in this sector was still intact, even though Smelkov's 134th Howitzer Regiment had lost one battery and Soviet artillerymen were told to "fire sparingly."[52]

On June 9, Hansen kept up the pressure, beginning with a bombardment of the Mekenzievy Mountain station area with 60cm, 42cm, 35.5cm, and 24cm heavy-artillery fire from Zuckertort's *Heeresartillerie*. Most of the Soviet bunkers were made of timber and stones and could not withstand a direct hit from large-caliber rounds. Then, instead of using Wolff's 22. Infanterie-Division as his main effort, as in the previous two days, Hansen brought up the relatively fresh IR 438 from Generalmajor Fritz Lindemann's 132. Infanterie-Division to mount a deliberate attack across the western end of the antitank ditch. Guz had been expecting Choltitz's IR 16 and Buhse's IR 47 to continue their direct advance down the rail line toward the station, and was caught by surprise by the German tactical flexibility in switching the *Schwerpunkt* from one unit to another. Infanterie-Regiment 438 attacked the antitank ditch near the boundary between the 95th and 345th Rifle Divisions – a typical German effort to exploit the weaknesses of Soviet inter-unit coordination. Two German battalions crossed the ditch and quickly overwhelmed the Soviet infantrymen from the 1163rd Regiment, who were still reeling from the effects of heavy artillery. Using rolling Stuka attacks that lasted for over an hour, Richthofen's Fliegerkorps VIII also disrupted Guz's ability to shift his reserves to deal with the German breakthrough on his left flank. Once the Germans were across the antitank ditch, they began spreading out laterally to roll up Guz's forward defense, while pioneers began filling in the ditch. Once this was accomplished, assault guns moved up to support the soldiers. With the Soviet defensive line tottering, Wolff attacked with his 22. Infanterie-Division, and Guz's entire line began to give way. Choltitz's IR 16 surged across the antitank ditch and overran the Mekenzievy Mountain station and the artillery barracks, despite the presence there of a battery of four 76.2mm antitank guns from the 674th Anti-Tank Regiment. The German advance was so rapid that a number of Russian artillery officers were captured near the train station. Under interrogation, they revealed a great deal about the location and condition of the Soviet artillery to the 22. Infanterie-Division's Ic (intelligence officer).[53] On Choltitz's left flank, Buhse's IR 47 advanced, pushing back the 2nd Perekop NIR. The 50. Infanterie-Division mounted a supported attack that captured the Forsthaus from the 79th NIB. Between the train station and the Forsthaus, German troops encountered Soviet Coastal Battery 704, which was equipped with two 130mm turrets from the sunken cruiser *Chervona*

Ukraina. Commanded by Lieutenant V. I. Durikov, the battery put up a good fight against the German infantry and assault guns, but it was eventually overrun and Pavlov was killed.[54]

The third day of the German ground offensive ended as another stunning tactical success everywhere except on the flanks. In the west, the 95th Rifle Division stood like a rock atop the "Neuhaus" hill and its 241st Rifle Regiment repulsed efforts by the 132. Infanterie-Division to reach Coastal Battery No. 30. Hansen's main effort had broken through a portion of the Soviet second defense line and captured 381 prisoners at the relatively low cost of 961 casualties, including 216 dead or missing.[55]

Hansen's corps had achieved remarkable success in the first three days of the ground offensive. The only really discordant note came from the 24. Infanterie-Division, which had consistently underperformed, while suffering excessive casualties. Generalleutnant Hans von Tettau's 24. Infanterie-Division had fought a nearly private battle with Kolomiets' ostensibly elite 25th Rifle Division *Chapaevskaya*. The terrain in this sector was very hilly and wooded, which made tactical movements slow and costly, and greatly aided the defense. Nor had Tettau's division been allocated as much artillery or air support, since they were assigned only a supporting role. Yet there was little doubt that the *Chapaevskaya* had given Tettau's division a bloody nose.

What was the condition of the frontline infantry units on each side after three days of intensive combat? Most infantrymen had got by on only a few hours of sleep in the past 72 hours, and poor-quality sleep at that, although experienced troops could sleep in the bottom of trenches or bunkers despite ongoing bombardments. As Obergefreiter Gottlob Bidermann in IR 437 remembered, "one lived only on cigarettes, cold coffee, tea, and the sparse battle rations that were issued daily to those in the foremost lines. It was impossible to wash regularly or to shave."[56] Thus, filthy, sleep-deprived, and underfed troops were expected to continue expending enormous amounts of energy and maintain combat alertness, day after day. A battle like Sevastopol became an endurance contest, won by the side with the best stamina. While Guz's 345th Rifle Division had not yet suffered heavy losses, Laskin's 172nd Rifle Division had been broken into pieces and was only fighting as uncoordinated company and battalion-size battle groups. Potapov's 79th NIB had lost roughly half its strength but was still holding the line near the Forsthaus, along with a battalion from the 2nd Perekop NIR. In Sector IV, the 95th Rifle Division had been forced to reform its flank into an L-shaped defense, but was still solid despite the destruction of one of its battalions. Soviet troops were still fighting tenaciously and the Germans had taken only 1,509 prisoners in this area. On the German side, some accounts have attempted to depict the German infantry as burnt-out after a few days of combat, but their losses – while heavy – were not unexpected. Hansen's LIV Armeekorps suffered 6,024 casualties, including 1,383 dead or missing, or about 13 percent losses from its starting strength of 45,500 combat troops.[57] Wolff's 22. Infanterie-Division, which had been rebuilt to nearly full strength before the battle, still had over 11,600 troops in the line. Hansen's main concern was with the understrength 132. Infanterie-Division, which was unable to break through the 95th Rifle Division's defenses in front of Coastal Battery No. 30. In order to reinvigorate this effort, Hansen brought up Oberst Otto Hitzfeld's Infanterie-Regiment 213 from reserve; once again, Hitzfeld would be employed to spearhead a critical attack. Despite heavy casualties, both sides' troops still had plenty of fight left in them.

The battle slowed down on June 10 as Hansen redistributed and reorganized his forces, but Buhse's IR 47 was able to gain some ground in conjunction with the 50. Infanterie-Division near the Forsthaus. Hansen adopted an economy-of-force stance against the Soviet Sector IV, bringing the entire 132. Infanterie-Division and Hitzfeld's regiment to crush the 95th Rifle Division's forces south of the Bel'bek River while leaving only reconnaissance troops to screen the 2-mile-wide front against the Soviet positions still north of the river. It would have been prudent for Petrov to order Kapitokhin to pull his 95th Rifle Division back toward Coastal Battery No. 30 and abandon the positions north of the river, which now served no purpose, but he was unwilling to voluntarily cede ground to the enemy. Instead, Petrov believed that Hansen's divisions were spent and overextended and that a major counterattack could retake much of the lost ground. Soviet tactical reporting was often flagrantly dishonest at this stage of the war, in an effort to conceal setbacks from superiors, and Petrov apparently accepted exaggerated reports from his frontline divisions. Whereas Hansen and Manstein were observing the battlefield every day from observation posts like the "Eagle's Nest," Petrov was out of touch in his distant bunker.

On the morning of June 11, a series of Soviet counterattacks did develop against Hansen's frontline divisions. Potapov's 79th NIB attacked the 50. Infanterie-Division's positions near the Forsthaus and some naval infantrymen managed to penetrate 600 yards before being stopped by German artillery fire and the assault guns from Sturmgeschütz-Abteilung 190. Although the armored train *Zhelezniakov* supported the attack with its three 76mm guns, coordination with two artillery regiments assigned to support the attack was ineffective because the naval infantrymen lacked tactical radios. Guz committed two battalions from his reserve regiments, the 1165th and 1167th Rifle Regiments, but their efforts to advance toward the Mekenzievy Mountain station were repulsed. Kapitokhin staged a two-battalion counterattack against the 132. Infanterie-Division's IR 437, which gained a little ground, but otherwise changed little. However, the main result of the disjointed Soviet counterattacks – none of which were properly coordinated – was that Soviet infantrymen emerging out in the open were exposed to German air attacks and artillery fire. Richthofen's pilots scattered antipersonnel bombs over attacking Soviet units, causing heavy casualties. Once the Soviet counterattacks were spent, Hansen ordered Wolff to hit Guz's reeling division, and Buhse's IR 47 managed to advance nearly half a mile, while Choltitz's IR 16 got close to Fort Stalin. Buhse's forward units were now about a mile from the northern shore of Severnaya Bay and even closer to the railroad tunnel next to a road loop known as the Serpentine; inside the tunnel were a number of headquarters units, artillerymen, engineers, and supply troops. At great cost, Hansen had succeeded in driving a deep wedge into Petrov's Sector III.

Despite much talk of "fortress Sevastopol" for propaganda purposes, Petrov's remaining defenses north of Severnaya Bay were really just a ramshackle collection of fortified hilltops, badly knocked-about coastal batteries, and archaic forts left over from the Crimean War. Guz's 345th Rifle Division's defense was now based upon a bevy of positions known as "Stalin," "Volga," "Siberia," "Molotov," "GPU," and "Ural." Virtually none of these positions were designed to repel ground attacks, and certainly not from the north. Choltitz's IR 16 had attacked the so-called "Fort Stalin" in December 1941 and failed, but that was due to fading German strength rather than the strength of the position itself. Hansen's next step was to eliminate Fort Stalin, from which Soviet observers were directing fire on the train station below, and then to move against Coastal Battery No. 30.

Ironically, Lieutenant Nikolai A. Vorobyev, the heroic commander of the 365th Antiaircraft Battery atop the 60-yard-high hill known by the Germans as Fort Stalin, was seriously wounded by artillery fragments on the first day of the German ground offensive and evacuated. He was replaced by Lieutenant Ivan S. Pyanzin. The battery consisted of four 76mm antiaircraft guns, mounted on concrete pads, but without overhead cover. The battery had been fortified with a small concrete command bunker in the center of a circular perimeter and three concrete pillboxes with machine guns on its eastern and southern perimeter, while its 60 personnel were provided with underground shelters and slit trenches. Furthermore, the troops were almost all veterans, and deliberately included a number of handpicked communists. A 4-yard-wide barbed-wire obstacle belt surrounded the position, as well as some wooden antipersonnel mines. For close support, Guz assigned the 1st Battalion/1165th Rifle Regiment to defend the approaches to the battery. While the 365th Antiaircraft Battery was fortified, it certainly was no fort, since it did not have all-round protection. Dorahad fired six 80cm rounds at the battery but without much effect; one round fell within 38 yards of one of the flak-gun positions, but the others missed by 140–280 yards.[58]

Hansen began "softening up" Fort Stalin on the afternoon of June 12 with a series of Stuka attacks, followed by 11 42cm rounds – which knocked out three of the four antiaircraft guns. In the evening, the 22. Infanterie-Division concentrated all its guns against Fort Stalin, supplemented by a battery each of 30.5cm and 21cm mortars. The bombardment also struck Fort Volga, a Soviet antiaircraft machine-gun position located further south on the same hill as Fort Stalin. Wolff selected Choltitz's IR 16 to assault Fort Stalin since this regiment had consistently displayed great tactical aggressiveness and ingenuity in overcoming fortified positions since the fighting at Perekop nine months before. Despite the loss of five company commanders since June 7, Choltitz still had 813 combat-ready troops available and his men had been given a brief rest in reserve. However, Choltitz decided not to employ all his troops for this attack, but only the best leaders and troops, in two carefully tailored assault battalions. He selected Major Johannes Arndt's I./IR 16 as his main effort; in addition to 105 infantrymen in three companies, Arndt was provided with five StuG III assault guns from Hauptmann Cäsar's 1./Sturmgeschütz-Abteilung 190, 35 engineers from Oberleutnant Heyer's 3./Pionier-Bataillon 744, and a *Panzerjäger* team with two 3.7cm Pak guns. Hauptmann Hermann-Albert Schrader's III./IR 16 would follow and support Arndt's battalion with two infantry companies and one machine-gun company, totaling 89 infantrymen and 20 engineers. Thus the assault force comprised only 194 infantrymen and 55 engineers.[59] Choltitz also formed a fire-support *Kampfgruppe* with the machine gunners of Oberleutnant Nahrwold's 14. Kompanie and regimental 7.5cm and 15cm infantry guns to suppress the enemy mortars suspected to be located in the so-called Wolf's Ravine southeast of Fort Stalin. After briefing Arndt and Schrader on the attack plan, Choltitz moved with two of his battalions to an assembly area near the train station, while the heavy artillery was pounding Fort Stalin during the afternoon of July 12.

German artillery continued to pound Fort Stalin during the night of June 12/13. At 0300hrs on June 13, Choltitz ordered his two assault battalions to begin moving toward the hill. The plan was for Arndt's battalion to infiltrate up the hillside in small groups, but soldiers from 1st Battalion/1165th Rifle Regiment were alert, and detected them. The Red Army soldiers responded with flares, then automatic-weapons fire at the intruders. Under the glare of the dangling pyrotechnics, they also called for mortar fire from the battery hidden in the Wolf's Ravine. Arndt's soldiers began to suffer heavy casualties – including his two lead company commanders – so he shifted westward to avoid the worst of the enemy fire, but ran into Schrader's battalion in the dark. The two battalions became mixed up, as often happens in a night attack, and the situation became very confused. Via radio, Arndt requested that Choltitz use Nahrwold's fire-support group to suppress the enemy mortars and machine gunners, but they were not successful. Yet this was one of those critical moments where the training of the German small-unit leaders really paid off. Sorting out the two battalions while under fire, the remaining officers and sergeants reorganized assault groups and closed in on the antiaircraft battery at the top of the hill. Cäsar's assault guns moved up the hill too, with infantry moving alongside and behind. The Soviet troops bravely defended their positions, but rather passively, letting the Germans come to them.

Once the German *Stossgruppen* reached the northern perimeter of Fort Stalin, Heyer's pioneers took over and began to blast holes in the barbed wire. The three machine-gun bunkers could not cover this angle, so the obstacle was only defended by small-arms fire. By 0400hrs several groups of German infantry had entered the perimeter and begun to assault each bunker with hand grenades and satchel charges. It turned out that the Soviets had reinforced their positions with tree trunks, which absorbed a great amount of any blast. In one case, soldiers from Schrader's battalion simply piled large stones against a bunker door, sealing the occupants within. German pioneers had some success using smoke grenades to flush Soviet troops out of underground shelters, who were mostly shot down as they emerged. Only 14 prisoners were taken on Fort Stalin.[60] The assault guns were able to approach and engage some of the outer timber fighting positions and blast them with 7.5cm high-explosive rounds, but they could not reach the three inner machine-gun bunkers. Instead, the Germans brought up their *Panzerjäger* team, who dragged a 3.7cm Pak gun up the hill and through one of the breaches. Using the new Stielgranate 41 hollow-charge round, they attacked each bunker from behind at a range of only 15 yards and blew their back doors off. Close combat and hand-to-hand fighting continued within Fort Stalin's small perimeter for 90 minutes, but by 0530 Soviet resistance was broken. A few Soviet positions, including Pyanzin's command bunker, held out for another ten hours. Pyanzin maintained a tenuous radio link with his battalion headquarters and he requested artillery fire on his own position, for which he later received the Hero of the Soviet Union. However, Heyer's pioneers gradually moved in and blew in the sides of his bunker around 1530hrs, silencing Pyanzin forever.

The assault troops had suffered heavily, and every officer in Major Arndt's battalion was either dead or wounded, so Choltitz sent the battalion adjutant, Oberleutnant Bringewatt, up the hill to reorganize the survivors. It is axiomatic that after seizing a well-defended position, the attackers must immediately prepare a hasty defense and reorganize their depleted forces, lest an enemy counterattack retake the position before the victors have regained their composure. It was not long before the Soviets realized that Fort Stalin had fallen. Fort Volga, located 465 yards southwest of Stalin, began to fire mortars and antitank fire at the Germans, who were now visible in the light of dawn. Three assault guns were quickly hit – one being destroyed – and the others were obliged to withdraw back down the hill. Yet the 2nd Battalion/1165th Rifle Regiment, which was located at Fort Volga, made no effort to intervene in the fight for Fort Stalin. Around 0630hrs a small Soviet counterattack was launched out of the "Wolf's

Ravine" on the east side of Stalin, but was repulsed with machine-gun fire from Nahrwold's support group. Soviet divisional artillery batteries also began to pound Fort Stalin, and this fire killed Hauptmann Schrader, who had previously been awarded the *Ritterkreuz*. Choltitz declared Fort Stalin secured around 0700hrs although mopping-up continued for the rest of the day. The assault had cost his regiment 32 killed, 136 wounded, and two missing – about half of the infantry committed. Virtually all of the German infantry officers in the attack had become casualties, including Arndt. By noon, Arndt's I./IR 16 had only 45 infantrymen still combat-ready on the objective out of the 105 that began the attack. Companies were reduced to just 15–17 soldiers, led by a *Feldwebel*.[61] Surprisingly, Generalmajor Wolff made his way to the top of the exposed hill in order to congratulate the assault troops and to personally hand out iron crosses to the survivors, including Hauptmann Cäsar.[62] In contrast, Petrov was so far removed from this critical point that he failed to realize how weak the Germans were on Fort Stalin, and thus failed to launch even a battalion-size counterattack from nearby positions, even though Guz's 345th Rifle Division still had plenty of troops in the area. It is apparent that German senior leadership at Sevastopol was more "hands-on" than on the Soviet side, and that this contributed to the outcome.

With Fort Stalin taken, Hansen turned to deal with Sector IV and the stubborn 95th Rifle Division, as well as Coastal Battery No. 30. Kapitokhin's 95th Rifle Division had built strong defensive positions atop a prominent ridge just 600 yards east of Captain Aleksandr's fortified command post known as Bastion I. Soviet troops still held the north–south stretch of antitank ditch in this sector and they had an advantage in terms of holding the high ground – any German movement brought instant fire. Nor did the introduction of Hitzfeld's IR 213 improve the German situation in this sector, and the regiment suffered over 400 casualties between June 11 and June 13, which was half as much as they lost at Perekop in September 1941. Indeed, the Soviet 90th and 161st Rifle Regiments kept repeatedly counterattacking Hitzfeld's positions atop Haccius Ridge and even succeeded in pushing them back several hundred yards on June 13. In response, II. and III./IR 437 from the 132. Infanterie-Division mounted a night attack on June 14 that succeeded in capturing the Neuhaus Heights from the 241st Rifle Regiment and threatened to outflank the ridge defenses protecting Aleksandr's Coastal Battery No. 30.

Obergefreiter Gottlob H. Bidermann, serving as a *Panzerjäger* in IR 437, was part of this push against the 95th Rifle Division's flank and described how "each foot of ground was hotly contested in attempts to capture the commanding Neuhaus heights." He also mentioned that, "the dead from both sides lay thick in the ravines and due to the danger from enemy snipers they could not be removed or recovered for burial. The oppressive heat soon bore with it the sickly sweet smell of decaying flesh."[63] Military historians rarely mention how a battlefield smells, but to the infantrymen on both sides at Sevastopol, the stench of unburied corpses was certainly one of their most poignant memories.

Once the Neuhaus Hill was captured, the 132. Infanterie-Division committed elements of IR 436 to exploit this success by pushing further west toward the next ridgeline. Oberfeldwebel Popp, from 10./IR 436, was in the lead assault squad and he encountered a deeply entrenched position with 13 concrete-and-earth bunkers. Initially, the Soviets were surprised by this sudden appearance of German troops and their resistance was ineffective. It was a confused pre-dawn action, fought at close quarters, and Popp soon found himself isolated from his company and in the middle of an alerted Soviet position. Gathering up a mixed unit of German troops who had fought their way into the Soviet trench system, including Obergefreiter Mersch from 2./IR 436, Popp tried to hold the position until German reinforcements arrived, but the Soviets counterattacked in force and overwhelmed them. Both Popp and Mersch were reported missing in action.[64] During the course of Operation *Störfang*, AOK 11 reported over 1,500 of its troops as missing in action.

Although most Soviet troops were still fighting tenaciously, there was an increasing number of Red Army soldiers deserting to the enemy after the fall of Fort Stalin. German intelligence officers were quick to note that many of the Ukrainians, Georgians, Chechens, and other minority recruits from the Caucasus were less than enthusiastic to serve in the Red Army or sacrifice themselves for Sevastopol. On the night of June 14/15, Serzhant Nikolai Voroshun, a flak soldier, crossed the lines and provided a great deal of information about the location of the remaining Soviet artillery in the sector, which assisted LIV Armeekorps in preparing its push westward toward Coastal Battery No. 30.[65] Kapitokhin had responded to Lindemann's economy-of-force move of withdrawing all but his reconnaissance troops from the positions north of the Bel'bek River by doing exactly the same – which allowed him to concentrate all his infantry south of the river. If Manstein had another regiment available, this would have been an excellent time to strike the thinned-out left flank of Sector IV, but he did not. Instead, it was Petrov who sent some of his last reserves – the half-strength 1st and 2nd Battalions of the 7th Naval Infantry Brigade – to reinforce the weakened front line near the Neuhaus. By June 15, Kapitokhin had six battalions deployed on a 1¼-mile-wide north–south front, from the bombed-out artillery barracks to the Bel'bek River, against Hansen's nine battalions.

After a week of intense ground combat, Hansen's strength was beginning to fade. Zuckertort's artillery was still providing daily artillery bombardments, but the heaviest weapons such as the 60cm Karl mortars and the pair of 42cm howitzers had expended all their ammunition by June 13. The Soviet troops in Sectors III and IV had taken hard knocks, but were still holding their ground. Manstein was concerned that the German offensive might culminate before reaching Severnaya Bay due to heavy casualties, so he ordered Hansen to reinvigorate his main effort by stripping forces from less essential areas. Since the 24. Infanterie-Division was achieving little in its sector, Hansen shifted Tettau's division onto the defense and transferred battalions from IR 31 and IR 102 to reinforce the 132. Infanterie-Division's front. Manstein directed the Romanian 4th Mountain Division to take over the front line formerly held by these troops. In addition, Manstein transferred I. and III./IR 97 from the idle 46. Infanterie-Division, which was once again guarding Kerch. Thus, Lindemann's 132. Infanterie-Division would have 12 or more infantry battalions to use against the flank of Kapitokhin's division. On June 15, Hansen pulled some of his battalions out of the line briefly to refit and prepare for the next offensive pulse. He intended to mount an all-out attack with both the 22. and 132. Infanterie-Divisionen and all the support he could muster in order to reach Severnaya Bay.

Despite ferocious resistance for over a week, Kapitokhin's troops were in worse shape than Hansen's, and he barely had 1,000 troops in the five battalions guarding the approaches to Coastal Battery No. 30. Hundreds of his wounded had been brought inside the reinforced concrete block of Bastion I, which was proof against virtually all the German artillery. Kapitokhin's division was bleeding to death, and he was now holding too much frontage with too few men. The real weak spot in the defense lay south of the Neuhaus Heights, where the remnants of Laskin's 172nd Division held the positions known as Molotov, GPU, Siberia and Volga. Guz's 345th Rifle Division had suffered significant losses but was still the strongest Soviet unit on the north side of Severnaya Bay – unfortunately, it was in the wrong place. Most of Guz's division was focused on opposing the slow advance of the 50. Infanterie-Division toward the railroad tunnels near the Serpentine (a section of the main road that consisted of several hairpin turns), but this area was not a priority for the Germans. Petrov also committed his only fresh unit – Major Petr Zielinski's 138th Naval Infantry Brigade – to this sector as well. Zielinski's brigade had been brought to Sevastopol by two convoys between June 12 and June 15 and was not ready to be sent to the front until June 16. On paper, 138 NIB was a very strong formation, with four 716-man rifle battalions, a battalion of 16 76mm guns, two mortar battalions, and an antitank battalion. However, many of the ethnic Caucasian troops in the unit were not particularly loyal to the Soviet regime, and morale was a problem from the moment they arrived in Sevastopol.

Instead of beginning his all-out assault with the usual artillery bombardment from Zuckertort's *Heeresartillerie*, Hansen opted for the subtlety of infiltration tactics. At 0200hrs on June 17, *Stossgruppen* from II. and III./IR 213 and Pionier-Bataillon 132 began infiltrating through the 95th Rifle Division's thinly held front and headed straight for Bastion I. Infantrymen moving stealthily at night move very slowly, often pausing if contact with the enemy appears possible, and it took these assault troops over five hours to move 600 yards. Nevertheless, as the sun began to rise, the troops were within sight of their objective. Meanwhile, the rest of the 132. Infanterie-Division mounted a full-scale attack at 0700hrs with artillery support that kept the rest of the 95th Rifle Division's frontline units occupied. Four battalions from Tettau's 24. Infanterie-Division attacked the 172nd Rifle Division's front, along with IR 65 and IR 16 from 22. Infanterie-Division, and quickly overwhelmed Laskin's paper-thin defenses. Hansen provided these *Stossgruppen* with considerable armored support: 19 StuG III assault guns from Sturmgeschütz-Abteilung 190, a similar number from Sturmgeschütz-Abteilung 197, and two companies of Pz IIIJ tanks from Panzer-Abteilung (FL) 300. Fort Siberia, which was originally an earthen redoubt built by the Russians during the Crimean War, was taken by surprise and overrun by an infiltration attack by III./IR 65 at 0710hrs. The neighboring Fort GPU was overrun by I./IR 31, with some help from Panzer-Abteilung (FL) 300 and a *Kampfgruppe* of Brandenburg infiltrators, at 0700hrs. For the first time, German pioneers used the new BIV remote-control demolition vehicles in combat, but with disappointing results; one exploded prematurely and two were lost on mines. Two of the control Pz IIIJ tanks were also destroyed on mines. Fort Molotov, which was an antiaircraft command post built in the early 1930s, consisted of an octagonal perimeter with a dense barbed-wire obstacle belt and some concrete bunkers, but no heavy weapons. I./IR 102 overran Molotov at 0945hrs, then pressed on to take Battery "Cheka." Once Laskin's front was shattered, the German advance surged toward Bartenyevka and Severnaya Bay. The 22. Infanterie-Division also began rolling up the 345th Rifle Division's open left flank, enabling IR 16 to capture the antiaircraft position at Fort Volga by 1930hrs.

Around 1100hrs, three battalions from IR 436 and 437 broke through the 95th Rifle Division's right flank, overran the forward trenches of the 514th Rifle Regiment, and advanced boldly toward the sea. By 1200hrs, Kapitokhin's entire flank had given way, and he ordered the remnants of his division to fall back toward Coastal Battery No. 12 (also known as Battery Schishkovka). However, 21 soldiers from the 1st Battalion, 90th Rifle Regiment fell back toward Bastion I. Altogether there were about 200 Soviet troops, including Aleksandr's remaining battery personnel and a medical team with six female medics, sheltered in or around his fortified command post.[66] In addition to the command post, Bastion I included the battery's large rangefinder and a transformer substation, both of which had been knocked out by the shelling. Bastion I was equipped with an electrical elevator and stairs that led 40 yards below ground to an underground tunnel, which connected it to the gun block 710 yards away. In between the Bastion I and the gun block, there was a large underground air-raid shelter. Aside from the two 305mm gun turrets, most of the gun block was buried underground and protected by a thick layer of dirt and concrete that even "Thor's" 60cm shells could not penetrate. According to Soviet accounts, at least one turret under the command of Chief Petty Officer F. P. Dovbysh was still operational and firing as the battle surged toward it, but even if correct, the turrets were designed to engage enemy battleships miles away, not small groups of infantrymen 100 yards away. Furthermore, the battery was almost out of ammunition.[67]

Initially, the two battalions of IR 213 that had broken through to Coastal Battery No. 30 focused on mopping up the outlying enemy infantry positions around Bastion I. Gradually, the Soviet troops fell back into the underground complex, ceding the surface to the Germans by mid-afternoon on June 17. The Germans requested an airstrike to neutralize any remaining resistance nests, and at 1530hrs 27 Ju-87 Stukas attacked the battery; one bomb scored a direct hit on the eastern turret and disabled it. Once the surface of the battery was secure, Hitzfeld's infantrymen turned to 1./Pionier-Bataillon 173 to reduce the trapped Soviet troops inside the battery. Initial attempts with flamethrowers and satchel charges proved ineffective against the thick concrete hide of the Bastion, and the pioneers settled in for a long siege. One group focused on breaking into Aleksandr's command post in Bastion I, while another group worked to attack the turrets themselves. Inside the battery, Aleksandr and his men could do little, since all four exits were covered by enemy machine-gun teams.[68] Furthermore, a large proportion of his men were either wounded or had no close-combat experience. By the end of June 17, Hansen had achieved another dramatic success and virtually demolished the Soviet forces in Sector IV. His corps had suffered another 836 casualties, but the battle on the north side of Severnaya Bay had been decided.

The Germans knew that a Soviet naval convoy had recently brought the fresh 138th Naval Infantry Brigade into Sevastopol, and Hansen moved quickly to mop up resistance on the north side of Severnaya Bay before Petrov could introduce these reinforcements. His first order of business was to eliminate Coastal Battery No. 12 (Battery Schishkovka) and the remnants of Kapitokhin's 95th Division, which were dug in around the battery. It consisted of four 152mm coastal guns mounted on-line in open-air pedestal mounts, but by the time German troops approached all four were inoperative. Instead, the strength of the position lay in its reinforced concrete casemates and underground shelters, which had been reinforced with trenches, earthworks, and belts of barbed wire. The combined force of naval gunners and infantrymen was armed with five heavy and 18 light machine guns. Lindemann's 132. Infanterie-Division planned a deliberate assault against the battery with IR 436 and two pioneer companies. The German after-action report describes the assault in vivid detail:

The battalion ordered that a platoon from the 2. Pionier-Kompanie would lead the 132. Infanterie-Division's assault. Oberfeldwebel Palle contacted IR 436 and told the platoon leaders to be ready immediately for removing mines or assault operations. At 1100hrs, the platoon and the regiment attacked the northeast side of the heavily reinforced work. Oberfeldwebel Palle captured three large shelters and penetrated into the position, regardless of the violent defensive fire and became involved in close combat.

Despite the pressure of strong enemy counterattacks and heavy flanking fire from the southern forts and the surrounding field positions, Oberfeldwebel Palle was able to hold the northern part of the work. On instructions from the division in the afternoon, the pionier force was reinforced with the rest of the 2. Pionier-Kompanie [under Oberleutnant Heinz-Peter Wack] for the capture of the work.

After equipping itself with plentiful pionier weapons, the company attacked the northern part of the battery at 1900hrs. Simultaneously, part of IR 436 and IR 437 advanced and attacked the field positions on the east and west sides of the work.

With exemplary boldness, Oberleutnant Wack led the assault platoon from the front and penetrated into the work despite strong enemy defensive fire from the south. Again and again they succeeded, by combining the firepower of our companies even against strong flanking fire from machine guns and riflemen … and meter by meter, the fortifications were silenced.[69]

Wack's pioneers were unable to complete the conquest of the battery by nightfall and spent the night involved in close combat. At dawn, Wack led a platoon-size raid that overwhelmed the remaining defenders and captured the battery. Most of the garrison fought to the death, but 36 naval gunners emerged from an underground shelter and surrendered. Wack's company had suffered eight dead or missing and 14 wounded in the assault, but demonstrated the kind of small-unit leadership and aggressiveness that wins battles. Immediately after the fall of the battery, both IR 436 and IR 437 were pulled out of the line to refit. Gottlob Bidermann noted that by this point his division was spent, and that one company was reduced to only two NCOs and a few enlisted men.[70] While the 132. Infanterie-Division eliminated Coastal Battery No. 12 and the remnants of the 95th Rifle Division, the 24. Infanterie-Division cleared the town of Bartenyevka and closed in on the final cluster of Soviet-held fortifications on the north side of Severnaya Bay.

Meanwhile, the engineers of 1./Pionier-Bataillon 173 spent June 18 trying to demolish Coastal Battery No. 30's two damaged 305mm turrets with fuel drums and satchel charges, but they succeeded only in causing cracks in the armored plates on the turrets. Unable to force their way into Bastion I, even with flamethrowers, the German engineers did succeed in damaging the air-handling system, and the underground bunkers soon filled with smoke. At first a few soot-covered Soviet soldiers emerged from an exit, then more, until 108 had surrendered. However, Aleksandr remained inside with about 90 more that refused to surrender.

Petrov did commit Major Petr P. Zelinsky's 138th Naval Infantry Brigade to try and regain some ground on the northern side of Severnaya Bay on June 18, but in typical fashion the counterattack was poorly planned. Only three of Zelinsky's four rifle battalions had arrived near the Serpentine when the attack was ordered and almost none of his artillery. His infantrymen attacked the 22. Infanterie-Division's combat outposts, which simply pulled back to their main line of resistance (known as the *Hauptkampflinie*, or HKL) and called in copious amounts of artillery fire upon Zelinsky's naval infantrymen. All three attacking battalions were decimated and forced to retreat, leaving 400 prisoners for the Germans. This ill-advised and hasty attack crippled Petrov's last major intact unit on the northern side of Severnaya Bay.

On June 19, two battalions from IR 97 moved southwest from Coastal Battery No. 12, with their right flank on the Black Sea. Enemy resistance was fairly light, but the German troops were increasingly wary of mines by this point and the infantry was unwilling to advance too far without engineer support. Engineers were still busy reducing Coastal Battery No. 30 as well as mopping up Battery No. 12, so only 1./Pionier-Bataillon 132 was initially available to support the advance of IR 97. By the afternoon of June 19 the German infantry came within sight of the North Fort, a large octagonal fort that was built before the Crimean War. Adjoining the west side of the North Fort was the position known as Lenin (a fortified antiaircraft battalion command post) and Coastal Battery No. 2 (equipped with four 100mm guns). Although the idea of a hasty attack was considered, the Germans decided to wait until they had sufficient artillery and engineer support to mount a proper deliberate attack on the morning of June 20. The attack began at 0900hrs, with two pioneer companies in the lead. Howitzer batteries were brought up to fire directly at the fort. It took nine hours of fighting to break into Lenin and the North Fort, but it took until 1030hrs on June 21 before these objectives were secure. The pioneers and assault guns were the key players in these mop-up battles, which tended to resemble urban warfare. Another result of these actions was that a good portion of Sevastopol's air-defense umbrella was overrun at Lenin, Molotov, Volga, and Stalin, which allowed Fliegerkorps VIII to completely dominate the skies over the battlefield.

Once the North Fort fell, Petrov ordered all remaining Soviet troops to evacuate the north side of Severnaya Bay, and German troops reached the shoreline on June 22, more than two weeks after beginning the ground offensive. The final action was fought at Fort Konstantinovsky, another archaic relic built in 1840 that guarded the entrance to Severnaya Bay. Major Ivan P. Datsko, commander of the 161st Rifle Regiment, made it to the fort with a handful of his men, and joined up with a motley collection of sailors, engineers, and political staff for a dramatic three-day last stand against IR 97. A naval officer, Captain 3rd Rank Mikhail E. Yevseyev, was nominally in charge of the fort. The defenders did have one advantage: the fort was located at the end of a small peninsula and the Germans could only approach across a narrow 100-yard strip of land, which was covered by a ravelin. The Germans methodically brought up artillery to knock down the fort's walls, and Stuka attacks ruined the barracks in the interior. Yevseyev's men eventually ran out of ammunition, and the last 26 men surrendered on the morning of June 23. Sevastopol's Sector IV had been eliminated and all that remained of Sector III was Guz's 345th Rifle Division and the 138th NIB holding on to the Serpentine tunnel and the Martynovski Ravine at the northeast corner of Severnaya Bay. German artillery now had a clear view to shell any target in the city or harbor.

Wolff's intelligence officers learned from prisoner interrogations that the 138th Naval Infantry Brigade's command post and two to three battalions of Soviet troops were located in the railroad tunnel a mile south of the Mekenzievy Mountain train station. Hansen ordered Wolff to eliminate the Soviet forces in the tunnel as a prelude to moving against the remnants of the Sector III forces. On the evening of June 21, pioneers from 3./Pionier-Bataillon 22 accompanied a *Stossgruppe* that would attack the west end of the tunnel. Prisoners had noted that the entrance to the 400-yard-long tunnel was barricaded and protected by bunkers and trenches, so the pioneers came loaded with flamethrowers, grenades, and 50kg hollow charges. At 0230hrs on June 22 the attack on the western end of the tunnel began, but the pioneers were surprised to find the entrance unguarded. The pioneers then began moving cautiously into the dark tunnel, expecting to find hundreds of armed Soviet soldiers:

> One hears one's own heartbeat … the tunnel floor is littered with dead Russians and craters are evidence of the work of our artillery and the Luftwaffe. A pionier finds six antipersonnel mines and disarms them… Now we light up the first 50 meters of the tunnel with rounds from a flare pistol. Still nothing stirred. We send some machine gun fire into the interior of the tunnel. In many cases, the rounds echo, but no Russkies can be seen. Now we throw hand grenades and smoke grenades.[71]

Eventually, a few Soviets remaining in the tunnel appeared and surrendered. They informed the pioneers that the Soviet troops had abandoned the tunnel and retreated toward the Martynovski Ravine. The German troops were relieved that they did not have to fight a point-blank battle in the darkened tunnel with a large enemy force.

As a postscript to the fighting on Mekenzievy Mountain, Aleksandr's group trapped underground in Coastal Battery No. 30 died a slow death. The German engineers continued to try and burn or blast them out for three days, but the battery's demise was precipitated by a commissar who detonated one of the underground ammunition rooms in an effort to destroy both the garrison and the besieging Germans. The blast killed many and wrecked the interior of the battery. A few survivors emerged, and the Germans believed that no one else was left alive inside. In fact, Aleksandr and 20 of his men were still inside, and they waited until June 25 before exiting the battery through a drainage pipe on the side facing the Bel'bek River. Aleksandr may have been dressed in civilian clothing – his interrogation report does not mention it – but they broke into small groups and tried to infiltrate east along Haccius Ridge. They did not get far – Aleksandr was captured by German pioneers on the morning of June 26 and thoroughly interrogated.[72] The interrogation makes no mention of his fate, but Manstein was angry that Coastal Battery No. 30 had proven so obstinate, and ordered Aleksandr turned over to the Sicherheitsdienst (SD), who executed him. Later, when Aleksandr was lionized as a hero of Sevastopol's defense, Manstein lamely claimed that he had been "shot while trying to escape."

Sevastopol's fate was decided in the two-week slugfest for the high ground around Mekenzievy Mountain. Both sides suffered thousands of casualties, but the Germans had triumphed due to superior small-unit leadership and plentiful air and artillery support. For the most part, the Soviet soldiers fought well and died well on Mekenzievy Mountain – there was no shortage of heroes in their ranks, either. Hundreds simply disappeared, buried in shell craters and rubble. Even in recent years, diggers in Sevastopol continue to unearth dozens of remains of fallen Red Army soldiers on the mountain.

Whereas the fighting on Sevastopol's northern front was often characterized by extreme violence and significant gain or loss of terrain, the fighting on the southern front was a war of position. Since December 1941, the front line in Sevastopol's Sectors I and II had been a revisit to the trench warfare of World War I, with advances measured in yards. There was little glory to be had here for either side – no *Ritterkreuz* or Red Star – since it was a sideshow to the main fight on Mekenzievy Mountain. The inclusion of the Romanian Mountain Corps further highlighted that fact for General der Artillerie Maximilian Fretter-Pico's XXX Armeekorps. Fought atop the same soil where some of the most dramatic moments of the Crimean War of 1854–55 had transpired, the fight between XXX Armeekorps and two Soviet divisions entered obscurity even as it was occurring. Yet the three weeks of fighting on the Balaklava front was very much a soldier's battle, where the mettle of each side was sorely tested.

Manstein assigned a supporting role to Fretter-Pico's XXX Armeekorps and the Romanians, with the intent of preventing Petrov from transferring any units from Sector I or II to reinforce the fight for Mekenzievy Mountain. Unlike Hansen's LIV Armeekorps, Fretter-Pico had to make do with significantly less air and artillery support, and Manstein made it clear that he would get no reinforcements. Fretter-Pico had taken over XXX Armeekorps just after the culmination of the December 1941 offensive and had not yet commanded a multi-division offensive. Now he would command three infantry divisions: General der Infanterie Johann Sinnhuber's 28.leichte-Infanterie-Division, Generalleutnant Philipp Müller-Gebhard 72. Infanterie-Division, and Generalleutnant Erwin Sander's 170.

Infanterie-Division. In addition to Fretter-Pico, two of his three infantry division commanders (Sinnhuber and Sander) were career artillery officers and relatively new to maneuvering infantry on a battlefield. By nature, artillerymen are very by-the-book and checklist oriented, rather than the risk-taking style of a born maneuver soldier, and this attitude was very evident in the methodical manner that XXX Armeekorps fought its battle.

While Manstein had not allowed the Romanians to play much of a role in his first two attempts to take Sevastopol, he was now forced to include General-Major Gheorghe Avramescu's Mountain Corps in *Störfang*. Avramescu had been working with AOK 11 since the beginning of *Barbarossa* and was well acquainted both with German operational methods and arrogance. He knew that the Germans were quick to blame the Romanians for any mistakes and to treat their troops in a condescending manner. Yet in order for Hansen's LIV Armeekorps to mass AOK 11's best forces against Sectors III and IV, and for Fretter-Pico to mass his lesser forces against Sector I, the Romanians would have to deal with Sector II with only limited German help. Avramescu's corps was a mixed bag: the 1st Mountain Division was a good unit, well suited to the terrain and mission, and the Corps artillery was quite good by Crimean standards. The Romanian mountain-infantry battalions had proven themselves to be aggressive and reliable in the December fighting, and were capable of capturing fortified positions if decently supported. On the other hand, Avramescu's other formation – the 18th Infantry Division – had negligible combat experience, and its reservist infantrymen were better suited for static defensive missions. The 4th Mountain Division was still dealing with remaining pockets of resistance from the Sudak landing and partisans, but would be sent to join Avramescu's corps in mid-June.

Fretter-Pico's main opponent was General-Major Petr G. Novikov, commander of the 109th Rifle Division and the SOR's Sector I, which ran from Balaklava to the Yalta–Sevastopol road, north of Kamary. Novikov was no rookie: he had commanded an infantry battalion in the Spanish Civil War, a rifle regiment in the Russo-Finnish War, and then a rifle division during *Barbarossa*. His 109th Rifle Division had been formed in Sevastopol in January 1942 from remnants of the 2nd Cavalry Division, NKVD border troops, and reservists. All three of his rifle regiments were in the front line and holding the high ground that blocked German entry into Balaklava. Colonel Nikolai A. Shvarev's 388th Rifle Division had two regiments protecting the sector around the destroyed village of Kamary, while his 782nd Rifle Regiment was in reserve on the Sapun Heights. Like Novikov, Shvarev was an experienced veteran, having been an NCO in the Tsarist Army during 1915–17, then having joined the Red Guards after the Bolshevik Revolution. During the Russo-Finnish War, he commanded a rifle regiment involved in breaching the Mannerheim Line. The 388th Rifle Division was a typical Caucasian outfit, with its Armenian, Azeri, and Georgian troops organized in segregated companies with Russian officers. Novikov was essentially a rifle-corps commander, but he did not have the resources of a corps commander. His artillery support was limited to two artillery regiments with 27 guns (eight 152mm, six 122mm, and 13 76.2mm), along with some help from Morgunov's local batteries. Blagoveshchensky's 9th Naval Infantry Brigade was assigned as a reserve for Novikov's sector, but most of its battalions were deployed in coastal-defense duties, due to Petrov's fear that the Germans would attempt an amphibious landing to get behind Balaklava.

The Germans had seized some, but not all, of the high ground overlooking Balaklava harbor on November 17. The most important position was Hill 212, on which the old Balaklava North Fort sat, and which gave the Germans excellent observation of Balaklava and the vicinity. Adjacent to Hill 212, Lieutenant-Colonel Gerasimos A. Rubtsov's 456th Rifle Regiment (NKVD) held a craggy, boulder-strewn ridge known to the Germans as "Sulzbacher Hill" protecting the harbor mouth, located near the old Genoese Cembalo fortress. Rubtsov's troops were atop the same area where the 93rd (Highland) Regiment made its famous "Thin Red Line" stand to defend Balaklava harbor from Russian cavalry in October 1854. Another key Soviet position was Fort Kuppe, atop a hill that had been Redoubt 1 in 1854; this position was heavily fortified behind a thick barrier of mines and barbed wire. At the boundary between Novikov's Sector I and Colonel Nikolai F. Stutel'nik's Sector II, Colonel Zhidilov's 7th Naval Infantry Brigade held the same ground where Russian artillery had repulsed the Charge of the Light Brigade in 1854. In this sector, Zhidilov's defense was based on holding Chapel Hill, an important point with a ruined church that overlooked the Yalta–Sevastopol road. Stutel'nik also had his own 386th Rifle Division to defend the Chernaya River valley.

When the artillery preparation for *Störfang* began on June 2, XXX Armeekorps' fire was directed by General der Artillerie Robert Martinek's Arko 110. His heavy firepower was limited to two Czech 30.5cm mortars, six 21cm mortars, and 12 Czech-made 14.9cm s.FH 37(t) howitzers from schwere Artillerie-Abteilung 154. He also had 36 Nebelwerfers from Werfer-Regiment 70. The Romanian Mountain Corps contributed its corps-level artillery: three battalions with 33 Czech-made M1934 15cm howitzers. Martinek could not afford to be extravagant with his artillery preparation, as Zuckertort had done, so he massed his fires against a few of the most important positions, such as "Sulzbacher Hill" and Fort Kuppe. Novikov's artillery remained silent during Martinek's preparation bombardment, so it was impossible for Fretter-Pico to determine if the enemy's defense had been weakened.

Manstein did not want Fretter-Pico to launch an all-out ground offensive until Hansen's LIV Armeekorps had made progress, but apparently he did not exercise sufficient supervision over XXX Armeekorps' planning for *Störfang*. Uncertain of the enemy's strength, Fretter-Pico timidly began his ground offensive by making two separate single-battalion probing attacks by Sinnhuber's 28. leichte-Infanterie-Division. Just after dawn on June 7, III./Jäger-Regiment 83 attacked Rubtsov's NKVD troops atop the Sulzbacher Hill, which meant crossing hundreds of yards of steep, open ground. The men were surprised when the NKVD troops opened up with direct fire with flak guns that had been brought onto the hill during the spring; the attack was repulsed with heavy losses. Ivan I. Bogatir', a renowned NKVD sniper in the 456th Rifle Regiment, inflicted numerous casualties upon the enemy before he himself was wounded and evacuated.

Meanwhile, III./ Jäger-Regiment 49 used a more stealthy approach to push north toward the fortified Blagodat State Farm, which was held by 2nd Battalion, 381st Rifle Regiment. In this case, they were able to seize a small hillock overlooking the farm and begin to fortify it before the Soviets noticed what was going on. Yet once the German infiltration was detected, the 381st Rifle Regiment acted energetically to repel the enemy intrusion. Lieutenant Nikolai I. Spirin's machine-gun company laid down heavy fire upon the Germans, supplemented by mortar and artillery fire, which inflicted heavy casualties. It turned out that Martinek's artillery preparation had failed, and now Novikov used his own artillery to break up the German attacks, as well as to inflict painful losses on Martinek's artillery. After a day of being pounded in no man's land, the Germans withdrew after suffering 500 casualties for no gain. Two of the hardest-hit companies in JR 49 had been reduced to just 20–30 survivors each.[73] The Romanian 1st Mountain Division also began an effort to seize two hilltops known as "North Nose" and "Sugarloaf," which controlled a crossing site over the Chernaya River valley. The initial small-scale attack was repulsed, but the Romanians were determined to contribute to the fall of Sevastopol.

When he learned about the lack of success by XXX Armeekorps and the heavy losses suffered by the 28. leichte-Infanterie-Division, Manstein ordered Fretter-Pico to cease any further such piecemeal attacks and to concentrate his forces to seize limited objectives. Yet Fretter-Pico failed to form a *Schwerpunkt* in any one sector and spent the next three days committing the 28. leichte-Infanterie-Division to probing attacks against the 381st Rifle Regiment's positions around the Blagodat State Farm. Meanwhile, Fretter-Pico's other two infantry divisions sat on their hands for the first four days of *Störfang*. After four days of indecisive fighting, XXX Armeekorps had suffered over 1,000 casualties and seized none of its objectives. Novikov's troops had stood up very well during these opening days, inflicting heavy losses and mounting spirited counterattacks that knocked the Germans back on their heels.

However, by June 11, Manstein reckoned that it was time for Fretter-Pico's corps to begin larger-scale offensive operations. Thus, Fretter-Pico attacked the center of Novikov's front near Kamary with three battalions (I. and III./IR 401 from Sander's 170. Infanterie-Division and I./IR 266 from Müller-Gebhard's 72. Infanterie-Division), supported by eight assault guns from 2./Sturmgeschütz-Abteilung 249 and 13 Pz IIIJ tanks from Panzer-Abteilung (FL) 300. The attack on the right by I./IR 401 near Chapel Hill went surprisingly well and succeeded in capturing Ruin Hill from the 602nd Rifle Regiment. The two-battalion attack further south gained a few hundred yards before being stopped by counterattacks from the 782nd Rifle Regiment. By day's end, the Germans had formed two small salients north and south of the fortified town of Kamary, which was held by two battalions from the 778th Rifle Regiment. The next day, Müller-Gebhard added in fresh troops from his IR 124 to reinforce the concentric attack against Kamary, which was being attacked from the east and the south. Martinek also focused most of XXX Armeekorps' artillery against Kamary, which inflicted significant losses on the 778th Rifle Regiment.

Novikov decided that the 778th Rifle Regiment was in poor shape and was uncertain that they could hold Kamary. This may have been one of those cases where ethnic prejudices against the combat capabilities of Caucasian troops helped to shape tactical decisions. In any case, Novikov decided upon the risky maneuver of a relief-in-place: he would pull out the 778th Rifle Regiment during the night of June 12/13 and replace them with steadier troops from his flank regiments. This was a difficult task for even veteran troops, and it did not go well in this case. The Germans detected movement around Kamary, and Müller-Gebhard immediately launched an attack at 0430hrs with his IR 124. The Soviets had emplaced a dense obstacle belt in front of Kamary, consisting of barbed wire and mines, but an obstacle's value is greatly reduced if it is not covered by fire. For reasons unclear, the 778th Rifle Regiment did not leave sufficient rearguards to cover the obstacles, and the pioneers attached to IR 124 were able to create lanes through the obstacles by 0700hrs. German artillery fire pounded the town, disrupting the Soviet relief-in-place. Jäger-Regiment 49 also launched a supporting attack against the 381st Rifle Regiment positions on Vermillion Hill, southwest of Kamary, which prevented them from transferring troops to help the 782nd Rifle Regiment. Under great pressure, the center of Novikov's line began to buckle.

Fretter-Pico requested Fliegerkorps VIII to make a concerted effort against Novikov's reserve positions at Fort Kuppe, which made it difficult for the Soviets to reinforce the threatened sector. The Germans knew from prisoner interrogations that the command posts of both the 602nd and 782nd Rifle Regiments were located at Fort Kuppe, which was about 1,300 yards behind the frontline. By late afternoon on June 13, with the Soviet defenses greatly weakened and their command and control disrupted, Fretter-Pico put all his cards on the table. North of Kamary, Sanders massed all three battalions of IR 401 against the 602nd Rifle Regiment defending the causeway road, just west of Ruin Hill. IR 401 was supplemented with assault guns, Pz IIIJ tanks, and a small mobile group comprised of bicycle infantry and a few armored cars. At 1600hrs he began his attack. Even though the 602nd Rifle Regiment was a veteran unit on good defensive terrain, it was quickly overwhelmed and forced to fall back. At this point, chaos and confusion took over the battle. Novikov probably tried to get his defeated regiments to withdraw to their secondary positions and form a new front, but troops were moving rearward with little direction. Sanders's mobile group aggravated the situation by aggressively pushing over half a mile down the causeway road, which turned the retreat of the 602nd Rifle Regiment into a stampede. Sensing a breakthrough, Sanders committed his reserve – II./IR 266 – to pursue the broken enemy. Adding to the Soviet discomfiture, the 28. leichte-Infanterie-Division and the Romanian mountain troops mounted supporting attacks against the flanks of the breakthrough zone. Amazingly, II./IR 266 reached the outskirts of Fort Kuppe by 1745hrs and began to methodically clear the position.[74] Novikov's requested air support and the VVS-ChF flew some strafing runs against the Germans, but it was too late. By nightfall, both Kamary and Fort Kuppe had fallen and Fretter-Pico's assault troops had created a deep salient in Novikov's lines. Hundreds of Soviet troops were captured in this debacle.

Novikov could take solace in the fact that his flanks still held firm: the 381st Rifle Regiment on Rose Hill and the Blagodat State Farm in the south, and Zhidilov's 7th Naval Infantry Brigade on the high ground overlooking the Chernaya River valley in the north. Despite the temporary blowout in the center, most of the Soviet defenses were still solid and full of fight. Fretter-Pico decided to keep up the pressure on the weakened Soviet center, while continuing fixing attacks on the flanks. On June 14, Sanders committed part of Oberstleutnant Richard Daniel's IR 391 from reserve to reinforce the push westward, which now included elements of two regiments each from the 72. and 170. Infanterie-Divisionen. At the forefront of this advance was Oberleutnant der Reserve Georg Bittlingmaier, commander of I./IR 391; it was unusual for a junior reserve officer to be leading an infantry battalion at this stage of the war, but Bittlingmaier was an unusual officer. No scion of Prussian gentry, Bittlingmaier had enlisted in the Reichswehr in 1921 and worked his way up to the NCO ranks. After the French campaign, he was awarded a reserve commission for his outstanding leadership qualities and then given command of a battalion in April 1942 when the previous officer was relieved. Photos show Bittlingmaier wearing a steel helmet instead of an officer's usual soft cap, and he had a scraggly beard – here was a former NCO and "trench rat" that the troops respected and believed in. Bittlingmaier's own 18-year-old son also served in his battalion – another rarity in the Wehrmacht.

Slowly, the Germans advanced another 1,420 yards and reached the outskirts of the town of Kadykovka by the next day. Novikov's line was bent back sharply, and the 381st Rifle Regiment in the Blagodat State

Farm was nearly encircled. Although Novikov's troops dug in their heels on June 15, they could not maintain this front line and they lacked the resources for a major counterattack. On June 16, Novikov finally bowed to the inevitable and evacuated the farm and Rose Hill, and he pulled his forces back 1,000–1,500 yards to create a shortened line that was centered on Kadykovka. Meanwhile, Stutel'nik continued to hold on to his original frontline positions in Sector II against small-scale Romanian attacks.

Fretter-Pico's forces pursued slowly, cautiously winding their way through minefields and mopping up small pockets of resistance. The main German advance was up the elevated causeway road, with troops in both the north and south valleys as well. On June 18, Radfahr-Abteilung 72 – an ad-hoc mounted unit under Major Karl Baake – was able to exploit a gap in Novikov's front and reach a position known as the "Eagle's Perch," only half a mile from the Sapun Heights. However, Fretter-Pico's troops were spent after incurring 5,235 casualties between June 7 and June 20, including 1,010 dead or missing. Fretter-Pico decided to revert to the defense on June 22 until he could gather sufficient strength to assault the Sapun Heights. Novikov's losses were probably heavier, and the 388th Rifle Division was virtually demolished in the fighting withdrawal. At least 1,800 Soviet troops from Sector I were captured in this period.[75] The heroic Colonel Pavel P. Gorpishchenko, commander of the 8th Naval Infantry Brigade, was seriously wounded during this phase of the fighting and was evacuated; Regimental Commissar Prokofiev I. Silant'ev took over the brigade.

The Romanian Mountain Corps finally made a major attack against Sector II's defenses in the lower Chernaya River valley on June 18. The 1st Mountain Division struggled mightily for three days to gain control of two hilltops – "North Nose" and "Sugar Loaf" – with the battle swinging back and forth as Zhidilov's 7th Naval Infantry Brigade and the 386th Rifle Division counterattacked regularly to retake any lost ground. Eventually, the Romanians were able to capture and hold both hills by June 20, which helped to secure XXX Armeekorps' right flank. Lacking assault guns or extensive air support, the Romanians suffered thousands of casualties for these two small objectives. On June 21, Fretter-Pico was able to gain two battalions of IR 420, which were temporarily loaned from Heeresgruppe Süd, to mount a sudden night attack on the Fedyukhiny Heights in conjunction with the Romanian 1st Mountain Division. Before Skutel'nik could react his single regiment on the heights was overwhelmed; the Axis had won a cheap tactical victory that put them one step closer to gaining the Sapun Heights.

While XXX Armeekorps rested on June 22–28, Avramescu's Mountain Corps mounted a major effort to clear the Chernaya River valley northeast of the Fedyukhiny Heights. This was the first time in the battle of Sevastopol that the Romanians employed all their forces, and they gradually eliminated several Soviet positions and forced the rest of Skutel'nik's Sector II forces to retreat. Indeed, the Romanians made an important contribution at this point, in mopping up positions that the Germans no longer had the forces to reduce themselves. By late June, Novikov's Sector I had been pushed back about 3 miles in the center, but he still had a firm grip on Balaklava in the south, while Skutel'nik's troops held the Sapun Heights. During the fighting in the south Soviet soldiers and small-unit leaders had demonstrated great resiliency in positional warfare, and the German infantry had been able to make significant advances only when they had assault guns and air support. On the other hand, German regiment and division-level leaders had proven adept at exploiting fleeting opportunities made by enemy mistakes. This kind of combat dynamic shaped a battle that was characterized by heavy casualties and sudden spasms of maneuver.

A brief lull settled over most sectors of the Sevastopol battlefield in late June, as both sides prepared for the final act. Both XXX and LIV Armeekorps temporarily shifted to the defense as they reorganized their decimated assault troops. Richthofen and his Fliegerkorps VIII staff had already left the Crimea on June 23, and some of the Luftwaffe units were departing as well, although the VVS-ChF was no longer able to contest air superiority over the city. The remaining Luftwaffe units were running out of bombs, meaning that bomber sorties were no longer flown with full loads. Zuckertort's largest artillery pieces, including Dora, the two Karl mortars, and the 42cm howitzers were no longer in the fight, having expended all their ammunition. Petrov's gunners were also running out of ammunition for their medium artillery, but there was still plenty of 76mm and 82mm ammunition. Hitler wanted *Störfang* completed by the end of June, as his main summer offensive, *Fall Blau*, was about to begin and he wanted Manstein's AOK 11 to be available soon for employment outside the Crimea. For the frontline soldiers, most were appreciative still to be on their feet and have all their limbs after three weeks of intense combat. Victory or defeat was now within their grasp, but one more blood deposit was required.

After the collapse of Sector IV, all forces that remained from Sector III fell back into the Martynovski Ravine, southeast of the Serpentine tunnel. The strongest unit – the 138th Naval Infantry Brigade – held the two railroad tunnels located on either side of the Serpentine and the western flank of Kolomiets' perimeter. In the center, the 2nd Perekop and 79th Naval Infantry Brigade were both reduced to about 20 percent of their authorized strength. On the eastern end, the 25th Rifle Division still had two depleted rifle regiments and most of its artillery, but its right flank was open. Altogether, these forces amounted to perhaps 6,000 combat troops, and they blocked the direct path into Sevastopol from the north. Hansen's LIV Armeekorps was in desperate need of rest and replacements, but he was still able to assemble some troops to keep the pressure on Kolomiets' forces. Schmidt's 50. Infanterie-Division was in the best shape of Hansen's four divisions, so he deployed that unit to clear the Serpentine and the Martynovski Ravine, assisted by part of the 132. Infanterie-Division and the Romanian 4th Mountain Division.

By chance, two platoon leaders from the 138th Naval Infantry Brigade – Lieutenants Sultan Sultanov and Filip Onelytschenko – deserted to the Germans and provided the Ic of the 22. Infanterie-Division with the strength and dispositions of the remaining Soviet troops around the Martynovski Ravine.[76] At 0530hrs on June 22 Hansen used this information to mount a carefully planned attack with the 50. Infanterie-Division, which overran the Serpentine and reached the railroad tunnel. German pioneers cleared out the tunnel with flamethrowers. Another German *Stossgruppe* from the 132. Infanterie-Division, assisted by assault guns from Sturmgeschütz-Abteilung 190, turned the 25th Rifle Division's open flank and advanced 1¼ miles. Heavy fighting raged around the Martynovski Ravine on June 23, but the disorganized Soviet units were defeated piecemeal, with at least 725 captured.[77] The equivalent of four battalions' worth of troops escaped southward to Inkerman, but the 345th Rifle Division was trapped on the north side of the bay and overrun. Much of the Soviet divisional artillery was lost in the retreat to the

Inkerman position, due to a lack of prime movers. As a result of this defeat, Petrov massed what little infantry and artillery he had left to hold Inkerman, with almost nothing in reserve. In the south, the defense was dependent upon holding the Sapun Heights.

During June 24–28 both sides licked their wounds and prepared for the final round. Three Black Sea Fleet destroyers succeeded in bringing in Major Sergei E. Kovalev's 142nd Naval Infantry Brigade over the course of two nights – the last reinforcements to reach Sevastopol. However, Kovalev's 3,550 troops were not intended to reinforce the front line but to establish a defensive perimeter around the port in case an evacuation became necessary. The Stavka was already beginning to consider an evacuation if Petrov could not hold the city, and wanted to salvage troops for use in the Caucasus. Yet Petrov was now so short of troops that he committed five construction battalions to reinforce the defenses at Inkerman. Thousands of his troops were wounded and in the 47th Medical Battalion's hospital, which was located in the champagne factory and catacombs at Inkerman. Now this hospital was on the front line, and there was no way to move large numbers of wounded. Most of his divisions no longer existed as such, and were reduced to regimental-size battle groups. Furthermore, Petrov's air and artillery support was now minimal and it was clear that no more reinforcements would make it through the Luftwaffe's blockade.

Although Manstein had gradually destroyed Petrov's defenses piece by piece in the first three weeks of *Störfang*, the offensive was rapidly approaching a culminating point where it would no longer have the strength to overwhelm the final defenses. Ironically, the Soviet defensive position at Inkerman was a natural fortress – far stronger than anything that LIV Armeekorps had overcome yet. Inkerman had very steep, rocky cliffs that overlooked both the road and rail bridges over the upper Chernaya River. Remnants of the 25th Rifle Division still held the Gaytani Heights, just across the river from Inkerman, which acted as a ravelin. Any attacking troops would have to cross 500 yards of open ground, most of which was marsh-like and laced with antipersonnel mines, then cross an 80-yard-wide river under fire. Even if the Germans could cross the Chernaya River, the cliffs at Inkerman were up to 100 yards higher than the river valley and consisted of vertical rock faces, making rapid ascent impossible. If anything, Inkerman was a mission for glider troops – but

Manstein did not have any. Faced with a tough enemy defensive position, Manstein adopted his standard solutions to such intractable problems: risk and maneuver.

Manstein knew that Petrov's forces were in bad shape as well, and that the Soviet commander would mass everything he had left to hold Inkerman and the Gaytani Heights. However, Petrov could not possibly protect the entire length of the southern side of Severnaya Bay, and Manstein believed that an assault crossing of the bay might catch the Soviets flat-footed and cause the defense at Inkerman to collapse, just as had occurred during Operation *Trappenjagd*. When Manstein raised this idea with Hansen and Wolff, whose 22. Infanterie-Division would have to mount the crossing, they were aghast. Wolff's division was completely spent, with fewer than 400 infantrymen still combat-ready. Even the energetic Choltitz was badly wounded in the arm. Hitzfeld's IR 213 was attached to the 22. Infanterie-Division, but, having suffered 70 percent losses, it too was judged "unsuitable for attack missions."[78] Nevertheless, the 902 and 905 Sturmboote-Kommando assembled a total of 130 assault boats, which were enough to move one battalion across the bay at a time, each crossing taking at least 20 minutes. Hansen and Wolff believed it highly likely that the Soviets would detect a night crossing, and even a few machine guns and mortars would be enough to decimate the single assault battalion. Or worse, one battalion might make it across, then find itself isolated and overwhelmed once the Soviets reacted to the landing. Yet Manstein knew that he had neither the time nor the resources to blast his way through Inkerman, so he ordered Hansen and Wolff to begin preparations for a crossing. In order to further increase the chances of a Soviet collapse, he ordered Hansen to prepare an assault upon Inkerman with the 50. Infanterie-Division when the time was right and for Fretter-Pico's entire XXX Armeekorps and the Romanians to simultaneously attack Novikov's forces on the Sapun Heights. Manstein reckoned that one last all-out attack by AOK 11 would break Petrov's defenses. If it did not, AOK 11 would be fought out and unable to complete its mission.

Petrov and Oktyabrsky were aware of the possibility of enemy landings, but did not expect them in Sevastopol. Instead, they were worried about an effort to outflank the defenses at Balaklava, and Manstein fed this fear by ordering Mimbelli's MAS boats to demonstrate off Cape Fiolent on the night of June 27/28. Italian naval activity near Balaklava was duly reported to Petrov and Oktyabrsky, who then alerted Morgunov's coastal defenses in that area. However, the southern shore of Severnaya Bay was guarded only by the survivors of Potapov's 79th Naval Infantry Brigade and the 2nd Perekop Naval Infantry Regiment, which together numbered no more than 600–800 troops. At 0200hrs on the night of June 28/29, German pioneers began to lay a smoke screen on the north side of Severnaya Bay to conceal the activity of the assault boats being brought to the water's edge and the troop loading. Overhead, German aircraft noisily attacked the area around Inkerman to further distract the defenders. On the northern side of the bay, 380 troops from Kampfgruppe Buhse (Choltitz had been wounded in the arm and Buhse temporarily took over the assault elements of IR 16, while Choltitz remained on the north side of the bay) loaded into the assault boats and started across.[79] No artillery preparation was made, in order to avoid alerting the Soviets on the southern side of the bay. It must have been a very tense and weird experience as the first wave of German troops made their way across the bay, threading their way through half-sunken ships and wreckage in the water, and expecting enemy flares and automatic-weapons fire at any moment. Yet Potapov's sailors – who were spread very thinly along the coast, were not terribly alert and did not detect the crossing until it was too late. Around 0220hrs the first German assault troops landed on the southern side of Severnaya Bay and quickly scrambled up the heights above the beach. One of Potapov's positions overlooked the landing site, but the troops – exhausted after weeks of combat – were apparently asleep, and the Germans stealthily approached and then eliminated the outpost before it could raise an alarm. The assault boats then turned around and went back for the second wave, which consisted of Kampfgruppe Schitting (IR 65), and then a third wave consisting of Kampfgruppe Hitzfeld. It was not until 0300hrs, by which point over 700 German troops were on the south side of Severnaya Bay, that Potapov became aware of the landings, when several of his outposts began firing red flares. The Soviet naval infantrymen began firing at boats in the water as well as troops on the shore, but the Germans had already seized a viable beachhead. Once Potapov's men were driven off the high ground overlooking the beaches, they could no longer bring direct fire upon the crossing sites. Soviet artillery fire damaged a quarter of the assault boats, but the crossing had cost the German pioneers only two boats destroyed, four men killed, and 29 wounded. In a major coup, the German assault troops succeeding in capturing Sevastopol's power plant, which brought an end to electrical power in the city. The next morning, the wounded Choltitz crossed the bay at 1000hrs in order to lead his regiment in the final fight for Sevastopol.[80]

Off to the south, flashes began lining the eastern horizon as Fretter-Pico's XXX Armeekorps began its assault on Sapun Ridge. When Martinek began his 60-minute artillery preparation he had an advantage: prisoner interrogations had revealed the exact location of Skutel'nik's 386th Rifle Division command post on the heights. The opening salvoes landed squarely atop Skutel'nik's command post, severely wounding him and his commissar, as well as disrupting Soviet command and control on the Sapun Heights. Next, Werfer-Regiment 70 laid a blanket of high-explosive and smoke rockets on the Sapun Heights, focusing on the area held by the 775th Rifle Regiment and the 7th Naval Infantry Brigade. Fretter-Pico had assigned Sanders the mission of storming the heights, and he had formed a special assault force consisting of three infantry battalions (I., and III./IR 399, and II./IR 420), supported by the assault guns of 2./Sturmgeschütz-Abteilung 249, a company of Pz III tanks, pioneers, and flak guns. While Martinek's barrage was still impacting on the ridge, the three assault battalions began to move forward, but they suffered casualties from unsuppressed Soviet mortars and machine gunners on the ridgeline. However, the assault troops moved in rapidly and infiltrated through weak points in the defenses. By 0340hrs, the German troops had reached the Soviet trenches on top of the Sapun Heights and began close-quarter fighting in the positions of the 7th Naval Infantry Brigade. Adding to the Soviet discomfiture, the Romanian 1st Mountain Division simultaneously launched a five-battalion attack against the left flank of Skutel'nik's 386th Rifle Division at the village of Novo Shuli. The Romanian mountain troops engaged in house-to-house fighting in Novo Shuli and cleared the objective by 0730hrs.[81]

Once both Petrov's flanks were reeling from simultaneous blows, Manstein ordered Schmidt's 50. Infanterie-Division to begin its attack at Inkerman at 0400hrs. Initially, Schmidt began by committing his IR 121 to clear the open areas north of Inkerman held by the combat outposts of the 138th Naval Infantry Brigade. Surprisingly, Soviet resistance began to melt away, so at 0505hrs Schmidt brought Kampfgruppe Walter (IR 32 and IR 122) and IR 123 into the fight to clear the Gaytani Heights and prepare to assault across the Chernaya River. Oberleutnant Erich Bärenfänger continued to aggressively lead III./IR 123, despite being wounded for the third time, but it was Major Willy Marienfeld's II./IR 123 that was the first to cross from Gaytani to Inkerman. The 47-year-old Marienfeld was an unusual battalion commander: he had fought at Verdun in 1916 and was twice awarded the Iron Cross, but had left the Wehrmacht after World War I and became a teacher. Returning in 1939, Marienfeld proved himself again in Poland, France, and the Balkans. As Schmidt was moving against Inkerman, Fretter-Pico sensed that Sander's three assault battalions were creating a breakthrough on the Sapun Heights, so he committed his reserve – IR 105 – to exploit this success. Far away in his command post, Petrov could not ascertain exactly what was going on, but he knew that his troops were under attack virtually everywhere. These were critical moments for Petrov, but he was uncertain what to do or where to commit his meager reserves. There were six T-26 light tanks from the 81st Separate Tank Battalion near the Severnaya Bay landings, but perhaps Potapov exaggerated the scale of the German landings. Some reports suggested that only a handful of enemy paratroopers had landed near the bay. Petrov decided to wait for daylight and more information.

As the sun came up, the Luftwaffe arrived in force to blast the Soviet positions at Inkerman and the artillery atop the Sapun Heights. Sander's assault units, reinforced by IR 105 and then IR 391, were tearing a wide breach in the now-leaderless 386th Rifle Division. Many troops from the 386th Rifle Division simply abandoned their positions and ran as the Germans closed in. The former NCO-turned-battalion-commander, Oberleutnant der Reserve Georg Bittlingmaier, led his I./IR 391 onto the Sapun Heights and succeeded in capturing a large bunker, but he was mortally wounded during the climax of the battle. Manstein unveiled another trick at 0605hrs: he had brought up IR 42 and IR 72 from the 46. Infanterie-Division at Kerch – another calculated risk – to mount an attack across the middle section of the Chernaya River between Inkerman and the Sapun Heights. This sector was held by the 8th Naval Infantry Brigade. Despite some intense defensive fire, the two German regiments were able to cross the river and begin enveloping the 8th NIB. Once Soviet resistance along the river was revealed to be weaker than expected, Schmidt sent the III./IR 123 across the river, and this battalion was able to seize an old Crimean War-era fort south of Inkerman by 0700hrs. By 0715hrs, Soviet resistance on the Sapun Heights was broken, and Sander's units fanned out to roll up the entire Soviet southern defensive line. Petrov's defenses began to crumble everywhere, all at once, as troops realized that German troops had broken through the final line of defense and were advancing upon the city. All thought now turned from fight to flight.

Despite the presence of nearly 5,000 Soviet troops around Inkerman, Schmidt's 50. Infanterie-Division seized the Chernaya River bridges and the heights overlooking them by noon on June 29. Thousands of Soviet troops remained isolated in pockets of resistance, but Hansen ordered Schmidt to ignore them for the moment, and, instead, send Kampfgruppe Walter to link up with the beachhead on Severnaya Bay. Potapov's naval infantrymen failed to seriously interfere with the German beachhead, which had grown to four regimental *Kampfgruppen*, reinforced with *Panzerjägers* and flak by the time that Kampfgruppe Walter reached them around 1700hrs.[82] At this point, Manstein directed Hansen and Fretter-Pico to spend the rest of the day mopping up isolated Soviet units, before moving toward the city itself. Fretter-Pico did send Jäger-Regiment 49 in pursuit, and they reached the old English cemetery by nightfall. The day had been a debacle for Petrov and a triumph for Manstein. Over 4,700 prisoners had been taken and, aside from the uncommitted 142nd Naval Infantry Brigade which might have played a significant role if used to counterattack the landing in Severnaya Bay, and Petrov had no formed units left near the city. Novikov's 109th Rifle Division was still relatively intact, but concentrated around Balaklava. German losses for June 29 had totaled 1,227, including 135 dead, between both corps.

During the night of June 29/30, many Soviet troops who had been cut off by the German breakthroughs tried to reach the city, resulting in a night of sporadic skirmishing. The entire staff of the 25th Rifle Division was still in the cellar of the champagne factory at Inkerman, collocated near the 47th Medical Battalion's hospital, which had 2,000 wounded soldiers inside. Kolomiets and his staff succeeded in exfiltrating in the darkness through the German lines to reach Sevastopol, abandoning their troops and the wounded. However, Lieutenant-Colonel Sergei R. Gusarov, commander of the 3rd Naval Infantry Regiment, made an incredible decision before leaving the champagne factory – he ordered his sappers to detonate stores of ammunition hidden in the catacombs so that they would not fall into German hands. Gusarov made this decision without any thought for the wounded in the hospital, and when the ammunition detonated, an entire section of the cliff face collapsed, burying the Soviet hospital under the rubble. By happenstance, a German reconnaissance team from Aufklärungs-Abteilung 132 that was approaching the champagne factory was also killed by the explosion.[83] On the neighboring Gaytani Heights, German observers were shocked to see the massive explosions, and prisoners soon revealed Gusarov's complicity in this gruesome incident. The destruction of the Inkerman depot eliminated much of the Maritime Army's last ammunition reserves. Gusarov also ordered a group of 50 soldiers to drag howitzers that had been abandoned near Inkerman; when they refused, he had them executed.

By 1800hrs on June 29 it was apparent that Sevastopol's defenses had been breached and that the city could no longer be held. Petrov and Oktyabrsky ordered most of the division and brigade commanders to report to Coastal Battery No. 35 – which left their units without senior leadership. Then they updated the Stavka on the day's events. After some deliberation, at 0950hrs the next morning the Stavka authorized the evacuation of Sevastopol. Stalin personally ordered all senior military and political leaders to leave the city as soon as possible. Once word of the evacuation got out, Petrov later admitted that panic began to spread among the officers, and chaos took over. No more food or ammunition reached the frontline troops, so many began to abandon their positions. Some units began to sabotage equipment in order to prevent it from falling into enemy hands; at Cape Fiolent, air-defense troops pushed two RUS-2 radars off a cliff into the sea. On the Sapun Heights, Fretter-Pico's XXX Armeekorps completed mopping-up operations and began to push toward Sevastopol's outskirts with both the 28. leichte-Infanterie-Division and Sanders' 170. Infanterie-Division. The 28. leichte-Infanterie-Division succeeded in capturing the English cemetery, which had been converted into a Soviet artillery position.[84] Realizing that he was about to be cut off, Novikov abandoned Balaklava and forced-marched his 109th Rifle Division toward Coastal Battery No. 35 on the Chersonese Peninsula. Novikov was able to form a tenuous perimeter near the battery, protecting the airstrip at Chersonese, which was the last link with Novorossiysk. Amazingly, a few Li-2 (license-built copies of the American DC-3) transports made it through to the airstrip, delivering 12 tons of ammunition and some food, but this was a drop in the ocean. The last 17 operational aircraft from 3 OAG, including six Yak-1 fighters and seven Il-2 Sturmoviks, flew out of the airstrip that afternoon to the Caucasus, leaving Sevastopol without any air defense. Meanwhile, Hansen's LIV Armeekorps spent the day mopping up around Inkerman, but was pushing into the outskirts of Sevastopol by nightfall. Prisoners were now falling into Axis hands in large numbers, as Soviet resistance crumbled.

At 2000hrs on June 30, the Military Council of the Black Sea Fleet held its last meeting in Sevastopol in a casemate at Coastal Battery No. 35. Oktyabrsky, Petrov, and Morgunov voted to evacuate the city as soon as transport arrived. Senior military and political leaders, including Boris A. Borisov and his KOS, would be included, but the council decided that the Black Sea Fleet would be unable to evacuate any of the troops or the wounded. Oddly, no effort was made to use the 142nd NIB for its intended purpose of securing an evacuation site, and Oktyabrsky ruled out any large-scale evacuation as unfeasible. Petrov designated Novikov as the new commander of the Maritime Army, which was clearly being abandoned by its leadership. A group of Li-2 transports flew in from the Caucasus after midnight, but their appearance caused a mad scramble for the planes. A VVS Major put in charge of organizing the airlift was one of the first onboard, and groups of sailors appeared, using their fists to fight their way on to the aircraft. Oktyabrsky and General-Major Aleksei P. Ermilov, chief of rear services, managed to get on one transport, and all the aircraft flew out by 0130hrs on July 1. Once the aircraft left, Petrov and the rest of the senior leadership had to make their way through a crowd of nearly 10,000 soldiers, sailors, and civilians that had gathered around Battery No. 35. After more pushing and shoving – and one can imagine the faces of men watching their leaders abandon them – Petrov and his leadership cadre went through a tunnel in the battery to reach a jetty at the base of the cliff. There, small boats took them out to two submarines that had surfaced. The *Shch-209* was the first to arrive and departed with 63 personnel at 0259hrs, followed by the *L-23* at 0847hrs with 117 men. Altogether, about 200 senior leaders escaped Sevastopol, including Petrov, Morgunov, Kolomiets (25 RD), Kapitokhin (95 RD), Laskin (172 RD), Shvarev (388 RD), Zhidilov (7 NIB), and Potapov (79 NIB).[85]

Shortly after the Soviet leadership fled, German infantry from Oberst Ernst Maisel's IR 42 began advancing into the shattered and burning ruins of Sevastopol, followed by IR 72. Captain-Lieutenant Aleksei P. Matyukhin's battery of two 130mm guns located on the edge of the city on the Malakhov Hill fired as long as they could against advancing German troops, but was overrun when it ran out of ammunition. Matyukhin was captured. Nearby, the armored train *Zhelezniakov* was found abandoned in a tunnel. There was negligible resistance inside the city. By 1313hrs a German flag was flying over the southern part of the city, and by 1400hrs Axis troops were pouring in. Major Willy Marienfeld, commander of II./IR 123, reached the center of the city and radioed his division command post that, "the target was reached." In an awkward moment for Axis cooperation, Manstein tried to prevent the Romanians from participating in this photo moment – he wanted the fall of Sevastopol to be seen as a purely German victory – but a column from the 4th Mountain Division ignored German orders, made its way into the city, and hoisted a Romanian flag on the prominent Nakhimov Monument. Over 12,000 Soviet prisoners were taken on July 1, and by the end of the day most of the city was in Axis hands. At 2100hrs Berlin radio announced the fall of Sevastopol to the world.

As the Germans moved into Sevastopol they encountered numerous Soviet wounded, as well as civilians. The treatment of these individuals depended upon the unit. Choltitz, having won a splendid reputation as commander of IR 16 throughout the Crimean campaign, was not about to spoil that reputation with war crimes against a vanquished foe. He ordered his troops to ignore the standing order to execute commissars, and directed his medical personnel to treat Soviet wounded. However, other German units were less chivalrous, and treated Soviet wounded in expedient fashion – with a bullet. Later, Choltitz recalled that 30,000 Jews were executed after the fall of Sevastopol, although most of these were probably Soviet POWs and local communist officials.[86]

Novikov retreated into the Chersonese Peninsula with about 50,000 troops from the Maritime Army and the naval base, intent upon making a last stand. The peninsula, which was about 5 miles long and a mile wide, was very heavily fortified, but Coastal Battery No. 35 had expended its last rounds on July 1. The only reasonably intact Soviet units were Major Nikulshin's 1st Battalion from 9 NIB, which had been assigned to defend the Chersonese airstrip, and a VVS-ChF security battalion. As Sanders' 170. Infanterie-Division approached the Chersonese they did not expect much resistance, but were astounded when the survivors of the 386th and 388th Rifle Divisions mounted a powerful counterattack at 1700hrs against the vanguard of IR 399 and IR 401, which inflicted 600 casualties. Thereafter, Fretter-Pico resolved to simply seal off the Soviet forces in the Chersonese and rely upon artillery and aerial bombardment to finish them off. Yet the Soviet mood for a suicidal last-stand evaporated quickly. Captain Aleksandr Leshchenko, commander of Coastal Battery No. 35, decided to detonate the powder magazines on the night of July 1/2, which completely demolished the battery and its turrets.

Could the Black Sea Fleet have conducted a "Dunkirk-style" evacuation from the Chersonese Peninsula and saved thousands of Soviet troops? If Oktyabrsky had committed the entire fleet, it is likely that a sizeable number of troops could have been evacuated over several nights, although the fleet would have suffered damage. Yet Oktyabrsky was unwilling to lose more warships, and rejected the idea of an evacuation. Nevertheless, a number of small craft from Gorshkov's Azov Flotilla made runs to the Chersonese at night to try and extract some survivors. At least two minesweepers, a survey vessel, three trawlers, and ten MO-IV type sub-chasers made runs to Cape Chersonese during July 2–4, saving several hundred members of the garrison. When the MO-IV sub-chaser SKA-112 arrived around 0100hrs on July 2, Novikov decided that discretion was the better part of valor and boarded it in an attempt to escape, but he had no luck. Off Yalta, SKA-112 was intercepted by Birnbacher's S-Boats and, after a running fight, the Soviet vessel was sunk and Novikov was captured. However, Nikolai Blagoveshchensky, commander of the 9th NIB, succeeded in evading the Axis dragnet aboard another MO-IV boat and made it to Novorossiysk. Several small craft were sunk or damaged by German air attacks, but the Axis blockade was not effective in stopping many of these vessels. A tugboat loaded with 77 troops made for the Turkish coast; under Soviet diplomatic pressure, the Turks allowed the vessel to proceed through their coastal waters to Batumi.

The remnants of the Coastal Army died a slow death in the Chersonese Peninsula, clustered around the airstrip and the lighthouse. One of those lost in this final stand was Lieutenant-Colonel Sergei R. Gusarov, commander of 3 NIR, whose orders had resulted in the death of many Soviet wounded at Inkerman just four days before. When German troops finally broke into the Chersonese, the last Soviet survivors huddled beneath the cliffs, while the Germans tossed hand grenades at them. Another Soviet group, formed around Lieutenant-Colonel Gerasimos A. Rubtsov's 456th

Rifle Regiment (NKVD), made a last stand around Coastal Battery No. 18, but were finally eliminated. By the evening of July 4, all Soviet organized resistance in the Crimea was finished. The next day, Manstein presided over an Axis victory parade at Livadiya to commemorate the conquest of the Crimea. Major Nikulshin and 11 of his naval infantrymen managed to escape the Chersonese in a small boat, and rowed across the Black Sea to internment in Turkey.

The fall of Sevastopol released AOK 11 for reassignment to other fronts – the only occasion in the Russo-German War where a complete German army became available, which was a unique opportunity – but AOK 11 was in no condition to accomplish any follow-on missions. The 33-day battle of Sevastopol had cost AOK 11 a total of 35,866 German casualties, including 5,786 dead or missing, or about 18 percent of its starting strength. All four infantry divisions in Hansen's LIV Armeekorps had suffered at least 30 percent casualties and their infantry battalions were almost all reduced to combat-ineffective status. Losses among officers and NCOs were particularly severe, with over 200 officers killed and 570 wounded – it would take months to replace these small-unit leaders. In Choltitz's IR 16 – one of the best regiments in AOK 11 – there were only 347 troops still fit for duty from an original strength of 3,000 men in June 1941. Oberleutnant Erich Bärenfänger's III./IR 123 was reduced to only 169 troops after the battle, and I./IR 121, which suffered over 70 percent casualties, was reduced to a battle strength of just 70 men.[87] Unable to replace these of losses, most of the German infantry divisions were forced to eliminate one battalion from each regiment and transfer the survivors to the two remaining battalions, which made for less-capable divisions. Indeed, the divisions that Hitler received back from the Crimea were not the same ones that he had sent there in September 1941.

Even among the troops who were not wounded, the effects of a month of sustained, close-quarter fighting in terrain strewn with corpses, rotting in the hot Crimean sun, was catastrophic. Many, such as Bärenfänger, came down with the "Wolhynian Fever" or "Trench Fever," which laid them up for one or two months.[88] Among the few soldiers still on their feet, they were granted local leave to enjoy the beaches at Yalta – no longer under regular nightly bombardment from Soviet destroyers – and to swill captured Crimean wine. A few, such as Gottlob Bidermann, were granted furloughs to return to Germany.[89] As was customary after a big, costly battle, the surviving victorious troops went on a week-long binge to forget their experiences. Manstein excused himself from the Crimea, first to collect his Generalfeldmarschall's baton from a grateful Führer, then to go on holiday in Romania.

Hitler hoped that once AOK 11 had rested and received replacements it could be employed either to reinforce the advance into the Caucasus by Heeresgruppe A or to reinforce Heeresgruppe Nord for Operation *Georg* to capture Leningrad. Yet it took far longer to rehabilitate these divisions than expected, and none were ready to redeploy until late August. Then, inexplicably, AOK 11's component formations were split up: the 24., and 28. leichte, 132., and 170. Infanterie-Divisionen were sent with Manstein to Leningrad, but *Georg* was cancelled and they were used to block a Soviet offensive that sought to open a corridor to the besieged city. The 72. Infanterie-Division was diverted to reinforce AOK 9 at Rzhev and the 46. and 50. Infanterie-Divisionen were kept in the Crimea unril October 1942, then sent to the Caucasus just as the advance there was sputtering out. Amazingly, Wolff's 22. Infanterie-Division was sent to garrison Crete – a complete waste of a fine infantry unit, but probably also an indication that heavy losses had made the unit unsuited for further offensive use. Thus, instead of being used en masse to achieve some operationally significant task, AOK 11 was broken up and its veteran divisions scattered. Yet, if instead AOK 11 had been compltely rebuilt and kept together, it would have provided Hitler and the OKH with a very powerful strategic reserve – this could have been a real game-changer when the crisis at Stalingrad developed in November 1942.

The fact that the Romanian Army had also bled considerably for Sevastopol – suffering a total of 8,454 casualties, including 1,874 dead or missing during *Störfang* – received considerably less attention from the German propaganda machine, which sought to portray the victory at Sevastopol as primarily a German triumph. The Romanian troops were afforded less opportunity to enjoy the fruits of victory. Instead, they were assigned to hunt down any of Petrov's troops who had escaped through the ring around Sevastopol before it fell in an effort to reach the partisans in the mountains, or to guard the long coastlines. German officers turned a blind eye to the post-battle drunkenness and looting of their own soldiers, but loudly complained if Romanian troops were caught doing the same. Sevastopol itself was a burning, smashed ruin when the Axis entered the city, with gas mains shattered, no electricity, and rubble preventing vehicles from driving down streets. It would take a tremendous clean-up effort to restore even minimal functions to the city.

On the Soviet side, the entire Maritime Army had been destroyed, with seven rifle divisions and six naval infantry units lost. Altogether, German sources indicate that they captured 97,000 Soviet prisoners, of which about one-third were wounded, which would suggest that about 18,000 Soviet soldiers and sailors died in the final battle for Sevastopol. What exactly happened to these prisoners is not exactly clear, but the survival rate for Soviet prisoners captured in 1941–42 was very low. Data from AOK 11 records for July indicate that 36,000 prisoners were transported to Dnepropetrovsk, 76,000 remained in AOK 11's POW cages (likely including some left over from *Trappenjagd*), and 5,000 were *Hilfswilliger*, who volunteered to serve as laborers to repair infrastructure in the Crimea.[90] Many of the *Hiwis* were Ukrainians or Caucasian troops, who had little loyalty for the Soviet regime. However, it appears that many Soviet prisoners such as commissars and other designated enemies of the Reich were turned over to the SD for summary execution, and their bodies buried in the antitank ditches on Mekenzievy Mountain or in the numerous bomb craters scarring the local landscape.

The loss of the Crimea was a bitter blow for Stalin, who had believed reports that Sevastopol was impregnable. Coming so soon after the stunning defeat at Kerch, he was dumbfounded that Manstein's AOK 11 had captured the entire region so quickly. In Stalin's mind, this kind of defeat could be explained only by criminal negligence, treachery, or both, but recriminations could wait. Foremost in his mind was the necessity of concealing from the Soviet people the fact that Sevastopol's troops and civilians had been abandoned by their military and party leadership – that could hurt morale – so that the truth would be carefully whitewashed from history for many decades to come. Instead, Stalin mandated that revenge was the order of the day and that the liberation of the Crimea would be a priority when the Soviet counteroffensive began. Despite losing his enire army, Petrov was given command of the survivors of the 44th Army that had escaped from Kerch in May, and he was instructed to prepare the defenses of the northern Caucasus. Oktyabrtsky remained as commander of the Black Sea Fleet, although his star was much diminished, while Gorshkov's was beginning to rise.

Altogether the conquest of the Crimea from the attack at Perekop to the fall of Sevastopol cost AOK 11 over 96,000 casualties, including 21,600 dead or missing. When the Romanian Army's 19,000 casualties are added in, it is clear that the Axis suffered at least 115,000 casualties in the Crimea in 1941–42. However, a far more important cost to the Axis cause was the loss of valuable time and resources poured into securing what amounted to a secondary objective. The diversion of so much Luftwaffe and artillery firepower to reduce Sevastopol was a luxury that the Wehrmacht in Russia could ill afford. Soviet losses in the Crimea in 1941–42 were catastrophic: five armies destroyed and with overall casualties aproaching 500,000. Even worse, the Soviets failed to achieve any of their operational-level objectives in the Crimea in 1941–42, and that theater proved to be a bottomless pit for resources. Nevertheless, the Soviet Union could better afford the manpower and resources wasted in pursuit of holding the Crimea than the Third Reich could afford the cost of seizing it. The German conquest of the Crimea would prove to be both expensive and, ultimately, empty.

CHAPTER 7

The German Occupation of the Crimea, 1942–44

"The Crimea should be freed from all foreigners and inhabited by Germans."
Adolf Hitler, July 19, 1941

"The Judaeo-Bolshevik system should be destroyed once and for all, so that it never threatens our vital European space ... the [German] soldier should understand the necessity of punishing the Jews – the carriers of the very spirit of Bolshevik Terror."
Erich von Manstein, Top Secret Directive to AOK 11, November 20, 1941

The Wehrmacht did not come to the Crimea to liberate its population, but to take control over a region that was regarded as having strategic, military, and economic value, and then exploit it for the benefit of the Third Reich.

Hitler was particularly adamant that those members of the local population who were designated enemies of the Third Reich – Jews, Gypsies, communists, and "uncooperative Slavs" – would be eliminated, while the survivors would be put to work repairing war damage and paving the way for German colonization of the Crimea. Generalplan Ost, the master plan for ethnic cleansing in the Soviet Union, envisioned the elimination of two-thirds of the Ukrainian population within a few decades after a German victory and their replacement by *Volksdeutsche* colonists. Hitler envisioned the Crimea as eventually being transformed into "Gotengau": a Germans-only Black Sea resort, with autobahns being built by forced labor to provide access for German tourists in a future post-war world. There was no room in this exalted vision of the Crimea for non-Germans, so their removal became an important prerequisite to realize Hitler's dream.

As AOK 11 moved into the Crimea in November 1941, it was followed by *SS-Gruppenführer* Otto Ohlendorf's Einsatzgruppe D. This 600-man unit (not including local auxiliaries) was already responsible for the murder of over 40,000 civilians in Ukraine during the first four months of Operation *Barbarossa*. Although some German sources have attempted to portray *Einsatzgruppe* activity as unrelated to Wehrmacht operations, Einsatzgruppe D was attached directly to AOK 11 and was dependent upon it for logistical support. The Korück 553 (Commander Army Rear Areas) under Generalleutnant Heinrich Döhla, which was established to operate the logistical network behind Manstein's AOK 11 in the Crimea, regularly provided resources to Einsatzgruppe D. Furthermore, Manstein issued his top secret directive to AOK 11's senior leadership on November 20, 1941, which identified Jews and Bolsheviks as one and the same and directed his troops to cooperate with repressive measures. Ohlendorf also met with Manstein and his staff frequently, both for coordination purposes and social reasons – Ohlendorf and Manstein both enjoyed playing bridge. There was also a certain amount of horse-trading between the Wehrmacht and the SS: Ohlendorf would ask Manstein for trucks and ammunition to support his "special actions," while Manstein asked Ohlendorf to provide AOK 11 with winter clothing and wristwatches from the victims.

When the Germans first entered the Crimea, the region's population numbered just under one million, of which roughly 65,000–85,000 were considered Jews under Nazi legal statutes.[1] There were two small sub-groups, the Krymchaks (whom the SS regarded as Jews) and the

Karaites (whom the SS designated as non-Jews), who had adopted elements of Tatar language and customs. Initially, Ohlendorf had to send half his small unit to support Kleist's push towards Rostov, and entered the Crimea with two company-size *Sonderkommandos*. He set up his group command post in Simferopol, not far from Manstein's headquarters, just two weeks after AOK 11 occupied the city. Given the small numbers of personnel he had at his disposal, he spent the first week gathering information about the Jewish population and communist sympathizers in the Crimea. Ohlendorf was quick to note in his regular reports to Berlin that the local Tatars were "positively inclined towards the German occupying forces" and willing to provide information about the Reich's enemies. It was at this point that the memory of OZET and the Red Terror hung like a noose about the neck of the Jewish community in the Crimea.

Ohlendorf moved first against Feodosiya and Kerch, which had only recently been cleared of Red Army units. In Feodosiya, Ohlendorf's men began registering and then liquidating about 1,000 persons over the course of a few weeks, but in Kerch he began the Crimean Holocaust in earnest. All Jews in Kerch were ordered to report to Haymarket Square in the center of the city for registration on November 29, 1941. About 7,000 civilians went to the square and were promptly arrested. Women and girls who were particularly attractive were separated from the group and detained elsewhere; they were raped by men from the SS Sonderkommando, and then shot. The bulk of the arrested population were moved by trucks borrowed from the XLII Armeekorps to Bagerovo, 2½ miles west of Kerch, on December 1. There, the SS had set up an execution area in an abandoned Red Army antitank ditch. On a crisp December morning, with the ground lightly dusted with snow, the SS brought groups of civilians to the ditch, shot them, and tossed the bodies in. Approximately 7,000 civilians were murdered by Ohlendorf's men at Bagerovo. As usual, there were a few survivors who escaped. By chance, this area was liberated by Soviet troops just a month later – before the Germans had the opportunity to conceal evidence – and they found the antitank ditch, "for the length of a kilometre, four meters wide and to a depth of two meters, filled with dead bodies of women, children, the elderly, and adolescents. Near the trench there were frozen puddles of blood. The area was also littered with children's hats, toys, ribbons, torn-off buttons, gloves, bottles with nipples, shoes, galoshes, arms, legs, and other body parts. All this was splattered with blood and brains."[2]

After Kerch, Ohlendorf concentrated his personnel for a major action against the Jewish population and communists in the Simferopol area. Ohlendorf requested military police, 25 trucks, and ammunition from Korück 553 in order to conduct the operation, and Generalleutnant Döhla provided them. A company of military policemen from Feldgendarmerie-Abteilung 683 were to help round up Jews in Simferopol and then secure the execution site, located at an old Soviet antitank ditch 9 miles northeast of Simferopol, while 20 personnel from Gruppe Geheime Feldpolizei 647 (Secret Field Police) were chosen to assist the executioners. Ohlendorf put Sturmbannführer Werner Braune and his Sonderkommando 11b in charge of the operation at Simferopol. The round-ups began in Simferopol in early December, and Braune's unit executed approximately 1,500 Krymchaks and 600 Gypsies on December 9–10. However, the main killing began on December 13, and continued for several days. The total number of civilians murdered at Simferopol was approximately 12,000–14,000. Not only did Wehrmacht troops participate in the massacres, but army leaders described the liquidation of the Simferopol Jews as "necessary" in order to avoid famine in the Crimea.[3] Although some Jews went into hiding, they were often betrayed by Crimean Tatars or other minorities who resented the loss of farmland to OZET in the 1930s. In his report to Berlin on January 2, 1942, Ohlendorf claimed that Einsatzgruppe D had executed 21,185 people in the Crimea between November 16 and December 15, 1941.[4] In addition to Jews and Gypsies, the SS also eliminated at least 212 Communist Party members and former officials rounded up near Simferopol. Since Einsatzgruppe D had no counter-intelligence capabilities or ability to sort out local loyalties, the SD dispatched 700 personnel to the Crimea in December 1941.

Once Simferopol was "pacified," Ohlendorf moved on to Yalta, which had only a small Jewish population. Lidiya I. Chyernih, a 14-year-old girl in Yalta, remembered that the SS detachment ordered the Jews to assemble on the embankment, where they were shot. A number of Komsomol members and communists were also hanged on the embankment.[5] Chyernih noted that some of the executioners were Tatars and former Russian policemen. It is estimated that the SS murdered about 1,500 civilians in Yalta on December 18. Thereafter, Ohlendorf and his Sonderkommando appear to have taken a Christmas holiday for more than a week, while they left *Feldgendarmerie* to round up the Jews in Feodosiya, with help from an infantry platoon.[6] Officials from Korück 553 apparently complained to Ohlendorf about a forgotten displaced-persons camp at Dzhankoy, which was still drawing rations at a time when food was very short in AOK 11. Ohlendorf promptly sent a Sonderkommando, which shot 455 Jews at the camp. AOK 11 expressed its gratitude for the expeditious response. Ohlendorf even claimed that the executions were popular with the non-Jewish population in the Crimea: "In general, the shooting of the Jews has been positively received after the initial fear of similar treatment for the rest of the population has subsided."

The Soviet amphibious landings at Kerch, Feodosiya, and Yevpatoriya temporarily put Einsatzgruppe D's activities on hold. After the landing at Yevpatoriya was crushed in January 1942, teams from Einsatzgruppe D and the SD were sent into the city to make an example of civilians who had assisted the Soviet landing force. About 1,300 civilians were rounded up – Jews, Ukrainians, and Russians – and executed. Thereafter, Einsatzgruppe D continued with its ethnic-cleansing operations in the Crimea, but AOK 11 increasingly called upon these professional executioners to inflict punitive measures upon non-Jews who cooperated with either the partisans or the Red Army. Terror became part of the Wehrmacht's panoply of tools, just like Karl or Dora, to crush all forms of resistance in the Crimea. In the last two weeks of February, Ohlendorf claimed that his group shot 1,515 people, including 729 Jews, 271 communists, 74 partisans, and 421 Gypsies or other "anti-social elements." Although the Holocaust would continue in the Crimea until the Soviet liberation in 1944, the SS confidently reported on April 16, 1942 that, "*Die Krim ist judenfrei*" (the Crimea is Jew-free). Only Sevastopol remained to be cleansed of enemies of the Reich. In fact, the SD killed 1,029 Jews and 11 communists in Kerch in July 1942, and was still finding holdouts months later.[7]

Ohlendorf left the Crimea before the fall of Sevastopol and most of Einsatzgruppe D followed the army into the Caucasus, but the SS and SD retained a strong presence in the occupied Crimea. Although the Wehrmacht established military *Ortskommandantur* (OK) in each occupied city in the Crimea, the real power was SS-Brigadeführer und Generalmajor der Polizei Ludolf von Alvensleben. A scion of Saxon aristocracy, Alvensleben had been an early adherent to the Nazi cause, joining the party and the SA in 1929, then the SS in 1934. He rose quickly in the SS hierarchy and took to the ethnic-cleansing mission with relish; he helped to orchestrate the first large-scale murder of civilians in Poland in October 1939. In 1941, Alvensleben was involved in organizing forced labor in Ukraine in an effort to get the region working for the Third Reich. When he arrived in Sevastopol in August 1942, Alvensleben was put in charge of all SS-Police units in the Crimea and was responsible for rooting out any remaining enemies of the Reich. Forced labor and "special actions" were his tools of choice. It was also part of his mandate to begin adapting the Crimea for German colonization.

The occupied Crimea was reorganized in August 1942 as the Generalbezirk Krim (General District) and subordinated to the Reichskommissariat Ukraine. The Austrian Nazi leader Alfred Frauenfeld was put in charge of the Generalbezirk Krim, which he operated as a semi-independent personal fiefdom. Frauenfeld was less vicious than Alvensleben, but viewed ethnic transformation as vital to German success in the Crimea and sought to import *Volksdeutsche* settlers into the occupied territory. Since virtually all of the Crimean Germans had been removed to the Urals by the NKVD in August 1941, the colonists would have to come from existing *Volksdeutsche* settlements in areas such as the Tyrol and Moldava. Frauenfeld had announced that Italians were "in all respects equivalent to *Volksdeutsche*," and sought to gather up ethnic Italians from Ukraine.[8] However, the task of gathering colonists for the Crimea proved far more difficult than expected, and by August 1943 only about 4,000 had been transported to the peninsula. Frauenfeld hoped to get 38,000, but even if he had, they would still have been only a tiny minority.[9] Efforts to organize economic projects such as "Arbeitsgruppe Krim" sounded great in reports to Berlin, but the reality on the ground was different. In May 1942, Frauenfeld established two small demonstration economic projects in Simferopol – a leather tannery and a textile factory, which together employed 250 workers.[10] Later, small quantities of coal were extracted from the region, as well as some foodstuffs, but the "colonies" remained dependent upon German supplies, draining resources from military projects. Frauenfeld was willing to cooperate with the Tatars, but he was very enamored of introducing or "re-discovering" Gothic culture in the Crimea, which would be renamed Gotengau. He encouraged amateur German archaeologists to come to the Crimea in the hope of discovering ancient Gothic artifacts in the region, which would demonstrate cultural links to the modern Germany and justify the post-war annexation by the Third Reich. While committed to making this fantasy into reality, Frauenfeld was less adept at restoring the region's agriculture, which had been nearly ruined by collectivization, war, and neglect. Throughout the war, the Crimea barely produced enough food to feed the Axis occupation forces, never mind the local population. One thing that the Crimea did produce in abundance was forced labor, and Frauenfeld provided Robert Ley, the Reich's labor minister, with over 60,000 forced laborers from the Crimea. Ley openly discussed the possibility of building summer resort camps for German youth groups in the Crimea, in another retreat from wartime reality.

The Wehrmacht established the *Befehlshaber Krim* under General der Infanterie Franz Mattenklott to control all military forces, exclusive of the SS, in the Crimea. Once AOK 11 left for Leningrad, he was left with a hodgepodge collection of *Feldgendarmerie*, coastal artillery, flak, pionier, signal, and supply units to act as an occupation force. In Sevastopol, Ortskommandantur 290 (OK 290) was established under the artillery officer Oberstleutnant Haensch. However, it was the SS, SD, and Abwehr who really ran occupied Sevastopol. Only five days after the end of organized Soviet resistance in the SOR, an SD detachment led by SS Obersturmbannführer D.M. Frick arrived and announced that all citizens left in Sevastopol would register within 48 hours or "be shot." Assisted by AOK 11's Gruppe Geheime Feldpolizei 647, the SD used the registration process to identify Komsomol members, communists, and Red Army survivors trying to hide among the population. In order to protect the Wehrmacht from Soviet stay-behind espionage networks, an Abwehr unit known as "Darius 305" arrived in Sevastopol to conduct the counter-intelligence mission. Approximately 1,500 Jews and communists were identified in Sevastopol by July 12 and turned over to Sonderkommando 11a for liquidation. The SD was also put in charge of 20 POW camps established around Sevastopol and Simferopol and, after filtering out useful collaborators, began eliminating the prisoners in August 1942. SD detachments took small groups of POWs out for labor details to clear rubble, and then shot them.

Despite the harsh measures inflicted during the occupation, there was some degree of local collaboration, even from ethnic Russians and Ukrainians. The teenager Lidiya I. Chyernih noted that, "among them [the Germans], there were good and bad people," and went on to describe how German troops employed Russian civilians as cooks, laundry help, and for other odd jobs, which provided a source of food. However, Chyernih noted that Romanian troops were more brazen and more likely to loot or rape. Gottlob Bidermann, whose unit was lodged with Crimean Tatars in the winter of 1941/42, noted a similar dynamic: German soldiers got on fairly well with the local population, but the Romanians were prone to misbehavior. As the Germans found elsewhere in Eastern Europe, there were always people – even Communist Party members – willing to work with the occupiers in return for food or other privileges. In Sevastopol, P. Supryagin was appointed the head of a puppet city council and willingly assisted the Germans in rounding up individuals targeted for elimination. The Germans established a small local auxiliary police force in Sevastopol, with volunteers taken from POW camps, as they did in other Crimean cities. In Yalta, Colonel Viktor I. Maltsev, a captured VVS officer, willingly volunteered his services to the Germans to "fight the Bolsheviks"; Maltsev had been arrested and tortured by the NKVD in 1938–39. Eventually, he would join Vlasov's anti-Soviet forces.

Nevertheless, the mythical Gotengau never materialized in the Crimea. A few *Volksdeutsche* colonies were established to harvest cotton, and Alvensleben began referring to Sevastopol as "Theodorichhafen" and Simferopol as "Gotenburg" – names that the Wehrmacht never used. Organization Todt was brought to the Crimea, but instead of refurbishing Soviet fortifications or port facilities, they wasted most of their efforts on ridiculous civil-engineering projects. Frauenfeld and Alvensleben tried to erase traces of the old Crimea and replace it with a new Gothic-inspired creation, but the Third Reich proved more adept at destruction than creation. When Reichsführer-SS Heinrich Himmler visited the Crimea in spring 1943, he was pleased with the progress made in removing the indigenous population and the arrival of a small number of *Volksdeutsche* settlers to begin the colony of Gotengau. Himmler visited a farm and was shown a cotton crop that was nearly ready for harvesting, proof that the German investment in the Crimea was about to bloom. He was less pleased when a local German army commander complained that he didn't have enough troops to defend the coastline from possible Soviet amphibious raids, but that Alvensleben was pressuring him to divert men and vehicles to assist with his colonization scheme. Himmler turned away from the *Generalmajor* without saying a word, thinking that the military mind could not understand what the Third Reich was trying to build here in the Crimea.

A German sniper looks for targets in the opposite hills around Sevastopol. Note that he is using a captured SVT-40 sniper rifle – which was highly prized by German soldiers. Positional warfare afforded ample opportunity for snipers on both sides to rack up a significant number of "kills." (Süddeutsche Zeitung, 00059506)

The "Thor," one of two 60cm "Karl"-type super-heavy mortars deployed to reduce Soviet defenses at Sevastopol. The two mortars fired a total of just 122 rounds during the siege, and fired their last rounds on June 9, 1942, against Coastal Battery 30. While these 60cm mortars gathered a great deal of publicity, they were not really practical battlefield weapons due to their very short range. (Author's collection)

A modern view of the rebuilt Coastal Battery 30, with the rangefinder in the foreground and the two turrets in the background, facing the Black Sea. The Germans assaulted the battery from this angle and the photo gives a good indication of the constricting nature of the ridge. (Author's collection)

A Luftwaffe ground crew prepares to load an SC 1000 bomb on a Ju-88 bomber. The Luftwaffe primarily relied upon 250kg and 500kg general-purpose bombs and did not have a large number of super-heavy or specialized bombs designed for attacking fortified targets. Consequently, the reduction of Soviet concrete gun batteries took multiple air attacks. (Nik Cornish, WH 1250)

The transport *Abkhazia* was sunk by German bombers in Severnaya Bay on June 9. The ammunition bunkers located behind the wreck of the *Abkhazia* in the chalk-faced cliffs are known as "White Cliff" – which was the target of the German 80cm Dora rail gun on June 6–7. Note that there is no evidence of a massive explosion as claimed by some German sources. (Author's collection)

With all the attention given to "Dora" and "Karl," it is often missed that the siege of Sevastopol represented the first opportunity for the Germans to employ massed *Nebelwerfer* rocket barrages in support of infantry attacks. Previously, they had been used only in small numbers, but at Sevastopol up to three or four battalions were simultaneously used to suppress a single enemy position. (Süddeutsche Zeitung, 00403714)

Dead Soviet troops inside one of Sevastopol's concrete forts. The German air and artillery bombardments inflicted only modest casualties on the well dug-in Soviet troops, but served to suppress positions, which could then be overrun by German combined-arms assault groups. (Author's collection)

The Soviets employed three armored trains during the fighting in the Crimea in 1941–42. The *Zhelezniakov* was the most powerful, armed with five 100mm naval guns and numerous 12.7mm DShK heavy machine guns. These trains provided mobile firepower, but were extremely vulnerable to air attack. (Author's collection)

Soviet naval infantrymen counterattacking to regain lost ground. Note the mixed weapons: a PPSH-41 submachine gun, SVT-40 automatic rifle, and captured German MP-40. German troops were often unnerved by the sudden onslaught of Soviet naval infantrymen, who could emerge from terrain that was thought to have been cleared and then conduct near-suicidal close-quarter assaults.

Romanian troops in the hilly terrain outside Sevastopol in June 1942. The performance of the Romanian Corps was decent, when properly supported by artillery and close air support. Without the participation of the Romanian mountain infantry, Manstein's 11. Armee would have had a difficult time overwhelming Petrov's Coastal Army. (Süddeutsche Zeitung, 00403679)

German infantry scramble up to the top of a shell-cratered hill outside Sevastopol, June 1942. Note that the German leader, armed with an MP-40, has a vertical white stripe painted on the back of his helmet. (Süddeutsche Zeitung, 00403689)

A German 10.5cm le.FH18 howitzer methodically shells Fort Constantine on June 24, 1942. By this point, German artillery clearly dominated Sevastopol's harbor area and could strike targets almost anywhere in the city. Note that the German howitzer is deployed on a forward slope in broad daylight – apparently there was no fear of Soviet counterbattery or air attack by this point. The German artillerymen are acting as if they are on a range shoot. (Author's collection)

Soviet troops emerging from the ruins of shattered positions during the final fighting in late June 1942. The German 11. Armee captured 95,000 Soviet troops at Sevastopol, but very few officers above the rank of colonel. After bravely resisting for months against superior firepower, the soldiers of the Coastal Army were abandoned by their commanders, who slipped away in the dead of night. (Süddeutsche Zeitung, 00403653)

Empfänger	Datum	An-lagen	Kurzer Inhalt	Bemerkungen	Verbleib
	17.3.		Dankschreiben für Tagebuch		
			Zu den Akten		36
	17.3.		Zur Bearbeitung abgegeben		18
	12.7. 13.5.		Abgabebescheid zur Bearbeitung		13
			Zu den Akten		
			Zu den Akten		
			Zu den Akten		36
	17.3.		Dankschreiben für Denkschrift		36
	11.2.	2	Abschrift des Schreibens und Anzeige an die genge.		15
			Zu den Akten		18
			Zu den Akten		36

Part of the daily log from a German security unit in the Crimea, for March 17, 1942. Note the numerous notations for "*Juden Akten*" or Jewish Action, indicating liquidation operations against local civilians. The banality of evil is quite evident on this piece of bureaucratic memorabilia, with the most interesting touch being that the Germans actually used a stamp for ethnic-cleansing activities. (NARA)

German R-Boats. The Kriegsmarine transferred the 3. Räumbootsflotille to the Black Sea in July 1942, and these small warships played a major role in the operations around the Crimea in 1943–44. Although intended primarily for coastal minesweeping, the R-Boats proved quite useful as convoy escorts, anti-submarine vessels, and even in surface combat against the Azov Flotilla's motor gunboats. (Nik Cornish, WH 1180)

German high-speed landing barges (MFP) unloading troops on the Sea of Azov, 1943. As a bonus from the aborted Operation *Sealion*, the versatile MFP proved well-suited to the shallow waters off the Crimea. Soviet naval forces never had much luck in efforts to interdict MFP coastal traffic, and it was not until the Luftwaffe lost its bases in the Crimea that Soviet air power could inflict significant losses on these craft. (Author's collection)

A Soviet MO-IV sub-chaser, SKA-038, operating off the Crimea. The Black Sea Fleet had 42 vessels of this type in service at the start of the war and built another 75 in 1941–44. This 50-ton, wooden-hulled vessel served as a jack-of-all trades in the Black Sea and was useful for landing troops and for escort duties. Although armed with two 45mm 21K guns, the MO-IV boats were much slower than the German *Schnellboote*, but about evenly matched with the R-Boats. (Author's collection)

Scouts from the 2nd Guards Rifle Division "Tamanskaya" land near Yenikale on November 4, 1943. Small groups of scouts were landed on the rocky coastline by light vessels from the Azov Flotilla, but the Soviets lacked the amphibious craft to land tanks or heavy artillery across this type of terrain. The failure to secure the port of Kerch in the initial phase of the Kerch–Eltigen operation greatly delayed the Coastal Army's breakout from their lodgment. (Author's collection)

Troops of the 346th Rifle Division crossing the Sivash on November 1, 1943. Soldiers had to link arms during the crossing, lest they become mired in the soft bottom. It took over two hours to walk across this 1½-mile wide ford, but the Soviet crossing was initially unopposed and took the Germans completely by surprise. Note that all the infantrymen are armed with PPSH submachine guns, and the flat Crimean coast in the distance. (Author's collection)

The Soviet 10th Rifle Corps had great difficulty in moving heavy weapons across the Sivash, and boats were nearly useless. Here, a 45mm anti-tank gun and two horses are being transported on two small boats, which must be pushed across the mud, rather than floated. It is interesting that German engineers thought that the Sivash could not be crossed by a large unit, and the ability of the Red Army to adapt and persevere in this kind of situation often dumfounded the more conventional German approach to warfare. (Author's collection)

Tanks from the 19th Tank Corps race through Simferopol on April 13, 1944, after the breakout from the Sivash bridgehead. Vasilevsky's decision to transfer this tank corps across the Sivash bridge rendered the German stand at Perekop futile and caused the entire Axis position in the Crimea to disintegrate virtually overnight. The 19th Tank Corps started the operation with 221 tanks and assault guns, including 63 British-built Valentine tanks. (Author's collection)

The freighter *Totila* under attack by Il-2 Sturmoviks on the morning of May 10, 1944, off Sevastopol. When it sank, it took an estimated 3,000 German and 1,000 Romanian troops with it. Soviet aircraft did not seriously interfere with the Axis evacuation from the Crimea until the final stages of the operation, but the concentration of Axis merchant shipping off the Chersonese was an easy target. (Author's collection)

A group of smiling female partisans in the Crimea, May 1944. Soviet partisans participated in the liberation of some of the coastal cities, such as Yalta and Alushta, which were close to their operating areas, but they completely failed to interfere with the retreat of V Armeekorps through the Yaila Mountains. Had the partisans delayed this German retreat by even a few days, the Red Army would almost certainly have overrun Sevastopol before the Axis had a chance to evacuate the rest of AOK 17. (Author's collection)

Soviet troops from the 2nd Guards Army in Sevastopol, May 10, 1944. The destroyed StuG-III assault gun in the foreground was probably blown up by the retreating Germans. Note that the building at left is the same one that the destroyer *Svobodnyi* was photographed next to in June 1942. (Author's collection)

German troops emerge from shattered buildings in Sevastopol to surrender on May 9–10, 1944. It is unclear exactly how many Axis troops were captured in the final days in the Crimea, but probably in the neighborhood of 8,000–10,000. (Author's collection)

Soviet naval infantrymen entering Sevastopol near Nakhimov Square, May 10, 1944. Fort Constantine can be seen in the background. At the end, the Germans put up no real resistance inside Sevastopol but instead made a beeline for the evacuation beaches. (Nik Cornish, RA 190)

Two Germans who attempted to flee from the Chersonese on a raft are captured by a Soviet naval infantryman. A handful of Germans escaped on improvised rafts or floating debris, but most fell victim to strafing attacks by Soviet fighters. Hitler's refusal to authorize an earlier evacuation condemned much of AOK 17's troops to death or capture. (Author's collection)

A Ukrainian BTR-70 armored personnel carrier occupies a defensive position near the Perekop Isthmus, March 2014. As in previous Crimean campaigns, control of the Perekop Isthmus is key terrain that both sides moved quickly to block.

Russian airborne troops arrived quickly in the Crimea in March 2014 in order to secure key facilities, but wore masks to conceal their identity. Nevertheless, their equipment – including RPG launchers – clearly identified them as regular troops and not the local patriots claimed by Russian television. Once the Crimea was annexed, Russian President Putin admitted that these men were, in fact, Russian troops.

The face of Russian imperialism in the 21st century looks remarkably like it did in the previous three centuries. Russian agitators used violence to terrorize anyone in the Crimea who opposed their annexation plan. Note the Cossack wielding a whip – ample proof that very little has changed in the age-old game to dominate the Crimea.

"For twenty years we were prisoners of the godless Soviets and we have hungered and worked day and night. Now we wish to help the German Army with all our strength and with our hearts."

Aliev Nambed, Tatar Volunteer in II./IR 399

After years of Soviet oppression, many Crimean Tatars welcomed the Germans as liberators. Manstein was willing to grant special status to the Crimean Tatars, and he ordered his troops to respect their religion and customs – but in return, he expected the Tatars to assist AOK 11 in identifying and pacifying pro-Soviet elements in the Crimea. He authorized the creation of Muslim committees – which had no real authority – in occupied Crimean towns, in order to give the appearance of some autonomy. For strategic reasons, the German Foreign Ministry also favored cooperation with the Crimean Tatars, since they viewed their assistance as useful for getting Turkey to join the Axis coalition arrayed against the Soviet Union. To this end, in November 1941 the German Foreign Ministry invited three Crimean Tatar exiles in Turkey – Edige Kirimal, Cafer Seidahmet, and Mustecip Ulkusal – to visit Berlin for consultations. Eventually, the pro-German Kirimal was selected to be a representative for Crimean Tatar interests. In 1940 it was estimated that there were 218,000 Crimean Tatars out of the Crimea's total population of 1,126,800. The Wehrmacht also regarded the Tatars as a potential source of military manpower, although no mention was made of Hitler's long-term plans for the Crimea, which would eventually result in their land being taken.

In October 1941, AOK 11 began forming the first Tatar volunteers into an 80-man security detachment, which was soon expanded to a 345-man unit once most of the Crimea was overrun.[11] In November, Manstein ordered that POWs of Crimean Tatar origin were to be released. Other Tatars supported the Wehrmacht in unarmed roles as well: as truck drivers, manual laborers in quartermaster units, interpreters, and guides. The Tatars also proved willing to identify communists, Jews, and Soviet agents among the general population. However, the initial recruiting and training efforts were haphazard, producing security units with negligible capabilities.

On November 23, 1941, the Simferopol Muslim Committee was established. The rump administration included recruitment and propaganda departments, intended to bolster the authority of the German occupation – not local autonomy. The AOK 11 referred to the civil administration they established in the Crimea using the old Ukrainian term "Starosta," in order to suggest continuity with traditional communal councils.[12] In January 1942, the committee was allowed to begin distributing a newspaper known as *Azat Krym* ("Free Crimea"), which regularly included pro-German and anti-Semitic items.

Once it became clear in January 1942 that the Wehrmacht was going to be operating in the Crimea for a while, AOK 11 began a serious effort to form Tatar volunteers into more useful units. The Germans began a widespread recruiting campaign in rural Tatar villages, using the local Muslim committees, and among the thousands of captured Red Army prisoners. Eventually, over 9,000 Tatars volunteered for service as auxiliaries in the Wehrmacht, which enabled AOK 11 to form 14 self-defense companies (*Schuma*). Some of these companies participated in mopping up the Soviet landing around Sudak, where they ruthlessly hunted down isolated Red Army soldiers. Some Tatars were recruited to fill combat losses in AOK 11. Saterov Vetut was assigned to 3. Kompanie of Pionier-Bataillon 132, and wrote that, "From now on things will be better for us than ever would have been possible under the Soviets. For us Tatars comes a new, good era. In the future we will no longer work for others, but for ourselves."[13]

After the fall of Sevastopol, the Wehrmacht began referring to the Crimean Tatars as an "allied people" and decided to increase the level of support provided to arming the Crimean Tatars. By November 1942, these original companies were expanded to eight *Schutzmannschaft* battalions and assigned to populated areas; these auxiliary troops were provided German uniforms and captured Soviet small arms, led by older German reservists. The *Schutzmannschaft* battalions proved useful for manning numerous checkpoints throughout the Crimea, coast watching, and conducting local security sweeps.[14]

Some Crimean Tatars took to the German occupation very quickly, and openly collaborated in return for not having their property confiscated. Others were even more enthusiastic and saw the German conquest as an opportunity to even old scores with Russian oppressors. Allegedly, some of the Tatar committees orchestrated the murder of large numbers of ethnic Russian communities in the Crimea in retaliation for earlier ethnic-cleansing operations; yet hard data on these allegations – made after the Soviet liberation of the Crimea in 1944 – is lacking. It is clear the Einsatzgruppe D recruited Crimean Tatar auxiliaries to assist in their ethnic-cleansing operations. Allegedly, Schutzmannschaft Bataillon 152 (tatarische) operated the "Red Farm" concentration camp in 1942–43 near Simferopol, where thousands of civilians with suspected links to the Soviet partisan movement in the Crimea were tortured and murdered. After the war, Soviet authorities unearthed hundreds of human skeletal remains at this site, but like the Katyn Forest situation, the Soviets attempted to mask who murdered these victims. Perhaps they were victims of Crimean Tatar retribution, but it is also possible that they were victims of the Red Terror in the 1920s or even Soviet ethnic cleansing in 1944.

Yet not all Crimean Tatars were so cozy with the German occupation. Dr Ahmet Ozenbasli, a Crimean Tatar nationalist who had been imprisoned in the Soviet Gulag in 1928–34, was made chairman of the Muslim committee in Simferopol in 1942. Although appreciative that the Red Army was gone, he was suspicious of German motives and ultimate intentions in the region. Like many Crimean Tatars, he regarded himself as a nationalist, not a collaborator, since he owed no allegiance to Stalin's regime. Ozenbasli pushed the Germans for more Crimean local autonomy, and when it was refused he began to speak out against German policies in the region. Unwilling to make a martyr of him and anger the Crimean Tatar populace, the Germans simply marginalized him. A few Crimean Tatars openly opposed the German occupation and ran off to the mountains to join the partisans.

As the war began to go against the Third Reich, the Wehrmacht and SS became increasingly eager to create Eastern European volunteer units for frontline combat duty. While the Crimean Tatars were regarded as "allies," the existing *Schutzmannschaft* battalions were only recruited for local service in the Crimea. By late 1942, the SS were interested in forming a Crimean Tatar brigade, and used personnel from the SD and Einsatzgruppe D to interview members of the *Schuma* units and Tatar POWs to identify potential recruits.[15] The SS also used the Tatar local committees to assist their recruiting drive in the rural areas. However, most Crimean Tatars volunteered to defend their local communities, not to join the SS or fight outside the Crimea. Recruitment was slow, and once the German retreat in the Caucasus began in January 1943, many Tatars began to reconsider collaboration. As the Red Army closed in on AOK 17 in the Kuban, discipline in the *Schutzmannschaft* battalions became problematic, and desertions increased. Consequently, the Wehrmacht was forced to disband several *Schutzmannschaft* battalions and execute those who encouraged disaffection. Other unreliable Crimean Tatars were deported as forced labor.

In 1943, SS efforts to form Crimean Tatar regular units progressed slowly, and did not succeed in attracting enough volunteers until the Red Army returned to the Crimea in 1944. At that point, some volunteers "voted with their feet" and deserted, but many of the *Schuma* men could not afford to fall into Soviet hands and had little choice but to remain loyal to the Wehrmacht. As Sevastopol was falling in May 1944, about 2,200 Crimean Tatar volunteers were evacuated to Romania and then Germany, where they were formed first into the Tataren-Gebirgsjäger-Regiment der SS, then the Waffengruppe Krim. In July 1944, the unit was redesignated as Waffen-Gebirgs-Brigade der SS (Tatar Nr. 1), but this formation was disbanded in December 1944 without ever seeing combat. As the war ended, the Crimean Tatar volunteers were apparently dispatched to the Italian front in 1945, but the formation disappeared in the final months of the war.[16]

In the end, collaboration between the Crimean Tatars and the German occupation authorities in 1942–43 became a justification for the Soviet authorities to inflict collective punishment upon the entire Tatar population when the Red Army returned to the Crimea in May 1944. The Tatars were singled out as traitors and made the scapegoats for Red Army defeats in the Crimea in 1941–42; allegedly the desertion of Crimean Tatars, as well as Chechens and other Caucasian minorities serving in the Red Army, fatally undermined the Soviet defense. By blaming the Crimean Tatars for the German conquest of the Crimea, the Soviet leadership could absolve themselves of any responsibility for their own mistakes in the region.

It is difficult to assess the Crimean Tatars simply as victims, since some of their community willingly assisted the SS in the Holocaust, but one thing is certain: in cooperating with the Germans, they got far more than they bargained for.

In August 1941, Boris A. Borisov's Communist Party (CPSU) committee in Simferopol, in conjunction with local NKVD authorities, began to discuss the possibility of partisan warfare in the Crimea, but no real action was taken for the next two months. Most of the available manpower had already been called up to fill the four militia divisions raised in the Crimea, and the CPSU was unwilling to arm the civil populace unless absolutely necessary. Everything changed when the Germans broke through at Ishun in late October, and Borisov's committee in Simferopol realized that it was necessary to act immediately. The committee selected Aleksei V. Mokrousov to head the partisan movement in the Crimea – the very same anarchist sailor who had delivered Sevastopol to the Bolsheviks in December 1917 and ruthlessly murdered Tsarist naval officers and Tatar nationalists in 1918. Mokrousov did have experience in leading irregular warfare, having led a partisan group against Wrangel's White forces in 1920, but he had no real military training, and discipline was not a strong suit for an anarchist. He had served in Spain as an advisor in 1936–37, but spent most of the interwar period in odd jobs for the Communist Party, including exploring Siberia. When the Germans reached the Crimea, Mokrousov was working as a hatchet man for Borisov's CPSU committee in Simferopol, tasked with helping the NKVD to hunt down enemies of the state. He was almost certainly involved in the massacre of Tatar prisoners at the NKVD prison in Simferopol in October 1941. Given Mokrousov's violent and erratic temperament, Borisov's committee selected NKVD Major Georgy L. Seversky as his military deputy and trusted party member Serafim V. Martynov as political commissar. As the CPSU officials evacuated post haste to Sevastopol or Yalta, Mokrousov announced that there would be five partisan zones formed in the Crimea, and a total of 29 units created. Then he and his handful of lieutenants sped off to the Yaila Mountains in the south, with no plan or supplies.

During November 1941, the anti-German partisan movement began to coalesce in the southern Crimean mountains, based upon small groups of cut-off Soviet soldiers, NKVD Border Guards, and civilians who fled from the towns to avoid German round-ups. Commissars also encouraged underage Komsomol members from the Sevastopol–Balaklava area to join partisan units. The guerrillas went into the mountains with plenty of patriotic enthusiasm but little else, particularly food. Weapons were limited to small arms, without much ammunition. Major Seversky apparently led one of the first partisan attacks near Alushta, where a few German supply trucks were ambushed. However, Manstein was focused on taking Sevastopol and not interested in wasting resources chasing partisans in the mountains, so he left most of the rear-area security mission to the Romanian mountain-infantry units, who were well suited to this task. The Axis learned that lone vehicles were at risk from partisan attacks, but that groups of three or four were fairly safe.

The Crimean partisans were almost totally ineffective in the winter of 1941/42 due to the lack of food and weapons. Most of the new recruits were teenagers, like 15-year-old Vilor P. Chekmak, eager to display their patriotic ardour, but completely untrained and amateurish. Chekmak blew himself up with a hand grenade when approached by a German patrol – heroically according to the Soviet version, but more likely due to mishandling the weapon. Winter hit the unprepared partisans hard, and many starved or froze to death in the mountains, while others were reduced to eating corpses. Virtually all of the enthusiastic Komsomol teenagers from Sevastopol and Simferopol were dead before spring arrived. Mokrousov aggravated an already bad situation by refusing to allow any Tatars to join his partisan groups and raiding Tatar villages to steal food – which helped to encourage the Tatars to assist Axis anti-partisan measures. On January 6, 1942, the Red Army conducted a regiment-size landing at Sudak, southwest of Feodosiya. The landing was ultimately a failure, but a good number of isolated troops from the landing force joined the partisans. In late February 1942, Soviet commissars ordered the Crimean partisans to assist an attempt by Petrov's Coastal Army to break through the siege lines around Sevastopol. A total of 134 partisans were sent to attack AOK 11's rear areas and 117 were killed – it was a complete fiasco. Soviet commanders viewed the partisans as a "Fifth Column" that could attack enemy rear areas, but the German appreciation of them as "Bandits," suitable only for raiding unarmed villages or lone Axis vehicles, was closer to the truth. In March 1942 a single Soviet plane landed with medical supplies, food, and ammunition for the partisans, but this was clearly a drop in the ocean. The main German anti-partisan unit in early 1942 was Feldgendarmerie-Abteilung 683, which was more concerned with hunting down paratroopers than partisans. Romanian anti-partisan operations rolled up hundreds of half-starved partisans, too weak to escape. Further weakening the partisan effort, Mokrousov defined the partisan struggle in the Crimea as a "two-front war" – against the Axis occupiers and against Tatar collaborators.[17]

By mid-1942 it was apparent that the Crimean partisans had achieved nothing of note, and that Mokrousov's erratic command style prevented effective recruiting or operations. Partisan strength in the Crimea dropped to fewer than 600. Soviet accounts are unusually candid about Mokrousov's continual drunkenness and casual execution of his own partisans for various alleged infractions. Indeed, under Mokrousov, the Crimean partisan movement was floundering, and was no hindrance at all to the Axis. Mokrousov sent communications to the North Caucasus Military District that blamed the Crimean Tatars for his failures due to their collaboration with the enemy. With the destruction of the Crimean Front in May 1942 and the fall of Sevastopol in July, Mokrousov's inability to orchestrate an effective partisan campaign in the Crimea was no longer tolerable to the Stavka. A plane was sent into the Crimea to collect Mokrousov from a clandestine landing strip on July 8, and he was flown back to the Caucasus. Although some officers wanted to put Mokrousov before a military tribunal, he had plenty of party and NKVD friends who protected him. Instead, Petrov promoted him to Colonel and made him the chief of intelligence for the North Caucasus Front.

While the partisan movement languished in the Yaila Mountains, there was resistance in other places in the Crimea. Colonel M. Yagunov, commander of the rearguard at Kerch in May 1942, had retreated into the Adzhimushkay Quarry. These underground limestone quarries had been used as hiding places by local partisans in the winter of 1941/42, as well as underground storage shelters for artillery ammunition. Yagunov pulled his small command back into the underground quarry, which consisted of deep catacombs that had been excavated for decades and were impervious to bombing. Other Soviet troops that had been abandoned in Kerch, as well as civilians, made their way to the Adzhimushkay Quarry, swelling Yagunov's "command" to purportedly between 10,000 and 13,000 people. Soviet sources claim that these resistance forces held out in the Adzhimushkay Quarry for 170 days with negligible water and supplies, and stole what they need from nearby German units. Claims are also made that the resistance in the Adzhimushkay Quarry tied down large numbers of German troops. Unfortunately, this version of what happened at the Adzhimushkay Quarry is a patriotic exaggeration. Although water was a major problem for those in the quarry, post-war excavations revealed that the defenders succeeded in digging deep wells through the rock.

However, XXXXII Armeekorps quickly discovered the Soviet presence in the Adzhimushkay Quarry, and surrounded the area with barbed wire and mines. German pioneer units made a few attempts to smoke or burn out the defenders, which caused some within the quarry to exit and face capture. However, the records of Ortskommandantur 287 in Kerch reveal that the Germans were little concerned about the Adzhimushkay Quarry, and simply assigned a reinforced Romanian infantry company to keep an eye on the place.[18] Indeed, OK 287 was far more concerned about Soviet air and artillery attacks from the Taman Peninsula than they were about some holdouts in a cave. German reports described the protracted defense of the Adzhimushkay Quarry as "tenacious" but "absurd." As supplies ran low, Yagunov was forced in desperation to mount a sortie on the night of July 8/9 to try and gain water and food from outside the quarry, but he was killed in the process. Afterwards, the defenders of the Adzhimushkay Quarry died a slow death of starvation and dehydration. On October 23, OK 287 noted that a single officer emerged from the cave to surrender, but that a handful were still alive inside.[19] By October 30 the Germans finally entered the caverns, as resistance from the starved defenders collapsed. At least 48 survivors were captured and sent to the Red Farm death camp near Simferopol, where they were probably executed. Soviet-era sources claim that 10,000–15,000 people died in the Adzhimushkay Quarry, but this claim is very unlikely. Based upon the known losses for the Crimean Front and OK 287's registration of the civilian population of Kerch in July 1942, it is unlikely that more than a few thousand were ever in the quarry at any one time, and that many left long before the end of the 170-day siege. Recent excavations suggest about 1,200 persons in the quarry. It is likely that most belonged to Yagunov's rearguard, along with a few hundred local civilians. Certainly the Germans would not have left a single Romanian company as a blocking force against 10,000–15,000 Soviets, and the matter-of-fact references to the quarry in German reporting suggests that is was not a large enemy force trapped inside. In any case, their resistance was certainly brave, but futile. Even though Yagunov had a radio and was in contact with Soviet forces on the

Taman Peninsula, no effort was made to help his group. Interestingly, the whole incident of the Adzhimushkay Quarry was initially suppressed from Soviet historiography after the war, because all references to the crushing defeat of Kozlov's Crimean Front were still raw and the fact that these people were abandoned to die in an underground quarry did not reflect well on the party or senior military leaders.

By November 1942 the partisan movement in the Crimea had all but sputtered out, with only 150 members still active. During the year, at least 398 partisans were killed, 473 starved to death, and hundreds more missing or deserted. A few brave souls remained, particularly in the occupied cities of the Crimea. In Sevastopol, Petty Officer Vasiliy D. Revyakin had been captured when the city fell in July 1942 but had managed to escape and be hidden. In March 1943, in conjunction with sympathetic civilians, he formed a resistance cell in Sevastopol that was grandiloquently named the "Communist Underground in the Rear of the Germans" (the KPOVTN). Working with dockyard workers like Paul D. Silnikova, who had a secret printing press, the group focused on political agitation and propaganda via leaflets. This was a typical communist tactic, but it did not accomplish much, and the Germans took little interest in the group until they started committing sabotage against rail lines. Once German logistics in the Crimea were threatened, the SD swooped in, arresting Silnikova in October 1943, which led to further arrests. In March 1944, Revyakin was betrayed by an informer and tortured to death by the SD. The underground resistance in Sevastopol was broken, just before liberation arrived.

Despite utter failure in 1942 and disappointments through much of 1943, the partisan movement began to revive once the Germans evacuated the Caucasus and the advance of the Red Army isolated the Germans in the Crimea in November 1943. Air resupply operations via short takeoff and landing aircraft like the Po-2 and R-5 biplanes increased in 1943, and succeed in preventing the partisans from either starving to death or running out of ammunition.[20] Lidiya I. Chyernih, a teenage girl from Yalta, joined the partisans in November 1943, at age 16. There were many female partisans, but Lidiya did not carry a weapon and served in a support role. She did note that, by this point, the partisans were forming into ten-person squads and were regularly receiving arms and supplies by air, as well as political commissars to direct them. Seven partisan brigades were formed in late 1943 and several clusters of active partisan areas appeared between Simferopol and Feodosiya. The partisans concentrated on attacking traffic on the Simferopol–Feodosiya and Simferopol–Sevastopol stretches of road, both of which ran through mountainous terrain. Most of the road security consisted of *Feldgendarmerie* and *Schuma* units. In late November 1943 the partisans began attacking in groups of up to 200 fighters, and inflicted 75 casualties on the Axis, but suffered 310 themselves.[21] In December 1943 a partisan offensive inflicted another 155 casualties on the Axis, but lost over 200 of their own. For the first time, the Axis had to seriously worry about road and rail security in the Crimea. By January 1944 there were 3,700 Soviet partisans in the Crimea, of which at least 630 were Tatars. Partisan tactics were still quite amateurish, resulting in heavy losses, but they were becoming increasingly bold, and the Axis had to devote significant forces to secure their supply lines to Sevastopol.

Soviet-era claims about the achievements of the Crimean partisan movement are only appropriate for the last six months of their fight against the Axis occupation. Throughout 1941–43, the Crimean partisans were badly led and mostly ineffectual, and only became a threat once the Red Army had isolated the German forces in the Crimea.

Nazi empire builders were not the only ones in the Third Reich that tried to convert fantasy into reality in the Crimea. Despite having done little to win the Crimea until the final weeks of Operation *Störfang*, the Kriegsmarine leadership became very interested in using the occupied Crimea to turn the Black Sea into a German-dominated lake, which could also provide future access to the Mediterranean. Although Sevastopol was a shattered ruin by the time it fell into German hands, the Kriegsmarine believed that it could be rebuilt into a "German Gibraltar" that would solidify the German hold on the region. Even before Sevastopol fell, Konteradmiral Heinz-Heinrich Wurmbach, titular commander of Kriegsmarine forces in the Black Sea, moved his headquarters from Bucharest to Simferopol. Wurmbach had a varied background, which included service on U-Boats in 1917–18, minesweepers, and diplomatic service in Rome in 1934–36, but at heart he was a "big ship" sailor and had commanded the pocket battleship *Admiral Scheer* just before the war began. When he arrived in Simferopol in late June 1942, Wurmbach had no intention of leading a "paper command" from a dusty and desolate Crimean provincial city.

On the opposite side, the Black Sea Fleet was seriously hurt by the loss of its shipbuilding facilities at Nikolayev in 1941 and its main base at Sevastopol in 1942. After the loss of the Crimea, the fleet was forced to retreat to the minor ports of the Caucasus – Poti, Sochi, Tuapse, and Batumi – which had minimal repair and support facilities. These facilities had been intended to provide a support base for a few minesweepers and patrol boats, not battleships and heavy cruisers. The larger port facilities at Novorossiysk became untenable soon after the loss of the Crimea due to frequent Luftwaffe attacks, and were no longer useable. Although Oktyabrsky had succeeded in evacuating some of the stocks of ammunition, torpedoes, and spare parts from Sevastopol during the winter of 1941/42, the Black Sea Fleet lost a great deal of its material when Sevastopol fell. Without decent bases or supplies, the operational effectiveness of the remaining large Soviet warships was severely impaired. Oktyabrsky's flagship, the battleship *Parizhskaya Kommuna*, would spend more than a year hiding in the small port of Poti, but her 305mm gun barrels were worn out and could not be replaced.[22] For the next year, Oktyabrsky's fleet was reduced to two cruisers, eight destroyers, and 20 submarines, of which only about half were operational at any one time. The Soviet merchant marine had also been gutted trying to keep Sevastopol supplied, meaning that naval transport and supply capabilities in the Black Sea would be insufficient for the rest of the war. Instead, most of the Soviet naval effort in the Black Sea after the fall of Sevastopol focused on occasional raids by cruiser–destroyer groups against the Crimean coastline and a stepped-up offensive by the Black Sea Fleet submarine flotillas against Axis merchant traffic in the Black Sea. However, the greatest weakness of the fleet remained their vulnerability to air attack, and as long as the Luftwaffe maintained a credible anti-shipping force in the Crimea, the Black Sea Fleet could not seriously contest the waters around the peninsula.

This weakness was amply demonstrated on the night of August 2/3, 1942, when Oktyabrsky sent the heavy cruiser *Molotov* and the destroyer leader *Kharkov* to bombard the port of Feodosiya, where the Kriegsmarine was believed to be assembling an amphibious force. Although the two warships travelled at high speed, the long summer days did not give them sufficient hours of darkness to make the entire transit in one night. The Soviet warhips were spotted by German reconnaissance aircraft and the defenses at Feodosiya were forewarned. As they approached the port, the *Molotov* was suddenly attacked by two Italian MAS boats and forced to turn away. The *Kharkov* lobbed 59 unaimed 130mm rounds at the port and then fled as well. For six hours the two warships were attacked by the Luftwaffe, and an He-111H from 6./KG 26 finally scored a torpedo hit that tore off the *Molotov's* stern.[23] It was a painful lesson, which sidelined one of Oktyabrsky's best warships for more than a year.

The Kriegsmarine naval build-up in the Black Sea accelerated after July 1942, as regular supply convoys began between the Romanian port of Constanta and Sevastopol–Balaklava–Feodosiya. In addition to Birnbacher's six S-Boats, which moved to Ivan Baba near Feodosiya, the 3. Räumbootsflotille arrived with five R-Boats and estlablished themselves in Balaklava harbor. Both the R- and S-Boats were about the same size, but they had different capabilities. While the S-Boats were built for high-speed torpedo attacks, the R-Boats were designed as coastal minewsweepers and were also useful as general-purpose escorts. No more S-Boats were sent to the Black Sea, but 12 more R-Boats were sent in late 1942. Initially, the Kriegsmarine was capable only of conducting sea-denial missions with its handful of S-Boats, but the arrival of the R-Boats enabled Wurmbach to attempt more aggressive operations. In August 1942, the Kriegsmarine launched Operation *Regatta*, in which a group of R- and S-Boats ran through the Kerch Straits – past Soviet artillery positions on the Taman Peninsula – to attack Soviet coastal shipping in the Sea of Azov. This operation assisted Heeresgruppe A's advance into the Caucasus and inflicted heavy losses on Gorshkov's Azov Flotilla.

Heeresgruppe A wanted the Kriegsmarine to support its advance into the Caucasus by conducting amphibious attacks across the Kerch Strait to seize the Taman Peninsula, but Wurmbach lacked the resources to pull this off according to the army's schedule. Unrealistically, Heeresgruppe A wanted five divisions from AOK 11 to be sent across the strait in August, but Wurmbach's Kriegsmarine forces did not have the ability to mount amphibious operations of such scale. However, the Kriegsmarine had invested heavily in developing amphibious craft for the aborted Operation *Sealion* in 1940, and that investment was about to bear fruit in a different area than intended. In 1940, the Kriegsmarine had developed the

Marinefährprahm (MFP) and Siebel ferries, both motorized barges built from bridging pontoons and aircraft engines, to carry troops across the English Channel. Both were modular designs that were easier to disassemble and transport by rail than standard vessels, and large numbers were transferred via the Danube to the Black Sea. By early September 1942, Kapitänleutnant Max Giele's 1. Landungs-Flotille had arrived in the Crimea with 24 MFPs; since each MFP could carry either two medium tanks or 200 troops, that meant that the Kriegsmarine had gained the ability to mount a brigade-size amphibious landing in the Black Sea. On September 1, 1942, the Kriegsmarine began Operation *Blucher II*, with the 24 MFPs transporting part of the 46. Infanterie-Division across the strait to land on the Taman Peninsula, escorted by four S-Boats. The operation was a great success, and the growth of Kriegsmarine capabilities significantly assisted army operations in the Caucacus. Nor were Gorshkov's light forces able to significantly interfere with German amphibious operations. Soviet motor torpedo boat (MTB) raids against German convoys found that their torpedoes passed harmlessly under the shallow-draft MFPs, and the Soviet MTBs were armed only with one or two machine guns. Giele soon began to mount 2cm or 8.8cm flak guns on some of his MFPs to repel Soviet MTB raids, and 10.5cm howitzers on others to provide naval gunfire support to the army. More and more amphibious craft were transferred to the Black Sea command, until by mid-1943 there were four landing flotillas with the ability to move nearly a division – this would become very useful in time.

Yet the Kriegsmarine wanted to be more than a mere adjunct to Heeresgruppe A, and kept pouring resources into the Black Sea area even after the Crimea was occupied and Novorossiysk had fallen. At great effort, the Kriegsmarine had begun transporting six disassembled Type IIB U-Boats by barge to the Black Sea in April 1942, and they were re-assembled at Constanta in Romania. The first U-Boat, *U-9*, became operational on October 28, 1942, followed by *U-19* in November, but the other four would not be ready until mid-1943. Although large surface warships could not be transported to the Black Sea, the Kriegsmarine sought to resurrect damaged Soviet warships that had fallen into its hands. The Kriegsmarine picked over the remains of the abandoned shipyards at Nikolayev and considered trying to launch the hull of the partially complete 59,000-ton battleship *Sovyetskiy Ukraina*, but this was eventually rejected as too difficult a task. Instead, the materials from two incomplete Soviet destroyers were plundered to build complete two incomplete troopships acquired from Hungary, which were named the *Totila* and the *Teja*. At Sevastopol, the Kriegsmarine put great effort into trying to salvage the wrecked cruiser *Chervona Ukraina*, which they thought could be restored to operational condition. However, none of these salvage efforts produced useful warships before the Crimea was liberated in 1944. In its quest for a true flagship for the Kriegsmarine in the Black Sea, German diplomats approached neutral Turkey about selling the obsolescent battlecruiser *Goeben/Yavuz* back to Germany, but this was ignored.

The Black Sea Fleet responded to the Axis naval build-up in the Black Sea by mounting numerous submarine patrols off the Crimea and the Romanian coast, but the results were disappointing even though Axis anti-submarine warfare (ASW) capabilities were minimal. Between June 1941 and December 1942, the Black Sea Fleet was able to sink only about 33,500 tons of Axis shipping, but lost 20 of its 43 submarines in the process. Soviet submarines laid only 60 mines in the Black Sea in the first eight months of the war, but laid 176 in Crimean waters in the months right after the fall of Sevastopol.[24] Most Soviet submarine losses were due to Axis mine barrages, which their submarines kept blundering into. Soviet submarines had great difficulty attacking moving vessels, and had a tendency to sink neutral Turkish vessels. In the most egregious incident, the submarine Shch-213 sank the refugee vessel *Struma* just 10 miles off Istanbul on February 24, 1942, killing 781 Jewish refugees trying to flee to Palestine. In 1943, the Black Sea Fleet had far fewer submarines operational, but the ones they had were more effective, sinking 27,500 tons of Axis shipping. Eventually, the loss of several Romanian merchantmen to Soviet submarines and the threat of mines being laid to block the use of Sevastopol caused the Kriegsmarine to create an anti-submarine capability in the Black Sea. In June 1943, the 1. Unterseebootsjagd Flotille was based at Sevastopol with 18 armed trawlers. A number of Soviet submarines were damaged and destroyed by this improvised ASW force, which made it increasingly difficult for the Soviets to attempt to operate near the approaches to Sevastopol. The Luftwaffe also finally deployed a naval-reconnaissance unit with six BV 138 flying boats to Sevastopol in July 1943, which were well suited to spotting submarines or mines.

While the Kriegsmarine had achieved a certain amount of sea control in the Black Sea by mid-1943 due to Luftwaffe support and the weakened condition of the Soviet Black Sea Fleet, this success was erased by Heeresgruppe A's failure to conquer the Caucasus. By February 1943, Generaloberst Richard Ruoff's AOK 17 had fallen back to the Kuban bridgehead, which it managed to hold for the next seven months against Petrov's North Caucasus Front. However, AOK 17 was gradually pushed back in heavy fighting, and although the Kriegsmarine was capable of keeping them supplied – unlike the Luftwaffe's failure to supply AOK 6 at Stalingrad – it was increasingly clear that this large formation was being wasted in the Kuban. The German military situation in Ukraine deteriorated very rapidly in southern Ukraine after the battle of Kursk in July 1943 and the beginning of an all-out Soviet multi-front offensive to reach the Dnepr River. Heeresgruppe Süd suffered over 159,000 casualties in July and August, and was straining to hold its front. Yet Hitler was reluctant to withdraw AOK 17 from the Kuban – still harboring delusions about making another push for the oil of the Caucasus – and did not authorize an evacuation of the Kuban until September 4. By that point, the northern part of Heeresgruppe Süd was retreating toward the Dnepr while AOK 6 was bleeding to death trying to stop a Soviet advance along the Sea of Azov. Once Hitler authorized the evacuation of the Kuban, the Kriegsmarine was ordered to transport AOK 17 to the Crimea, after which most of the German divisions would be transferred to reinforce AOK 6 while the Romanian divisions would remain to defend the Crimea.

On September 12, 1942, the Kriegsmarine began Operation *Brunhild* to evacuate AOK 17, and by this point it had four amphibious groups with a large number of MFPs and Siebel ferries. It was a complicated, three-phase operation, to be conducted over 38 days. AOK 17, now under General der Pioniere Erwin Janecke, had to hold off repeated Soviet attacks by Petrov's North Caucasus Front while the Kriegsmarine began evacuating one corps at a time across the Kerch Straits. Soviet efforts to interfere with the evacuation failed miserably, although Soviet aircraft sank a few MFPs and barges. Over the course of four weeks, the Kriegsmarine succeeded in evacuating 15 divisions with more than 239,000 German and Romanian troops across the Kerch Strait, plus most of their equipment, artillery, and vehicles. By October 9, 1943, Petrov's forces had liberated the entire Kuban, but AOK 17 had slipped away. Operation *Brunhild* was a major operational-level sucess for the Germans at a point after the battle of Kursk when they enjoyed few successes, but it is almost unknown today. Although the Kriegsmarine was unable to fulfill its dream of creating a Gibraltar in the east, it had succeeded in creating a general-purpose naval force that was capable of accomplishing astonishing results with very limited resources.

In contrast, the Black Sea Fleet became increasingly irrelevant. On October 5, the fleet decided to dispatch the destroyers *Kharkov*, *Sposobnyi*, and *Bezposhchadny* under Captain 2nd Rank G. P. Negoda from Tuapse to bombard German coastal traffic between Yalta and Feodosiya. As Negoda's squadron approached Feodosiya around 0530hrs, they ran into the German *S-28*, *S-42*, and *S-45*; a brief naval skirmish resulted in no damage to either side. However, it was clear that the element of surprise was lost, and after briefly shelling Yalta Negoda's squadron beat a hasty retreat. The VVS-ChF managed to provide three fighters for cover over the squadron, and they managed to shoot down a German reconnaissance plane at 0810hrs. Nevertheless, Ju-87 Stukas from III./StG 3 found the destroyers at 0900hrs and crippled *Kharkov* with three bomb hits. Negoda tried to tow the *Kharkov*, but his squadron suffered repeated air attacks, damaging the other two destroyers. At 1413hrs, the *Bezposhchadny* was hit by four bombs and broke in two. The other two destroyers were sunk by 1835hrs. Altogether, three destroyers with 716 sailors were lost for no appreciable gain, and once again the Black Sea Fleet proved unable to operate in daylight in waters controlled by the Luftwaffe. When he learned of this naval disaster, Stalin ordered that all major warships of the Black Sea Fleet be placed in reserve and used only with his permission – effectively putting Soviet naval capabilities in the Black Sea on par with the Kriesgmarine.

CHAPTER 8

The Red Army Returns to the Crimea, 1943

"The Crimea is the largest prison camp in the world."
Soviet radio propaganda broadcast, winter 1943/44

General der Pioniere Erwin Jaenecke was an unusual German army-level commander since he came from the engineers, not the infantry, cavalry, or artillery. He took command of AOK 17 in June 1943, just five months after being badly wounded at Stalingrad and being flown out on one of the last transport planes. The 53-year-old Jaenecke had spent most of his military career since 1911 in engineer or logstic assignments. He saw no frontline service in the first two years of World War II, and was a senior staff officer in Paris until February 1942. Jaenecke was also a good friend of Friederich Paulus, commander of AOK 6, with whom he had served in pre-war staff duty. Despite never having commanded infantry units before, Jaenecke was given command of the newly raised 389. Infanterie-Division and sent to the Eastern Front, where he participated in the advance to the Volga and the vicious city fighting around the tractor works in Stalingrad.

Like many German soldiers who found themselves encircled at Stalingrad in the winter of 1942/43, Jaenecke became critical of Hitler and his conduct of the war. He openly urged his friend Paulus to disobey Hitler's orders and attempt a breakout, saying that, "your own head is nothing compared to the lives of so many soldiers."[1] Paulus ignored him and all other advice. Jaenecke was badly wounded on January 17, 1943, and was fortunate to be flown out a week later. After three months convalescing in France, he returned to the Eastern Front as summer 1943 arrived. Assigned to a backwater theater in the Kuban and given command of another army threatened with isolation and encirclement, Jaenecke was less than enthusiastic about his situation.

When Operation *Brunhild* began on September 12, Jaenecke lost control over parts of AOK 17 as it was transported from the Kuban to the Crimea. XXXXIV Armeekorps was the first major formation to be transported to the Crimea, where the OKH immediately transferred it to AOK 6 to reinforce its crumbling front. As more divisions were evacuated from the Kuban, they kept getting transported to other threatened sectors in Ukraine, until finally, eight of the ten German divisions in AOK 17 were transferred to other commands. In the Crimea, Jaenecke's AOK 17 was left with just the 50. and 98. Infanterie-Divisionen and six Romanian divisions. Even those units were incomplete; Major Erich Bärenfänger's Grenadier-Regiment 123 was detached from the 50. Infanterie-Division and sent by truck across the Chongar bridge to reinforce XXXXIV Armeekorps at Mariupol. In small compensation, AOK 6 transferred Generalmajor Wilhelm Kunze's worn-out 336. Infanterie-Division to AOK 17 for rebuilding in the Crimea, but it had only four battalions and almost no artillery.[2] Of the seven Romanian divisions subordinate to AOK 17, the three mountain divisions were in decent shape in terms of personnel and equipment, but the Germans no longer put much faith in the Romanians to fulfill any but the most basic missions after the defeat at Stalingrad. In addition, the Befehlshaber Krim contributed the 153. Feldausbildungs-Division and the 1st Slovakian Infantry Division, both of which had minimal combat capabilities. By late October 1943, there were over 200,000 Axis military personnel in the Crimea, but only about one-fifth of these were combat troops. Over 27,000 personnel were assigned to quartermaster and logistic units, Fliegerkorps I had over 5,000 Luftwaffe personnel and the Kriegsmarine had over 4,000 in the Crimea.

In addition, the SS, SD, and Abwehr still had a very strong presence in the Crimea, with over 6,000 assigned personnel, but their military effectiveness was negligible.

Jaenecke had only just settled into his new headquarters in Simferopol when the entire situation around him spun out of control. AOK 6, including the recently arrived XXXXIV Armeekorps, was badly defeated at Melitopol by General Fyodor I. Tolbukhin's 4th Ukranian Front on October 24 and began to retreat toward the lower Dnepr. Tolbukhin let loose his armor and cavalry in pursuit – the 11th and 19th Tank Corps and the 4th Guards Cavalry Corps – which came rolling across the barren Nogai Steppe at great speed. It was quickly apparent that the Soviets would make for the traditional entrances to the Crimea – Perekop and the Chongar Narrows – to isolate AOK 17. Amazingly, the only Axis forces near Perekop was a battlegroup of the 1st Slovak Division and a few replacement battalions from Generalmajor Kurt Gerock's 153. Feldausbildungs-Division, while the Chongar Narrows were virtually unguarded.[3] For once, it was the Wehrmacht caught with its pants down, with the entrances to the Crimea wide open.

Axis command and control in the Crimea was in a muddle in the last days of October 1943. Jaenecke controlled General der Gebirgstruppe Rudolf Konrad's XXXXIX Gebirgs-Korps, but Konrad had no troops near Perekop or Chongar, which were still designated "Rear Areas" under control of the Befehlshaber Krim. Generalleutnant Friedrich Köchling, an experienced infantryman, arrived from Berlin to take over the Befehlshaber Krim just two weeks before the Soviets arrived at the approaches to the Crimea. The command relationship between Jaenecke and Köchling was rather fuzzy, with each controlling some of the troops in the Crimea – a clear violation of the principle of unity of command. There were also separate Romanian, Kriegsmarine, and Luftwaffe chains of command, with no clear senior authority (this same phenomenon of poor inter-service coordination and inter-allied relations had plagued the Wehrmacht in North Africa as well). Köchling was observant enough to notice the threat to Perekop and Chongar and he agreed to move his available units, meager though they were, into blocking positions. Jaenecke displayed no sense or urgency at all and openly talked about a plan named "Michael" that his staff had prepared for evacuating AOK 17 from the Crimea, even though this was not authorized.[4] In fact, Hitler expressly forbade evacuation on October 28.[5] Yet Hitler did not bother consulting with the Romanian dictator Ion Antonescu about his opinion of keeping seven Romanian divisions isolated in the Crimea. By chance, elements of Kunze's 336. Infanterie-Division were not too far from the northern coast of the Crimea and Jaenecke acquiesced to it establishing a few blocking positions, but he was slow to order either the 50. Infanterie-Division or the two Romanian corps to detach any reinforcements. Jaenecke was looking to exit the Crimea, not defend it.

Kunze began establishing a blocking position at Sal'kove, at the northern entrance to the Chongar Peninsula, with a battery of four 8.8cm flak guns and two companies from his Panzerjäger-Abteilung 336, while his division pioneers prepared the railroad bridge for demolition. He sent the other company from Panzerjäger-Abteilung 336 to link up with an 8.8cm flak battery at Ishun. Indeed, Generalleutnant Wolfgang Pickert's 9. Flak-Division, which had 134 8.8cm and 334 light flak guns, would play a crucial role in the defense of the Crimea. Yet Kunze had very little infantry in his decimated division and was initially able to provide only 100 troops from Grenadier-Regiment 686 for the Chongar blocking position. The replacement formations under Köchling's Befehlshaber Krim had devolved into essentially school and convalescent depots during the past year, with personnel always in transit and minimal equipment on hand – not combat-ready formations. Gerock's 153. Feldausbildungs-Division had three *Feld-Ersatz Bataillone* (FEB) near Perekop, which were ordered to dig in along the old Tatar Wall, assisted by a battalion of construction troops. Artillery support was limited to two batteries of 10.5cm howitzers. The Slovak Tartarko Combat Group, with 800 troops, was also assigned to the Perekop position. Köchling sent Generalmajor Weber from a school unit in Yevpatoriya to take command of the defenses at Perekop, while combing out more ad hoc infantrymen from units as far as Feodosiya. Kunze ordered his II./Grenadier-Regiment 687 to reinforce Gruppe Weber. By October 28, two rudimentary blocking positions were established at Perekop and Sal'kove, but neither was capable of sustained defense against a superior enemy force. After all the effort wasted on trying to colonize the Crimea, the Germans had actually made no provision to defend it. As an afterthought, a *Kampfgruppe* from Luftwaffen-Jäger-Regiment 10 was assigned to guard Genische'k and the Arabat Spit.[6]

Meanwhile, General-Lieutenant Ivan D. Vasil'ev's 19th Tank Corps was rapidly approaching the Perekop Isthmus, with Kirichenko's 4th Guards Cavalry Corps (4GCC) close behind. Tolbukhin assigned General-Lieutenant Iakov G. Kreizer's 51st Army the mission of breaking through any defenses at Perekop, while General-Lieutenant Aleksei A. Grechkin's 28th Army would penetrate the defenses on the Chongar Peninsula. Tolbukhin hoped to take the Crimea on the run – and he stood a good chance given the level of German unpreparedness – and he knew that Petrov would soon mount an amphibious crossing of the Kerch Strait. While both Kreizer's and Grechkin's armies had suffered heavy losses in the Melitopol offensive, they were still infinitely stronger in tanks, infantry, and artillery than the ad hoc formations thrown together to defend the Crimea. The VVS was also much stronger than in 1942, and the 8th Air Army could provide effective fighter cover and ground support over the Crimea. If the two Soviet armies could break through at Perekop and Chongar, followed by Petrov landing at Kerch, the entire German defense in the Crimea could collapse in a matter of days. However, the Soviet advance into the Crimea was a secondary operation, while the Stavka focused most of its attention and resources on crossing the Dnepr River and liberating Kiev.

October 30, 1943, was a cool, overcast day in the Crimea. Several of Gerock's battalions were still arriving at Perekop, giving Gruppe Weber a total of six battalions, but all very understrength. Köchling was able to get the Kriegsmarine to agree to send some coastal artillery to Perekop, and they were enroute. Another odd unit, the III./Gebirgsjäger-Regiment Bergmann (an *Abwehr* unit comprising Azerbaijani and Georgian volunteers), also arrived at Perekop. At the Chongar Narrows, Kunze managed to force-march Fusilier-Bataillon 336 to reinforce the Sal'kove blocking position, and he had the rest of Grenadier-Regiment 686 on the way. Soviet reconnaissance aircraft were already flying over the Crimea, and they detected the German effort to fortify the entrances. Grechkin's 28th Army was the first to reach the entrance to the Crimea, in the late afternoon. Elements of the 347th Rifle Division forced the Luftwaffe field troops out of Genische'k and began pushing down the Arabat Spit, while the 118th Rifle Division appeared a mile north of the Sal'kove blocking position. Kunze took the risky course of action of splitting his forces; he ordered his pioneers to ferry I./Grenadier-Regiment 686 and some

Pak guns across the lagoon to defend the Arabat Spit, while II./ Grenadier-Regiment 686 remained to hold the Chongar Narrows. The move was accomplished during the night, to minimize risk of air attack.

Although Soviet scouts began probing the Chongar position during the night, the information about the Sal'kove blocking position was apparently not disseminated. Around 0900hrs, a column of 14–16 Soviet trucks approached Sal'kove and drove straight into the German engagement area. German 7.5cm Pak guns and 8.8cm flak guns tore the column to pieces, destroying every vehicle. Five hours passed before the 118th Rifle Division responded to this ambush, when it sent two dismounted rifle companies supported by mortars against the blocking position, but the result was a desultory exchange of fire for the rest of the afternoon.[7] The Soviet advance down the Arabat Spit also stopped when they encountered Koch's single battalion of grenadiers. By this point, Jaenecke was finally facing the reality that he was going to have to defend the Crimea, and he ordered Generalleutnant Friedrich Sixt to send a *Kampfgruppe* from his 50. Infanterie-Division to reinforce Gruppe Weber at Perekop. One-third of the division, organized as Gruppe Krieger, remained to defend Feodosiya. Belatedly, the Romanians were finally included in the picture, and the Romanian Mountain Corps dispatched Gruppe Balan (three mountain battalions, an artillery battalion, an antitank company, and a company of Skoda-built light tanks) to guard the Sivash coastline between Perekop and the Chongar Narrows. The situation had become a race to see who could get their forces into place fast enough.

On the morning of November 1, the lead elements of Vasil'ev's 19th Tank Corps arrived within sight of Perekop. Lieutenant-Colonel Nikolai Lebdev's 220th Tank Brigade was the vanguard, and he attacked immediately at 0620hrs, with 11 T-34s and 300–400 troops. Since the beginning of the war, Soviet tank commanders had often attacked aggressively and impulsively with poor results, but this time was different. Pickert's 8.8cm flak guns were still back at Ishun and only light artillery and Pak guns had arrived at the Perekop position. Nor were any mines in place yet. Lebdev's tank brigade smashed into the center of the enemy position at the Tatar Wall, panicking one of the Slovak battalions. Contrary to some sources, the Slovaks were not annihilated defending the Tatar Wall, but simply retreated, opening a large gap in the Axis front line. Since Gruppe Weber had not received authorization to destroy the road and rail bridges over the Tatar Ditch – which were still intact – Lebdev's tankers raced across them and penetrated over a mile into the Axis position, being stopped only at the outskirts of Armyansk. Part of the 40th Cavalry Regiment from Kirichenko's 4GCC also arrived to reinforce the breakthrough, but Soviet reinforcements were insufficient to exploit this tactical success, which gave the Germans a chance to recover.

Hauptmann Werner Streck was a 30-year-old reserve officer who had just returned from home leave in Germany after being wounded for the fourth time, and found himself placed in command of Feldersatz Bataillon 81 (FEB 81); this was a 1,500-man replacement unit divided in four companies and armed only with small arms and light machine guns. Streck's battalion was holding the west end of the Tatar Wall and he moved quickly to seal off Lebdev's breakthrough as best he could. A small counterattack even managed to capture a few prisoners at the Tatar Wall, who revealed important details about the Soviet forces en route to Perekop.[8] Streck and a few other replacement battalions managed to patch together a new front around the Soviet breakthrough, while waiting for three battalions from the 50. Infanterie-Division to arrive.

While the Germans had won the race to block the three traditional entrances into the Crimea, they were too late to protect the coastline along the Sivash. Lieutenant-Colonel Polikarp E. Kuznetsov, chief of intelligence of Generalmajor Konstantin P. Neverov's 10th Rifle Corps, had been tasked by General-Lieutenant Kreizer to find useable fords across the Sivash. Due to wind and tidal conditions, the Sivash was very unpredictable. Gathering up 30 volunteers, Kuznetsov began reconnoitering the coastline, and had the good fortune to find a local fisherman who identified a crossing site from the mainland to Cape Dzhangar. Kuznetsov sent three scouts across the 1½-mile-wide stretch of muddy water, which was ankle deep, and they confirmed the fisherman's information. The next morning (November 1), Kuznetsov led his small detachment across the Sivash at 1000hrs. It was slow going, and it took the men nearly two hours to cross the muck, but they made it to the opposite shore and Kuznetsov lit a signal fire to alert Neverov's 10th Rifle Corps to begin crossing. Major P. F. Kaymakova was the first to cross with a battalion of the 1168th Rifle Regiment and the rest of the 346th Rifle Division soon crossed as well, followed by the 216th and 257th Rifle Divisions. Nesterov's troops could not use rubber boats because the water was too shallow and the soldiers had to cross the Sivash on foot, with linked arms to avoid becoming stuck in the mud. A few heavy weapons were brought across on shallow-draft pontoons, including some 45mm antitank guns, but the troops were mostly limited to what they could carry. There were no Axis troops within 3 miles of the crossing site, and even though it began in broad daylight, the enemy was ignorant of the Soviet crossing of the Sivash for hours.[9]

As Nesterov's 10th Rifle Corps crossed the Sivash, Kuznetsov pushed on ahead and captured a German officer in his staff car, who had been sent to select positions for the Romanian Gruppe Balan, en route to guard the Sivash coast. By the time that the Romanians began to arrive, Nesterov's corps had already seized a large bridgehead on the southern side of the Sivash. Two ad hoc German formations, Gruppe Grote and Gruppe Beetz, were detached to reinforce the Romanian blocking force and to seal off the Soviet bridgehead at Cape Dzhangar. Since Nesterov's troops had no tanks and a small number of mortars, they had only a limited ability to attack until pontoon bridges could be built across the Sivash. The handful of Romanian mountain-infantry battalions, along with a sprinkling of German replacement troops, was able to build a screen around Nesterov's beachhead for the moment. It would take Nesterov more than two weeks to organize and supply his forces, by which point the German 336. Infanterie-Division had reinforced the Romanians. Colonel Petr G. Panchevsky's 12th Assault Engineer Brigade was brought up to build a pontoon bridge across the Sivash, but the task proved exceedingly difficult and the bridge was not completed until December 9, 1943.

More Soviet units began to arrive in front of Perekop on November 2, including Colonel Peter S. Arkhipov's 79th Tank Brigade and the rest of General-Major Boris S. Millerov's 10th Guards Cavalry Division. The Soviets mounted another attack at 1400hrs against the center of the Tatar Wall with 30 tanks and 2,000 troops; they succeeded in getting both troops and tanks across the ditch. German flak guns knocked out four tanks and inflicted "bloody losses" on the attackers, but the Soviets succeeded in pushing a large salient into the center of the German defenses.[10] The next day, Millerov sent another 1,000 dismounted cavalrymen across the Tatar Wall, along with more tanks. However, by November 3, Pickert had brought up several 8.8cm flak batteries to reinforce the defense and Gruppe Konrad had arrived with seven StuG IIIs from 2./Sturmgeschütz-Abteilung and additional infantry. Luftflotte 4 was able to commit Stukas for ground-support missions at Perekop, despite intense Soviet air opposition, which enabled Gruppe Weber to stabilize their defense at Perekop by November 4. German flak and antitank troops claimed to have knocked out about 80 Soviet tanks at Perekop between November 1 and November 4, although Pickert's flak gunners had suffered considerable losses, including five 8.8cm and four 2cm guns. When Stalin found out that the Soviet breakthrough at Perekop was not exploited in a timely manner, he had General-Lieutenant Nikolai Kirichenko relieved of command of the 4th Guards Cavalry Corps for failing to move up his troops quickly enough. Oddly, Vasil'ev, commander of the 19th Tank Corps, was awarded the Hero of the Soviet Union for the breakthrough at Perekop, although he had been slow to get the rest of his corps into the fight.

On November 6, reinforcements from the 50. Infanterie-Division had finally reached Gruppe Weber, and the Germans began an all-out attack against the Soviet salient from east, west, and south with six battalions. Although the Germans were able to recover the ancient Fort Perekop near the center of the line, they suffered very heavy losses and could not eliminate the Soviet salient. Hauptmann Streck, leading his FEB 81, was wounded for a fifth time, and this time he was sent home permanently – with the *Ritterkreuz* in recognition of his role in saving the line at Perekop. On November 7, Gruppe Weber shifted back to the defense and the front at Perekop stabilized, as it already had at Chongar and on the Arabat Spit. Although probing attacks would occur regularly, the front line settled into static, positional warfare for the next five months with little change. Gruppe Sixt from the 50. Infanterie-Division eventually took over the defenses at Perekop, while Gruppe Weber and the 336. Infanterie-Division took over the Sivash and Chongar sectors. The Axis had been extremely lucky, particularly at Perekop, but AOK 17 had been granted a temporary reprieve. However, AOK 17 was now isolated in the Crimea and completely dependent upon naval supply across the Black Sea from Romanian ports. Furthermore, just as the Axis were fending off this series of probing attacks by Tolbukhin's 4th Ukrainian Front, they also had to confront an old, more familiar crisis – Petrov's troops were crossing the Kerch Straits.

The Kerch-Eltigen landings, November 1943

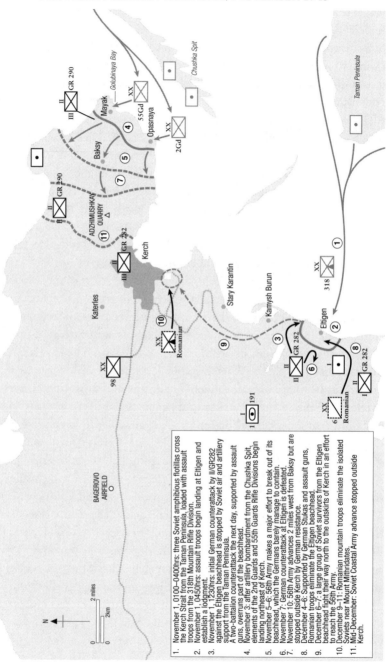

1. November 1, 0100–0400hrs: three Soviet amphibious flotillas cross the Kerch Strait from the Taman Peninsula, loaded with assault troops from the 318th Mountain Rifle Division.
2. November 1, 0450hrs: assault troops begin landing at Eltigen and establish a lodgment.
3. November 1, 1230hrs: initial German counterattack by II/GR282 against the Eltigen beachhead is stopped by Soviet air and artillery support from the Taman Peninsula.
   A two-battalion counterattack the next day, supported by assault guns, overruns part of the beachhead.
4. November 3: after artillery bombardment from the Chushka Spit, elements of the 2nd Guards and 55th Guards Rifle Divisions begin landing northeast of Kerch.
5. November 5–6: 56th Army makes a major effort to break out of its beachhead, which the Germans barely manage to contain.
6. November 7: German counterattack at Eltigen is defeated.
7. November 10: 56th Army advances 2 miles west from Baksy but are stopped outside Kerch by German resistance.
8. December 4–6: Supported by German Stukas and assault guns, Romanian troops eliminate the Eltigen beachhead.
9. December 6–7: a large group of Soviet survivors from the Eltigen beachhead fight their way north to the outskirts of Kerch in an effort to reach the 56th Army.
10. December 9–11: Romanian mountain troops eliminate the isolated Soviets near Mount Mithridates.
11. Mid-December: Soviet Coastal Army advance stopped outside Kerch.

Jaenecke assigned General der Infanterie Karl Allmendinger's V Armeekorps to defend the eastern Kerch Peninsula, although this was a very threadbare formation consisting solely of Generalleutnant Martin Gareis's tired 98. Infanterie-Division. Gareis' division had four battalions guarding 61 miles of coastline, with another four battalions in reserve.[11] Allmendinger had very little artillery support, but he had one ace up his sleeve: Hauptman Alfred Müller's veteran Sturmgeschütz-Abteilung 191, which had racked up an impressive combat record during the defensive fighting in the Kuban.[12] In addition, the Romanian Cavalry Corps was subordinated to Allmendinger's, but only the 6th Cavalry Division and part of the 3rd Mountain Division were in the eastern Kerch Peninsula. Allmendinger could count on a fair amount of support from the Kriegsmarine in coastal defense, although German naval leaders wanted to conserve their strength for an evacuation operation. Luftflotte 4 still had about 185 combat aircraft in the Crimea, including 84 He-111H bombers in three *Gruppen*, 33 Bf-109G in I./JG 52, and 63 ground attack aircraft in II./StG 2 and III./SG3. All of the ground-attack aircraft were at Bagerovo airfield, within easy reach of potential landing beaches in the Kerch Peninsula. The Germans knew that Soviet amphibious capabilities were very limited due to heavy losses over the past two years, so Jaenecke was not particularly concerned about a Soviet attack across the Kerch Strait just yet. However, the Red Army did not always play by the book, and the Stavka was insistent that Petrov mount an amphibious operation at the same time as Tolbukhin's forces reached Perekop and Chongar.

General-Colonel Petrov had begun planning for a crossing operation over the Kerch Strait just three days after the last elements of AOK 17 evacuated the Kuban. His basic plan was to transport elements of the 18th and 56th Armies simultaneously across the strait and seize beachheads north and south of Kerch – which was quite similar to the December 1941 landing operation. Unfortunately, neither Gorshkov's Azov Flotilla nor the Black Sea Fleet had the resources to mount a proper amphibious landing, and from the start, the operation later known as the "Kerch-Eltigen landing" was run on a shoestring and was more dependent upon luck than logistics. Relatively little shipping was available in the Caucasus and it consisted primarily of trawlers, fishing boats, tug boats, and barges. Gorshkov's flotilla could provide coastal minesweepers, motor torpedo boats, and various gunboats. Amazingly, after three years of war, the Soviet

Navy still did not have a proper landing craft available, particularly one that could transport tanks or heavy artillery. Nor did they have anything in the Black Sea comparable to the German MFPs. While the Western Allies did provide over 500 DUKW amphibious trucks that would have been perfect for crossing the Kerch Strait, they were sent elsewhere. Marshal Aleksandr Vasilevsky, chief of the Soviet General Staff, opposed Petrov's under-resourced amphibious operation across the Kerch Strait since he assessed it as too risky, and instead advocated concentrating all effort against the northern entrances to the Crimea, but he was overruled.

While Gorshkov and Vice-Admiral Lev Vladimirsky gathered up all the available shipping, Petrov positioned virtually all the artillery from the 56th Army – over 400 guns – on the narrow Chushka Spit to support the main landing near Yenikale. A smaller artillery group with 50 howitzers from the 18th Army was deployed on the lower Taman Peninsula to assist the secondary landings at Eltigen. Petrov intended to first make his main landing with the 56th Army near Yenikale, northeast of Kerch, on October 31, but this effort was delayed due to a bungled loading process by the Azov Flotilla. Another effort on the morning of November 1 was aborted due to unexpected losses to enemy mines. Instead, the 18th Army's secondary landing at Eltigen was the only one ready to go on the morning of November 1. Colonel A. D. Shiryaev's 137th Rifle Regiment from the 318th Mountain Rifle Division loaded at Krotovka on the lower Taman Peninsula throughout the night of October 31/November 1 and proceeded into the Kerch Strait around 0100hrs in six small landing flotillas. Each vessel loaded as many troops as it could carry on its deck, and none of the Soviet troops were issued life jackets or any form of flotation device. Off Cape Panajia, the Soviet flotillas ran into a German minefield that sank two vessels, killing over 200 troops, including Shiryaev and most of his regimental staff. The Soviet formations became disordered in the darkness, and the different speeds of vessels – some troops were even rowing across in longboats – pulled the formations apart. In mid-crossing, the flotilla encountered the German K-12 barrage, which had 120 moored contact mines – causing several more Soviet vessels to blow up. Although the Germans had several coastal batteries from Marine-Artillerie-Abteilung 613 to cover the straits, they did not notice the explosions. The Kriegsmarine also had several S-Boats on alert, but none near the straits. Despite heavy losses, the battered Soviet flotillas continued their crossing.

Petrov's staff had selected the sandy beach at Eltigen, south of the previous landing site of Kamysh Burun used in 1941, to land the assault elements of the 318th Rifle Division and the 386th Naval Infantry Battalion. Around 0330hrs, seven I-15 and two I-153 fighter-bombers from the VVS-ChF's 62 IAP strafed and bombed the beach area around Eltigen. Two Il-4 bombers also dropped incendiary bombs near the beach to provide a beacon for the landing force. At 0420hrs, the artillery support group on the lower Taman Peninsula opened a 35-minute artillery preparation against the opposing shore. This would have been a good time for the Black Sea Fleet's cruisers and destroyers to make an appearance and provide naval gunfire support, but the Stalin edict after the disaster of October 6, 1943, found them restricted to base. At 0450hrs, the first vessels approached the beaches at Eltigen. Due to lack of proper reconnaissance, Petrov's staff had failed to note that there was a sandbar located about 50 yards from the shore, and the first wave of troops began disembarking on the sand bar. When they enthusiastically rushed forward in the darkness, troops fell into 3 yards of deep water, and many heavily laden soldiers drowned. Initially, there was no resistance, but the surf was rough and made beaching difficult. By 0505hrs, small groups of troops had made it to the beach, which was covered with barbed-wire obstacles, but no Germans fired on them. Most soldiers arrived on the beach in the dark with only their personal weapon, and in small squad-size gaggles.

The beach around Eltigen was guarded by 5. Kompanie from II./Grenadier-Regiment 282, but its level of alertness was woefully inadequate. It took about 15 minutes before they realized that there was activity on the beaches. Finally, someone noticed something and called for artillery to fire illumination rounds over the straits at 0520hrs. The flares revealed dozens of Soviet craft on the water, which provoked a barrage of German artillery fire. The 2. Batterie of Marine-Artillerie-Abteilung 613, with four 17cm cannon, was located a mile southwest of the Soviet landing, and it began firing large-caliber rounds into the flimsy Soviet flotillas. The coastal artillerymen inflicted tremendous losses on the landing force, including sinking the barges carrying the artillery battalion's 12 76mm guns. Nevertheless, the Soviets managed to land enough troops to secure a lodgment, and a battalion from the 1339th Rifle Regiment and the 386th Naval Infantry Battalion managed to overrun a battery of two Romanian 75mm howitzers on the northern end of the beachhead.

Another Soviet battalion from the 1331st Rifle Regiment landed too far south, near the German 17cm gun battery, but the Germans could not see the troops on the beach in front of them due to cliffs, and the Soviet troops marched along the shoreline to link up with the main landing force. Once the sun rose, the Soviets were forced to suspend further landings at Eltigen until the next night. It is estimated that no more than 2,900 Soviet troops landed at Eltigen out of 5,700 dispatched, and that only a few 45mm antitank guns and mortars reached the shore. At least one-third of the landing craft were sunk or damaged, and hundreds of troops had drowned.[13]

Allmendinger was not particularly alarmed by the landing at Eltigen, which was incorrectly assumed to be a battalion-size diversionary force, so he ordered Oberst Karl Faulhaber's Grenadier-Regiment 282 to mop it up. Inside the bridgehead, Major Dmitri S. Koveshnikov found himself the senior officer at Eltigen, with elements of several battalions mixed together. Initially, Koveshnikov had no radio contact with his division command post on the Taman Peninsula or with his subordinate units. Oberst Faulhaber pulled together the spread-out 5. and 7. Kompanie for a counterattack at dawn, but quickly realized that he was not dealing with a small diversionary force. By 1130hrs, Faulhaber had assembled a battalion-size counterattack with some artillery support, but in the interim Koveshnikov had finally established radio contact with the artillery on the Taman side, which he directed to pound the German positions around the beachhead. Soviet aircraft also continually strafed every attempt by Faulhaber to mass troops for a counterattack. Around 1230hrs, six StuG III assault guns from Sturmgeschütz-Abteilung 191 arrived and led an advance against the northern side of the Eltigen beachhead. A Soviet penal company was overrun and destroyed, and Major Koveshnikov's front line began to crumble. Only timely artillery support from the Taman Peminsula forced the Germans to break off the counterattack late in the afternoon. When night arrived, Petrov began sending more troops across to reinforce the Eltigen beachhead, and, despite serious losses due to mines and artillery fire, another 3,200 troops and nine mortars were landed. Among the new arrivals was Colonel Vasily F. Gladkov, commander of the 318th Mountain Rifle Division, who took command of the Eltigen beachhead. Again the Kriegsmarine failed to interdict the crossing operation.

Dawn on November 2 found Gladkov with three poorly armed battalions holding a half-mile-deep and 1½-mile-wide strip of land. In mid-morning, Gareis's 98. Infanterie-Division began a counterttack with two infantry battalions (I. and II./GR 282), supported by six StuG IIIs, pioneers, and flak guns. Luftflotte 4 also managed to scrape up some air support, although the Soviet 4th Air Army strenuously contested the air space over the beachhead. Attacking both ends of the beachhead, the Germans were able to reduce Gladkov's lodgment by half during the day, but Soviet artillery support from the Taman Peninsula inflicted significant losses on the German infantry, halting the counterattack. Faulhaber's Grenadier-Regiment 282 suffered 110 casualties in the first two days of fighting at Eltigen.[14] The next day Gareis continued counterttacking, and he received Stuka support from III./SG3 at Bagerovo airfield, but could not overwhelm the beachhead at Eltigen. By this point, the German forces surrounding the beachhead were heavily outnumbered by the encircled Soviet forces, but Gladkov's troops lacked the tanks or heavy weapons necessary to affect a breakout.

Meanwhile, Petrov was finally able to begin his main landing effort with the 56th Army on the night of November 3/4. It began with a massive artillery preparation with over 600 guns and rockets from the Chushka Spit, bombarding German positions near the beaches. Then assault elements of the 2nd Guards and 55th Guards Rifle Divisions, along with the 369th Naval Infantry Battalion, began crossing the straits. The Germans detected the crossing operation, and coastal artillery from Marine-Artillerie-Abteilung 613 opened fire and inflicted losses, but could not stop the crossing. The easternmost part of the Kerch Peninsula was guarded only by 9. and 11. Kompanie of III./Grenadier-Regiment 290, supported by three batteries of 10.5cm guns and one battery of 17cm cannon. When the 55th Guards Rifle Division began landing at Golubinaya Bay near Mayak, 9. Kompanie immediately fell back toward the battalion headquarters in Baksy. It was much the same at Opasnaya, where the 2nd Guards Rifle Division routed the sole German company in the area. Almost 4,000 Soviet troops were landed on the first day, seizing a lodgment area by evening that was 8 miles wide and up to 5 miles deep. Allmendinger hurriedly shifted two companies of fusiliers, some replacement units, and a pioneer outfit to create a thin screen around the Soviet beachhead, but he knew that he would need virtually all of Gareis's 98. Infanterie-Division to contain the new Soviet beachhead. Consequently, he ordered Faulhaber's Grenadier-Regiment 282 to make one more effort against the Eltigen beachhead, reinforced by Pionier-Bataillon 46 and two Romanian battlegroups from the 6th Cavalry Division. Allmendinger's staff developed a counterattack plan known as "Komet," which would crush the Eltigen beachhead, then redeploy all forces to contain the new Soviet landings. Allmendinger also pressed the Kriegsmarine to attack Soviet convoys in the Kerch Straits, but it was reluctant to risk its limited number of warships in the face of Soviet air and artillery attacks.

While Allmendinger struggled to employ his limited combat resources, Petrov ordered the 56th Army to expand its beachhead before the German defense could stabilize. On November 4 the town of Baksy was captured and the thin German center shoved backward. Gareis committed his fusilier and pioneer battalions, which prevented a complete collapse, but it was obvious that the equivalent of four battalions could not contain the 56th Army for long. Soviet reinforcements continued to pour across the Kerch Strait every night, enabling General-Lieutenant Mel'nik's 56th Army to mount a major breakout effort on November 5–6. Somehow, Gareis's thin screen of fusiliers and pioneers repulsed all attacks for two days, until Mel'nik's forces expended most of their ammunition. Thereafter, Petrov called off further attacks until he could get more troops, tanks, artillery, and supplies across the straits.

The Axis implemented "Komet" at Eltigen on November 7 and it was an utter failure. The promised Luftwaffe support went instead to Gruppe Konrad at Perekop, and Gladkov's troops heavily outnumbered the German and Romanian units that attacked the northern and southern perimeter. The only positive aspect of "Komet" was that the Kriegsmarine was finally prodded into operating in the Kerch Straits again, and the S-Boats and R-Boats began to seriously interfere with resupply missions to the Eltigen beachhead. Furthermore, it was clear to Petrov that Eltigen could not be expanded into a larger lodgment area, so no more reinforcements would be committed into this tactical dead end. After the failure of "Komet," Grenadier-Regiment 282 was withdrawn and the Romanian 14th Machine-gun Battalion and 6th Cavalry Division took over the perimeter defense. The Kriegsmarine also began to erect a fairly impenetrable blockade around Eltigen, using light warships, armed MFPs, and mines, which gradually starved the Soviet forces in the beachhead.

The battle of Kerch–Eltigen was shaped by the struggle for air supremacy over the beaches and the Kerch Straits in November and December 1943. Although Fliegerkorps I only had a single fighter unit at any one time in the Crimea during this period, it was the cream of the Luftwaffe's fighter arm. The Germans began the battle with I./JG 52, but Hauptmann Gerhard Barkhorn's II./JG 52 took their place on November 13, and his unit remained in the Crimea until April 1944. Barkhorn was already one of the top Luftwaffe aces, with 177 victories claimed by the end of October 1943. Although his *Gruppe* of 40 Bf-109G fighters was outnumbered by more than 10-1 by the fighters from the VVS-ChF and the 4th and 8th Air Armies, Barkhorn's pilots ripped into the Soviet air units operating over the Kerch Peninsula. In November and December 1943, Barkhorn personally claimed 51 enemy aircraft shot down and II./JG 52 inflicted over 200 losses on the VVS in exchange for 17 Bf-109s lost. Due to the ferocious resistance put up by Barkhorn's fighters, the VVS failed to deliver adequate air support to either beachhead.

Once a lodgment in the Crimea was created, the 56th Army was redesignated the Coastal Army and Petrov took personal command. On November 10, Petrov made a major attack against the center of the German perimeter west of Baksy and pushed it back 2 miles. Gareis's had a hodgepodge of company-size detachments from eight different battalions, but no complete units, so his defensive line had little integrity. The first ten T-34 tanks were brought across the Kerch Strait on barges on November 10/11, but Petrov had only limited armor support for some time. He continued to push westward, and by November 12 the Coastal Army was on the outskirts of Kerch. Major Erich Bärenfänger's Grenadier-Regiment 123, which had been detached to AOK 6, was now flown back into Bagerovo airfield by Ju-52 transports to reinforce Gareis's flagging line. Bärenfänger's regiment was reduced to a battalion-size *Kampfgruppe* after the heavy fighting at Mariupol, but this consisted of first-class veterans. When Petrov brought his armor into play on November 13–14, they ran straight into Bärenfänger's grenadiers. With his usual preference for close combat, Bärenfänger participated in knocking out a T-34 with Teller mines and 3kg demolition charges, and his battalion knocked out a total of nine tanks in one day. Bärenfänger was wounded again but remained with his troops, and his battalion was responsible for knocking out 24 enemy tanks between November 14 and November 20.[15] The Red Army also had heroes. Mladshiy Serzhant Tatiana I. Kostyrin, a 19-year-old female sniper in the 691st Rifle Regiment, had gained a reputation as a lethal killer during the fighting against Bärenfänger's battalion on the outskirts of Kerch. On November 22 Kostyrin led a local counterattack near the Adzhimushkay Quarry when her commander became a casualty, and she charged the German positions. She was killed in the action, but the Soviets claim that her bravery helped to achieve a favorable tactical outcome and she was posthumously awarded the Hero of the Soviet Union. Around the same time, German pioneers apparently tested a new weapon system known as the *Taifun-Gerät*, which was similar in effect to a fuel-air explosive and which was used against Soviet underground tunnels near the Adzhimushkay Quarry. Although not very effective, the Soviets regarded it as a chemical weapon.

Although Petrov was eventually able to replace his armor losses, he had to suspend his efforts to take Kerch until reinforcements arrived. Just as his forces were preparing to renew the offensive, the weather and the Kriegsmarine saved Allmendinger's V Armeekorps from being overwhelmed. Six R-Boats of Kapitänleutnant Helmut Klassmann's 3. Räumbootsflotille and five S-Boats from Korvettenkapitän Hermann Büchting's 1. Schnellbootsflottille proved a major thorn in the operations of Gorshkov's Azov Flotilla and gradually sank or damaged a considerable number of vessels crossing the Kerch Straits. Armed MFPs, equipped with 2cm or 3.7cm flak, also proved effective in the blockade mission, although 11 out of 31 committed were sunk, mostly by mines or air attacks. In skirmish after skirmish, the German R- and S-Boats picked off Soviet shipping, which seriously impeded the Coastal Army's build-up, and doomed the Eltigen beachhead.

By early December the situation at Kerch had become deadlocked, and Allmendinger took steps to finally eliminate the troublesome Eltigen beachhead. The Germans provided Sturmgeschütz-Abteilung 191 with 12 artillery batteries and Stukas to support Brigadier-General Corneliu Teodorini's 6th Cavalry Division's attack against Eltigen at 0500hrs on December 4. Two mountain-infantry battalions from the Romanian 3rd Mountain Division spearheaded the attack on the southern end of the beachhead, which gained ground. Attacks on the northern end of the beachhead failed. Gladkov's troops had limited ammunition due to the Kriegsmarine blockade, and the troops had been on limited rations for weeks. Continuing the attack on December 5, the Romanians slowly rolled up the beachhead from north to south. On December 6 Teodorini committed all his forces, and the Soviet perimeter began to crumble. After three days of heavy fighting, Gladkov decided that he would lead a breakout attempt to reach the Soviet positions near Kerch. This was a desperate decision, entailing a march of more than 12 miles through Axis lines. On the night of December 6/7, Gladkov led a group of more than 1,500 troops through the Romanian 14th Machine-gun Battalion's lines and succeeded in breaking clean through the enemy perimeter. The next morning, the Romanians overran the Eltigen beachhead by 0715hrs and took 2,294 prisoners. Teodorini's Romanian units suffered at least 865 casualties in reducing the Eltigen beachhead, but Soviet losses were much larger.

Gladkov managed to make it to the south side of Kerch before running into elements of Faulhaber's Grenadier-Regiment 282, which blocked their path. Although only 4 miles from Soviet lines, Gladkov's exhausted troops could not fight their way through the city of Kerch. Instead, he formed them into a perimeter along the water's edge, just east of Mount Mithridates. Although some Soviet sources refer to this action as the battle of Mount Mithridates, the Soviet troops were not on the mountain itself and instead clustered near the water, hoping for rescue. It did not take long for the Axis to figure out what had happened, and Brigadier-General Leonard Mociulschi's 3rd Mountain Division was assigned to eliminate the Soviet group. He quickly surrounded Gladkov's group with three mountain battalions, while German artillery and Stukas pounded the trapped enemy into submission. After four days of this, Mociulschi's 3rd Mountain Division overran the Soviet position on December 11 and took 820 prisoners. Gladkov was not among the dead or the prisoners, having been evacuated by sea just before the end.

Petrov had succeeded in creating a firm army-size lodgment at Yenikale that Allmendinger's V Armeekorps could not defeat, which greatly added to the strain on AOK 17's limited resources. However, the Eltigen beachhead was a clear defeat that cost Petrov a reinforced division, as well as a great deal of Gorshkov's diminished naval transport. Yet the Axis ground forces had proved to have very little offensive capability left – just enough to defeat troops who lacked armor and artillery support. Given the Soviet lodgment across the Sivash and the lodgment across the Kerch

Straits, it was obvious by mid-November 1943 that a force as weak as AOK 17 could not possibly survive an all-out Soviet offensive once Tolbukhin and Petrov had gathered sufficient forces and supplies. However, Hitler had no intention of giving up the Crimea without a fight.

The Third Reich's military situation on the Eastern Front deteriorated rapidly in late 1943, as the Red Army crossed the Dnepr River at several points before the Wehrmacht could establish a coherent defense. Kiev was liberated on November 6 and it was evident that Germany had lost the strategic initiative. Faced with one disaster after another, Hitler dug in and refused to consider withdrawals, even when military common sense dictated otherwise. He also failed to appreciate the reduced capabilities of his armies, and believed that they could still operate with the kind of superiority they enjoyed over the Red Army in 1941–42. In looking at the Crimea, Hitler saw terrain that was eminently defensible and a full army to defend it – why should AOK 17 evacuate the Crimea? Adding to his misperception, the Kriegsmarine assured him that they could supply the army in the Crimea indefinitely or evacuate it if necessary. Thus, in Hitler's mind, AOK 17's situation was not analogous to AOK 6's situation at Stalingrad, one year earlier.

In a letter sent to Romanian dictator Antonescu on November 28, Hitler informed him of his intent to defend the Crimea "by all means" and to supply AOK 17 by sea. Hitler also promised to send reinforcements by sea to rebuild AOK 17 and that at some point, Heeresgruppe Süd would re-establish ground communications with the Crimea. Hitler did send reinforcements: low-quality cannon-fodder units such as II./Grenadier-Regiment 583 from France and I./Grenadier-Regiment 759, a newly raised fortress unit. Obviously, a few battalions of overage static troops was little more than a gesture, and a pathetic one at that. While it was true that AOK 6 still maintained the Kherson bridgehead on the east side of the Dnepr as a springboard for a potential counteroffensive to re-establish rail links with the Crimea, the Wehrmacht could barely maintain its current front, never mind recover lost territory. Thus, the Crimea was going to remain isolated, and AOK 17's only realistic options were either to evacuate (and use the troops elsewhere on the Eastern Front) or hold to the death.

If AOK 17 had been comprised primarily of German troops Hitler might have been more open to evacuation, but since the bulk of the combat units were Romanian, he regarded them as having negligible value if deployed elsewhere. By holding the Crimea, AOK 17 was tying up three much stronger Soviet armies, as well as two air armies and much of the Soviet naval capabilities in the Black Sea. If the Crimea was evacuated prematurely, the OKH feared that the Soviets might conduct amphibious attacks against Heeresgruppe Süd's coastal flanks. Thus, there was a brutal military logic to Hitler's intransigence over evacuating the Crimea, since the logistical infrastructure was available to sustain operations there for some time.

Throughout the winter, the Soviets contained to pound against the German defenses of the Crimea, particularly near Kerch. Prodded by the Stavka to break out from his Kerch lodgment, Petrov mounted an ill-planned amphibious landing behind the V Armeekorps lines at Cape Tarhan on the morning of January 10, 1944. The winter weather was predictably awful, and broke up the Azov Flotilla's landing force. Colonel Georg Glavatsky, who had been awarded the Hero of the Soviet Union for his bravery at Balaklava in 1942, led over 1,700 troops from his 166th Guards Regiment ashore, but lacked the equipment to seriously threaten the Germans. Furthermore, the VVS-ChF failed to protect the beachhead, and German Ju-87 Stukas and Fw-190F ground-attack aircraft had a field day shooting up the Azov Flotilla and Glavatsky's regiment. German ground troops moved in the next day and crushed the landing force, although Glavatsky and some of his troops escaped. Petrov tried to reach Glavatsky's beachhead using a battalion of T-34 tanks that he had just received, but Sturmgeschütz-Abteilung 191 was repositioned to counter this effort and knocked out 16 T-34s. On January 20 Petrov began a serious attack with his 16th Rifle Corps against the southern end of the German HKL, but Füsilier-Bataillon 98 put up fanatical resistance that held the line and inflicted heavy losses on Petrov's assault troops. Bärenfänger's Grenadier-Regiment 123, now just a battalion-size *Kampfgruppe*, also put up great resistance, which resulted in Bärenfänger being awarded the Oak Leaves to his *Ritterkreuz*. German losses were also quite heavy, including Bärenfänger, who was wounded for the sixth time; he was sent home to recover and received his award directly from Hitler.[16]

On the night of January 22/23, Petrov attempted a coup de main against Kerch, with the Azov Flotilla transporting two naval infantry battalions into the harbor. Although the Soviet naval infantrymen briefly seized part of the port, the battalions were too far apart to support each other and Allmendinger's V Armeekorps destroyed them piecemeal. Fighting continued for several days as Petrov's troops tried to reach the naval infantrymen in Kerch, but every effort by the 339th Rifle Division was repulsed. Two German junior officers, Hauptmann Hans Richter and Hauptmann Hans Neumayer, were each awarded the *Ritterkreuz* for their role in stopping this Soviet offensive. Stalin was incensed when he learned about the double failures at Cape Tarhan and Kerch; both Petrov and Vice-Admiral Lev Vladimirsk, commander of the Black Sea Fleet, were relieved of command and demoted. Instead, Stalin sent one of his favorites, General Andrei I. Eremenko, to take over the Coastal Army on February 6, while Vice-Admiral Oktyabrsky was brought back to command the Black Sea Fleet once again. Rear-Admiral Sergei Gorshkov (still the same rank after three years of constant combat experience) somehow managed to avoid serious censure, and a subordinate took most of the blame for faulty naval execution.

In the Sivash lodgment, the Soviet 10th Rifle Corps also made several large breakout attempts, beginning with a night attack on February 4, but made no progress. Fortunately for the Germans, it was a relatively mild winter in the Crimea, and the Sivash did not freeze over – if it had, AOK 17's fragile defenses would have been outflanked and overwhelmed. Another Soviet breakout attempt, in the middle of a snowstorm on March 28, also failed. Gruppe Konrad sealed off the lodgment with the Romanian 10th Infantry Division on the eastern side and the 336. Infanterie-Division on the western side. Although the Soviet 10th Rifle Corps outnumbered the Axis forces encircling it, the Soviet formation lacked the heavy weapons to achieve a breakout. As part of a reorganization Tolbukhin assigned General-Lieutenant Georgy F. Zakharov's 2nd Guards Army to take over all the forces in the Perekop sector, allowing Kreizer's 51st Army to focus exclusively on the Sivash sector.

Whether or not AOK 17 could hold the Crimea depended far more upon the Kriesgmarine and the Luftwaffe than Jaenecke's worn-out divisions. The Kriegsmarine and Royal Romanian Navy had opened a regular convoy route from Constanta to Sevastopol in August 1942, but the bulk of supplies to the Crimea had come via rail. Once the Crimea was isolated, bulk supplies now had to come by sea, while personnel would come by Luftwaffe air transport. Generalmajor Fritz Morzik, who had run both the Demyansk and Stalingrad airflifts, was picked to command the air-transport operation to the Crimea. Morzik was an energetic and talented aviation leader, and by 1943 the Luftwaffe had built up a very robust air-transport capability on the Eastern Front. Seven air-transport groups with 268 aircraft were subordinated to Morzik, who established regular runs from Odessa and Uman to the Crimea. Unlike the Stalingrad airlift, the winter weather was milder over the Crimea and, aside from fog, did not seriously disrupt operations. Nor did the VVS initially make much effort to intercept Morzik's transports, even though they were flying in daylight. Typically, transport planes could fly one-way to the Crimea in 2½hrs. The main purpose of the airlift was to fly in replacements for AOK 17 and fly out wounded. In addition, they also flew in high-priority cargo, such as replacement parts for the StuG III assault guns and trucks. The Germans still had over 9,000 vehicles in the Crimea, and they managed to keep 80 percent of them operational.[17] Although complete statistics are not available, the Ju-52s of just one group – III./TG 2 – flew in 30,838 troops to the Crimea in the period November 5, 1943 to February 2, 1944, and flew out 17,140 wounded personnel, while losing only two Ju-52s to enemy action.[18] Morzik's air-transport fleet also included Major Günther Mauss's I./TG 5, equipped with 19 Me 323 Gigant transports; the Me-323 was capable of carrying a 10-ton load, such as an 8.8cm flak gun or up to 130 troops. Indeed, Morzik's air-transport fleet was not severely stressed during the first several months of the airlift, and its capacity exceeded demand.

Heavy equipment and bulk fuel had to come by sea. Since Hitler intended to replace AOK 17's material losses, in mid-November 1943 the Kriegsmarine and Royal Romanian Navy organized a large naval convoy from Constanta to Sevastopol designated "Wotan." One vessel, the German steamer *Santa Fe* (4,627 tons), carried 12 StuG III assault guns intended for Sturmgeschütz-Abteilung 191 in the Crimea. Yet, despite the presence of a strong escort, including a Romanian destroyer, a minesweeper, and three German R-Boats, the *Santa Fe* was struck by a torpedo (probably from the Soviet submarine *D-4*) off the west coast of the Crimea on November 23. After catching fire, the vessel exploded and broke in two, taking her vital cargo with her. The Soviets sent more submarines to patrol off the Crimea, but aside from the *Santa Fe*, they achieved only occasional successes. In response, the Germans stepped up their anti-submarine efforts by deploying more sub-hunters to Sevastopol; the submarine *D-4* was depth-charged and sunk less than two weeks after sinking the *Santa Fe*. Yet aside from occassional large convoys, the Germans tended to rely upon their shallow-draft MFPs for the bulk of their logistical pipeline to the Crimea since these craft could operate in coastal waters too shallow for enemy submarines. Turkey turned a blind eye as German and Italian merchantmen passed through the Dardanelles to increase Axis merchant shipping in the Black Sea.

Between November 1943 and March 1944, AOK 17 suffered 21,970 casualties, including 6,077 dead or missing, but was receiving a monthly average of about 3,500 replacements. In February 1944, Sturmgeschütz-Abteilung 279 was brought in by sea, doubling the anti-armor capability of AOK 17. In mid-March, the Kriegsmarine was even able to transfer large elements from the 73. and 111. Infanterie-Divisionen from Odessa to the Crimea, to reinforce AOK 17; both units were battered and understrength. The 111. Infanterie-Division deployed a 5,000-man group to the Crimea by MFP and air transport, but suffered a painful loss when an Me-323 loaded with an 80-man artillery battery crashed, killing everyone aboard. The OKH directed Jaenecke to restructure all five of his German infantry divisions according to the revised 1944 table of organization (which included 1,181 *Hiwis* in the structure), but none of his divisions were even close to the standard. His strongest unit, Generalleutnant Friedrich Sixt's 50. Infanterie-Division, had only four of its own infantry battalions, plus four replacement battalions (FEB), two Slovak battalions, two Bergmann battalions made of Caucasian troops, and two German battalions from other commands. Sixt's artillery regiment had all its 10.5cm l.FH 18 howitzers, but only three of its 15cm s.FH 18 howitzers.[19] The 336. Infanterie-Division was in even worse shape, with only three of its own infantry battalions and six Romanian battalions attached directly to it. Large numbers of *Hiwis* and Tatars were also incorporated into German units. Aside from relying heavily upon captured or local troops, the quality of most German replacements by this point in the war was problematic, and replacing a junior infantryman was one thing, but replacing veteran NCOs and junior officers was quite another. Jaenecke was also forced to employ odd formations like Landesschützen-Bataillon 876 and the Kriegsmarine's

Marine-Infanterie-Bataillon Klüver, which lacked the equipment or training to go toe-to-toe with the Red Army. Once the Wehrmacht lost its advantage in combat-experienced junior leaders, its ability to withstand the Red Army's hammer blows was forfeit.

However, not all the replacements flown into the Crimea were inexperienced. Some veterans who had been evacuated earlier for wounds voluntarily opted to return to their units in the Crimea, even though they had opportunities to be re-assigned elsewhere. Hauptmann Karl-Otto Leukefeld, who had been awarded the *Ritterkreuz* for his accomplishments as a company commander with the 50. Infanterie-Division during the fighting at Sevastopol in the winter of 1941/42, had been assigned to instructor duty in France after he recovered from wounds. Yet in March 1944 he requested to return to his old regiment in the Crimea. He was flown in and took command of I./Grenadier-Regiment 123 in reserve near Perekop. The German concept of *Kameradschaft*, or comradeship, was a key factor that held units together under the stressful combat conditions on the Eastern Front. Regimental identity and loyalty remained strong among officers and NCOs, serving as a combat multiplier as long as trusted leaders remained. Although the Red Army had many brave soldiers, regimental-level political commissars ensured that loyalties were reserved for Stalin, the Communist Party, or the *Rodina*, not military leaders or organizations – that kind of loyalty was considered dangerous in the Soviet Union.

Unlike other isolated Axis armies, the forces in the Crimea did not suffer great privations, since food and fuel remained readily available. The troops of AOK 17 were never forced to eat their horses. There was no starvation among Axis troops in the Crimea, and a deliberate effort was made to ensure that food was brought in for local civilians. Special attention was made by AOK 17 to protect the pro-Axis Tatar population from unnecessary privations.[20] Local fishing craft were employed to supplement rations with coastal fishing, and even the Tatars were forced to contribute livestock and produce. Nevertheless, the Germans did take the best of the supplies for themselves, and tended to give less of everything to the Romanians. Naval convoys also brought in over 100 tons of S- and T-mines to fortify the northern entrances to the Crimea, as well as large shipments of the new *Faustpatrone* antitank rocket, which significantly increased the antitank firepower of even weak infantry units. Yet the greatest logistic challenge for AOK 17 in the Crimea was obtaining an adequate supply of artillery ammunition. Due to the diversity of German and Romanian weapons, as well as flak guns, coastal artillery, and captured pieces, the artillery supply was nothing like the lavish standards of 1942. At best, quartermasters were able to prioritize a few ammunition types, like 10.5cm rounds for the German l.FH 18 howitzer, but even this mainstay of the German division-level artillery received a gross total of only 1,500 tons of ammunition per month.[21]

The morale of the 65,000 Romanian troops in the Crimea was deteriorating for a number of reasons, of which isolation was only one. It was increasingly clear that Germany was losing the war and that the Red Army would soon reach the Romanian border. Antonescu was quietly sending out peace feelers to the Western Allies, and he did not allow any replacements to go to the Romanian forces in the Crimea. By January 1944 most of the Romanian units in the Crimea were seriously understrength and their vehicles non-operational. For example, the 10th Infantry Division was reduced to 30 percent of authorized strength, with just 4,989 troops. Jaenecke attached some of the better Romanian mountain battalions directly to German divisions and attached low-quality German battalions to reinforce Romanian divisions. Anxious to keep the Romanians in the Crimea from lapsing into apathetic non-involvement in the war, Jaenecke put the Romanian Mountain Corps in charge of suppressing the Crimean partisans during the winter of 1943/44.

Once the Red Army reached the entrances to the Crimea, the partisan forces there became increasingly aggressive in attacking Axis lines of communication. Ambushes by groups of 30–100 partisans on the road from Simferopol to Feodosiya and near Yalta inflicted painful losses on Axis rear-area units, which threatened AOK 17's supply lines. In late December 1943, six Romanian mountain battalions, with limited German support, began a week-long search-and-destroy mission in the rough terrain east of Simferopol. Apparently, the partisans were taken by surprise and had unwisely concentrated their forces in brigade-size base camps, which were identified and destroyed one at a time. The 4th Partisan Brigade had an 800-person camp identified near Sudak. The operation was a major success, inflicting over 3,700 casualties on the partisans, at a cost of 232 Romanian casualties. However, when the Romanians attempted to replicate this success by attacking three partisan brigade areas southwest of

Simferopol in mid-January, the results were less promising: 651 casualties were inflicted on the partisans against 88 Romanian casualties. A final anti-partisan operation conducted in early February was a disaster, with the partisans evading the Axis dragnet and inflicting significant losses on the German-Romanian units involved. Altogether, the Romanian-led anti-partisan operations in early 1944 neutralized about half of the Soviet partisan forces in the Crimea and temporarily reduced attacks against AOK 17's lines of communications. However, the partisans also managed to tie down the bulk of the three best Romanian divisions in rear-area security duties, which was a win for the Red Army.

In addition to partisan attacks, the Soviet VVS formations used their substantial superiority in air power to wear down the Axis forces in the Crimea with almost daily air attacks. Soviet bombers, mostly DB-3s and Pe-2s, began appearing over Sevastopol and Feodosiya in squadron-size strength in November 1943 and regularly pounded the harbor facilities, warehouses, and airfields. By December 1943, Luftflotte 4 decided to pull most of its bombers out of the Crimea, and then the Fliegerkorps I headquarters, which transferred to Romania. Oberst Joachim Bauer was left in charge of the remaining fighters and ground-attack aircraft based in the Crimea. Barkhorn's II./JG 52 was blessed with an incredibly skilled cadre of *Experten* – 11 of its pilots had scored over 40 victories and three had over 100 – which enabled them to fend off an enemy who enjoyed a 10-1 numerical superiority over the Crimea.[22] Hauptman Werner Dörnback's II./SG-2, equipped with Fw-190F ground-attack fighters, also played a critical role in defeating Soviet probes against the Crimea's defenses during the winter of 1943/44. For his part, Hitler attempted to live up to his pledge that the forces in the Crimea would continue to receive adequate replacements, and Bauer's squadrons received 120 replacement aircraft during the winter, while losing a similar number. Yet VVS strength had grown so overwhelming by the onset of spring 1944 that even the best Luftwaffe units, equipped with the best aircraft and flown by the best pilots, could no longer delay the inevitable.

Both sides used the winter to prepare for the battles in the spring. In January, the Soviets completed another bridge across the Sivash, capable of of handling tanks and heavy artillery. The Soviet lodgment across the Sivash was a miserable, muddy place, with cold winds and completely flat terrain. Troops could not dig trenches because the ground consisted of clay soaked with salty brine, making them particularly vulnerable to German artillery and air attacks. Troops remained cold and wet for days, leading to trench foot. General-Major Peter K. Koshevoi, commander of the 63rd Rife Corps, arrived in the lodgment and was shocked by the conditions:

> Soon, the army commander [Kreizer] went with me to the south bank of the Sivash in order to get acquainted with the situation in the bridgehead. Here the picture was quite bleak. There was not a tree or bush… Around us stretched a boundless steppe as flat as a table and a drained white expanse of shallow salt lakes. There were not even any weeds visible. Only here and there was a sparse tuft of reddish-gray sage. We could see all the way to the horizon. It seemed that the troops were completely open to enemy observation and fire. To the south of our front line the enemy was located on ancient Scythian burial mounds … and our scouts have repeatedly noticed the gleaming glass of binoculars. Nor were there any sources of fresh water in the bridgehead.[23]

The Germans were indeed watching and listening. German radio intercepts enabled Jaenecke to keep up with Soviet developments. He knew that Koshevoi's 63rd Rifle Corps had reinforced the 10th Rifle Corps in the Sivash lodgment and that Petrov's Coastal Army near Kerch was reinforced to eight rifle divisions and two tank brigades, with 75,000 troops and 80 tanks.[24] Jaenecke did succeed in rebuilding AOK 17's units to some extent, although the overall balance was now so unfavorable that even full-strength units would have difficulty holding the Crimea. One of his efforts to create more effective combat units was the authorization of Gebirgs-Jäger-Regiment Krim (GJRK) in late March 1944; this three-battalion unit was formed under Major Walter Kopp from FEB 94 and FEB 125, plus remnants of the 4. Gebirgs-Division stranded in the Crimea.[25] Kopp's regiment was assigned to Allmendinger's V Armeekorps to provide it a real reserve, in case of more Soviet landings on the coast.

German intelligence estimates believed it was possible that the Soviets would attempt more amphibious landings on the Crimean coast when spring came, but concluded that the most dangerous threat was a breakout attack from their Sivash bridgehead, followed by an outflanking maneuver against the Perekop position. Although a German retreat to Ishun might have reduced this threat, Hitler refused to authorize any more withdrdawals in the Crimea. Instead, Jaenecke's staff used the winter to begin work on a fallback position known as the Gneisenau Line, to protect the approaches to Sevastopol in case of a Soviet breakout from the Sivash, but this effort received little priority. By spring 1944, the Gneisenau Line consisted of seven company-size *Stützpunkt*, each armed with a few antitank guns and Romanian howitzers – at best, a delaying position.[26] Jaenecke and his chief of staff, Generalmajor Wolfdietrich Ritter von Xylander, also worked on a variety of evacuation schemes, renamed first *Litzmann*, then *Rudderboot*, then *Gleiterboot*, then *Adler*. [27] All these plans were designed to organize an emergency Dunkirk-style evacuation from the Crimea once an all-out Soviet offensive began in order to save as much of AOK 17 as possible, but they remained little more than staff studies since Hitler would not authorize an evacuation. Holding the Crimea was more important to him than the risk to AOK 17.

CHAPTER 9

German Defeat in the Crimea, 1944

"History shows that there are no invincible armies."
Josef Stalin

Once spring weather arrived, the German goose in the Crimea was pretty well cooked. Tolbukhin and Eremenko had met with Stalin in Moscow during March to discuss the Crimea, and the basic plan of attack had been decided. Zakharov's 2nd Guards Army would mount a strong deliberate offensive against Gruppe Konrad's defenses at Perekop, while Kreizer's 51st Army would stage a breakout attack from its Sivash bridgehead. Once the German front was broken, Vasil'ev's 19th Tank Corps would exploit southward to Simferopol. Eremenko's Coastal Army was intended merely to fix Allmendinger's V Armeekorps at Kerch during the first phase of the Crimean Offensive and then exploit the situation as circumstances permitted.[1] Compared to previous Soviet offensives, the 1944 Crimean Offensive was very well planned and coordinated. Zakharov's troops had spent the winter months training intensively on breach operations, and were well provided with wire cutters, sapper platoons, and plenty of support weapons. On the Perekop front, the 2nd Guards Army had been busy digging approach trenches, which narrowed the width of no man's land from 700–1,000 yards to just 150–200 yards. From their trenches, the Germans watched apprehensively as the distance narrowed.

Gruppe Konrad had prepared a defense in depth, consisting of three lines across the Perekop Isthmus. Indeed, this was a luxury that the Germans rarely enjoyed on the Eastern Front, but here the narrowness of the isthmus allowed them to concentrate their forces. Sixt's 50. Infanterie-Division deployed in a standard "two up, one back" style, with Grenadier-Regiments 121 and 122 still holding the eastern and western ends of the Tatar Ditch, and the town of Armyansk in the center turned into a fortified *Stützpunkt*. Further back, two batteries of StuG III assault guns from Major Gerhard Hoppe's Sturmgeschütz-Brigade 279 waited in reserve. Sixt's other regiment, Grenadier-Regiment 123, was positioned even further back, where it could either reinforce at Armyansk or act as a reserve for the defenses on the Sivash. Oberstleutnant Willy Marienfeld, the former schoolteacher who was awarded the *Ritterkreuz* for being one of the first German officers into Sevastopol in 1942, was commander of Grenadier-Regiment 123. Hauptmann Walter Salzmann, another veteran company commander and *Ritterkreuz* recipient from the 1942 campaign in the Crimea, commanded Füsilier-Bataillon 50. Sixt's division might have been badly depleted from losses, but it still had very capable tactical leaders. The German front line consisted of a continuous row of trenches, surmounted by rows of barbed wire and antipersonnel mines – reminiscent of the last year of World War I. The second and third lines of defenses were built at Ishun, but manned only by Romanian troops. The Axis defenses on the Sivash front were broken into three distinct groups by the lake terrain: a western group (consisting of the Romanian 38th Infantry Regiment), a central group (the Romanian 23rd and 33rd Infantry Regiments, the German 336. Pionier Bataillon, and a battery of StuG III assault guns), and an eastern group (the Romanian 94th and 96th Infantry Regiments, supported by two StuG IIIs). In all these sectors, the terrain was flat and constricted by water, which favored the defense.

Tolbukhin knew that airpower would be the crucial element of this operation, and he wanted to take the Luftwaffe out of the battle as quickly as possible. Hoping for a knockout blow, Tolbukhin decided to begin his

Crimean offensive with a massive air attack by 8th Air Army on April 7 against the Luftwaffe bases and German artillery positions on the Perekop. Having learned the value of a specialist close-air-support unit from Fliegerkorps VIII, the 8th Air Army was provided with General-Major Vasiliy Filin's 7th Ground Attack Aviation Korps (7 ShAK), which possessed 108 Il-2 Sturmoviks. Barkhorn was away on leave at the start of the Soviet offensive and II./JG 52 was apparently caught off guard by the scale of the Soviet onslaught; it got only a few fighters in the air in time. Protected by dozens of Yak-7 fighters, groups of Soviet Sturmoviks came in low over the treeless Perekop Isthmus, shooting up artillery positions and anything else that was visible. Although the Germans claimed that flak inflicted heavy losses on the raiders, the VVS raids were not seriously disrupted.[2]

The next morning, April 8, 1944, the artillery of both the 2nd Guards Army and the 51st Army opened fire at 0800hrs. The Soviet artillery delivered a punishing 2½-hour-long prep fire against the Axis positions, from tube and rocket artillery, as well as heavy mortars. The 8th Army also returned again in strength, strafing and bombing the German positions. This time, II./JG 52 was able to intercept some of the Soviet bombers, although it made little difference. Soviet aircraft were everywhere over the Crimea. At 1030hrs, both Soviet armies commenced their ground attacks.

The 51st Army put its main effort against the center of the Axis perimeter around their Sivash lodgment, with the 91st Rifle Division and 32nd Guards Tank Brigade (32 GTB) attacking the Romanian 10th Infantry Division. The Romanian positions were well protected by mines and artillery, which broke up the Soviet attack. German StuG IIIs supporting the Romanian defense knocked out 27 of the 32nd Guards Tank Brigade's 53 tanks. Surprisingly, a supporting attack made by Koshevoi's 63rd Rifle Corps' 267th Rifle Division and the 22nd Guards Tank Regiment against the Romanian 19th Infantry Division on the eastern end of the lodgment was more successful. Upon Tolbukhin's specific recommendation, Koshevoi sent the 2nd Battalion/848th Rifle Battalion to wade across the shallow Lake Aygulskoe to outflank the Romanian positions. Although German sources claim that the Romanian 94th Infantry Regiment panicked and ran, Koshevoi notes that the enemy fell back slowly to a second line of defense and that only 550 prisoners were taken.[3] When Kreizer realized that he was achieving no success in the

Soviet breakout, April 1944

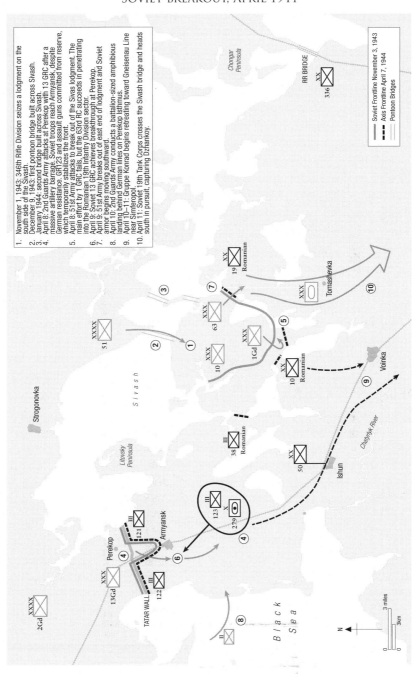

1. November 1, 1943: 346th Rifle Division seizes a lodgment on the south side of the Sivash.
2. December 9, 1943: first pontoon bridge built across Sivash.
3. January 1944: second bridge built across Sivash.
4. April 8: 2nd Guards Army attacks at Perekop with 13 GRC after a massive artillery barrage. Soviet troops reach Armyansk, despite German resistance. GR123 and assault guns committed from reserve, which temporarily stabilizes the front.
5. April 8: 51st Army attacks to break out of the Sivas lodgment. The main effort by 1 GRC fails, but the 63rd RC succeeds in penetrating into the Romanian 19th Infantry Division sector.
6. April 9: Soviet 13 GRC achieves breakthrough at Perekop.
7. April 9: 51st Army breaks out of east end of lodgment and Soviet armor begins moving southward.
8. April 10: 2nd Guards Army conducts a battalion-sized amphibious landing behind German lines on Perekop Isthmus.
9. April 10–11: Gruppe Konrad begins retreating toward Gneisenau Line near Simferopol.
10. April 11: Soviet 19th Tank Corps crosses the Sivash bridge and heads south in pursuit, capturing Dzhankoy.

Soviet Frontline November 3, 1943
Axis Frontline April 7, 1944
Pontoon Bridges

center but that the Romanian 19th Division was buckling, he shifted the depleted 32 GTB and more infantry to reinforce this sector.

At the Perekop Isthmus, Zakharov's 2nd Guards Army used relatively novel tactics. Instead of relying upon mass, as in previous offensives, Zakharov used only General-Major Porfiri G. Chanchibadze's 13th Guards Rifle Corps in the initial attack. Like Stalin, Chanchibadze was a Georgian and he had a similar tough outlook, which made him well suited for a breakthrough operation. While the 126th Rifle Division and the 87th Guards Rifle Division launched supporting attacks on the flanks, the heavily reinforced 3rd Guards Division (3 GRD), under General-Major Kantemir A. Tsalikov, made the main effort in the center. Rather than just futilely throwing tank brigades at the enemy front, as in the past, Zakharov kept Vasil'ev's 19th Tank Corps in reserve. The Soviet ground assault was preceded by artillery-delivered smoke rounds to reduce the accuracy of German automatic weapons, then the infantry rose up from the trenches and assaulted the enemy frontline trenches around Armyansk.[4] Another Soviet innovation was the use of the 512th Separate Tank Battalion equipped with 16 TO-34 flamethrower tanks and the 1452nd Self-Propelled Artillery Regiment with a mix of KV-85 tanks, JSU-152 howitzers, and Su-76 assault guns to support the infantry attacks. The 3 GRD concentrated all its effort against a single German battalion, II./Grenadier-Regiment 122. This time, German mortars and automatic weapons failed to stop the Soviet infantrymen from reaching the first line of trenches, which were quickly taken in a frenetic moment of hurled grenades and submachine-gun bursts. Soviet flamethrower tanks burned out German machine-gun nests and antitank guns in the rubble of Armyansk, which was quickly overrun. Indeed, the Soviet breakthrough was going better than expected until the supporting armor ran into a very large field of antitank mines located behind the German HKL, which knocked out eight tanks. As the Soviet attack bogged down in the minefield, *Panzerjägers* engaged the stalled tanks, knocking out five more. German artillery was also directed onto the Soviet penetration corridor, destroying two JSU-152s with direct hits. Yet despite these losses, the 13th Guards Rifle Corps had torn a large hole in the German front line that could not be repaired, and Zakharov fed more troops into the breach. Sixt scraped some infantry platoons together to counterattack the flanks of the Soviet breakthrough and committed Hauptmann Karl-Otto Leukefeld's

I./Grenadier-Regiment 123 from reserve, but could not regain any ground. Konrad then sent the two batteries of assault guns forward and they were able to stem the Soviet advance, but lost a number of their vehicles. By the end of the first day of the ground offensive, Tolbukhin's two armies had achieved local penetrations, but had not yet achieved a true breakthrough. Nevertheless, Gruppe Konrad had very little in the way of reserves left to influence the battle.

The next morning, both of Tolbukhin's armies continued to pound away at Gruppe Konrad. Even after the loss of Armyansk, the 50. Infanterie-Division still had a front line of sorts across the Perekop Isthmus, but it was crumbling on the western side. Zakharov simply kept attacking with infantry and artillery until the German line finally broke around 1600hrs. With the help of massed Sturmovik attacks and a brigade of BM31 multiple rocket launchers, Koshevoi's reinforced 63rd Rifle Corps overwhelmed the Romanian 19th Infantry Division as well, and by late afternoon a small group of tanks were heading south.[5] Konrad alerted Jaenecke that his forces could only delay the enemy and that he should activate plan *Adler* as soon as possible. After several hours of hesitation, Jaenecke activated *Adler* at 1900hrs on April 9 – without informing the OKH – and ordered Allmendinger's V Armeekorps to abandon its positions at Kerch and retreat immediately toward Sevastopol. Eremenko was quick to note the German preparations to retreat, which included destruction of the harbor facilities in Kerch, and immediately ordered his ground forces to advance and the 4th Air Army to attack German convoys heading westward. Tolbukhin also spotted preparations by Gruppe Konrad to withdraw to its second line of defenses at Ishun and ordered Vasil'ev's 19th Tank Corps to cross the bridge across the Sivash and enter the battle through the 51st Army's breakthrough zone. Although the crossing was slow, it caught the Germans completely by surprise.

While Gruppe Konrad was struggling to maintain its positions on the Perekop Isthmus, Zakharov decided to increase the pressure on the German defense by conducting an amphibious landing behind the German lines on the Black Sea. Before dawn on April 10, 512 troops from Captain Filipp D. Dibrov's 2nd Battalion/1271st Rifle Regiment were landed on the coast. As usual, the troops landed without heavy weapons and could hold only a small beachhead. Gruppe Konrad soon counterattacked with a company of infantry and several assault guns, but the Germans could not spare sufficient troops to eliminate the beachhead. Consequently, Dibrov's battalion was the final straw that convinced Konrad to abandon his remaining positions on the Perekop Isthmus and retreat to the second line of defense at Ishun. This retreat proved difficult, since some sub-units of Sixt's 50. Infanterie-Division were already bypassed and a number of artillery pieces and flak guns had to be abandoned. Indeed, Gruppe Konrad put up only token resistance at Ishun for a few hours, since the breakout of the 51st Army from the Sivash lodgment threatened to cut them off. Konrad, whose headquarters was in Dzhankoy, directed his forces to pull back to the Gneisenau Line.

Hauptmann Werner Dörnbrack's Fw-190F fighter-bombers from II./SG2 made every effort to stem the enemy breakthrough, and mercilessly attacked Soviet troops crossing into the Sivash lodgment. At 1000hrs on April 10, General-Major Nikolai V. Gaponov, commander of the 26th Artillery Division, was killed by a German air attack.[6] Vasil'ev went forward to personally reconnoiter the route that his 19th Tank Corps would have to follow, whereupon his vehicle was also strafed by German fighter-bombers and he was severely wounded. Nevertheless, his deputy took over and moved the 19th Tank Corps into forward-assembly areas on the evening of April 10. The 19th Tank Corps was heavily reinforced for the exploitation mission, with four tank brigades with a total of 221 tanks and assault guns (including 58 T-34s, 34 TO-34 flamethrower tanks, 44 Su-76s, and 63 Valentines) at the start of the operation. At dawn on April 11, the 19th Tank Corps advanced south between two lakes and pushed against weak resistance to Tomashevka. Overhead, the 8th Air Army provided excellent close air support, despite tenacious efforts by the *Experten* of II./JG 52. Fearful of being outflanked, the rest of the Axis units on the Sivash line fell back, along with those units defending the Chongar sector. By 1100hrs, the vanguard of the 19th Tank Corps reached Dzhankoy, capturing Konrad's supply dumps. It was apparent that Tolbukhin's front had achieved a successful breakthrough. All of Gruppe Konrad was now falling back toward the Gneisenau Line, although the lack of transport and incessant Soviet air attacks caused a great deal of material to be abandoned. In particular, the 50. Infanterie-Division suffered heavy losses in the retreat, since a number of its units were already cut off. Hauptmann Karl-Otto Leukefeld, commander of I./Grenadier-Regiment 123, was captured, along with some of his troops.

On the Kerch Peninsula, Allmendinger's V Armeekorps began retreating from its positions during the night of April 9/10. His troops had to retreat over 100 miles to reach relative safety around Sevastopol, and Eremenko's Coastal Army was hard on his heels. Eremenko had three rifle corps – the 3rd Mountain, 16th, and 11th Guards – comprising ten rifle divisions and two naval infantry brigades. His armor force was relatively small – just Colonel Aleksandr Rudakov's 63rd Tank Brigade, three independent tank regiments, and a self-propelled artillery unit – with a total of 204 tanks and assault guns. The German retreat was relatively sloppy, with no effort at deception, and Eremenko launched a hasty attack that destroyed FEB 85 and wiped out company-size rearguards from the 73. and 98. Infanterie-Divisionen. It was clear that Axis morale in the Crimea was collapsing and that no one wanted to be left behind – all thoughts were on getting to Sevastopol and the evacuation ships. In contrast, Soviet morale was sky-high, and Eremenko's Coastal Army had not suffered heavy losses. On the morning of April 11 Eremenko's troops entered Kerch to occupy an empty and devastated city. Meanwhile, the bombers of the 4th Air Army viciously attacked Allmendinger's retreating columns. Since there was only a single main road leading west, Allmendinger's entire corps was stretched out along it – making easy targets for low-level strafing. Most of the German artillery was horse-drawn, which could not retreat very fast. Oberst Karl Faulhaber's Grenadier-Regiment 282 formed the rearguard, reinforced with motorized flak guns and some antitank guns. Allmendinger was able to get his corps to the Parpach Narrows by April 12, but he could not remain at this position. With the 19th Tank Corps and 2nd Guards Army heading for Simferopol, it was clear that they would soon cut off Allmendinger's retreat path, so Jaenecke ordered him to instead head for Feodosiya or Sudak, where the Kriegsmarine could evacuate him by sea.

Despite the fact that AOK 17 was in full retreat on all fronts and suffering heavy losses, Hitler would still not authorize a full-scale evacuation of the Crimea. However, he did allow Jaenecke to begin evacuating wounded, as well as non-essential support personnel, but no able-bodied combat troops. In Hitler's mind, AOK 17 should be able to hold out in Festung Sevastopol for many months, just as Petrov's army had in 1941–42, although he ignored the fact that the defenses were in very poor condition. Hitler ordered the Luftwaffe to slow the Soviet advance in order to buy time for AOK 17 to organize a defense of the port, but Soviet tanks had already overrun German airfields at Bagerovo and Karankut, which seriously disrupted Luftwaffe air operations at a critical moment. All German air units in the Crimea were forced to relocate to the small airfields at Sevastopol. Fritz Morzik's transport fleet hurriedly brought in ammunition to replace the stocks lost in the Perekop and Sivash fighting, while evacuating hundreds of wounded troops. Hitler also order the Fliegerkorps I headquarters to return to the Crimea to control air operations, while directing Luftflotte 4 to provide air support from its bases in Romania. The He-111 bombers of KG 27 and Bf 110 fighters of II./ZG 1 intervened in an effort to stem the Soviet armored pursuit, but it was too little and too late.

On April 13 the Soviet pursuit reached its flood tide, as the 19th Tank Corps liberated Simferopol and Yevpatoriya. Jaenecke evacuated his headquarters from Simferopol just 12 hours before the Soviet tanks arrived. Eremenko pursued Allmendinger's V Armeekorps with the 227th Rifle Division and 257th Independent Tank Regiment in the lead. After liberating an abandoned Feodosiya, Eremenko's advance guard caught up with the tail end of Allmendinger's V Armeekorps near Stary Krim. Antitank gunners from Panzerjäger-Abteilung 198 ambushed and destroyed several T-34s, but the Soviets would soon overwhelm the rearguard unless something was done. Major Walter Kopp's Gebirgs-Jäger-Regiment Krim, relatively unengaged up to this point, was ordered to make a stand in the hilly terrain in order that the rest of the corps could escape unmolested to Sudak. Kopp's mountain troops put up a desperate resistance that temporarily halted Eremenko's pursuit, but most of Kopp's regiment was sacrificed in the process. The Germans also deliberately left supply dumps intact, knowing that the Soviet penchant for looting would slow their pursuit. At Sudak, MFPs from the 1. Landungs-Flotille arrived and began transfering troops from V Armeekorps to Balaklava. However, it was not long before the VVS-ChF detected the Kriegsmarine operation and sent its bombers to disrupt the evacuation. The Luftwaffe was too preoccupied relocating to alternate airbases, so they failed to protect the evacuation and Soviet bombers had a field day, ripping apart the slow-moving MFPs with bombs and cannon. About 10,000 troops from Allmendinger's corps were evacuated to Balaklava by sea, but the rest would have to retreat through the partisan-infested Yaila Mountains.

Surprisingly, the partisans did not seriously interfere with Allmendinger's retreat, after a few displays of firepower. This was a chance for the Crimean partisans to make a decisive contribution to victory, by delaying the retreat of V Armeekorps, but they missed it. Instead, they waited for the Red Army's tanks to appear, then emerged to join in the numerous photo opportunities that liberation afforded. Had the partisans inflicted delay upon Allmendinger's retreating corps, there is a good possibility that AOK 17 would have been unable to make even a brief stand at Sevastopol and that the city would have been overrun before a naval evacuation could occur.

Instead, Lieutenant-General Hugo Schwab, commander of the Romanian Mountain Corps, deployed two battalions to help cover the retreat of V Armeekorps along the coast road and to prevent sabotage by partisans. By the morning of April 14, V Armeekorps reached Alushta and continued to move through the town as the Romanian battalions formed blocking positions. Many of the remaining horses were shot in Alushta because they were slowing the retreat, and artillerymen removed the breechblocks from their guns and threw them into the sea. The Germans promised to evacuate the two Romanian rearguard battalions with MFPs from Alushta, but in the confusion of the retreat the Romanians were abandoned. At dawn on April 15, Eremenko's vanguard struck the Romanians in force, and, after several hours of a delaying fight, they began retreating toward the perceived safety of naval evacuation from Alushta. However, upon reaching the town, the Romanians found the Germans gone and Soviet troops blocking the coast road. The two Romanian battalions attempted to infiltrate westward along secondary roads in the mountains, but they were eventually encircled and destroyed – only three survivors made it to Sevastopol. Schwab was incensed that the Germans had allowed his rearguard battalions to be destroyed, and Axis relations began to deteriorate during the retreat. Meanwhile, the German V Armeekorps reached Yalta on April 15, and Eremenko's pursuit had fallen behind due to the sacrifice of the Romanian battalions. Allmendinger apparently felt safe enough in Yalta to pause for a good meal and a night's sleep in the officer's rest home, which had served as an R & R area for Axis troops since 1942. Generalleutnant Alfred Reinhardt, the commander of the 98. Infanterie-Division, had to remonstrate with Allmendinger to keep moving, lest the Soviet pursuit catch them bunched up on the coast road.[7] Schwab was further angered that the Germans found time to rest while the Romanian rearguard was being annihilated. Finally, after five days of retreating, V Armeekorps reached the eastern outskirts of Sevastopol on April 16. However, the cost of this successful retreat was very high, with over 70 percent of Allmendinger's artillery and heavy weapons lost, as well as thousands of troops – the survivors were in no shape to conduct defensive operations.

Meanwhile, Gruppe Konrad had fallen back precipitously from the Ishun position, but a good part of the artillery was saved thanks to the rearguard fought by two batteries of the Sturmgeschütz-Brigade 279. Elements of the Soviet 19th Tank Corps actually got ahead of the retreating Germans – just as Brigade Ziegler had done to Petrov's retreating army in 1941. German columns were forced to form all-around defensive hedgehogs at nightfall, lest they be surprised and attacked by marauding Soviet mechanized units. One Romanian battalion that did not form a hedgehog was caught by Soviet tanks and opted to surrender. In another ambush, the Soviets managed to knock out two StuG III assault guns, but the rest of Sturmgeschütz Brigade 279 fought its way out of the enemy ambush.[8] By the time that Gruppe Konrad reached the Gneisenau Line on April 12/13, it found its retreat route blocked by Soviet forces and was obliged to fight its way through the *Kessel* forming around them. Gruppe Konrad succeeded in fighting through the Soviet pincers, but only by retreating as fast as possible. The Romanian 19th Infantry Division was hard pressed by the Soviet tankers, and some of its battalions were destroyed.

Contrary to what Hitler thought, Sevastopol was not prepared for another siege. A total of seven Romanian mountain-infantry battalions were manning a thin outer perimeter, which was much weaker than the Soviet positions of 1942. German naval engineers had repaired a few flak positions and built some additional bunkers, but very little had actually been done to prepare the naval base for a ground attack. The man on the spot was Oberst Paul Betz, an engineer officer, who had been designated as commander of Festung Sevastopol just two weeks prior. Betz had spent six months with the Afrikakorps in North Africa, then spent much of 1942–43 as a senior pioneer leader for AOK 17 in the Caucasus. Upon the activation of *Adler*, he formed a *Kampfgruppe* from Feldausbildungs Regiment 615 (FAR 615), six flak batteries from Pickert's 9. Flak-Division, and the Luftwaffe's armored flak train "Michael." Betz moved his

Kampfgruppe to block the main road to Sevastopol, just south of Bakhchisaray. When the lead elements of Gruppe Konrad arrived late on April 13, Betz was given six of the last operational StuG III assault guns to reinforce his position. At dawn on April 14 the vanguard of the 19th Tank Corps arrived at Bakhchisaray, but Kampfgruppe Betz was able to delay them for 12 critical hours, while Gruppe Konrad withdrew into Sevastopol. Then, Betz broke contact and fell back under the cover of a barrage from Gruppe Konrad's artillery.

While the Germans retreated, Schwab deployed all three of his mountain divisions on Sevastopol's perimeter, with the 1st and 2nd Mountain Division barring the direct routes in from the north. On the morning of April 15, the 19th Tank Corps began probing attacks against the Romanian defenses, but the mountain-infantry battalions continued to display combat effectiveness and they knocked out 23 Soviet tanks. It took Konrad 24 hours or more to get the disorganized 50. and 336. Infanterie-Divisionen into the perimeter lines, which meant that it was the Romanians who defeated the initial Soviet attacks on their own. Tolbukhin continued probing the Romanians for the next week, but not in great strength. Tolbukhin apparently believed that the Axis defenses of Sevastopol were much stronger than they really were and that a deliberate attack was necessary, so he decided to wait for his artillery to arrive before mounting a serious offensive. In fact, Jaenecke had fewer than 20,000 organized combat troops left after the retreat. In just nine days, AOK 17 had suffered 29,873 casualties, as well as losing a great deal of its equipment. Allmendinger, who had begun to display odd behavior during the retreat, decided to go on leave for a week, and left V Armeekorps under temporary command of a Romanian mountain-infantry officer – a bizarre action for a German general. The two most effective German units, the assault-gun brigades, were reduced to only a handful of operational vehicles. Luftwaffe air support dwindled after the loss of 70 aircraft, and fewer than 50 aircraft remained operational in the Crimea, including 16 Bf-109s and 21 ground-attack aircraft. Simply put, AOK 17 was no longer capable of effective resistance.

The first phase of the Axis evacuation from the Crimea began on April 12, but was ostensibly restricted to non-combat personnel. The Germans initially committed nine merchant ships and all their remaining Kriesgmarine assets in the Black Sea to the operation, while the Romanians committed a good part of their merchant marine as well. For the first time in the war, the Romanian Navy also decided to risk its best warships on the Constanta–Sevastopol run, the Italian-built destroyers *Regina Maria* and *Regele Ferdinand*. Despite frequent Soviet air and submarine attacks, the evacuation was able to operate for nearly a week without loss. Most of the convoys consisted of two or three merchant ships with robust escort and sometimes fighter cover from Bf-110s based in Romania. By the time that Gruppe Konrad and V Armeekorps reached the perimeter of Sevastopol, the Kriesgmarine and Romanian Navy – as well Morzik's air transports – had already transferred more than 20,000 people from the Crimea to Romania, and the operation was in full swing.

Yet it was not until April 18 that the Soviets achieved any success against the Axis convoys. The VVS-ChF committed two units equipped with US-made A-20G Havoc bombers to the interdiction mission – the 36th Mine-Torpedo Aviation Regiment (MTAP) and 13th Guards Bomber Regiment (GDBAP). A two-ship Romanian convoy that was returning to Constanta was spotted by the Soviet submarine *L-6* about 90 miles southwest of Sevastopol around 1100hrs. The Soviet submarine fired a torpedo at the convoy but missed, and was apparently sunk by depth charges from the counterattacking escort *UJ-104*. However, four A-20G Havoc bombers from the 36th MTAP found the convoy at 1237hrs and put two bombs into the freighter *Alba Iulia* (5,700 GRT). Ironically, the freighter was loaded mostly with Soviet POWs, and about 500 of them died in the attack. Although the vessel was abandoned, it was recovered the next day and towed back to Constanta by the destroyer *Regele Ferdinand*. Although Hitler had decreed that no combat troops would be evacuated from the Crimea, the Romanians ignored him and proceeded to evacuate considerable numbers of their own combat troops, including mountain infantry. On April 22 both A-20 bomber groups mounted separate attacks against another convoy, which crippled the small German tanker *Ossag I* (3,950 GRT), and scored a lucky hit – which did not explode – on the destroyer *Regele Ferdinand*. Although the escorting German R-Boats tried to shepherd the crippled *Ossag I* and its vital cargo of fuel into Sevastopol, they were forced to scuttle it 17 miles southwest of the port. Three Soviet A-20G bombers were lost in the attacks.

Soviet submarines made repeated attacks on the convoys but failed to achieve any hits. The two A-20G bomber-equipped regiments continued to attack daily convoys, inflicting light damage but suffering regular losses. Once Soviet forces reached the perimeter of Sevastopol, the VVS also committed Il-2 Sturmovik ground-attack aircraft to attack the convoys when they were close to the coast. On April 23, Il-2s sank an MFP that was overcrowded with 1,000 troops – but due to prompt rescue efforts by the escort two-thirds of the men were saved. On April 27 two large convoys left Sevastopol with a strong escort, but were attacked 11 miles southwest of Sevastopol by five Soviet MTBs. The Soviets managed to torpedo the escort *UJ-104*, but two S-Boats from the 1. Schnellbootsflottille sank one of the Soviet boats and the rest retreated. The first phase of the Axis evacuation from the Crimea lasted from April 12 to 27, 1944, and succeeded in evacuating almost 72,000 personnel, including 28,394 German and 20,779 Romanian troops. Interestingly, fewer than a fifth of the military evacuees were wounded, indicating that many unauthorized personnel were leaving. A number of German combat troops from the assault-gun units and artillery battalions that had lost much of their equipment in the retreat were evacuated as well. The Axis also evacuated all the Slovak and Caucasian volunteer troops, as well as *Hiwis*, POWs, and civilians. The initial Axis evacuation from the Crimea was a staggering accomplishment, and was achieved with less than 2 percent losses.

Meanwhile, Jaenecke found himself in command of an army that was badly battered and shrinking daily. He was exasperated with Hitler's unwillingness to evacuate the entire army or to recognize that Sevastopol was a trap, not a fortress. Nevertheless, Jaenecke continued to toe the Führer's line, and on April 24 he issued a bombastic and inaccurate proclamation to his troops:

Soldiers of the 17th Army, the Führer ordered us to defend the Sevastopol fortress and, by doing so, trusted us with a very important and serious mission. Our mission has a huge importance. The enemy made the mistake of taking powerful forces and an overwhelming number of tanks from the important points of the Eastern Front to send against the Crimea. This superior force succeeded in breaking through our over-extended front on the Sivash only after a hard battle. The quick redeployment of our Army to Sevastopol succeeded in stopping the enemy, forcing them to assault against our determined defence, which caused them terrible losses, they lost 602 tanks between April 8 and April 23. Everything they lose here they will lack in their Western offensive against the heart of Romania.

The actions of the brave German and Romanian soldiers here in Crimea, through faithful duty and bravery, serve a greater purpose. The harder the enemy will struggle to conquer Sevastopol, the safer our country will be, shielded by our actions. We are all aware of the tough battle that lies ahead. The Führer will help us with weapons and reinforcements. But our strongest force is inside us, the determination and unity proved by us in hundreds of battles in the Caucasus, Kuban and the Crimea, by all of us, Germans and Romanians, ground forces, Luftwaffe and Kriegsmarine.

Our motto is: "Not a step back!" Victory is ahead while death lies in retreat. We will stay here as long as the Führer orders us, in this critical spot of the titanic battle. Whoever will try to leave this mission, who will leave his post, those responsible for reducing the limited combat strength of our army, will be executed. Let the Soviets come, they will be destroyed. Let their tanks advance, if you infantrymen cannot stop them, let them enter our positions, they will be easier destroyed there. Every man able to hold a weapon will be sent to the front. All the reserves are ordered to work day and night to fortify the positions in depth. The 17. Armee fights now in a place where thousands of our brave troops offered an example. We will succeed in our mission, like they did, for our country! Long live the Führer! Long live his Majesty King Mihai! Long live Marshall Antonescu!

There was little truth in Jaenecke's proclamation, and it is doubtful that he believed it himself. The Red Army lost a total of only 171 tanks during the period from April 7 to May 12, 1944, and overall Soviet losses in the Crimea had been relatively light, while Axis losses had been extremely heavy. Nor was Hitler going to send any more substantial reinforcements to the Crimea. The idea that the Soviets were diverting critical resources to liberate the Crimea was the converse of the fact that Hitler had consigned the AOK 17 to hold an untenable position in the Crimea, while the Wehrmacht was desperately short of troops all along the Eastern Front. The Soviets were in no hurry to liberate the Crimea before spring 1944 because they did not want AOK 17 evacuated and transferred to more critical parts of the Eastern Front; Soviet officers joking referred to the Crimea as "an ideal prison camp" where the inmates fed and guarded themselves. Rather than fighting for king and country, the German and Romanian troops in the Crimea were now fighting simply due to Hitler's unwillingness to face military logic.

Once inside Sevastopol's perimeter, the German and Romanian troops went underground in order to avoid enemy artillery and air attacks. Large stockpiles of food had accumulated in Sevastopol, and these were freely distributed to the troops in order to maintain morale. One German artillery officer from III./AR 117 stated that "we could not complain about our creature comforts. Chocolate, candy, canned food – as much as we would like. I drank a bottle of wine every evening in my cave." Some senior German officers still enjoyed sleeping on clean sheets in Sevastopol, despite incessant Soviet bombing and artillery fire.

Gerhard Barkhorn was in Germany for an extended period, and did not return to the Crimea until late April 1944. In the interim, II./JG 52 continued its daily combat with the VVS and inflicted painful losses, despite being badly outnumbered. On the morning of April 17, General-Major Ivan P. Vilin, deputy commander of the 214th Assault Aviation Division (Shad), personally led a low-level raid by four Il-2s against the Chersonese airstrip, but ran into a gaggle of Bf-109 fighters. Three of the Il-2s were shot down, but Vilin managed to reach Soviet lines before crashing; he was rescued but died of his wounds.[9]

On April 16 Eremenko was transferred to the Baltic front and the Coastal Army, now under General-Lieutenant Kondrat S. Mel'nik, was subordinated to Tolbukhin's 4th Ukrainian Front. Three days later, the Maritime Army launched a strong attack against the V Armeekorps positions around Balaklava while the 51st Army attacked the center of the Axis line, but neither made progress. Soviet artillery ammunition was still in short supply in the Crimea. On April 23 the Soviets attacked again, and the 2nd Guards Army seized ground on Mekenzievy Mountain, but the tanks of the 19th Tank Corps were stopped by dense minefields. After these attacks were repulsed, Jaenecke was given enough of a respite to reorganize his forces. Gruppe Konrad (XXXXIX Gebirgs-Korps), now consisting of the 50. and 336. Infanterie-Divisionen and the Romanian 1st and 2nd Mountain Divisions, was assigned to defend the northern sector of Sevastopol, including the area around Mekenzievy Mountain. Allmendinger's V Armeekorps, consisting of the 73., 98., and 111. Infanterie-Divisionen and Romanian 3rd Mountain Division, were assigned to defend the southeast approaches. Only small detachments of the Romanian infantry and cavalry divisions were still left, and they were rolled into the three mountain divisions. All five of the German divisions were reduced to about 30 percent of their authorized strength in personnel and equipment and both corps had only limited artillery left. Hitler made a token gesture of trying to replenish AOK 17's losses in men and equipment by sending 1,300 replacements, 15 antitank guns, and four howitzers, but this was a drop in the ocean.[10]

Despite his bombastic proclamation, Jaenecke knew that AOK 17 could not withstand a determined enemy assault, so he demanded to know when more reinforcements would arrive in the Crimea and requested "freedom of action" in the event that Tolbukhin launched an all-out offensive. This was too much for Hitler, and he ordered that Jaenecke personally report to him at Berchtesgaden on April 29. Once in Hitler's presence, Jaenecke argued that the rest of AOK 17 had to be withdrawn immediately or face destruction. Hitler was infuriated that a general would talk to him in this manner and began screaming at him. Jaenecke simply turned and left the room, slamming the door. Striding past Hitler's adjutant, Jaenecke said, "Tell the Führer I have left" and drove off to the airfield.[11] Jaenecke did not get far. Hitler had his plane stopped in Romania and ordered the *Generaloberst* placed under arrest. Hitler ordered that Generaloberst Heinz Guderian conduct a formal inquiry into Jaenecke's behavior and hold a formal court martial; Guderian obeyed the letter of the order, but in a deliberately slow manner. Meanwhile, General der Infanterie Karl Allmendinger was ordered to take command of AOK 17. Apparently believing that AOK 17 needed leaders made of firmer stuff, Hitler ordered that Generalleutnant Friedrich-Wilhelm Müller would fly from Crete to take over V Armeekorps. Müller had distinguished himself in the Crimea as a regimental commander in the 72. Infanterie-Division in 1942, but subsequently had earned a reputation as "the Butcher of Crete," which was the kind of man Hitler wanted in a tight spot. Müller did not arrive in the Crimea until May 4.

Tolbukhin steadily increased the pressure on Festung Sevastopol. On May 1, a major attack was launched by the 2nd Guards Army against the German defenses on the south side of the Bel'bek River. During the fighting, Generalleutnant Friedrich Sixt, commander of the 50. Infanterie-Division, was wounded by artillery fire while inspecting forward defenses on the Ölberg. Sixt was evacuated and Oberst Paul Betz took over the division. Mel'nik's Coastal Army also succeeded in liberating Balaklava. By this point, AOK 17 had only 64,000 troops left in the Crimea, against over 400,000 Soviet troops. On May 5, Tolbukhin commenced his final offensive at 0930hrs with a massive two-hour barrage by 400 artillery pieces concentrated against the XXXXIX Gebirgs-Korps front in the north. Generalmajor Wolf Hagemann's 336. Infanterie-Division managed to repulse attacks by five Soviet rifle divisions for the next two days, but Hagemann was badly wounded and was flown out.

While the attacks of the 51st Army focused German attention toward the center of their perimeter around Sevastopol, Mel'nik moved up General-Major Konstantin I. Provalov's 16th Rifle Corps and a large quantity of artillery into assault positions west of Balaklava. Provalov was an experienced infantry commander who had been awarded the Hero of the Soviet Union for leading a rifle regiment during the battle of Lake Khasan in 1938. On the morning of May 7, Provalov's 16th Rifle Corps attacked V Armeekorps after a heavy-artillery bombardment and quickly achieved a penetration in the center of the sector held by Generalleutnant Hermann Böhme's 73. Infanterie-Division. II./Grenadier-Regiment 170 was pummeled by volleys of rocket artillery then overrun by a massive assault spearheaded by the 83rd Naval Infantry Brigade. By evening, Provalov's troops had penetrated 1,500 yards into the German defense and reached their artillery positions near the village of Karan. V Armeekorps was so badly hurt by this attack that there was no option but to begin withdrawing to its second line of defense. On the same day, Zakharov's 2nd Guards Army reached the edge of Sevastopol's Severnaya Bay while Kreizer's 51st Army pushed back the northern part of the V Armeekorps' front line and reached the foot of Sapun Mountain with two rifle corps.

Kreizer attacked the German positions around the Sapun Heights with his 63rd Rifle Corps and 1st Guards and 11th Guards Rifle Corps, supported by a strong artillery concentration and considerable close air support. Starting at 0900hrs on May 7, Soviet artillery blasted the top of the heights – held mostly by the 98. and 111. Infanterie-Divisionen – with tube and rocket artillery. At 1030hrs, the Soviet infantry attacked but encountered very strong automatic-weapons and mortar fire from the still-intact German positions. One Soviet rifle-platoon leader, Lieutenant Mikhail Y. Dzigunsky from the 1372nd Rifle Regiment, succeeded in knocking out three German positions, but was killed attempting to knock out a stone machine-gun bunker; he was the first of six men to earn a Hero of the Soviet Union on the Sapun Heights. General-Major Peter K. Koshevoi's 63rd Rifle Corps attacked all day long, fighting its way through German barbed wire and trenches. By 1800hrs his troops were within 100–200 yards of the crest of the Sapun Heights, but his rifle and artillery units were almost out of ammunition. This was one of those moments where the enemy – not knowing that the attack had actually exhausted itself – made the mistake of pulling back to regroup. Koshevoi's troops surged forward and overran some of the German positions atop the ridge, and even captured the commander of Grenadier-Regiment 117. Nevertheless, the Soviet foothold was tenuous and Kreizer quickly brought up the 10th Rifle Corps to solidify the Soviet hold on the Sapun Heights. Tolbukhin also ordered the 19th Tank Corps deployed to support the Coastal Army's attack on May 8.[12]

During the night of May 7/8, Allmendinger scraped together Kampfgruppe Marienfeld and Kampfgruppe Faulhaber, supported by the last assault guns, to counterattack the flanks of the Soviet forces atop the Sapun Heights. The German counterattack began around 1000hrs and reached its climax around 1200hrs. Despite regaining some ground, the German counterattack was smothered under a barrage of Soviet artillery and Sturmovik attacks. Once it was clear that the counterattack had failed and that his last reserves were exhausted, Allmendinger reported to Generaloberst Ferdinand Schörner, the commander of Heeresgruppe Südukraine, that Sevastopol could no longer be held. The report was forwarded to the OKH, and at 2300hrs on May 8, Hitler grudgingly authorized the evacuation of AOK 17. One hour later, the Bradul 1 convoy left Sevastopol with 2,887 troops aboard, followed soon thereafter by the Bradul 2 convoy. Soviet artillery bombarded the harbor area, sinking the small German tanker *Prodromos* and several light craft. Two German battalions from the 50. Infanterie-Division had been isolated by Zakharov's 2nd Guards Army north of Severnaya Bay, but managed to cross the bay in small boats during the night of May 8/9. Oberst Paul Betz, commander of the 50. Infanterie-Division, personally led a counterattack to link up with these isolated units, which enabled them to escape southward.

On the morning of May 9, Mel'nik's Coastal Army continued its offensive with the added impetus of the 19th Tank Corps. Up to this point, Soviet armor had played little part in the battle, but now the tanks crashed through the retreating 73. Infanterie-Division and broke up the German front line. Provalov's 16th Rifle Corps and the tankers pursued these broken fragments back to the Chersonese Peninsula. In anticipation of a last stand, Jaenecke had ensured that the Chersonese Peninsula was well stocked with supplies of food, water, and ammunition. Sevastopol's last airfield was located here, and Axis ships could still load personnel from several beaches. With the defensive line collapsing, all elements of AOK 17 began retreating to the Chersonese Peninsula in the hope of evacuation. By 1600hrs the last German troops abandoned the ruins of Sevastopol, and Soviet troops from the 51st Army quickly moved in and reached the inner city. During the retreat, Major Willy Marienfeld, commander of Grenadier-Regiment 123, was badly wounded by a shell splinter and was flown out, but he later died of his wounds in Romania. Later that night, Oberst Paul Betz was also killed trying to make his way to the Chersonese Peninsula.

Once it was clear that Sevastopol had been liberated, Tolbukhin realized that he could no longer employ all three armies against the narrowing enemy front, and he gave Mel'nik's Coastal Army the mission of eliminating the remnants of AOK 17 in the Chersonese Peninsula. The Axis troops retreated to a final line of defense near the old Coastal Battery No. 35, where the peninsula's neck was only 875 yards wide. Provalov's 16th Rifle Corps could employ only the 383rd Rifle Division and 32nd Guards Rifle Division, supported by a tank brigade, against this narrow sector. Nevertheless, Tolbukhin's artillery could strike everywhere on the Chersonese Peninsula, including the airfield. Once Soviet artillery began impacting on the airfield, the Luftwaffe decided to withdraw its last fighters from JG 52 late on May 9, thereby depriving AOK 17 of air cover. Morzik's transports flew their last missions from Sevastopol on the night of May 9/10, and succeeded in flying out 1,000 wounded from the Chersonese.[13] After that, the skies over the Chersonese belonged to the VVS.

Despite Hitler's late endorsement of the evacuation option, the Kriegsmarine and Royal Romanian Navy had prepared as well as they could for this operation. Vizeadmiral Helmuth Brinkmann – who had commanded the heavy cruiser *Prinz Eugen* during the sortie of the *Bismarck* in 1941 – was *Admiral Schwarzes Meer*, commander of all Kriegsmarine forces in the Black Sea. Brinkmann, whose headquarters had moved from

Simferopol to Constanta in February 1944, coordinated with the Romanian Navy to ensure that there was more than enough merchant shipping available to evacuate 60,000 troops from the Crimea within a few days. He also put Konteradmiral Otto Schulz, nominally in charge of the Kriegsmarine coastal defenses in the Crimea, in charge of coordinating between AOK 17 and the naval forces involved in the evacuation operation. On the morning of May 9 the first evacuation convoys left from Constanta, with the Patria convoy sailing, and four more later in the day, involving 11 merchant ships and ten MFPs. It normally took a convoy 24 hours to cross the 250 miles from Constanta to Sevastopol, at an average speed of 9 knots. The Patria convoy, escorted by two Romanian destroyers, arrived off the Chersoneses Peninsula around 0200hrs on May 10 and began loading troops onto the merchantmen *Teja* and *Totila* (2,760 GRT). Small craft were used to ferry troops from the beaches out to the waiting merchantmen, while the warships kept alert for aerial, surface, and sub-surface threats. Soviet air attacks began at dawn, but did not score any hits, and the convoy set sail for Constanta at 0830hrs. Three German R-Boats escorted the *Teja* and *Totila,* which were loaded with 5,000 German and 4,000 Romanian troops. However, at 0930hrs 21 Il-2 Sturmoviks from the 8th Guards Ground Attack Regiment (GshAP) attacked and scored three hits with 100kg bombs on the *Totila*, which sank in a matter of minutes. The *Teja* and her escorts continued on, but five hours later 11 A-20G bombers from 13 GDBAP attacked and sank her. The R-Boats managed to rescue about 400 troops, but over 8,000 Axis troops were lost on the *Teja* and *Totila.*

The situation only grew worse for the other convoys approaching the Chersonese Peninsula on the night of May 10/11. Once the sun came up the VVS-ChF appeared in force, and Il-2s attacked and sank the Romanian minelayer *Romania* (3,152 GRT) and the freighter *Danubius* (1,489 GRT), while the German freighter *Helga* ran aground and was later destroyed. Lieutenant Commander Titus Samson's destroyer *Regele Ferdinand* attempted to protect the freighters with its 40mm Bofors antiaircraft guns, but it was itself targeted by numerous air attacks. One bomb struck the hull and killed 11 crewmembers, but did not explode. A Soviet 152mm howitzer battery also engaged the *Regele Ferdinand*, and Samson returned fire with his 120mm guns. By 1030hrs Samson was forced to quit the area due to damage and running low on antiaircraft ammunition – Axis ships could no longer survive in daylight hours in Crimean waters. The Romanians dispatched more merchant ships from Constanta and the evacuation continued on the night of May 11/12. Soviet artillery fired illumination rounds to light up the beach areas, which were then pounded with high explosives. The Romanian destroyer *Regina Maria* escorted the convoys back from the Chersonese on the morning of May 12, but the merchantman *Durostor* was attacked by 12 Pe-2 bombers and sunk. German and Romanian soldiers on the decks of the merchantmen were exposed to strafing, bombing, and artillery fire, which caused numerous casualties.

The German divisions held the narrow neck of the Chersonese Peninsula as long as they could, but were under constant attack. Sturmgeschütz-Abteilung 191 still had eight operational StuG III assault guns that made it to the Chersonese, but they were the target of constant air and artillery attacks. Meanwhile, the Soviets were already rejoicing in the liberation of Sevastopol and Marshal Aleksandr Vasilevsky, who had coordinated operations between Tolbukhin's 4th Ukrainian Front and the Coastal Army, was eager to tour the shattered city. However, Sevastopol was still littered with unexploded ordnance, and as Vasilevsky's staff car moved down the road across Mekenzievy Mountain on May 10 he had the ill luck of driving over a German mine.[14] Marshal Vasilvesky was wounded and evacuated to Moscow for military treatment – not an auspicious start to the liberation. However, the German troops isolated on the Chersonese Peninsula were unaware that they had succeeded in wounding a Soviet marshal and were instead focused on their fight to survive until they could be evacuated.

The Axis defense began to crumble late on May 11, as Tolbukhin's forces launched attack after attack. Some Romanian mountain troops were still in the fight, but the bulk of the 3rd Mountain Division had already been evacuated. By 2300hrs, all units were ordered to retreat to pre-designated embarkation points. However, this signal resulted in a disorderly race for the boats, and order and discipline began to collapse even in German units. The Soviet 19th Tank Corps was hard on the heels of the retreating Axis units, followed by the 383rd Rifle Division and 32nd Guards Rifle Division. Generalmajor Alfred Reinhardt, leading the remnants of his 98. Infanterie-Division, managed to load all his troops in an ordered manner by 0300hrs on May 12 and get away, but other units were less fortunate. In any evacuation operation, troops fear being forgotten or left behind. At this critical moment, Konteradmiral Schulz, who was operating from an S-Boat offshore, suffered communications problems that interfered with his ability to direct shipping to the right embarkation point at the right time. Insufficient transports arrived to pick up either the 50. or 336. Infanterie-Divisionen, and none at all for the 111. Infanterie-Division. Only about 2,800 troops from the 50. Infanterie-Division, including Hauptmann Walter Salzmann, commander of Füsilier-Bataillon 50, managed to escape. A 2,756-man Romanian detachment, with five mountain battalions from the 1st and 2nd Mountain Divisions, was also left behind. Some transports returned empty to Constanta, having failed to find the correct embarkation beaches. The remaining troops were left with their backs to the sea, often in tactically indefensible positions. Some officers committed suicide rather than face capture, while others tried to disguise themselves as enlisted men. On the morning of May 12 the Soviets rushed into the Chersonese Peninsula with tanks and infantry, crushing resistance nests. By 0945hrs, a large concentration of Axis troops was surrounded at the airstrip by the 19th Tank Corps. Flushed with victory, many Soviet troops shot surrendering German troops out of hand. Thousands of Germans and Romanian troops were captured, but the exact numbers are uncertain.

Generalmajor Erich Grüner, who had distinguished himself as a regimental commander during the second battle of Kharkov in May 1942, led the final stand of the abandoned 111. Infanterie-Division. When Soviet T-34s began overrunning his positions at the water's edge, he stood up and died on his feet, with his *Ritterkreuz* at his throat. Many of the rest of his troops surrendered. A group from the 50. Infanterie-Division managed to hold out for hours, until they were overwhelmed by Soviet OT-34 flamethrower tanks and heavy artillery. Generalleutnant Hermann Böhme's 73. Infanterie-Division managed to hold its positions throughout the day, expecting that more rescue ships would appear at nightfall. Lieutenant Commander Anton Foca's *Amiral Murgescu*, a modern 812-ton minelayer armed with 40mm and 20mm antiaircraft guns, was the last Romanian warship to arrive off the Chersonese, and it was able to take off about 1,000 troops, including General der Artillerie Walter Hartmann, the commander of the XXXXIX Gebirgs-Korps. Several other ships loitered in the waters off the Chersonese in the early morning hours of May 13, dodging artillery and air attacks, and collecting troops who paddled out to them in life rafts or swam. At 0330hrs, Konteradmiral Otto Schulz, aboard an S-Boat from the 1. Schnellbootsflottille, decided to terminate further rescue efforts and head out to sea before the sun rose.

Generalleutnant Böhme remained in his command post to the end, until it was overrun by Soviet troops on the morning of May 13. He was captured, but would eventually return to Germany many years later.

Between May 10 and May 13 the Kriegsmarine and Royal Romanian Navy evacuated another 47,825 personnel from the Crimea, including 28,992 German and 15,078 Romanians. Approximately 5,000 German and 3,000 Romanian personnel were lost at sea during the evacuation. Although the Romanians complained that the Germans favored their own troops in the evacuation, all three of the Romanian mountain divisions survived the debacle in the Crimea in better shape than any of the German divisions did. Of the five German division commanders, two were killed, one was wounded, and one was captured. Although detachments from each had been evacuated, these units had lost virtually all their vehicles and artillery and would require complete rebuilding. Although AOK 17 had not been destroyed as completely as AOK 6 was at Stalingrad, it was reduced to little more than a collection of poorly armed refugees. Thousands of trained troops were sacrificed just to hold the strategically useless Crimea for a few more months.

Soviet losses in the Crimea between April and May 1944 totaled 84,819, including 17,754 dead or missing.[15] As Soviet victories went, the liberation of the Crimea was a relatively cheap triumph, which inflicted heavier losses on the enemy. With the Crimea liberated, the 4th Ukrainian Front was disbanded and Tolbukhin was sent to spearhead the invasion of Romania.

Four days after the evacuation ended, Vizeadmiral Brinkmann and Konteradmiral Schulz were both awarded the *Ritterkreuz* for their role in organizing the evacuation. Wehrmacht leaders, particularly Allmendinger, were acrimonious about these awards and claimed that the Kriegsmarine had fouled up the evacuation because of the abandonment of some units. These protests need to be taken with a grain of salt, since Allmendinger's own performance in the Crimea had been far from stellar, and the senior leaders of AOK 17 had committed their own fair share of mistakes in the final week of the fighting around Sevastopol. Faced with defeat, Wehrmacht leaders were quick to point to the Kriegsmarine and the Romanians as scapegoats. German–Romanian relations deteriorated rapidly after the final campaign in the Crimea, and Romania was moving toward making an accommodation with Stalin before the Red Army crossed its borders.

Altogether, the fighting in the Crimea between 1941 and 1944 cost the Red Army something like 700,000 casualties. Five Soviet armies and numerous reputations were demolished in the Crimea. Axis losses in the Crimea were over 250,000, including at least 60,000 German and 15,000 Romanian dead or missing. Nevertheless, these horrendous military casualties have scant mention in the history of World War II. During their occupation of the Crimea, the Germans constructed elaborate cemeteries in Feodosiya, Yalta, and other locations for their soldiers killed in the 1941–42 campaign, but these were all eradicated after the Soviet liberation in 1944. Local Russians refused to bury German war dead in the Crimea, and either sent them back to Germany or dumped them in the Black Sea. Decades later, a warehouse near Sevastopol was found with the boxed remains of about 10,000 German military casualties. Finally, as German–Russian economic ties increased after the fall of the Soviet Union, a new German military cemetery was established near Sevastopol in 1998, where the remains of 11,000 Germans were re-interred.

Just two days after the liberation of Sevastopol, Stalin signed a top secret document, State Defense Committee (GKO) Decree No. 5859ss, which authorized a massive operation to punish the Crimea Tatars. The document stated that:

> During the Patriotic War, many Crimean Tatars betrayed the Motherland, deserting Red Army units that defended the Crimea and siding with the enemy, joining volunteer army units formed by the Germans to fight against the Red Army; as members of German punitive detachments, during the occupation of the Crimea by German fascist troops, the Crimean Tatars particularly were noted for their savage reprisals against Soviet partisans, and also helped the German invaders to organize the violent roundup of Soviet citizens for German enslavement and the mass extermination of the Soviet people.
>
> The Crimean Tatars actively collaborated with the German occupation authorities, participating in the so-called "Tatar national committees," organized by the German intelligence organs, and were often used by the Germans to infiltrate the rear of the Red Army with spies and saboteurs. With the support of the Crimean Tatars, the "Tatar national committees," in which the leading role was played by White Guard-Tatar emigrants, directed

their activity at the persecution and oppression of the non-Tatar population of the Crimea and were engaged in preparatory efforts to separate the Crimea from the Soviet Union by force, with the help of the German armed forces.

Stalin put Lavrentiy Beria, the sadistic head of the NKVD, in charge of the operation against the Crimea Tatars. Beria assembled a force of 32,000 NKVD troops in the rear of Tolbukhin's 4th Ukrainian Front and waited for German resistance in the Crimea to be extinguished. On May 18, Beria's NKVD troops moved to major Crimean Tatar settlements and began rounding up all the inhabitants at gunpoint. Most were given just a few minutes to gather a few items and then forced on to waiting trucks. In just three days, Beria's troops rounded up more than 150,000 Crimean Tatars, who were assembled at the rail stations at Simferopol and Dzhankoy for rail transport to Uzbekistan. Simultaneously, all ethnic Crimean Tatar troops serving in either the Red Army or Crimean partisan brigades were separated and dispatched to forced-labor camps in the Soviet Gulag system. Some remote Tatar settlements were not rounded up until later in the month, and some people hid in the mountains, but by the end of May 1944 the NKVD reported rounding up 183,155 Crimean Tatars. Another 10,000 were found in subsequent operations. Stalin intended to "Russify" the Crimea and remove the Tatar presence once and for all, and their collaboration with the Germans became the pretext for massive ethnic cleansing. The Tatars referred to their forced deportation as the *Sürgün* (exile).[16]

A few Tatars escaped the Soviet dragnet. The Tatar leader Edige Kirimal was in Germany when the Crimea was liberated by the Red Army, and had the good fortune to fall into the hands of the Western Allies in 1945. A few others made their way to Turkey or the Near East. Yet the bulk of the Crimean Tatar population was removed from the Crimea, and their deportation was conducted under very harsh conditions, little different from German round-ups of targeted groups. At least 6,400 Crimean Tatars perished en route to the labor camps in Uzbekistan, and 30,000 died within the first year. Within 30 months, more than half of those deported – 109,000 Crimean Tatars – were dead from illness, starvation, and mistreatment in NKVD-run camps.

However, Beria's ethnic-cleansing operations in the Crimea continued after the main operation against the Crimean Tatars. In June 1944 he received authorization from Stalin to round up Armenians, Bulgars, Greeks, and other non-Russian minorities; they too were put on trains and sent eastward. In mid-July, Beria was chagrined to learn that his NKVD troops had neglected to search the Arabat Spit, and that a number of Crimean Tatars were still there. Apparently, he had already reported to Stalin that all of the Crimean Tatars had been removed, and the discovery of these "un-persons" was an embarrassment. He hastily sent troops to round up the villagers on the Arabat Spit, but instead of loading them onto trains, they were loaded onto barges left over from the amphibious landings of 1943. Around July 20, 1944, the barges were towed out into the Sea of Azov and scuttled, drowning hundreds of civilians. Details of this event are still obscure. The Soviet ethnic-cleansing operations in the Crimea were a heinous crime that bore a striking similarity with the German "special actions" in the Crimea. Oddly, both Jews and Muslims in the Crimea faced persecution and extermination by the opposing sides, but as is well known, it is the victors who write history, so the German crimes in the Crimea have been exposed to the world, while Soviet crimes both before and after World War II have been hidden.

As if to reinforce their point that they were the victims, the Soviet regime decided to hold war-crimes trials in Sevastopol in November 1947. Generaloberst Erwin G. Jaenecke, the former commander of AOK 17, was the most senior German officer indicted by the Soviet tribunal, but it is interesting that the specific charges against him related to his use of the "Taifun" weapon system near Kerch in November 1943.[17] The Soviets claimed that "Taifun" was a chemical weapon, and Jaenecke was charged with authorizing its use. He was convicted by the Soviet tribunal and spent eight years in a Soviet work camp until released in 1955. The Soviets also tried and convicted a number of other Germans for offenses committed in the Crimea, but usually for reprisals against Soviet POWs or partisans, not for the ethnic-cleansing operations of 1941–42. While Stalin was alive, and even for many years afterwards, Soviet historians were reticent to raise the subject of the Holocaust, since it was too close a subject to other Soviet-era crimes.

CHAPTER 10

Postscript, 2014

"History repeats itself, first as tragedy, second as farce."
Karl Marx

In 1954, the Soviet Union legally transferred the Crimea to the Ukrainian Soviet Socialist Republic. Nikita Khrushchev believed that the "gift" of the Crimea would help to solidify Ukrainian support for the communist regime, which had been tenuous from the beginning. However, Khrushchev had not counted on the Soviet Union crumbling into the "ashbin of history" less than four decades later, leaving the whole question of Russian-Ukrainian solidarity a moot point. Instead of wistful notions of Slavic Brotherhood, the breakup of the Soviet Union in 1991 enabled the Ukraine to make a break for the open prison door in order to gain its independence and seek a different course. The new government in Kiev retained control over the Crimea, and Russia was too overwhelmed by internal chaos at the time to press its interests. Ironically, after using force to acquire the Crimea in 1920 and 1944, the Russians lost control over the region by peaceful means in 1991.

When Russia regained some of its internal stability in the mid-1990s, its leaders' first order of business was not territory, but to take back critical military assets that had been abandoned in the Ukraine. In December 1994, Russia, the United States, the United Kingdom, and the Ukraine signed the Budapest Memorandum, in which all signatories guaranteed the territorial integrity of the Ukraine in return for Ukraine returning Soviet-era nuclear weapons to Russian control. Leaders in Moscow were also concerned with the fate of the Black Sea Fleet and the naval base at Sevastopol, which had been languishing in limbo for years. Although the Black Sea Fleet was reduced to a worn collection of rusting and obsolescent warships, with very little military value and no mission, it retained an outsized political and ideological value to the leaders in the Kremlin. For the leaders in Moscow, the Black Sea Fleet is a status symbol, just as it was for the tsars. In May 1997, Ukraine and Russia signed the Partition Treaty, which divided the fleet between the two, and allowed Russia to maintain a lease on the base until 2017. Gradually, economic ties developed between Ukraine and Russia, with the former becoming very dependent upon Russian natural gas.

Ukraine's claim to the Crimea was based strictly upon Khrushchev's 1954 executive decision, not upon historical claims or demographics. In 2001, the bulk of the population in the Crimea were ethnic Russians with little love for the government in Kiev, and ethnic Ukrainians comprised less than a quarter of the region's population. The Crimean Tatars, numbering some 243,000, were in an even worse position. Even before the collapse of the Soviet Union, Mikhail Gorbachev allowed the remaining Tatars to return to the Crimea in 1989, but it was soon evident that they would be reduced to a despised minority. After returning to the Crimea, the Tatars found that all their former land had been appropriated by the state and given to others, often Red Army veterans or local Communist Party bureaucrats, leaving them to settle as squatters on the outskirts of Simferopol and Bakhchysaray. Local officials did everything they could to prevent returning Crimean Tatars from acquiring land or employment.[1]

Despite the appearance of peaceful coexistence between Russia and the Ukraine, many Russians never reconciled themselves to the loss of the Crimea and the former empire, and with the ascendancy of Vladimir Putin to the presidency in 2000, Russian irredentist aspirations found their champion. In the mindset of Putin – a hardcore Chekist – and his Russian nationalist supporters, the Red Army's liberation of the Crimea in May 1944 has been tarnished by the zeal of Ukrainian nationalists to lay claim over land bought and paid for with Russian blood. Initially, Putin hoped to reduce Ukraine to a vassal state by using the threat of natural-gas embargoes to weaken its economy, and by providing assistance to former communists such as Viktor Yanukovych, who became Ukraine's prime minister in 2002. Yanukovych favored close ties with Russia, and sought to keep Ukraine away from membership of NATO. When Yanukovych was elected president in 2010, he hurried to sign the Kharkov Accord with Russia, which extended the lease on the Sevastopol naval base until 2042. Putin could live with an independent Ukraine as long as it was run by a compliant pro-Russian such as Yanukovych, but everything changed when the Ukrainian people rose against his corrupt regime and the parliament deposed him on February 22, 2014. Yanukovych fled to Russian territory.

Without an ally in Kiev, Russia could no longer count on Ukraine staying out of NATO or maintaining access to Sevastopol. Putin suddenly began claiming that the Crimea was never really integrated into the country and should never have been part of an independent Ukraine – marking Khrushchev's gesture as a historic mistake.[2] He also regarded the political vacuum in Kiev as an excellent opportunity to correct this mistake. Only five days after Yanukovych was deposed in Kiev, ethnic Russian agitators – acting on Moscow's behest – seized control of the provincial capital of Simferopol. Once the locals had seized a base of operations, the first Russian airborne and Spetsnaz troops – without national markings – began entering the Crimea in order to reinforce the local Russian groups. The 18,000 Ukrainian troops stationed in the Crimea were caught completely by surprise and were quickly surrounded in their garrisons; lacking orders from the interim government in Kiev, they passively watched as Russian forces occupied the entire peninsula. Within three weeks, Russian forces were able to starve out the Ukrainian garrisons in the Crimea and seize the bulk of the Ukrainian Navy, with minimal bloodshed, but provoking a crisis with the West. On March 16, 2014, the new pro-Russian regime in Simferopol declared its independence from Ukraine, and on the next day formally joined with Russia. Two days later, the new Russian regime in Simferopol took immediate steps to target the remaining Crimean Tatars for ethnic cleansing, as their removal is a necessary prerequisite to stabilize the Russian claim to the region.[3] In short order,

Russian-sponsored violence encouraged many Crimean Tatars to begin relocating to the Ukraine or other countries. Once again, Russian territorial acquisition has been accompanied by ruthless ethnic cleansing.

However, the seizure of the Crimea was only the first step in unleashing a new confrontation between East and West that is likely to persist for many years. Now, in the second decade of the 21st century, we are witness to another confrontation at the Perekop Isthmus and Chongar Narrows, with Russian troops on one side and Ukrainian troops on the other. Suddenly, in the era of the Internet and GPS-guided bombs, an 18th century ditch dug by Crimean Tatars is again a relevant military feature. Once again, the Perekop Isthmus is mined and troops are on guard against a sudden assault. History is truly odd at times. Ukraine's leaders are resolved to regain the Crimea some day, and the West refuses to recognize this Russian land-grab, which sets the stage for a future East–West crisis, with the Crimea at the center of the storm.

Putin openly violated the Budapest Memorandum and risked a confrontation with the West in order to regain control over the Crimea and to ensure a future for the Black Sea Fleet. However, in order to make the Black Sea Fleet really viable, Russia will have to reclaim the shipbuilding facilities in Nikolayev and Odessa, as well as direct land access to the Crimea through the Nogai Steppe – something that would cause the collapse of an independent Ukrainian state. Consequently, the occupation of the Crimea was only a half-measure, and Putin is now intent upon dismembering Ukraine by any means necessary, which can lead only to conflict and bloodshed at some point. NATO is hardly likely to acquiesce to large-scale land grabs or the destruction of independent states, and the consequences may be very unpalatable for Russia in the long term. Poland will likely arm itself to the teeth, and Germany – if it sees no clear US commitment to prevent further Russian aggression – may also embark upon serious rearmament, including acquisition of a nuclear deterrent. A NATO that was nearly superfluous at the dawn of the 21st century has been given a new lease on life, thanks to Putin's decisions in the Crimea. A new Cold War beckons, and all hopes for greater East–West cooperation now lie dashed to pieces.

Despite the fact that competing efforts to gain control over the Crimea have yielded negligible strategic benefit to anyone for the past century, the idea that owning the Crimea is worth shedding copious amounts of blood and oppressing others for is going to retain ideological saliency for some time. Putin has learned nothing from the tragic history of the Crimea from 1917–45, and appears poised to repeat the mistakes of his predecessors. Amazingly, the Crimea is going to remain as a cockpit of war, with ancient fortifications refurbished and pressed back into service so that new generations of heroes can be asked to make sacrifices for an arid peninsula that has consistently proven to be an empty prize.

Appendices

Appendix A: Dramatis personae

Colonel Pavel P. Gorpishchenko (1893–1943). Commander of the 8th Naval Infantry Brigade at Sevastopol until seriously wounded in June 1942. He was evacuated and later commanded the 77th Rifle Division until killed at the Nikopol bridgehead on November 28, 1943. Gorpishchenko is now widely regarded as one of the great Soviet heroes of the 1941–42 Siege of Sevastopol, and his reputation did not suffer like other commanders, who abandoned their units when the city fell.

Captain Lieutenant Aleksei P. Matyukhin (1912–45). Commander of Battery 701 on the Malakhov Hill, who survived three years of captivity in the Gross-Rosen Concentration Camp until he was liberated at the end of the war. However the NKVD interrogated all former POWs and Matyukhin received a very rough welcome. He committed suicide in August 1945.

Aleksei V. Mokrousov (1887–1959). Soviet partisan leader in Crimea in 1941–42. After being relieved of command in mid-1942, he was given command of the 66th Guards Rifle Regiment and participated in the landings near Kerch in November 1943. After the liberation of the Crimea, he managed to get promoted to the rank of colonel but was quickly relegated to the reserves once the war ended. Post-war, Mokrousov used his connections with the Communist Party bosses in Simferopol to get himself a senior bureaucratic post. Given his hatred for the Crimean Tatars, he was likely one of the Communist officials who benefited from the appropriation of Tatar lands and property.

Marshal of the Soviet Union Fyodor I. Tolbukhin (1894–1949). Followed up the liberation of the Crimea with spearheading an invasion of Romania in August 1944 that caused that country to switch sides. Tolbukhin's forces eliminated much of the German presence in the Balkans and played a major role in the German defeat on the Eastern Front. However, after the war Tolbukhin was sent to command the backwater Transcaucasus Military District – a very minor post for a Marshal – where he died in 1949.

General Ivan E. Petrov (1896–1958). Given command of the 2nd Belorussian Front and later the 4th Ukrainian Front in 1944–45, but his career continued to suffer from ups and downs. He ended the war as a full general and was awarded the Hero of the Soviet Union, but only after the war was over. Like Tolbukhin, he was sent to a backwater posting in the Turkestan Military District from 1945–52. Petrov held a number of senior but supervisory-type assignments until his death in 1958. He was fortunate to keep his head after the debacles in the Crimea in 1941–42, and his role in the liberation of the Crimea restored his reputation somewhat, but he was still pigeonholed as a military mediocrity.

Admiral of the Fleet Sergei G. Gorshkov (1910–88). Despite remaining the commander of the second-string Azov Flotilla throughout much of the war, Gorshkov did very well in the post-war Soviet Navy. In 1956, Khrushchev appointed him commander-in-chief of the Soviet Navy, a post he held until 1985. Gorshkov had no experience of leading great fleets into battle, but he was an astute observer of naval strategy and operations. He was responsible for building up Soviet naval power, and after the humiliation in the 1962 Cuban Missile Crisis, he was determined to build a balanced fleet with aircraft carriers. However, the Soviet Union lacked the economic resources to build Gorshkov's ideal fleet, and by the time that he retired, Soviet power was in decline.

Marshall of the Soviet Union Petr K. Koshevoi (1904–76). Koshevoi was awarded the HSU for his leadership of the 63rd Rifle Corps in the capture of the Sapun Heights. He was awarded another HSU for his role in the capture of Königsberg in April 1945. After the war, he pointedly avoided taking senior positions in Moscow and preferred duty in East Germany and Siberia. In 1965, Koshevoi was given command of the Group of Soviet Forces in Germany (GSFG) and was promoted to Marshal of the Soviet Union in August 1968. Six days later, he led the invasion of Czechoslovakia. However, Koshevoi was relieved of command in the next year and was in reserve until his death in 1976. Despite his distinguished military record, Koshevoi was not buried in the Kremlin wall, as is customary for Soviet marshals.

General der Kavallerie Erik Hansen (1889–1967). Hansen remained in command of LIV Armeekorps on the Leningrad front until January 1943. Despite his excellent performance as a corps commander, Hansen was never given an army-level command and instead was sent to be the senior German officer in Romania during 1943–44. When Romanian dictator Ion Antonescu was overthrown in a coup in August 1944, Hansen was in the German embassy in Bucharest, which was quickly surrounded by Romanian troops. Soon, Hansen was handed over to the troops of Tolbukhin's advancing 3rd Ukrainian Front. He spent a decade in Soviet captivity, but returned to Germany in 1955.

Oberst Rudolf Buhse (1905–97). After the fall of Sevastopol in July 1942, Buhse was sent three months later with his regiment to join the DAK in North Africa. When Anglo-American forces defeated Axis forces in Tunisia in May 1943, Buhse was captured and spent 12 years in captivity. Upon returning to West Germany, Buhse joined the Bundeswehr in 1956 and served in several positions, including command of a *Panzergrenadier* brigade, until his retirement in 1962.

General der Infanterie Otto Hitzfeld (1898–1990). The intrepid commander of Infanterie-Regiment 213 of the 73. Infanterie-Division, who was later known as "the Lion of Sevastopol," rose rapidly after the Crimean campaign. Soon he became a division commander, then a corps commander, and finally in 1945 an army commander. Hitzfeld spent the last year of the war on the Western Front and was captured by American troops in 1945. He was released after only two years and eventually became the director of a chemical company.

General der Infanterie Dietrich von Choltitz (1894–1966). After his outstanding performance as a regimental commander at Sevastopol in 1941–42, he rose very rapidly and was made commander of XXXXVIII Panzerkorps in May 1943. Nevertheless, Choltitz became disillusioned with Hitler and the Nazis and he was approached by Oberst Claus von Stauffenberg in his efforts to organize an anti-Hitler resistance. Choltitz was sympathetic to the resistance but believed that Stauffenberg was too indiscrete and did not openly join the conspiracy. In early 1944, Choltitz was transferred to the Western Front and served famously as the last German commander of the Paris garrison, where he ignored Hitler's orders to destroy the city. After his surrender to the Allies in August 1944, he spent the next three years in relatively comfortable captivity in England and the United States. While a prisoner, Choltitz's conversations with other German senior prisoners were secretly taped and he unwittingly revealed that, "the worst job I ever carried out – which, however, I carried out with great consistency – was the liquidation of the Jews."[1] In arguments with pro-Nazi officers, Choltitz labeled the "scorched earth" tactics used by the retreating Wehrmacht as war crimes and said that Hitler was a criminal. After his release, Choltitz suffered from poor health – he had been wounded several times in the Crimea – and settled into a quiet retirement. Yet if any German officer learned something positive from his experiences in the Crimea, it was Dietrich von Choltitz.

Generalmajor Erich Bärenfänger (1915–45). After being evacuated from the Crimea in January 1944, Bärenfänger was awarded the swords to his *Ritterkreuz*, but due to his multiple wounds it was decided that he would not be sent back to the front. Instead, he was sent to train Hitler Youth recruits. During the battle of Berlin in April 1945, Hitler decided to promote Bärenfänger two ranks to *Generalmajor* and put him in charge of the defenses around the Reichstag. Bärenfänger led a *Kampfgruppe*, which took part in fierce counterattacks, but all he could do was prolong the agony. On May 1, the 30-year-old Bärenfänger and his wife committed suicide in the ruins of Berlin.

SS-Gruppenführer Ludolf-Hermann von Alvensleben (1901–70). After directing the ethnic cleansing of the Crimea in 1941–43, Alvensleben returned to Germany once the Crimea was isolated by the Red Army's advance. Although he was captured by British forces in April 1945, he managed to escape and make his way to Argentina, where he lived as a fugitive for the rest of his life. He was tried and sentenced to death in absentia by a Polish court for war crimes he committed in Poland in 1939, but was never held accountable for his crimes in the Crimea.

SS-Gruppenführer Otto Ohlendorf (1907–51). After murdering at least 90,000 people in and around the Crimea, Ohlendorf returned to staff positions in Germany in 1943. He remained close to Himmler and was captured with him in April 1945. He was tried and convicted for crimes against humanity by a US military tribunal and hanged in June 1951. Much of what we know today about Einsatzgruppe D's activities is based upon Ohlendorf's frank testimony, and he remained unapologetic about his actions.

General der Infanterie Karl Allmendinger (1891–65). Allmendinger was placed in reserve after the loss of the Crimea and received no further assignments. He was captured by US troops in 1945 but was released two years later.

Generalleutnant Johannes Zuckertort (1886–1969). Zuckertort continued to command HArko 306 until November 1942, at which point he was transferred to France. In May 1944 he was retired from the Wehrmacht and later died in East Germany.

Korvettenkapitän Karl-Heinz Birnbacher (1910–91). Commander of 1. Schnellbootsflottille until August 1942. In December 1943, he took command of the destroyer Z-24 at Bordeaux and survived when the ship was sunk by British bombers in August 1944. Afterwards, he commanded a naval battalion in the defense of the Fortress-South Gironde, which did not surrender to French troops until April 1945. Birnbacher was released from captivity in 1947 and joined the newly formed Bundesmarine in 1956. In 1959, he took command of the destroyer Z-1, West Germany's first major warship. He continued to serve in senior naval positions until his retirement in 1970.

Generalleutant Gerhard Barkhorn (1919–83). Three weeks after he left the Crimea, Barkhorn was shot down and badly wounded by Soviet P-39 fighters. He returned to flight duty in October 1944, flying defensive missions over the Reich. He began flying the Me-262 jet fighter in 1945 but scored no victories in it. By the end of the war he claimed 301 aerial victories, making him the second-highest-scoring Luftwaffe pilot of World War II. After brief captivity by US forces in 1945, Barkhorn joined the Bundesluftwaffe in 1956. He commanded the 31st Fighter-Bomber Wing, initially equipped with American-made F84F jet fighters, and then F-104 Starfighters, from 1957–62. He retired from the Luftwaffe as a *Generalleutnant* in 1976.

Appendix B: Comparative rank table

US Army rank	Wehrmacht rank	Soviet rank
General of the Army	Generalfeldmarschall	Marshal of the Soviet Union
General	Generaloberst	General-Armiyi
Lieutenant General	General der (Infanterie)	General-Polkovnik
Major General	Generalleutnant	General-Leytenant
Brigadier General	Generalmajor	General-Major
Colonel	Oberst	Polkovnik
Lieutenant Colonel	Oberstleutnant	Podpolkovnik
Major	Major	Major
Captain	Hauptmann	Kapetan
First Lieutenant	Oberleutnant	Starshiy Leytenant
Second Lieutenant	Leutnant	Mladshiy Leytenant
Master Sergeant	Oberfeldwebel	Starshina
Technical Sergeant	Feldwebel	Starshiy Serzhant
Staff Sergeant	Unterfeldwebel	--
Sergeant	Unteroffizier	Serzhant
Corporal	--	Mladshiy Serzhant
Private First Class	Obergefreiter	Yefreytor

Appendix C: The Black Sea Fleet in June 1941

Type	No.	Class	Name	Commissioned
Battleships	1	Gangut	*Parizhskaya Kommuna*	1914
Heavy cruisers	2	Kirov	*Molotov, Voroshilov*	1940–41
Light cruisers	4	Svetlana	*Krasny Krym, Krasny Kavkaz*	1928–32
		Admiral Nakhimov	*Chervona Ukraina*	1927
		Bogatyr	*Komintern*	1905
Flotilla leaders	3	Tashkent	*Tashkent*	1939
		Leningrad	*Moskva, Kharkov*	1938
Destroyers	14	Soobrazitel'ny (Type 7U)	*Smyshlyonyi, Soobrazite'ny, Sposobnyi*	1940–41
		Gnevny (Type 7)	*Bodry, Bystry, Bezuprechny, Bditelny, Boiky, Bezposhchadny*	1938–39
		Fidonisy	*Dzherzhinsky, Zhelezniakov, Shaumyan, Nyezamozhnik*	1924–25
		Derzky	*Frunze*	1914

Submarines	44	S-Class	*S-31, S-32, S-33, S-34*	1940–41
		L-Class	*L-4, L-5, L-6, L-23, L-24, L-25*	1931–41
		M-Class	*M-31* to *M-36, M51, M-52, M-54, M-55, M58* to *M-60, M-62*	1933 –41
		Shchuka	*Shch-201* to *Shch-216*	1932–38
		Dekabrist	*D-4, D-5, D-6*	1929
		AG-class	*A-1* to *A-5*	1922–30
Minesweepers	13	Tral-class	*T-401* to *T-413*	1936–41

Black Sea Fleet Naval Aviation (VVS-ChF)

62nd Fighter Brigade (62 IAB):

8th Fighter Regiment (8 IAP) at Yevpatoriya with 22 I-153, 19 I-15bis, 41 I-16, and 1 MiG-1

32nd Fighter Regiment (32 IAP) in Bel'bek Eupatorium with 31 I-153, 50 I-16, 3 I-15, and 5 TB-3

9th Fighter Regiment (9 IAP) near Sevastopol with 64 I-153 and I-15bis

119th Reconnaissance Regiment (119 OMRAP) with MBR-2 flying boats

63rd Bomber Brigade (63 BAB):

2nd Mine-Torpedo Aviation Regiment (2 MTAP) based at Sarabus and Karagoz [70x DB-3F]; only 12 of 62 aircrews were trained

40th Bomber Regiment in Sarabus (40 BAP) [47x SB-2]

3rd Training Aviation Regiment at Dzhankoy [11x SB-2, 10x I-15bis, 6x I-153]
16, 45, 60, 80, 82, 83 OMRAE [MBR-2 flying boats]

Appendix D: Coastal batteries at Sevastopol, 1921–42

Battery No.	305mm	203mm	152mm	130mm	120mm	100mm	Completed
2						4	
10 (Mamaschai)		4					1920
12			4				
13 (Shiskov)					4		1912
14			4	3			
18			4				1917
30	4						1934
35	4						1927

Appendix E: Order of battle at Perekop, September 24, 1943

11. Armee (General der Infanterie Erich von Manstein)
LIV Armeekorps (General der Kavallerie Erik Hansen)
46. Infanterie-Division (Generalmajor Kurt Himer, [DoW 4 April 1942])
Infanterie-Regiment 42 (Oberst Ernst Maisel)
Infanterie-Regiment 72 (Oberst Friedrich Schmidt)
Infanterie-Regiment 97 (Oberst Oscar Döpping)
73. Infanterie-Division (Generalleutnant Bruno Bieler)
Infanterie-Regiment 170 (Oberst Richard Schleußinger)
Infanterie-Regiment 186 (Oberst Ernst Klüg)
Infanterie-Regiment 213 (Oberstleutnant Otto Hitzfeld)
3./Sturmgeschütz-Abteilung 190 (Oberleutnant Reinhard Näther)

51st Army (General-Polkovnik Fyodor I. Kuznetsov)
9th Rifle Corps (General-Lieutenant Pavel I. Batov)
156th Rifle Division (Colonel Aleksandr I. Danilin)
361st Rifle Regiment (Colonel V.V. Babikov)
417th Rifle Regiment (Colonel Aleksandr Kh. Iukhimchuk)
530th Rifle Regiment (Colonel N. F. Zaivyi)
5th Tank Regiment (Major Mikhail P. Baranov)

Appendix F: Soviet naval infantry units at Sevastopol, 1941

Unit	Commander	Origin
7th Naval Infantry Brigade (four battalions)	Colonel Evgeny I. Zhidilov	Formed in Sevastopol, August 17, 1941
8th Naval Infantry Brigade	Colonel Vladimir L. Vilshansky	Formed from reservists September 13, 1941. Arrived from Novorossiysk October 30, 1941
Sevastopol 1st Naval Infantry Regiment	Colonel Pavel P. Gorpishchenko	Formed from ships' crews and naval students in Sevastopol, October 1941
2nd Naval Infantry Regiment	Major Nikolai I. Taran (captured July 4, 1942)	Formed in Sevastopol from Coastal Artillery Guard Battalion, NKVD detachment, and base personnel from Nikolayev and Ochakov
3rd Naval Infantry Regiment (3 Battalions)	Kapitan Kuzma M. Koryen'	Formed in Sevastopol from ships' crews and reservists, September 3, 1941

2nd Perekop Naval Infantry Regiment	Major Ivan I. Kulagin	Formed November 12, 1941, from one battalion of 7 NIB plus other base personnel
15th, 16th , 17th, 18th and 19th Naval Infantry Battalions	N. A. Stalberg G. I. Lvovsky Unchur Hovrich Chernousov	Formed from ships' crews and base personnel in Sevastopol, October 29, 1941. Personnel transferred to other units in late November 1941
79th Naval Infantry Brigade (three battalions)	Colonel Aleksei S. Potapov	Arrived in Sevastopol December 21, 1941

Appendix G: AOK 11 Heeresartillerie at Sevastopol, June 1942

schwere Artillerie-Abteilung (E) 672	1x 80cm Dora
schwere Artillerie-Abteilung 833	3x 60cm Karl mortars Major Freiherr Rüdt von Collenberg
schwere Artillerie-Batterie 458	1x 42cm Gamma howitzer
schwere Artillerie-Batterie 459	1x 42cm Skoda M17
schwere Artillerie-Abteilung 624	6x 30.5cm Mörser (Czech)
schwere Artillerie-Abteilung 641	1x 35.5cm M1 howitzer, 4x 30.5cm Mörser (Czech)
schwere Artillerie-Abteilung 815	6x 30.5cm Mörser (Czech)
Eisenbahn-Artillerie-Batterie 688	2x 28cm schwere Bruno railroad guns
schwere Artillerie-Batterien 741, 742, 743	each 2x 28cm Haubitze L/12
schwere Artillerie-Batterie 744	3x 28cm Küsten Haubitze L/12
I./schwere Artillerie-Abteilung 814	4x 24cm H39 howitzers (Czech)
II./schwere Artillerie-Abteilung 814	4x 24cm H39 howitzers (Czech)
917./ schwere Artillerie-Abteilung 767	3x 194mm (fr) GPF SP Gun
502./ schwere Artillerie-Abteilung 767	3x 17cm K18 M.L.
II./Artillerie Regiment 818	4x 15cm K39 cannon, 8x 10cm s.K 18
schweres Werfer-Regiment 1 (mot.)	54x 28/32cm Nebelwerfer 41
schweres Werfer-Regiment 2 (mot.)	18x 15cm Nebelwerfer 41
III. Werfer-Regiment 54	18x 15cm Nebelwerfer 41
II. Werfer-Lehr-Regiment	18x 15cm Nebelwerfer 41
Nebelwerfer Abteilung 1 (mot.)	18x 15cm Nebelwerfer 41

Appendix H: Order of battle, Sevastopol, June 7, 1942

AXIS

AOK 11 (Generaloberst Erich von Manstein)
LIV Armeekorps (General der Kavallerie Erik Hansen)
22. Infanterie-Division (Generalmajor Ludwig Wolff)
24. Infanterie-Division (Generalleutnant Hans von Tettau)
50. Infanterie-Division (Generalleutnant Friedrich Schmidt)
132. Infanterie-Division (Generalleutnant Fritz Lindemann)
Sturmgeschütz-Abteilung 190
Sturmgeschütz-Abteilung 197
XXX Armeekorps (General der Artillerie Maximilian Fretter-Pico)
28. Jäger-Division (General der Infanterie Johann Sinnhuber)
72. Infanterie-Division (General der Artillerie Philipp Müller-Gebhard)
170. Infanterie-Division (Generalleutnant Erwin Sander)
Sturmgeschütz-Abteilung 249

Romanian Mountain Corps (General-Maior Gheorghe Avramescu)
1st Mountain Division (General de Brigade Constantin Rascanu)
18th Infantry Division (General-Maior Radu Baldescu)
Fliegerkorps VIII (Generaloberst Wolfam von Richthofen)

SOVIETS
Coastal Army (General-Major Ivan E. Petrov)
Defensive Sector I:
   109th Rifle Division (General-Major Petr G. Novikov)
   388th Rifle Division (Colonel Nikolai A. Shvarev)
Defensive Sector II:
   386th Rifle Division (Colonel N. F. Skutel'nik)
   7th Naval Infantry Brigade (Colonel Y. I. Zhidilov)
   9th Naval Infantry Brigade (Colonel N. V. Blagoveschensky)
Defensive Sector III:
   25th Rifle Division (General-Major Trofim K. Kolomiets)
   345th Rifle Division (Colonel Nikolai Gus)
   8th Naval Infantry Brigade (Colonel P. F. Gorpishchenko)
   79th Naval Infantry Brigade (Colonel Aleksei S. Potapov)
Defensive Sector IV:
   95th Rifle Division (Colonel Aleksandr G. Kapitokhin)
   172nd Rifle Division (Colonel Ivan Laskin)

3 OAG, VVS-ChF (Colonel G. G. Dzyuba)

Appendix I: Order of battle, April 1944

AXIS
17. Armee (AOK 17) (General der Pioniere Erwin Jaenecke)
Gruppe Konrad (General der Gebirgstruppe Rudolf Konrad)
50. Infanterie-Division (Generalleutnant Friedrich Sixt)
336. Infanterie-Division (Generalmajor Wolf Hagemann)
Sturmgeschütz-Brigade 279 (Major Gerhard Hoppe)
Romanian 10th Infantry Division
Romanian 19th Infantry Division

111. Infanterie-Division (Generalmajor Erich Grüner)

V Armeekorps (General der Infanterie Karl Allmendinger)
73. Infanterie-Division
98. Infanterie-Division (Generalleutnant Alfred Reinhardt)
Gebirgs-Jäger-Regiment Krim (Major Walter Kopp)
Romanian 3rd Mountain Division
Romanian 6th Cavalry Division

Romanian Mountain Corps (Lieutenant-General Hugo Schwab)
Romanian 1st and 2nd Mountain Divisions
Romanian 9th Cavalry Division

9. Flak-Division

SOVIETS
4th Ukrainian Front (General Fyodor I. Tolbukhin)
2nd Guards Army (General-Lieutenant Georgy F. Zakharov)
   13th Guards Rifle Corps (General-Major Porfirii G. Chanchibadze)
      3rd, 49th, and 87th Guards Rifle Divisions
      1,452nd Self-Propelled Artillery Regiment
      512th Tank Battalion (Flamethrower)
   54th Rifle Corps
      126th Rifle Division
   55th Rifle Corps
      387th Rifle Division
   26th Artillery Division (General-Major Nikolai V. Gaponov)

51st Army (General-Lieutenant Iakov G. Kreizer)
    1st Guards Rifle Corps (General-Lieutenant Ivan I. Missan)
        33rd Guards Rifle Division
        91st and 346th Rifle Divisions
        32nd Guards Tank Brigade
    10th Rifle Corps
        216th, 257th, and 279th Rifle Divisions
    63rd Rifle Corps (General-Major Peter K. Koshevoi)
        263rd, 267th, and 417th Rifle Divisions
        22nd Guards Tank Regiment

19th Tank Corps (General-Lieutenant Ivan D. Vasil'ev)
    6th Guards Tank Brigade
    79th, 101st, and 202nd Tank Brigades

8th Air Army
    7th Ground Attack Aviation Corps (General-Major Vasiliy Filin)

Coastal Army (General Andrei Eremenko)
    11th Guards Rifle Corps (General-Major Serafim E. Rozhdestvensky)
        2nd and 32nd Guards Rifle Divisions
        414th Rifle Division
        83rd Naval Infantry Brigade
        85th Tank Regiment
    3rd Mountain Rifle Corps
        128th Guards Mountain Rifle Division
        242nd Mountain Rifle Division, 318th Rifle Division
        63rd Tank Brigade
    16th Rifle Corps (General-Major Konstantin I. Provalov)
        339th and 383rd Rifle Divisions
        255th Naval Infantry Brigade
        244th Tank Regiment
    Army Reserves:
        89th and 227th Rifle Divisions
        257th Tank Regiment

VVS-ChF
4th Air Army

Notes

Prologue

1. Isabel de Madariaga, *Ivan the Terrible: First Tsar of Russia* (New Haven: Yale University Press, 2006), pp. 265–266.

2. Robert K. Massie, *Peter the Great: His Life and World* (New York: Ballantine Books, 1980), pp. 91–92.

3. Massie, *Peter the Great: His Life and World*, p. 142.

4. Thomas Milner, *The Crimea: Its Ancient and Modern History: the Khans, the Sultans, and the Czars* (London: Longman, Brown, Green and Longman, 1855), pp. 200–201.

5. Milner, *The Crimea: Its Ancient and Modern History: the Khans, the Sultans, and the Czars*, pp. 220–222.

6. Milner, *The Crimea: Its Ancient and Modern History: the Khans, the Sultans, and the Czars*, p. 279.

7. W. Bruce Lincoln, *The Romanovs: Autocrats of all the Russias* (New York: Anchor Books, 1981), pp. 233–235.

8. John N. Lenker, *Lutherans in all lands: the wonderful works of God, Volume 2* (Milwaukee, WI: Lutherans in all Lands Company, 1896), pp. 450.

9. The Nautical Magazine and Naval Chronicle for 1855, Volume 24 (London: Simpkin, Marshall and Co., 1855), pp. 581–582.

10. Apollon G. Zarubin, *Bez Pobeditelei: Iz Istorii Grazhdanskoi Voiny v Krymu* [*Without Winners: From the History of the Civil War in the Crimea*] (Simferopol: Antiqua, 2008).

11. Peter Kenez, *Civil War in South Russia, 1919–1920: the Defeat of the Whites* (Berkeley, CA: University of California Press, 1977), p. 192.

12. Vladimir I. Lenin, *Protest to the German Government Against the Occupation of the Crimea, May 11, 1918*, Collected Works, 4th English Edition, Volume 27 (Moscow: Progress Publishers, 1972), pp. 358–359.

13. The German forces in the Crimea in 1918 included the Bavarian Cavalry Division, 15. Landwehr-Division and the 217. Infanterie-Division.

14. Stephen McLaughlin, *Russian and Soviet Battleships* (Annapolis, MD: Naval Institute Press, 2003), p. 308.

15. David Snook, *British Naval Operations in the Black Sea 1918–1920, Part 1*, Warship International, Volume XXVI, No. 1 (1989), p. 44.

16. J. Kim Munholland, *The French army and intervention in Southern Russia, 1918–1919*, Cahiers du monde russe et soviétique, Volume 22, Issue 1, 1981, pp. 43–66.

17. Snook, *British Naval Operations in the Black Sea 1918–1920, Part 1*, p. 45.

18. Snook, *British Naval Operations in the Black Sea 1918–1920, Part 1*, p. 45.

19. W. Bruce Lincoln, *Red Victory: A History of the Russian Civil War* (New York: Simon and Schuster, 1989), pp. 423–424.

20. Vladimir K. Triandafillov, "Perekopskaya Opyeratsiya Krasnoy armii" [Perekop Operation of the Red Army] in Boris Gulubev (ed.) *Perekop and Chongar* (Moscow: Military Publishing, 1933), p. 63.

Chapter 1

1. Mikhail V. Frunze, "Pamyat Perekop I Chongar" [Memories of Perekop and Chongar] in Boris Gulubev (ed.) *Perekop and Chongar* (Moscow: Military Publishing, 1933), pp. 23–32.
2. W. Bruce Lincoln, *Red Victory: A History of the Russian Civil War* (New York: Simon and Schuster, 1989), p. 449.
3. Vasiliy I. Achkasov and Nikolai B. Pavlovich, *Soviet Naval Operations in the Great Patriotic War 1941–1945* (Annapolis, MD: Naval Institute Press, 1981), p. 19.
4. Stephen McLaughlin, *Russian and Soviet Battleships* (Annapolis, MD: Naval Institute Press, 2003), p. 310.

Chapter 2

1. Richard W. Harrison, *The Russian Way of War: Operational Art, 1904–1940* (Lawrence, KS: University Press of Kansas, 2001), pp. 247–269.
2. Aleksandr B. Shirokorad, *Bitva za Krym* [*Battle of the Crimea*] (Moscow: AST, 2005).
3. Christer Bergström and Andrey Mikhailov, *Black Cross, Red Star: The Air War Over the Eastern Front, Volume 1* (Pacifica, CA: Pacifica Military History, 2000), pp. 67–69.
4. Hugh Trevor-Roper (ed.), *Hitler's War Directives 1939–1945* (London: Birlinn Ltd, 2004), p. 96.
5. Heather Pringle, *The Master Plan: Himmler's Scholars and the Holocaust* (New York City: Hyperion Books, 2006).
6. Trevor-Roper, *Hitler's War Directives 1939–1945*, pp. 143, 149.
7. Hilda Riss, *Germans from Crimea in Labor Camps of Sverdlovsk District*, Landsmannschaft der Deutschen aus Russland Heimatbuch, 2007/2008, pp. 58–91.
8. David M. Glantz, *The Battle for the Crimea: Combat Documents and Chronology, Volume 1, 9 September – 31 December 1941* (Self-published by David M. Glantz, 2008), p. 17.
9. Paul Carell, *Hitler Moves East 1941–1943* (Winnipeg: J.J. Fedorowicz Publishing, 1991), pp. 262–264.

Chapter 3

1. General Staff Order No. 001980, 15 September 1941, TsAMO, F. 48, Op. 3408, D. 4, L. 214.
2. Ia, Anlagenteil 4 z. KTB 2, *Möglichkeiten zum Angriff auf die Krim über den Ssiwasch*, September 1 – October 31, 1941, 11. Armee, NAM (National Archives Microfilm), series T-314, Roll 1340.
3. Franz Kurowski, *Sturmgeschütz vor! Assault Guns to the Front!* (Winnipeg: J. J. Fedorowicz Publishing, 1999), p. 43.

4. Ic, Tätigkeitsbericht, July 17 – November 16, 1941, 73. Infanterie-Division, NAM (National Archives Microfilm), series T-315, Roll 1065.

5. Ia, Anlagen z. KTB 7, Band 3, *Gefechtsbericht über den Einsatz des I.R. 213 beim Durchbruch durch die Lendenge von Perekop,* 27 September 1941, 73. Infanterie-Division, NAM (National Archives Microfilm), series T-315, Roll 1064.

6. Christer Bergström and Andrey Mikhailov, *Black Cross/Red Star, Volume 2* (Pacifica, CA: Pacifica Military History, 2001), p. 212.

7. Ia, Anlagen z. KTB 7, Band 3. *Bericht über den Einsatz des Pionier-Bataillons 173 beim Angriff auf die Landenge von Perekop in der zeit vom 24. – 28.9.41,* September 9 – October 4, 1941, 73. Infanterie-Division, NAM (National Archives Microfilm), series T-315, Roll 1064.

8. Ia, Anlagen z. KTB 7, Band 3. *Gefechtsbericht über den Angriff des Regiments auf die Landenge von Juschunj,* Infanterie-Regiment 213, September 9 – October 4, 1941, 73. Infanterie-Division, NAM (National Archives Microfilm), series T-315, Roll 1064.

9. Ic, Tätigkeitsbericht, July 17 – November 16, 1941, 73. Infanterie-Division, NAM (National Archives Microfilm), series T-315, Roll 1065.

10. Stavka Directive No. 002454, 29 September 1941, TsAMO, F. 148a, Op. 3763, D. 96, L. 52,53.

11. Kurowski, *Sturmgeschütz vor! Assault Guns to the Front!,* p. 43.

12. Bergström and Mikhailov, *Black Cross/Red Star, Volume 2,* pp. 225–226.

13. Ia, VII, Beilagenheft zum Kriegstagebuch Nr. 4, "*Gefechtsbericht der Brigade Ziegler, 28.10 – 7.11.41,*" XXXXII Armeekorps, NAM (National Archives Microfilm), series T-314, Roll 1669, frame 409.

14. Ic, Anlagen z. TB., Interrogation Report dated 30 October 1941, September 22 – 30 December 1941, LIV Armeekorps, NAM (National Archives Microfilm), series T-314, Roll 1350.

15. Vladimir L. Vilshansky, "Na ognyevom rubezhye" [On the Shooting Range] in Petr Ye. Garmash (ed.), *Ognennye dni Sevastopolya [Fiery Days of Sevastopol]* (Simferopol: Tavria Publishing, 1978), pp. 40–47.

16. Ia, VII, Beilagenheft zum Kriegstagebuch Nr. 4, "*Gefechtsbericht der Brigade Ziegler, 28.10 – 7.11.41,*" XXXXII Armeekorps, NAM (National Archives Microfilm), series T-314, Roll 1669, frame 409.

17. F. Perechnev and F. Vinogradov, *Na strazhe morskikh gorizontov* [*The Guardians of the Coast*] (Moscow: Soviet Mininstry of Defense, 1967), p. 42.

18. Alan W. Fisher, *The Crimean Tatars* (Stanford, CA: Hoover Institute Press, 1978), p. 154.

19. Gottlob H. Bidermann, *In Deadly Combat: A German Soldier's Memoir of the Eastern Front* (Lawrence, KS: University Press of Kansas, 2000), pp. 48–49.

20. Franz Kurowski, *Generalmajor Erich Bärenfänger: vom Leutnant zum General* (Würzburg: Fleschig Verlag, 2007), pp. 65–70.

21. Perechnev and Vinogradov, *Na strazhe morskikh gorizontov* [*The Guardians of the Coast*], p. 45.

22. Bidermann, *In Deadly Combat: A German Soldier's Memoir of the Eastern Front,* pp. 50–54.

23. Vilshansky, "Na ognyevom rubezhye" [On the Shooting Range] in Petr Ye. Garmash (ed.), *Ognennye dni Sevastopolya [Fiery Days of Sevastopol]* (Simferopol: Tavria Publishing, 1978), pp. 40–47.

24. Bidermann, *In Deadly Combat: A German Soldier's Memoir of the Eastern Front*, p. 57.
25. TsAMO f. 288, Op. 9912, 2.
26. Ia, VII, Beilagenheft zum Kriegstagebuch Nr. 4, "*Gefechtsbericht der Brigade Ziegler, 28.10 – 7.11.41,*" XXXXII Armeekorps, NAM (National Archives Microfilm), series T-314, Roll 1669, frame 409.
27. Charles C. Sharp, *Red Legions: Soviet Rifle Divisions Formed Before June 1941*, Soviet Order of Battle World War II Series, Volume VIII (Published by George F. Nafziger, 1996), pp. 54, 77.

Chapter 4

1. Report No. 877 of the Commander of the Forces of the Crimea to the Chief of the General Staff, 8 November 1941, TsAMO, F. 48a, Op. 3412, D. 720, L. 708–709.
2. David M. Glantz, *The Battle for the Crimea: Combat Documents and Chronology, Volume 1, 9 September – 31 December 1941* (self-published by David M. Glantz, 2008), p. 149.
3. Michel Ledet et al, "*Sébastopol: À l'assault de la forteresse*" Part 1, Batailles Aériennes, No. 36, April–June 2006, p. 6.
4. O.Qu., Anlage D z. KTB 4 u. 5, Zahlenmeldungen, AOK 11, Nov. 2 1941 – April 2, 1942, NAM (National Archives Microfilm), Series T-312, Roll 417.
5. Glantz, *The Battle for the Crimea: Combat Documents and Chronology, Volume 1, 9 September – 31 December 1941*, p. 185.
6. Sevastopol's Defensive Works, 17 December 1941, TsMVA, D. 1950, L. 244.
7. General Staff Order No. 2529/OP, 18 November 1941, TsAMO, F. 48a, Op. 3412, D. 706, L. 11.
8. Stavka Directive No. 004973, 19 November 1941, TsAMO, F. 148a, Op. 3763, D. 96, L. 89-91.
9. Gottlob H. Bidermann, *In Deadly Combat: A German Soldier's Memoir of the Eastern Front* (Lawrence, KS: University Press of Kansas, 2000), p. 63.
10. O.Qu., Anlage D z. KTB 4 u. 5, Zahlenmeldungen, AOK 11, Nov. 2 1941 – April 2, 1942, NAM (National Archives Microfilm), Series T-312, Roll 417.
11. F. Perechnev and F. Vinogradov, *Na strazhe morskikh gorizontov* [*The Guardians of the Coast*] (Moscow: Soviet Mininstry of Defense, 1967), p. 51.
12. Perechnev and Vinogradov, *Na strazhe morskikh gorizontov* [*The Guardians of the Coast*], p. 53.
13. Perechnev and Vinogradov, *Na strazhe morskikh gorizontov* [*The Guardians of the Coast*], pp. 54–55.

Chapter 5

1. Ia, XII. Beilagenheft z. KTB 4, Gefechtsbericht Infanterie-Regiment 42, XXXXXII Armeekorps, December 24, 1941 to January 1, 1942, NAM (National Archives Microfilm), Series T-314, Roll 1669.
2. Ia, Anl. Z. KTB 1, Lagekarten, December 4 – 31, 1941, AOK 11, NAM (National Archives Microfilm), Series T-312, Roll 367.
3. Ia, XII. Beilagenheft z. KTB 4, Befehle und Gefechtsberichte, XXXXXII Armeekorps,

December 24, 1941 to January 1, 1942, NAM (National Archives Microfilm), Series T-314, Roll 1669.

4.   Aleksandr B. Shirokorad, *Bitva za Krym* [*Battle of the Crimea*] (Moscow: AST, 2005).

5.   Ia, XII. Beilagenheft z. KTB 4, Befehle und Gefechtsberichte., *Auszug aus dem Kriegstagebuch J. R. 97 vom 26.12.41 bis 1.1.42*, XXXXXII Armeekorps, December 24, 1941 to January 1, 1942, NAM (National Archives Microfilm), Series T-314, Roll 1669.

6.   Ia, IV. Beilagenheft z. KTB U, Tagesmeldungen der Divisionen., XXXXXII Armeekorps, October 30, 1941 to March 31, 1942, NAM (National Archives Microfilm), Series T-314, Roll 1668.

7.   Aleksei M. Guscin, *Osyenyenniye gvardyeyskim styagom* [*Shaded Guards Banner*] (Moscow: Young Guard Publishing, 1975).

8.   Ia, IV. Beilagenheft z. KTB U, Tagesmeldungen der Divisionen., XXXXXII Armeekorps, October 30, 1941 to March 31, 1942, NAM (National Archives Microfilm), Series T-314, Roll 1668.

9.   Paul Carell, *Hitler Moves East 1941–1943* (Winnipeg: J.J. Fedorowicz Publishing, 1991), p. 284.

10.   Carell, *Hitler Moves East 1941–1943*, p. 285.

11.   Franz Kurowski, *Sturmgeschütz vor! Assault Guns to the Front!* (Winnipeg: J. J. Fedorowicz Publishing, 1999), p. 44.

12.   O.Qu., Anlage D z. KTB 4 u. 5, Zahlenmeldungen, AOK 11, Nov. 2 1941 – April 2, 1942, NAM (National Archives Microfilm), Series T-312, Roll 417.

13.   Kurowski, *Sturmgeschütz vor! Assault Guns to the Front!*, p. 44.

14.   Gottlob H. Bidermann, *In Deadly Combat: A German Soldier's Memoir of the Eastern Front* (Lawrence, KS: University Press of Kansas, 2000), p. 86.

15.   Erich von Manstein, *Lost Victories* (Novato, CA: Presidio Press, 1986), p. 228.

16.   David M. Glantz, *Forgotten Battles of the German-Soviet War, Volume II, The Winter Campaign* (Self-published by David M. Glantz, 1999), p. 128–129.

17.   O.Qu., Anlage D z. KTB 4 u. 5, Zahlenmeldungen, AOK 11, Nov. 2 1941 – April 2, 1942, NAM (National Archives Microfilm), Series T-312, Roll 417.

18.   Ia, Anlagenteil 3 z. KTB 4., January 1–31 1942, LIV Armeekorps, NAM (National Archives Microfilm), T-314, Roll 1344.

19.   David Kahn, *Hitler's Spies: German Military Intelligence in World War II* (Cambridge, MA: Da Capo Press, 2000), p. 189–190.

20.   F. Perechnev and F. Vinogradov, *Na strazhe morskikh gorizontov* [*The Guardians of the Coast*] (Moscow: Soviet Ministry of Defense, 1967), pp. 54–57.

21.   Christer Bergström and Andrey Mikhailov, *Black Cross/Red Star, Volume 2* (Pacifica, CA: Pacifica Military History, 2001), p. 81.

22.   Winter 1941/43 Dekaden-Übersicht der Wetterbeobachtungen, W. Geol. St. 16 Nr. 176/42, AOK 11, NAM (National Archives Microfilm), Series T-312, Roll 1692, Frame 650.

23.   O.Qu., Anlage D z. KTB 4 u. 5, Zahlenmeldungen, AOK 11, Nov. 2 1941 – April 2, 1942, NAM (National Archives Microfilm), Series T-312, Roll 417.

24.   Klaus Häberlen, *A Luftwaffe Bomber Pilot Remembers* (Atglen, PA: Schiffer Military History, 2001), p. 87.

25.   Aleksandr B. Shirokorad, *Bitva za Krym* [*Battle of the Crimea*] (Moscow: AST, 2005).

26. O.Qu., Anlage D z. KTB 4 u. 5, Zahlenmeldungen, AOK 11, Nov. 2 1941 – April 2, 1942, NAM (National Archives Microfilm), Series T-312, Roll 417.
27. Shirokorad, *Bitva za Krym* [*Battle of the Crimea*].
28. Bergström and Mikhailov, *Black Cross/Red Star, Volume 2*, p. 128.
29. O.Qu., Anlage D z. KTB 4 u. 5, Zahlenmeldungen, AOK 11, Nov. 2 1941 – April 2, 1942, NAM (National Archives Microfilm), Series T-312, Roll 417.
30. Manstein, *Lost Victories*, p. 229.
31. Simon Sebag Montefiore, *Stalin: The Court of the Red Tsar* (New York: Vintage Books, 2003), p. 413.
32. Ia, Anl. Z. KTB 1, Lagekarten, March 1 – 31, 1942, AOK 11, NAM (National Archives Microfilm), Series T-312, Roll 367.
33. Kurowski, *Sturmgeschütz vor! Assault Guns to the Front!*, pp. 58, 125.
34. Thomas L. Jentz, *Panzertruppen, Volume 1*(Atglen, PA: Schiffer Publishing Ltd., 1996), p. 228.
35. Ia, VII, Beilagenheft z KTB Nr. 4, October 30, 1941 – March 31, 1942, *Meldungen: Fliegermeldungen, Funkmeldungen, unterstellter einheiten*, XXXXII Armeekorps, NAM (National Archives Microfilm), series T-314, Roll 1,669.
36. la, Kriegstagebuch 1 u. 2, Krim, 29 January – 5 July 1942, 28. Jäger-Division, NAM (National Archives Microfilm), series T-315, Roll 834.
37. Kahn, *Hitler's Spies: German Military Intelligence in World War II*, p. 206.

Chapter 6

1. Christer Bergström and Andrey Mikhailov, *Black Cross/Red Star, Volume 2* (Pacifica, CA: Pacifica Military History, 2001), p. 153.
2. *Erfahrung und Auswirkung beim Einsatz der Luftwaffe in kampfe um Festungen*, OKL, Chef d. Genst./8 Abt./Teilkommando Wien, June 16, 1942, The Von Rohden Collection, NAM (National Archives Microfilm), Series T-971, Roll 18.
3. Franz Kurowski, *Sturmgeschütz vor! Assault Guns to the Front!* (Winnipeg: J. J. Fedorowicz Publishing, 1999), p. 44.
4. Ia Anlagen, z KTB Nr. 1, April 24 – 11 May 1942, AOK 11, NAM (National Archives Microfilm), Series T-312, Roll 1692, frames 69 and 77.
5. Aleksandr B. Shirokorad, *Bitva za Krym* [*Battle of the Crimea*] (Moscow: AST, 2005).
6. Shirokorad, *Bitva za Krym* [*Battle of the Crimea*].
7. Bergström and Mikhailov, *Black Cross/Red Star, Volume 2*, p. 158.
8. Shirokorad, *Bitva za Krym* [*Battle of the Crimea*].
9. Kurowski, *Sturmgeschütz vor! Assault Guns to the Front!*, p. 44.
10. David M. Glantz, *Forgotten Battles of the German-Soviet War, Volume II, The Winter Campaign* (Self-published by David M. Glantz, 1999), p. 154.
11. Ia Anlagen z KTB Nr. 1, O. Qu. Nr. 51/42, *Bericht über die Versorgunslage der 11. Armee nach beendigung der schlacht auf der Halbinsel Kertsch*, May 24, 1942, AOK 11, NAM (National Archives Microfilm), Series T-312, Roll 1692, Frame 622.
12. la, Verschuss beim Kampf urn Sewastopol, June 2 – July 1, 1942, LIV Armeekorps, NAM (National Archives Microfilm), Series T-314, Roll 1351.
13. *Erfahrung und Auswirkung beim Einsatz der Luftwaffe in kampfe um Festungen*, OKL, Chef d. Genst./8 Abt./Teilkommando Wien, June 16, 1942, The Von Rohden

Collection, NAM (National Archives Microfilm), Series T-971, Roll 18.

14. Shirokorad, *Bitva za Krym* [*Battle of the Crimea*].

15. *Erfahrung und Auswirkung beim Einsatz der Luftwaffe in kampfe um Festungen*, OKL, Chef d. Genst./8 Abt./Teilkommando Wien, June 16, 1942, The Von Rohden Collection, NAM (National Archives Microfilm), Series T-971, Roll 18.

16. *Erfahrung und Auswirkung beim Einsatz der Luftwaffe in kampfe um Festungen*, OKL, Chef d. Genst./8 Abt./Teilkommando Wien, June 16, 1942, The Von Rohden Collection, NAM (National Archives Microfilm), Series T-971, Roll 18.

17. Ic, Anlage F z. TB, Feindlage, Gefangenenvernehmung, 7 June 1942, 22. Infanterie-Division, NAM (National Archives Microfilm), Series T-315, Roll 781.

18. Vasiliy N. Eroshenko, *The Leader of the Tashkent* (Moscow: Military Publishing, 1966).

19. Eroshenko, *The Leader of the Tashkent*.

20. Alberto Rosselli, "Activities of the Italian MAS and Pocket Submarines in the Black Sea: 1942–1942," located at *www.regiamarina.net*.

21. Kriegstagebuch der 1. Schnellbootsflotille, 1-30.6.1942, NAM (National Archives Microfilm), Series T-1022, Roll 3207, PG/71131.

22. Kriegstagebuch der 1. Schnellbootsflotille, 1-30.6.1942, NAM (National Archives Microfilm), Series T-1022, Roll 3207, PG/71131.

23. Bergström and Mikhailov, *Black Cross/Red Star, Volume 2*, p. 204.

24. Ilya I. Azarov, *Nyepobyezhdyenniye [Undefeated]*, (Moscow: DOSAAF, 1973).

25. Bergström and Mikhailov, *Black Cross/Red Star, Volume 2*, p. 204.

26. Eroshenko, *The Leader of the Tashkent*).

27. "Oborona 79-I strelkovoi brigady pod Sevastopolem v iune 1942" [the Defense of the 79th Naval Infantry Brigade in Sevastopol in June 1942] in *Sbornik voenno-istoricheskikh materialov Velikoi Otechestvennoi voine* [*Collection of military history materials of the Great Patriotic War*] (Moscow: Military Publishing, 1954).

28. Ia, Kriegstagebuch 8, Teil I u. II., June 1 – July 5, 1942, LIV Armeekorps, NAM (National Archives Microfilm), Series T-314, Roll 1348.

29. Ivan A. Laskin, "Stoyat' nasmyert'!" ["Fight to the Death"] in Peter Ye. Garmash (ed.), *Ognyenniye dni Sevastopolya* [*Fiery Days of Sevastopol*] (Simferopol: Tavriya, 1978), pp. 196–217.

30. Ia, Kriegstagebuch 8, Teil I u. II., June 1 – July 5, 1942, LIV Armeekorps, NAM (National Archives Microfilm), Series T-314, Roll 1348.

31. "*Oborona 79-I strelkovoi brigady pod Sevastopolem v iune 1942.*"

32. Franz Kurowski, *Generalmajor Erich Bärenfänger: vom Leutnant zum General* (Würzburg: Fleschig Verlag, 2007), pp.104–105.

33. "*Oborona 79-I strelkovoi brigady pod Sevastopolem v iune 1942.*"

34. Ia, Anlagen I-IV z. KTB 10, Gefechtsmeldungen, April 1 – July 7, 1942, 22. Infanterie-Division, NAM (National Archives Microfilm), Series T-315, Roll 780.

35. Laskin, "Stoyat' nasmyert'!" ["Fight to the Death], pp. 196–217.

36. Franz Kurowski, *Sturmgeschütz vor! Assault Guns to the Front!* (Winnipeg: J. J. Fedorowicz Publishing, 1999), p. 45.

37. Laskin, "Stoyat' nasmyert'!" ["Fight to the Death"], pp. 196–217.

38. Ia, Anlagen I-IV z. KTB 10, Gefechtsmeldungen, April 1 – July 7, 1942, 22. Infanterie-Division, NAM (National Archives Microfilm), Series T-315, Roll 780.

39. *"Oborona 79-I strelkovoi brigady pod Sevastopolem v iune 1942."*

40. Ia, Kriegstagebuch 8, Teil I u. II., June 1 – July 5, 1942, LIV Armeekorps, NAM (National Archives Microfilm), Series T-314, Roll 1348.

41. Ia, Kriegstagebuch 8, Teil I u. II., June 1 – July 5, 1942, LIV Armeekorps, NAM (National Archives Microfilm), Series T-314, Roll 1348.

42. Ia, Kriegstagebuch 8, Teil I u. II., June 1 – July 5, 1942, LIV Armeekorps, NAM (National Archives Microfilm), Series T-314, Roll 1348.

43. Ia, Kriegstagebuch 8, Teil I u. II., June 1 – July 5, 1942, LIV Armeekorps, NAM (National Archives Microfilm), Series T-314, Roll 1348.

44. Markus Jaugitz, *German Remote-Control Tank Units 1940–1943* (Atglen, PA: Schiffer Military History, 1996).

45. Ia, Kriegstagebuch 8, Teil I u. II., June 1 – July 5, 1942, LIV Armeekorps, NAM (National Archives Microfilm), Series T-314, Roll 1348.

46. Ia, Kriegstagebuch 8, Teil I u. II., June 1 – July 5, 1942, LIV Armeekorps, NAM (National Archives Microfilm), Series T-314, Roll 1348.

47. Ia, Anlagen I-IV z. KTB 10, Gefechtsmeldungen, April 1 – July 7, 1942, 22. Infanterie-Division, NAM (National Archives Microfilm), Series T-315, Roll 780.

48. Ia, Verschuss beim Kampf urn Sewastopol, June 2 – July 1, 1942, LIV Armeekorps, NAM (National Archives Microfilm), Series T-314, Roll 1351.

49. Aleksandr V. Nemenko, *Sostav Primorskoy armii v Sevastopol'* [*The Composition of the Maritime Army in Sevastopol*] in Samizdat, February 2013.

50. *"Oborona 79-I strelkovoi brigady pod Sevastopolem v iune 1942."*

51. Ic, Anlage F z. TB, Feindlage, Gefangenenvernehmung, June 8, 1942, 22. Infanterie-Division, NAM (National Archives Microfilm), Series T-315, Roll 781.

52. Ic, Anlage F z. TB, Feindlage, Gefangenenvernehmung, June 10, 1942, 22. Infanterie-Division, NAM (National Archives Microfilm), Series T-315, Roll 781.

53. Ic, Anlage F z. TB, Feindlage, Gefangenenvernehmung, June 10, 1942, 22. Infanterie-Division, NAM (National Archives Microfilm), Series T-315, Roll 781.

54. F. Perechnev and F. Vinogradov, *Na strazhe morskikh gorizontov* [*The Guardians of the Coast*] (Moscow: Soviet Ministry of Defense, 1967), p. 61.

55. Ia, Anlagenteil 3 z. KTB 8, June 1 – July 5, 1952, LIV Armeekorps, NAM (National Archives Microfilm), Series T-314, Roll 1349.

56. Gottlob H. Bidermann, *In Deadly Combat: A German Soldier's Memoir of the Eastern Front* (Lawrence, KS: University Press of Kansas, 2000), pp. 135–36.

57. Ia, Anlagenteil 3 z. KTB 8, June 1 – July 5, 1952, LIV Armeekorps, NAM (National Archives Microfilm), Series T-314, Roll 1349.

58. Ia, Wegnahme der Verteidigungsanlage "Stalin' durch I. und III./IR 16, verstärkt durch die 3./Pi. Btl. 744, June 13, 1942, NAM (National Archives Microfilm), Series T-315, Roll 781.

59. Ic, Tätigkeitsbericht, Die Wegnahme des Forts "Stalin', April 1 – July 10, 1942, 22. Infanterie-Division, NAM (National Archives Microfilm), Series T-315, Roll 781.

60. Ic, Anlage F z. TB, Feindlage, Gefangenenvernehmung, June 14, 1942, 22. Infanterie-Division, NAM (National Archives Microfilm), Series T-315, Roll 781.

61. Ia, Wegnahme der Verteidigungsanlage "Stalin' durch I. und III./IR 16, verstärkt durch die 3./Pi. Btl. 744, June 13, 1942, 22. Infanterie-Division, NAM (National Archives Microfilm), Series T-315, Roll 781.

62. Franz Kurowski, *Sturmgeschütz vor! Assault Guns to the Front!* (Winnipeg: J. J. Fedorowicz Publishing, 1999), p. 45.

63. Bidermann, *In Deadly Combat: A German Soldier's Memoir of the Eastern Front*, pp. 132, 136.

64. Ia, Anlagen I-IV z. KTB 10, Gefechtsmeldungen, April 1 – July 7, 1942, 22. Infanterie-Division, NAM (National Archives Microfilm), Series T-315, Roll 781.

65. Ic, Anlage F z. TB, Feindlage, Gefangenenvernehmung, June 14, 1942, 22. Infanterie-Division, NAM (National Archives Microfilm), Series T-315, Roll 781.

66. Ic, Gefangenenvernehmung Nr. 259, June 19, 1942, 132. Infanterie-Division, NAM (National Archives Microfilm), Series T-315, Roll 1390.

67. Perechnev and Vinogradov, *Na strazhe morskikh gorizontov* [*The Guardians of the Coast*], p. 64.

68. Ia, Pionier Bataillon 132, Bericht über Vernichtung der Kampfanlagen der Panzerbatterie "Maxim Gorki" durch 1./Pi. 173, June 25, 1942. 132. Infanterie-Division, NAM (National Archives Microfilm), Series T-315, Roll 1389.

69. Ia, Pionier Bataillon 132, Bericht über Wegnahme der Batterie Schischkowa am 18. Und 19.6.1942, June 28, 1942, 132. Infanterie-Division, NAM (National Archives Microfilm), Series T-315, Roll 1389.

70. Bidermann, *In Deadly Combat: A German Soldier's Memoir of the Eastern Front*, p. 137.

71. Ia, Anlagen I-IV z. KTB 10, Gefechtsmeldungen, *Eine nicht alltägliche Pionieraufgabe: Kampf gegen einen tunnel,* April 1 – July 7, 1942, 22. Infanterie-Division, NAM (National Archives Microfilm), Series T-315, Roll 781.

72. Ic, Gefangenenvernehmung Nr. 11, June 27, 1942, 22. Infanterie-Division, NAM (National Archives Microfilm), Series T-315, Roll 781.

73. Ia, Anlagen z. KTB, Darstellung der Ereignisse, July 1–15, 1942, XXX Armeekorps, NAM (National Archives Microfilm), Series T-314, Roll 828.

74. Ia, Kriegstagebuch, May 21 – July 15, 1942, XXX Armeekorps, NAM (National Archives Microfilm), Series T-314, Roll 828.

75. Ic, Tätigkeitsbericht "Sevastopol," May 21 – July 15, 1942, XXX Armeekorps, NAM (National Archives Microfilm), Series T-314, Roll 827.

76. Ic, Gefangenenvernehmung Nr. 9, June 23, 1942, 22. Infanterie-Division, NAM (National Archives Microfilm), Series T-315, Roll 781.

77. Ic, Gefangenenvernehmung Nr. 10, June 25, 1942, 22. Infanterie-Division, NAM (National Archives Microfilm), Series T-315, Roll 781.

78. Ia, KTB 10, Beurteilung der Division, June 28, 1942, 22. Infanterie-Division, NAM (National Archives Microfilm), Series T-315, Roll 780.

79. Ia, Anlagen I-IV z. KTB 10, Gefechtsmeldungen, April 1 – July 7, 1942, 22. Infanterie-Division, NAM (National Archives Microfilm), Series T-315, Roll 780.

80. Ia, Anlagen I-IV z. KTB 10, April 1 – July 7, 1942, 22. Infanterie-Division, NAM (National Archives Microfilm), Series T-315, Roll 780.

81. Ia, Anlagen z. KTB, Darstellung der Ereignisse, July 1–15, 1942, XXX Armeekorps, NAM (National Archives Microfilm), Series T-314, Roll 828.

82. Ia, Anlagen I-IV z. KTB 10, April 1 – July 7, 1942, 22. Infanterie-Division, NAM (National Archives Microfilm), Series T-315, Roll 780.

83. Bidermann, *In Deadly Combat: A German Soldier's Memoir of the Eastern Front*, p. 141.

84. Ia, Anlagen z. KTB, Darstellung der Ereignisse, July 1 -15, 1942, XXX Armeekorps, NAM (National Archives Microfilm), Series T-314, Roll 828.
85. Shirokorad, *Bitva za Krym* [*Battle of the Crimea*].
86. Soenke Neitzel, *Tapping Hitler's Generals: Transcripts of Secret Conversations, 1942–1945* (St Paul, MN: MBI Publishing, 2007), p. 219.
87. Ia, Anlagen z. KTB 6, January 1 – July 10, 1942, 50. Infanterie-Division, NAM (National Archives Microfilm), Series T-315, Roll 947, frame 497.
88. Kurowski, *Generalmajor Erich Bärenfänger: vom Leutnant zum General*, p.117.
89. Bidermann, *In Deadly Combat: A German Soldier's Memoir of the Eastern Front*, p. 143.
90. AOK 11, NAM (National Archives Microfilm), Series T-312, Roll 1692.

Chapter 7

1. Norbert Kunz *"The Jews are completely destroyed": The Fate of Jewish Minorities in the Crimea in World War II in The Holocaust in Ukraine: New Sources and Perspectives* (Washington, DC: U.S. Holocaust Memorial Museum Center for Advanced Holocaust Studies, 2013).
2. Gitel Gubenko, *The Book of Sorrows* (GS Tanislav Co., Inc., 2003).
3. Andrei Angrick, *Besatzungspolitik und Massenmord: Die Einsatzgruppe D in der südlichen Sowjetunion 1941–1943* (Hamburg: Hamburger Edition Verlag, 2003), pp. 335–345.
4. Operational Situation Report USSR No. 150, Einsatzgruppe D, January 2, 1942.
5. Interview with Lidiya I. Chyernih on April 28, 2013 on the "I Remember" website, http://iremember.ru/partizani/chernikh-milko-lidiya-ivanovna.html.
6. Tätigkeitsbericht, Feldkommandantur 810, 19 December 1941, NAM (National Archives Microfilm), Series T-501, Roll 233, frames 409–410.
7. Tätigkeitsbericht vom 1-15.7.42, Feldkommandantur 287, 16 July 1942, NAM (National Archives Microfilm), Series T-501, Roll 233, frame 424.
8. Memorandum from Generalkommissar für die Krim to OKH, July 16, 1942, NAM (National Archives Microfilm), Series T-454, Roll 18.
9. Report from Generalkommissar für die Krim, August 18, 1943, NAM (National Archives Microfilm), Series T-454, Roll 18, frames 170–171.
10. Report from Generalkommissar für die Krim, May 8, 1942, NAM (National Archives Microfilm), Series T-454, Roll 28.
11. Antonio J. Munoz, *Forgotten Legions: Obscure Combat Formations of the Waffen SS* (New York: Axis Europa Books, 1991), p. 39.
12. Kommandant des ruckwartigen Armeege Metes 553, NAM (National Archives Microfilm), Series T-501, Roll 58.
13. Gottlob H. Bidermann, *In Deadly Combat: A German Soldier's Memoir of the Eastern Front* (Lawrence, KS: University Press of Kansas, 2000), p. 119.
14. J. F. Borsarello and W. Palinckx, *Wehrmacht & SS Caucasian – Muslim – Asian Troops* (Bayeux, France: Editions Heimdal, 2007).
15. O.Qu./Qu. 2, Report by Einsatzgruppe D of the Sicherheitspolizei about Rekrutierung der Krimtataren, April 4 –September 8, 1942, NAM (National Archives Microfilm), Series T-312, Roll 421.
16. Munoz, *Forgotten Legions: Obscure Combat Formations of the Waffen SS*, pp. 173–174.
17. Aleksandr B. Shirokorad, *Bitva za Krym* [*Battle of the Crimea*] (Moscow: AST, 2005).

18. Tätigkeitsbericht vom 1.-15.10.42, Feldkommandantur 287, 16 October 1942, NAM (National Archives Microfilm), Series T-501, Roll 233, frames 969.

19. Tätigkeitsbericht vom 16.-31.10.42, Feldkommandantur 287, 1 November 1942, NAM (National Archives Microfilm), Series T-501, Roll 233.

20. Shirokorad, *Bitva za Krym* [*Battle of the Crimea*].

21. Bandentätigkeit in der Zeit vom 1.-7.12.43, AOK 17, NAM (National Archives Microfilm), Series T-312, Roll 740.

22. Stephen McLaughlin, *Russian and Soviet Battleships* (Annapolis, MD: Naval Institute Press, 2003), p. 402.

23. Vasiliy I. Achkasov and Nikolai B. Pavlovich, *Soviet Naval Operations in the Great Patriotic War 1941–1945* (Annapolis, MD: Naval Institute Press, 1981), pp. 262–264.

24. Achkasov and Pavlovich, *Soviet Naval Operations in the Great Patriotic War 1941–1945*, pp. 258–259.

Chapter 8

1. Philipp Humberts, "Ich Bitte Ershossen zu werden," *Der Spiegel*, 5/1949, January 29, 1949.

2. Ia, Anlage 1 z. KTB Nr. 8, Kriegsgliederungen der Armee, AOK 17, Oct 12–Dec 11, 1943, NAM (National Archives Microfilm), Series T-312, Roll 738.

3. Ia, Anlage 9 z. KTB Nr. 8, Lagenkarten, AOK 17, Oct 10–Dec 31, 1943, NAM (National Archives Microfilm), Series T-312, Roll 740.

4. Ia, Anlagenband 2 z. KTB Nr, 8. Unternehmen "Michael" mit Sondervorgang, AOK 17, Oct 19–31, 1943, NAM (National Archives Microfilm), Series T-312, Roll 738.

5. Paul Carell, *Scorched Earth* (Atglen, PA: Schiffer Military History, 1994), p. 456.

6. Ia, Anlage 4 z. KTB Nr. 8, AOK 17, Oct 10–Dec 31, 1943, NAM (National Archives Microfilm), Series T-312, Roll 739.

7. Ia, 336. Infanterie-Division, October-December 1943, NAM (National Archives Microfilm), Series T-315, Roll 2,097.

8. Ic, Gefangenenvernehmung, AOK 17, November 1, 1943, NAM (National Archives Microfilm), Series T-312, Roll 741.

9. Anatoly N. Grylev, *Dnipro-Karpaty-Krym: Osvobozhdenie pravoberezhnoi ukrainy i kryma v 1944 gody* [*Dnepr-Carpathians-Crimea: The Liberation of the Right Bank of Ukraine and Crimea, 1944*] (Moscow: Nauka, 1970).

10. Ic, Tatigkeitsbericht, Verteidigung der Nordzugange zur Krim, XXXXIX Gebirgs-Korps, October 30 – December 31, 1943, NAM (National Archives Microfilm), Series T-314, Roll 1226.

11. Ia, Anlage 1 z. KTB Nr. 8, Kriegsgliederungen der Armee, AOK 17, Oct 12–Dec 11, 1943, NAM (National Archives Microfilm), Series T-312, Roll 738.

12. Franz Kurowski, *Sturmgeschütz vor! Assault Guns to the Front!* (Winnipeg: J. J. Fedorowicz Publishing, 1999), p. 53.

13. Andrei Kuznetsov, *Bolshoi desant Kerchensko Eltigenskaya operatsiya* [*The Large Landing at Kerch-Eltigen*] (Moscow: VECHE, 2011).

14. Ia, Anlage 4 z. KTB Nr. 8, AOK 17, Oct 10–Dec 31, 1943, NAM (National Archives Microfilm), Series T-312, Roll 739.

15. Franz Kurowski, *Generalmajor Erich Bärenfänger: vom Leutnant zum General* (Würzburg: Fleschig Verlag, 2007), pp. 146–147.

16. Kurowski, *Generalmajor Erich Bärenfänger: vom Leutnant zum General*, p.148.

17. O.Qu., Anlagenband LXX z. KTB Nr. 8, AOK 17, NAM (National Archives Microfilm), Series T-312, March 1944, Roll 744.

18. Fritz Morzik, *German Air Force Airlift Operations* (Honolulu: University Press of the Pacific, 2002), p. 240.

19. Ia, Anlagen z. KTB 9, Teil II, February 1–29, 1944, XXXXIX Gebirgs-Korps, NAM (National Archives Microfilm), Series T-314, Roll 1227.

20. O.Ou./VII, AOK 17, November 1, 1942–February 28, 1944, NAM (National Archives Microfilm), Series T-312, Roll 745.

21. O.Qu., Anlagenband LXX z. KTB Nr. 8, AOK 17, NAM (National Archives Microfilm), Series T-312, March 1944, Roll 744.

22. Christer Bergström, *Bagration to Berlin: The Final Air Battles in the East, 1944–1945* (Hersham, UK: Ian Allan Publishing, 2008), p. 46.

23. Peter K. Koshevoi, *v gody voennye* [*During the War*] (Moscow: Military Publishing, 1978).

24. Ic, Anlage 4 z. Tätigkeitsbericht, January 1–March 31, 1944, AOK 17, NAM (National Archives Microfilm), Series T-312, Roll 748.

25. Ia, Anlage 5 z. KTB Nr. 9, Besondere Vorgange, January 1–March 31, 1944, AOK 17, NAM (National Archives Microfilm), Series T-312, Roll 747.

26. Ia, Sonderband Nr. 4, z. KTB Nr. 9, Unternehmen "Gneisenau," January 8–March 23, 1944, AOK 17, NAM (National Archives Microfilm), Series T-312, March 1944, Roll 746.

27. Ia, Sonderband Nr. 5, z. KTB Nr. 9, Unternehmen "Litzmann," November 13–24, 1943, AOK 17, NAM (National Archives Microfilm), Series T-312, Roll 746.

Chapter 9

1. Anatoly N. Grylev, *Dnipro-Karpaty-Krym: Osvobozhdenie pravoberezhnoi ukrainy i kryma v 1944 gody* [*Dnepr-Carpathians-Crimea: The Liberation of the Right Bank of Ukraine and Crimea, 1944*] (Moscow: Nauka, 1970).

2. Christer Bergström, *Bagration to Berlin: The Final Air Battles in the East, 1944–1945* (Hersham, UK: Ian Allan Publishing, 2008), p. 46.

3. Peter K. Koshevoi, *v gody voennye* [*During the War*] (Moscow: Military Publishing, 1978).

4. Konstantin V. Sychev (ed.), *Boyeviye dyeystviya stryelkovoy divizii* [*The Fighting Infantry Division*] (Moscow: Military Publishing, 1958).

5. Grylev, *Dnipro-Karpaty-Krym: Osvobozhdenie pravoberezhnoi ukrainy i kryma v 1944 gody* [*Dnepr-Carpathians-Crimea: The Liberation of the Right Bank of Ukraine and Crimea, 1944*].

6. Aleksander A. Maslov, *Fallen Soviet Generals* (London: Frank Cass Publishers, 1998), p. 135.

7. Paul Carell, *Scorched Earth: The Russo-German War 1943–1944* (Atglen, PA: Schiffer Military History, 1994), pp. 462–463.

8. Franz Kurowski, *Sturmgeschütz vor! Assault Guns to the Front!* (Winnipeg: J. J. Fedorowicz Publishing, 1999), p. 139.
9. Maslov, *Fallen Soviet Generals*, p. 136.
10. Carell, *Scorched Earth: The Russo-German War 1943–1944*, p. 467.
11. Soenke Neitzel, *Tapping Hitler's Generals: Transcripts of Secret Conversations, 1942–1945* (St Paul, MN: MBI Publishing, 2007), p. 259.
12. Koshevoi, *v gody voennye* [*During the War*].
13. Carrell, *Scorched Earth: The Russo-German War 1943–1944*, p. 471.
14. Aleksandr M Vasilevsky, *Dyelo vsyey zhizhi* [*The Point of All Life*] (Moscow: Politizdat, 1978), p. 395.
15. Grigory F. Krivosheev, *Soviet Casualties and Combat Losses in the Twentieth Century* (London: Greenhill Books, 1997), p. 143.
16. Greta Lynn Uehling, *Beyond Memory: The Crimean Tatars' Deportation and Return* (New York: Palgrave Macmillan, 2004), pp. 80–81.
17. RG-06.025.05, N-19096, tom 1, Sevastopol, 1946–1947, Trial of Erwin Gustav Jaenecke, U.S. Holocaust Museum Archives.

Chapter 10

1. Greta Lynn Uehling, *Beyond Memory: The Crimean Tatars' Deportation and Return* (New York: Palgrave Macmillan, 2004), pp. 208–211.
2. "Ukraine Crisis: March 18 as it happened," *Telegraph*, March 18, 2014.
3. "Crimean Tatars will have to vacate their land, says Crimean deputy premier," RIA Novosti, March 19, 2014.

Appendices

1. Soenke Neitzel, *Tapping Hitler's Generals: Transcripts of Secret Conversations, 1942–1945* (St. Paul, MN: MBI Publishing, 2007), p. 192.

Bibliography

Primary Sources

National Archives and Research Administration (NARA) records for the German AOK 11 and AOK 17 and all major constituent corps and divisions in the period from September 1941 to May 1944.

Secondary Sources

Achkasov, V. I., and N. B. Pavlovich, *Soviet Naval Operations in the Great Patriotic War 1941–45* (Annapolis, MD: Naval Institute Press, 1981).

Antonescu, Jon, *Wir erobern die Krim: Soldaten der Krim-Armee berichten* (Pfälzische Verlaganstalt, 1943).

Bergström, Christer and Andrey Mikhailov, *Black Cross/Red Star, Volume 2* (Pacifica, CA: Pacifica Military History, 2001).

Bidermann, Gottlob H., *In Deadly Combat: A German Soldier's Memoir of the Eastern Front* (Lawrence, KS: University Press of Kansas, 2000).

Borisov, Boris A., *Podvig Sevastopol* [*Feat of Sevastopol*] (Simferopol: Crimea Publishing House, 1970).

Carell, Paul, *Hitler Moves East 1941–1943* (Winnipeg: J. J. Fedorowicz Publishing, 1991).

Egger, Martin, *Die Festung Sewastopol: Dokumentation ihrer Befestigungsanlagen und der Kämpfe 1942* (Cologne: Harry Lippman, 1995).

Garmash, Peter Ye., *Za rodnoi Krym: vospominanii a uchastnikov boev za Krym* [*For native Crimea: memories of the participants battle for the Crimea*] (Simferopol: Sonat Publishers, 2008).

Garmash, Peter Ye., *Za rodnoi Sevastopol* [*For Native Sevastopol*] (Moscow: the young guard, 1983).

Glantz, David M., *The Battle for the Crimea: Combat Documents and Chronology, Volume 1, 9 September – 31 December 1941* (self-published by David M. Glantz, 2008).

Grylev, Anatoly N., *Dnipro-Karpaty-Krym: Osvobozhdenie pravoberezhnoi ukrainy i kryma v 1944 gody* [*Dnepr-Carpathians-Crimea: The Liberation of the Right Bank of Ukraine and Crimea, 1944*] (Moscow: Nauka, 1970).

Hayward, Joel S., *Stopped at Stalingrad* (Lawrence, KS: University Press of Kansas, 1998).

Ignatovich, Evgeniy A., *Zenitnoe bratstvo Sevastopolya* [*The zenith of brotherhood in Sevastopol*] (Kiev: izdatelstvo politiceskoy literatury, 1986).

Karpov, Vladimir V., *Commander* (London: Brassey's, 1987).

Koshevoi, Peter K., *v gody voennye* [*During the War*] (Moscow: Military Publishing, 1978).

Krylov, Nikolai I., *Ne Pomerknet Nikogda* [*It Will Never Fade*] (Moscow: Military Publishing, 1984).

Kurowski, Franz, *Der Angriff auf die stärkste Festung der Welt 1942* (Friedberg: Podzun-Pallas, 2002).

Kurowski, Franz, *Generalmajor Erich Bärenfänger: vom Leutnant zum General* (Würzburg: Fleschig Verlag, 2007).

Lower, Wendy, *Nazi Empire-Building and the Holocaust in Ukraine* (Chapel Hill, NC: University of North Carolina Press, 2005).

Manstein, Erich von, *Lost Victories* (Novato, CA: Presidio Press, 1986).

Morgunov, Petr A., *Gyeroichyeskiy Sevastopol'* [*Heroic Sevastopol*] (Moscow: Nauka, 1979)

Moschansky, Savin I., *Bor'ba za Krim, syentyabr' 1941 – iyool' 1942 goda* [*Fight for the Crimea, September 1941–July 1942*] (Moscow: PKV, 2002).

Perechnev, F., and F. Vinogradov, *Na strazhe morskikh gorizontov* [*The Guardians of the Coast*] (Moscow: Soviet Mininstry of Defense, 1967).

Shirokorad, Aleksandr B., *Bitva za Krym* [Battle of the Crimea] (Moscow: AST, 2005).

Winkel, Walter, *Der Kampfe Um Sewastopol* (Berg am see: Kurt Vowinckel Verlag, 1984).

Periodicals

Hayward, Joel S., "A Case Study in Early Joint Warfare: An Analysis of the Wehrmacht's Crimean Campaign of 1942" in *The Journal of Strategic Studies*, Vol. 22, No. 4 (December 1999), pp. 103–130.

"Oborona 79-I strelkovoi brigady pod Sevastopolem v iune 1942" [the defense of the 79th Naval Infantry Brigade in Sevastopol in June 1942] in *Sbornik voenno-istoricheskikh materialov Velikoi Otechestvennoi voine* [*Collection of military history materials of the Great Patriotic War*] (Moscow: Military Publishing, 1954)

Rosselli, Alberto, "Activities of the Italian MAS and Pocket Submarines in the Black Sea: 1942–1943" on *www.regiamarina.net* website.

Snook, David, "British Naval Operations in the Black Sea," Parts 1 and 2, *Warship International*, Vol. 26, No 1 and No. 4 (1989).

Wernet, Dieter and Inge Wernet, "Maksim Gorky I: A Recent Example of the Re-use of Naval Turrets in Coast Defenses," *Warship International*, No. 1, 1997.

Index